volume
2

Story by
Surt Lim

Art by
Hirofumi Sugimoto

Lettered by
Monkey Square

BALLANTINE BOOKS ● **NEW YORK**

Kasumi volume 2 is a work of fiction. Names, characters, places, and incidents are the products of the author's imagination or are used fictitiously. Any resemblance to actual events, locales, or persons, living or dead, is entirely coincidental.

A Del Rey Manga Trade Paperback Original

Published in the United States by Del Rey Books, an imprint of The Random House Publishing Group, a division of Random House, Inc., New York.

ISBN 978-0-345-50359-6

Printed in the United States of America

www.delreymanga.com

9 8 7 6 5 4 3 2 1

Art Director—Stanley Adrianus
Translation—Harumi Ueno
Lettering—Monkey Square
Assistants—Natuki, Bon Komamiya

This book is dedicated in memory of my dad,
whose passion for life will always be my inspiration.

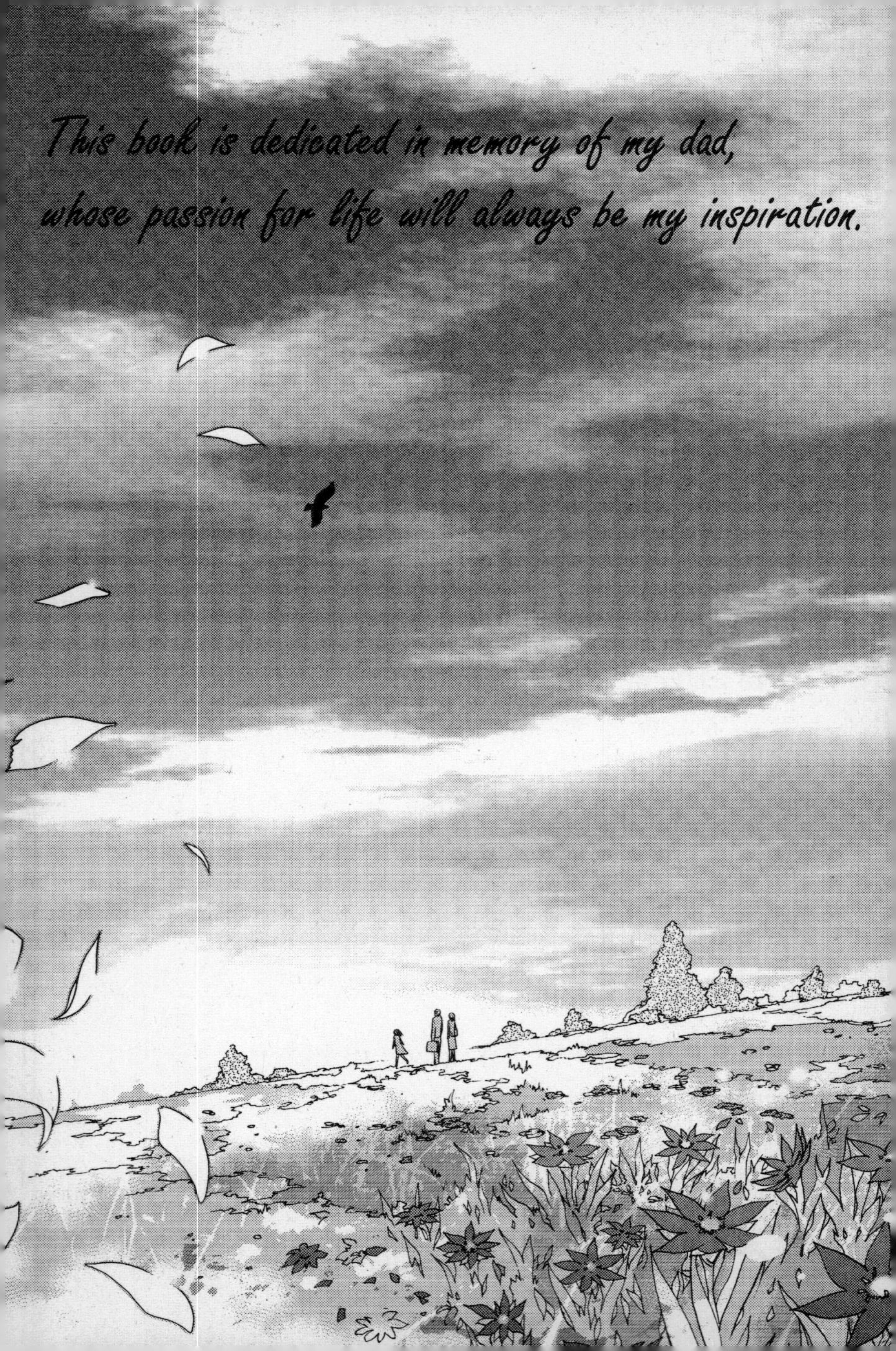

CONTENTS

HONORIFICS EXPLAINED

The following are some of the honorifics that come up in "Kasumi." By knowing these, you'll have a better understanding of the relationships between the characters.

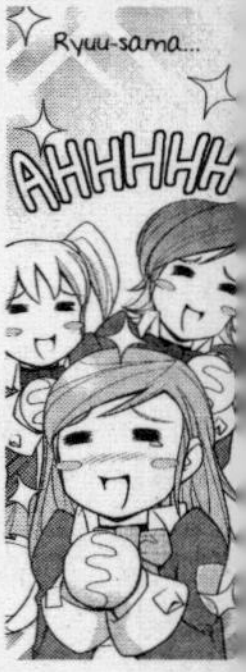

Ryuu-sama...
AHHHHH

-san This is the most common honorific and is equivalent to Mr., Miss, Ms., or Mrs. It is the all-purpose honorific and can be used in any situation where politeness is required. (E.g. Hasegawa-san)

-sama This is one level higher than "-san" and is used to confer great respect. (E.g. The RSF admires and respects Ryuuki-kun, and calls him "Ryuu-sama")

-kun This suffix is used at the end of boys' names to express familiarity or endearment. It is also sometimes used by men among friends, or when addressing someone younger or of a lower station. (E.g. Ryuuki-kun)

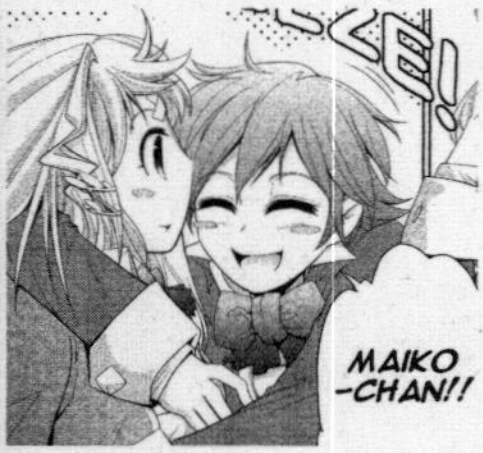

MAIKO -CHAN!!

-chan This is used to express endearment, mostly toward girls. It is also used for little boys, pets, and even among lovers. It gives a sense of childish cuteness. (E.g. Maiko-chan, fans calling Seiji senpai "Sei-chan")

Sensei This literally means "one who has come before." This title is used for teachers, doctors, or masters of any profession or art. (E.g. Yoshida-sensei)

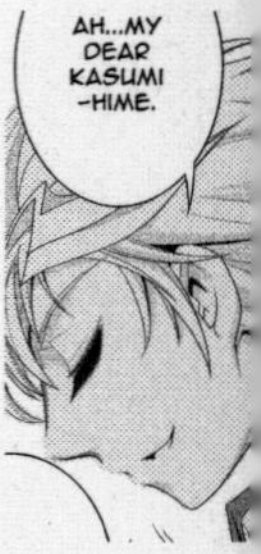

AH...MY DEAR KASUMI -HIME.

Sempai/ Senpai This title suggests that the addressee is one's senior in a group or organization. It is most often used in a school setting, where underclassmen refer to their upperclassmen as "sempai." It can also be used in the workplace, such as when a newer employee addresses an employee who has seniority in the company. (E.g. Seiji-senpai)

-hime This means "princess." It is used at the end of girls' names. (E.g. Kasumi-chan is called "Kasumi-hime" by Seiji-senpai)

Onesan/ Onechan This means "older sister." It can also be used for girls and women older than oneself in general. (E.g. Tsutomu-kun calling his sister Maiko-chan "Onechan" and calling Kasumi-chan "Kasumi-onechan")

Obaasan/ Obaachan This means "grandmother." It is used toward one's or someone's grandmother, and also for old women in general. (E.g. Maiko-chan's obaachan)

-[blank] This is usually forgotten in these lists, but it is perhaps the most significant difference between Japanese and English. The lack of honorific means that the speaker has permission to address the person in a very intimate way. Usually, only family, spouses, or very close friends have this kind of permission. Known as *yobisute,* it can be gratifying when someone who has earned the intimacy starts to call one by one's name without an honorific. But when that intimacy hasn't been earned, it can be very insulting. (E.g. Reina-san calling Kasumi-chan "MORIOKA"!)

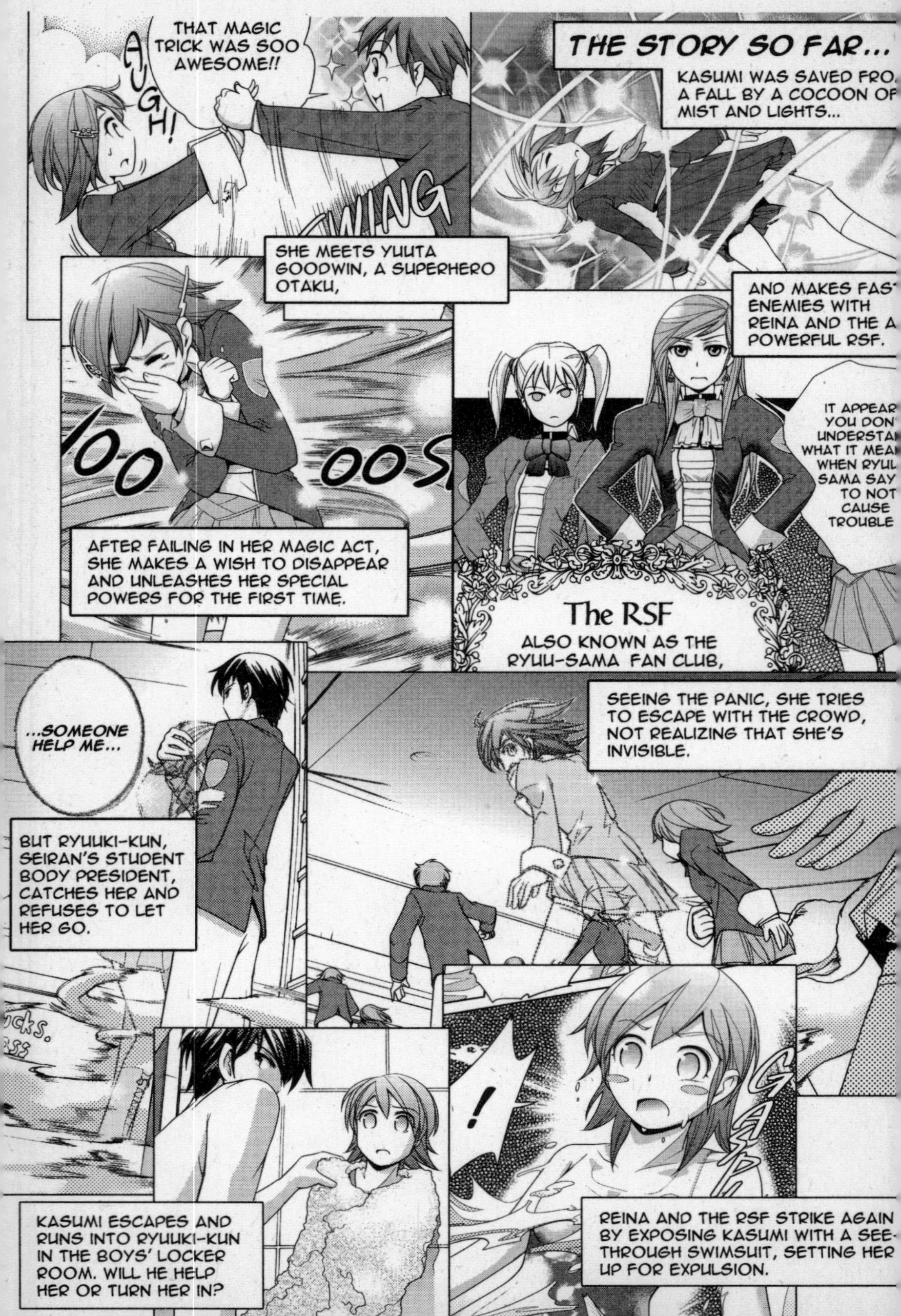
THE STORY SO FAR...
KASUMI WAS SAVED FRO A FALL BY A COCOON OF MIST AND LIGHTS...
THAT MAGIC TRICK WAS SOO AWESOME!!
AUGH!
WING
SHE MEETS YUUTA GOODWIN, A SUPERHERO OTAKU,
AND MAKES FAST ENEMIES WITH REINA AND THE A POWERFUL RSF.
IT APPEAR YOU DON' UNDERSTA WHAT IT MEA WHEN RYU SAMA SAY TO NOT CAUSE TROUBLE
The RSF
ALSO KNOWN AS THE RYUU-SAMA FAN CLUB,
OOS
OOO
AFTER FAILING IN HER MAGIC ACT, SHE MAKES A WISH TO DISAPPEAR AND UNLEASHES HER SPECIAL POWERS FOR THE FIRST TIME.
SEEING THE PANIC, SHE TRIES TO ESCAPE WITH THE CROWD, NOT REALIZING THAT SHE'S INVISIBLE.
...SOMEONE HELP ME...
BUT RYUUKI-KUN, SEIRAN'S STUDENT BODY PRESIDENT, CATCHES HER AND REFUSES TO LET HER GO.
GASP
!
REINA AND THE RSF STRIKE AGAIN BY EXPOSING KASUMI WITH A SEE-THROUGH SWIMSUIT, SETTING HER UP FOR EXPULSION.
KASUMI ESCAPES AND RUNS INTO RYUUKI-KUN IN THE BOYS' LOCKER ROOM. WILL HE HELP HER OR TURN HER IN?

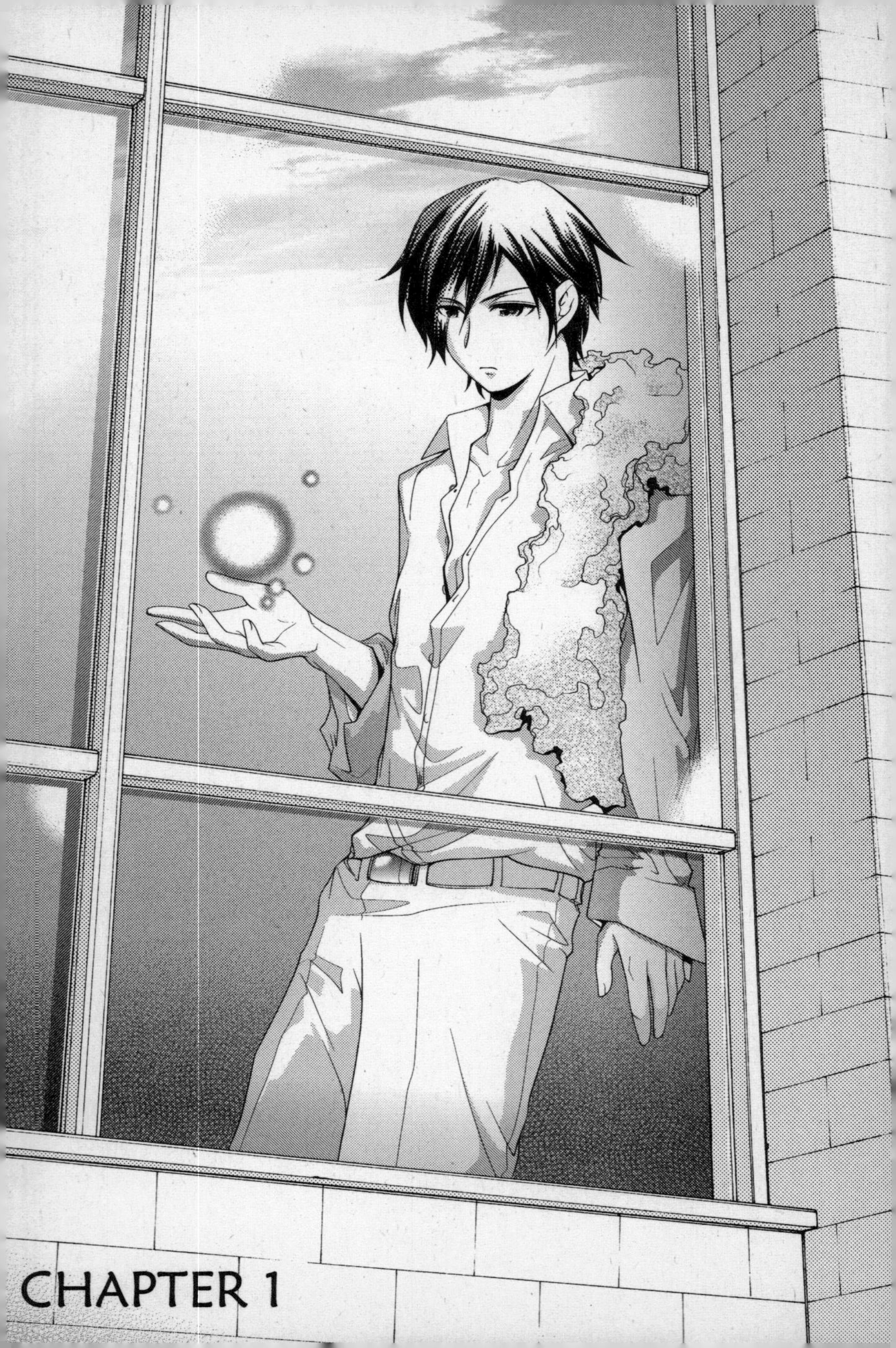

CHAPTER 1

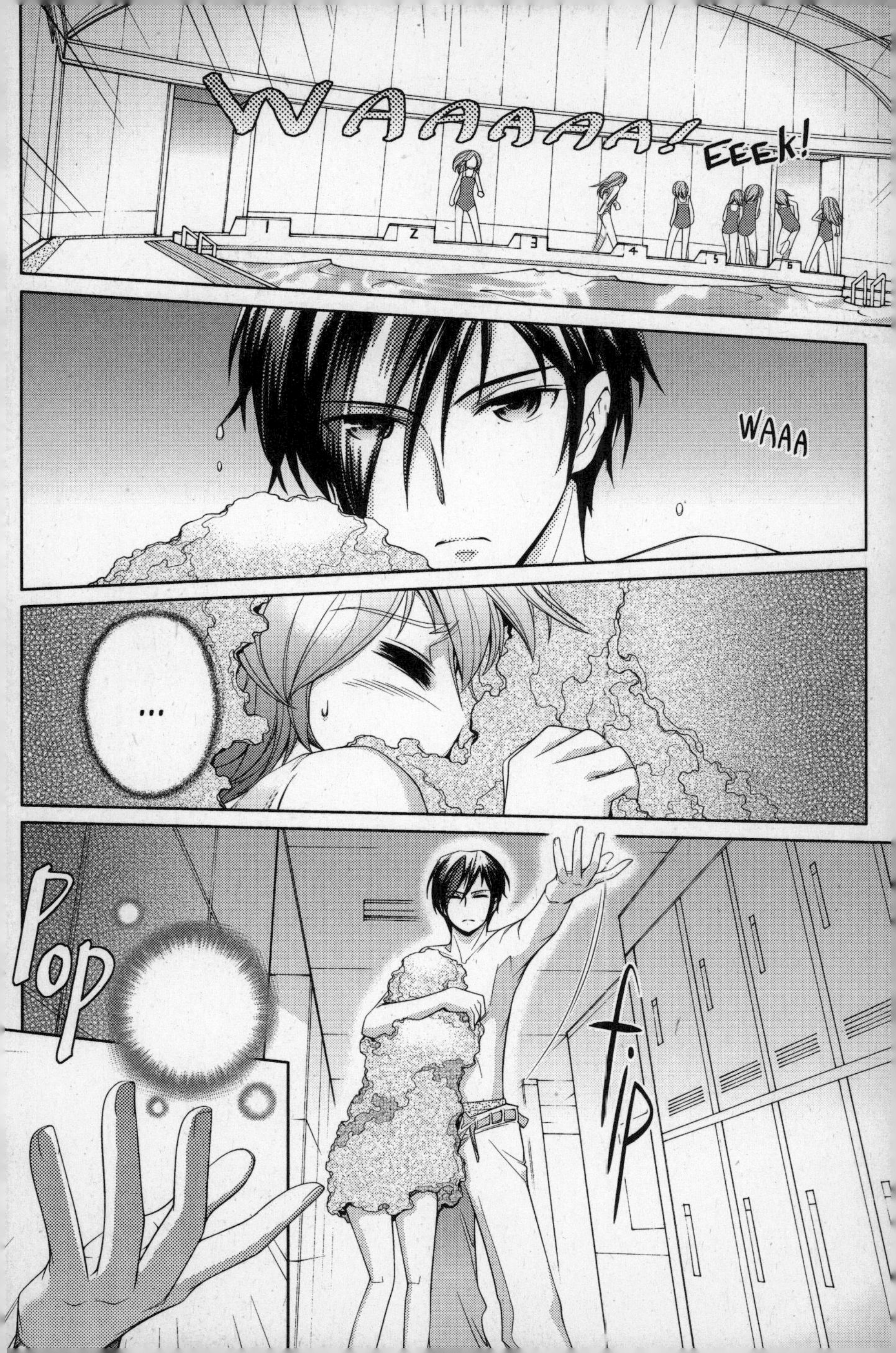
WAAAAAA!
EEEK!
WAAA
...
Pop
Flip

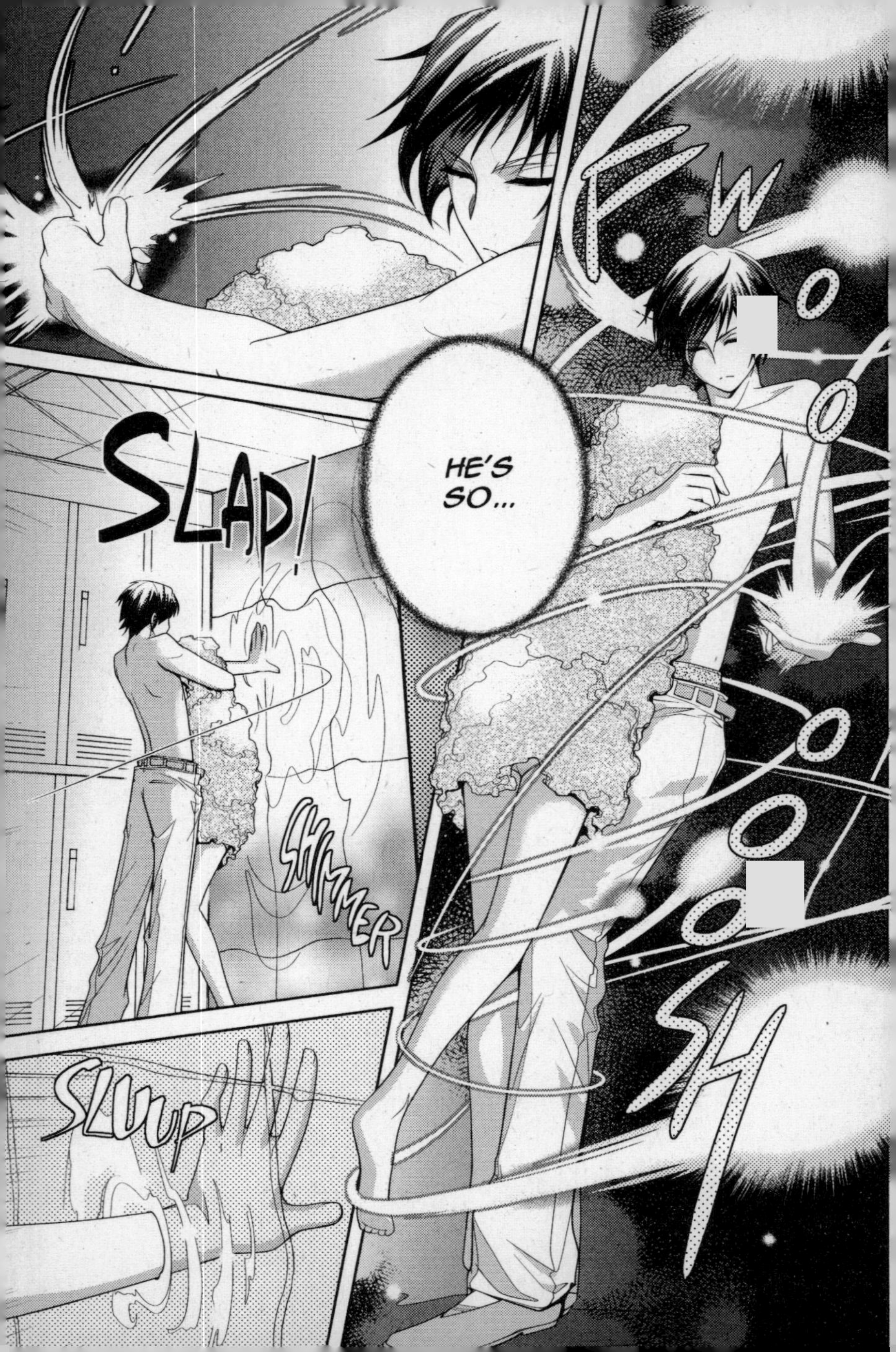
FWOOOOOOSH
HE'S SO...
!
SLAP!
SHIMMER
SLUUP

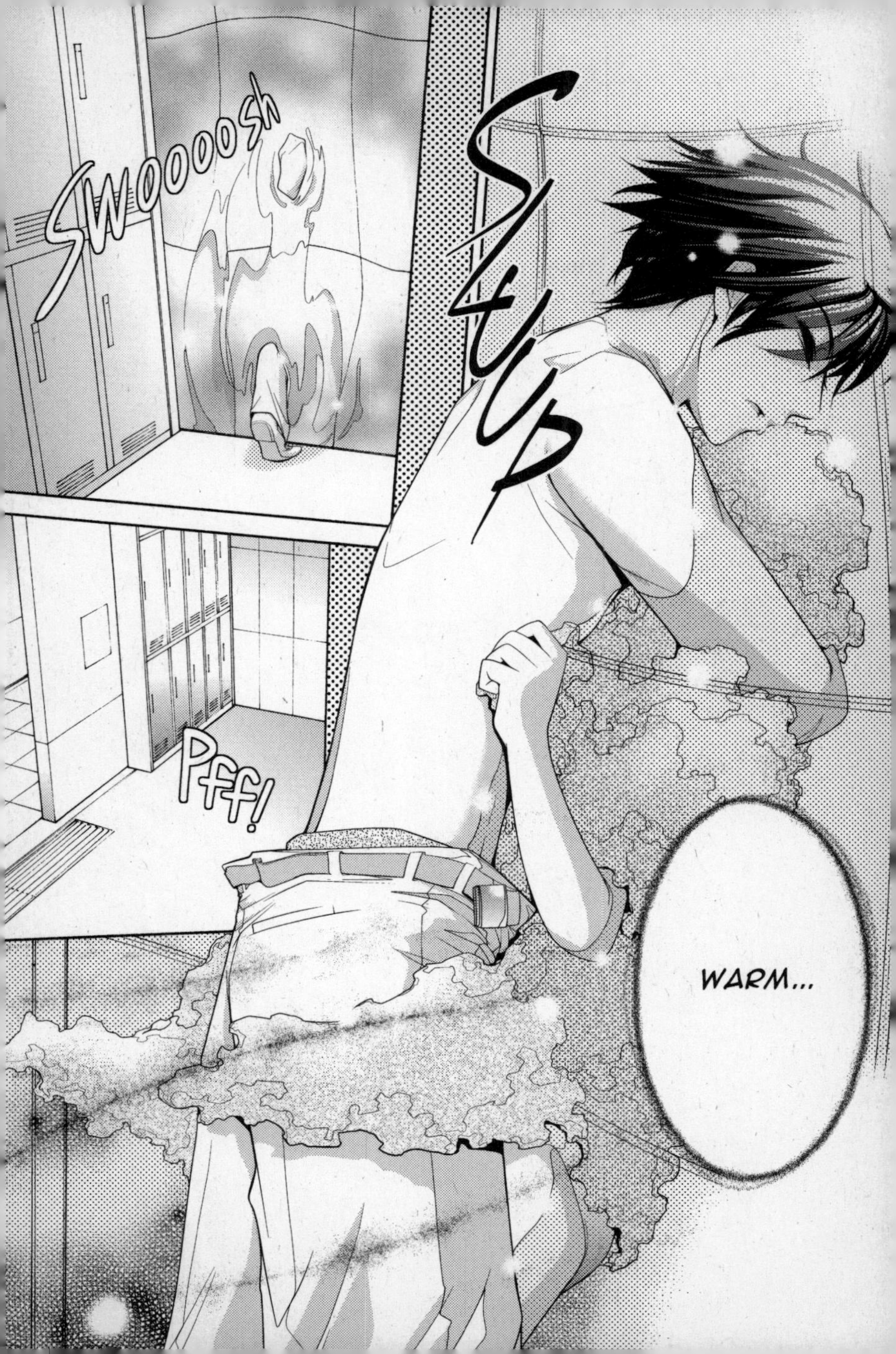
SLURP
WARM...
Swoooosh
Pff!

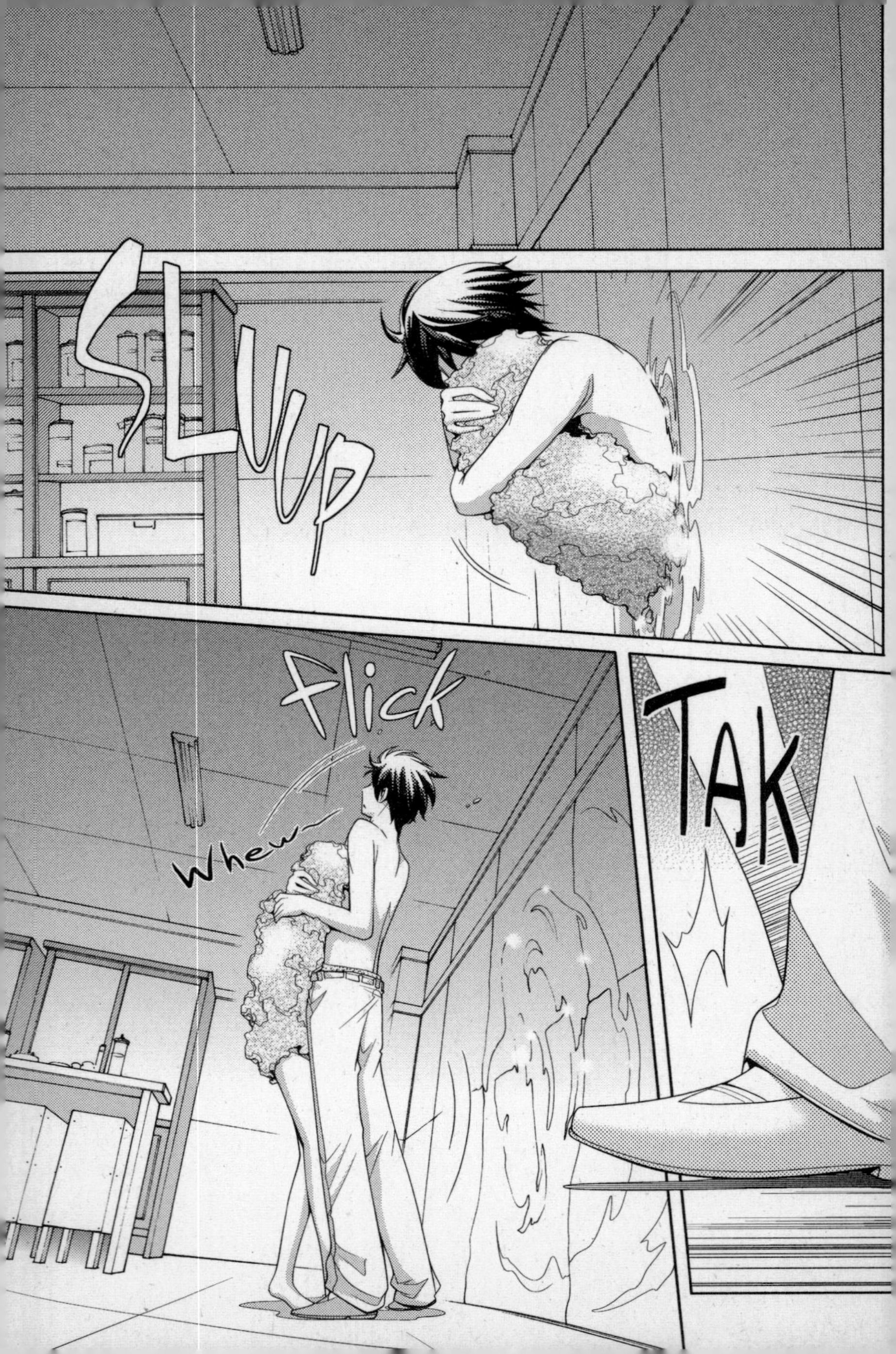
SLUUP
TAK
Flick
Whew~

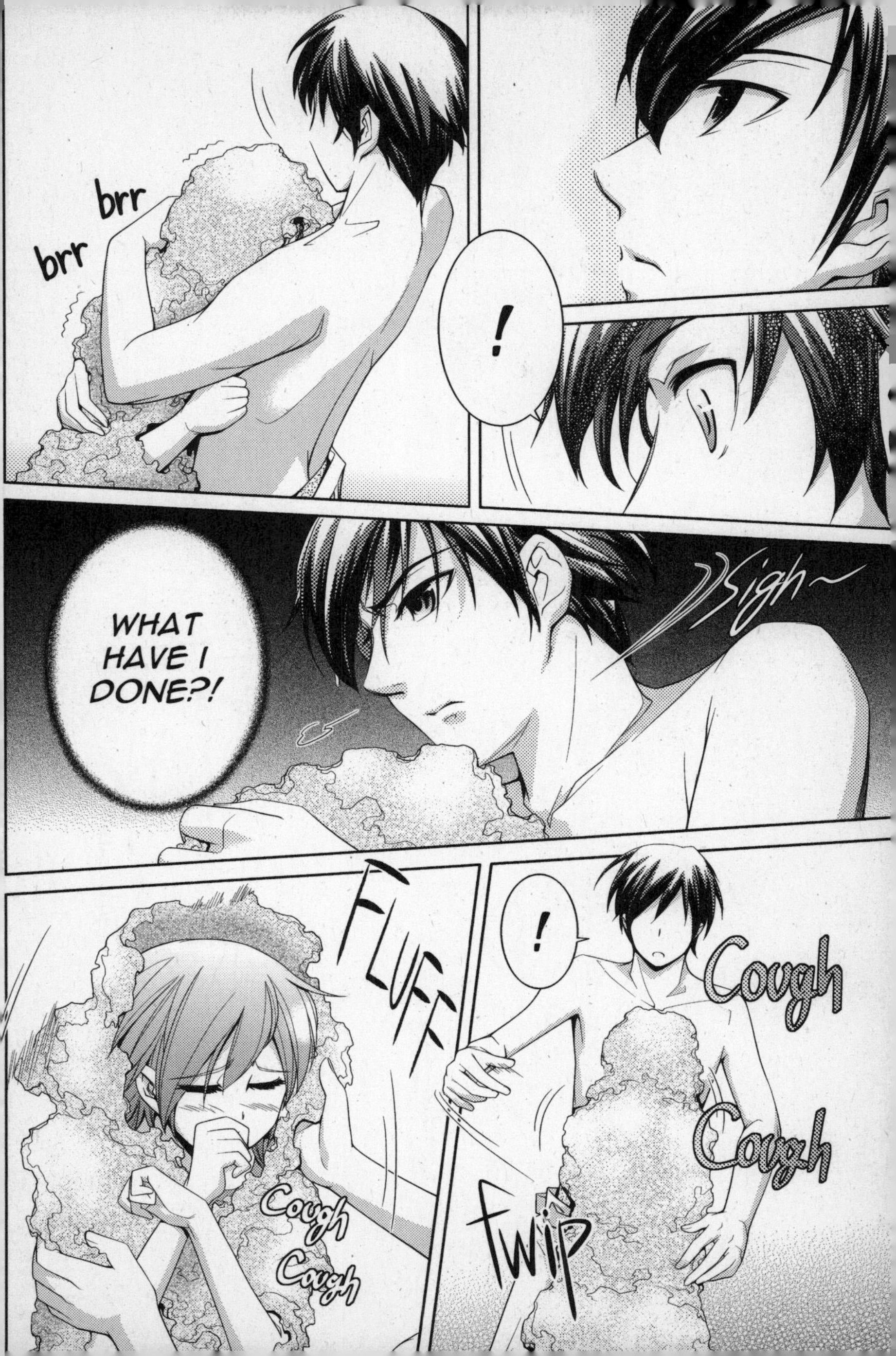
!
brr
brr
Sigh~
WHAT HAVE I DONE?!
!
Cough
Cough
fwip
FLUFF
Cough
Cough

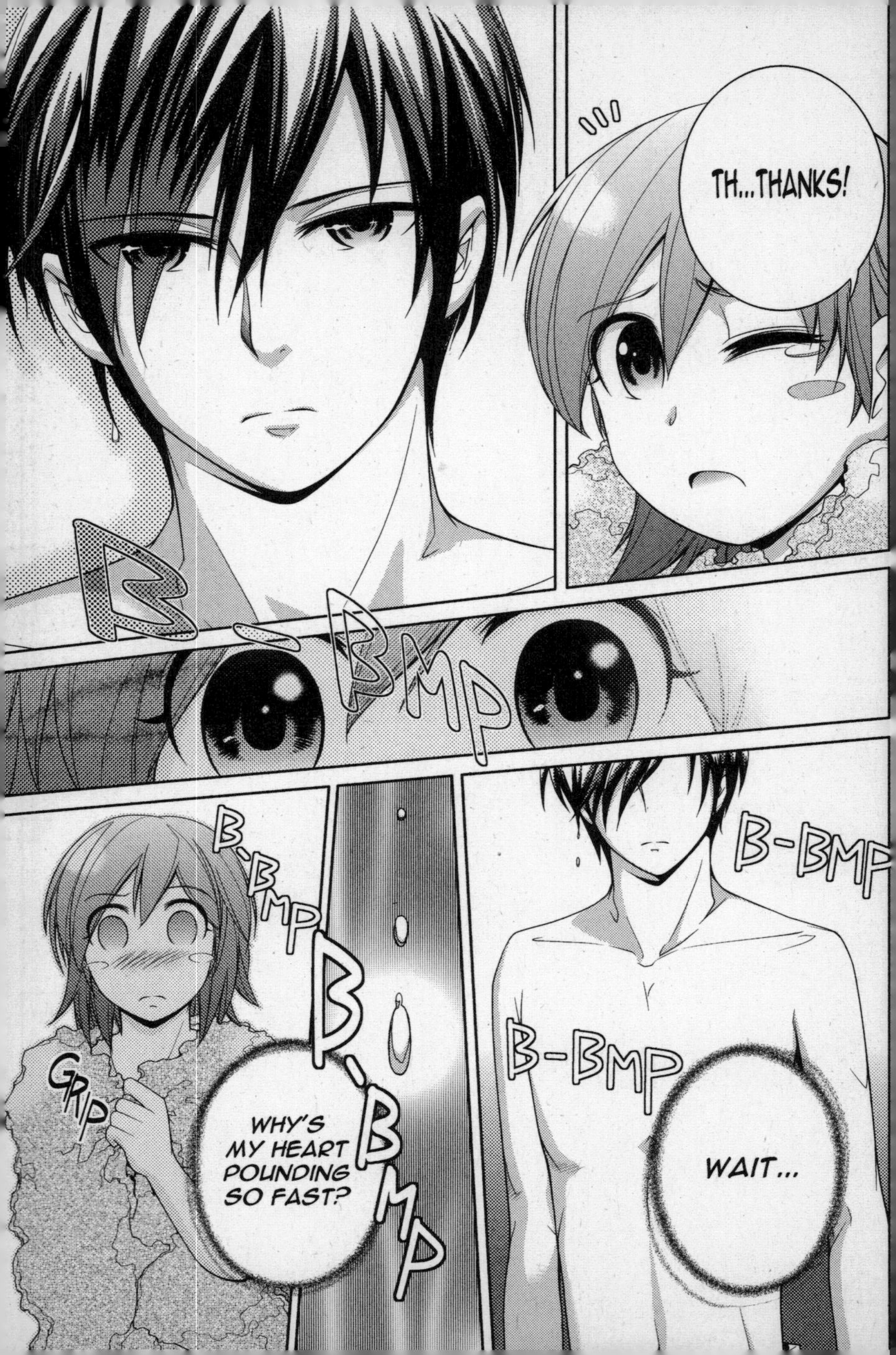
TH...THANKS!
B-BMP
B-BMP
B-BMP
WAIT...
B-BMP
B-BMP
GRIP
WHY'S MY HEART POUNDING SO FAST?

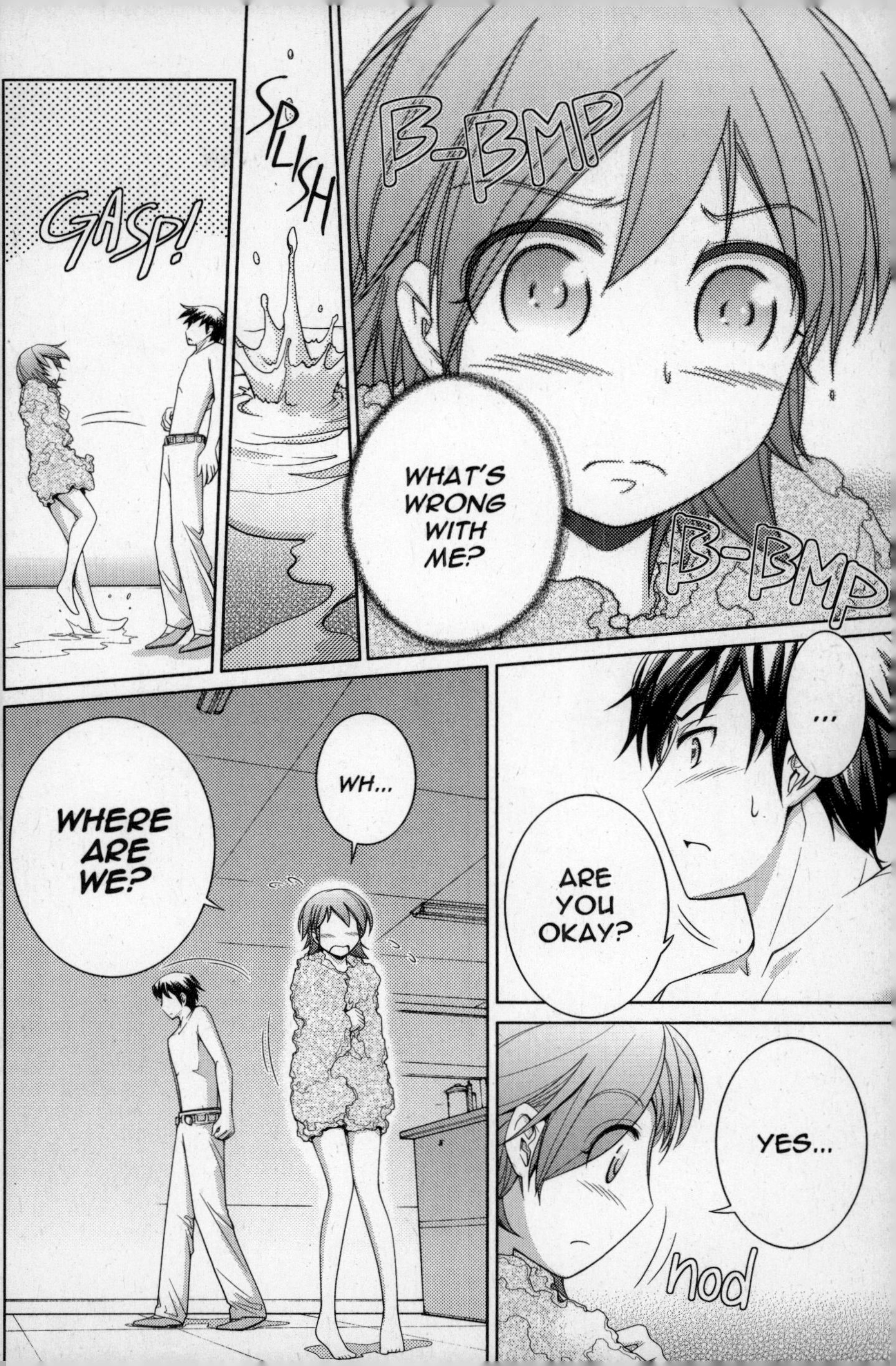
B-BMP
WHAT'S WRONG WITH ME?
B-BMP
SPLISH
GASP!
...
ARE YOU OKAY?
YES...
nod
WH...
WHERE ARE WE?

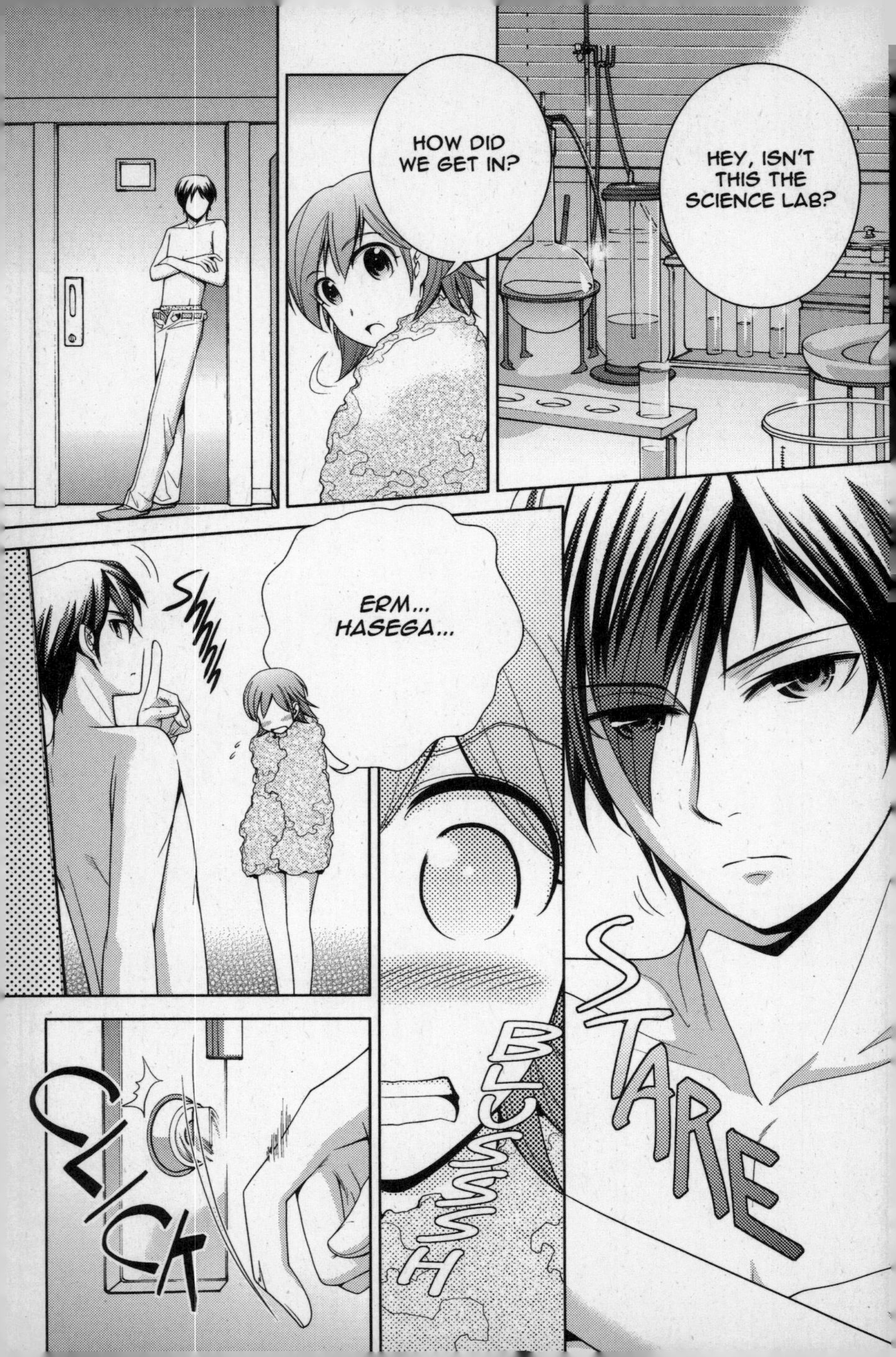
HEY, ISN'T THIS THE SCIENCE LAB?
HOW DID WE GET IN?
STARE
BLUSSSH
ERM... HASEGA...
Shhhh
CLICK

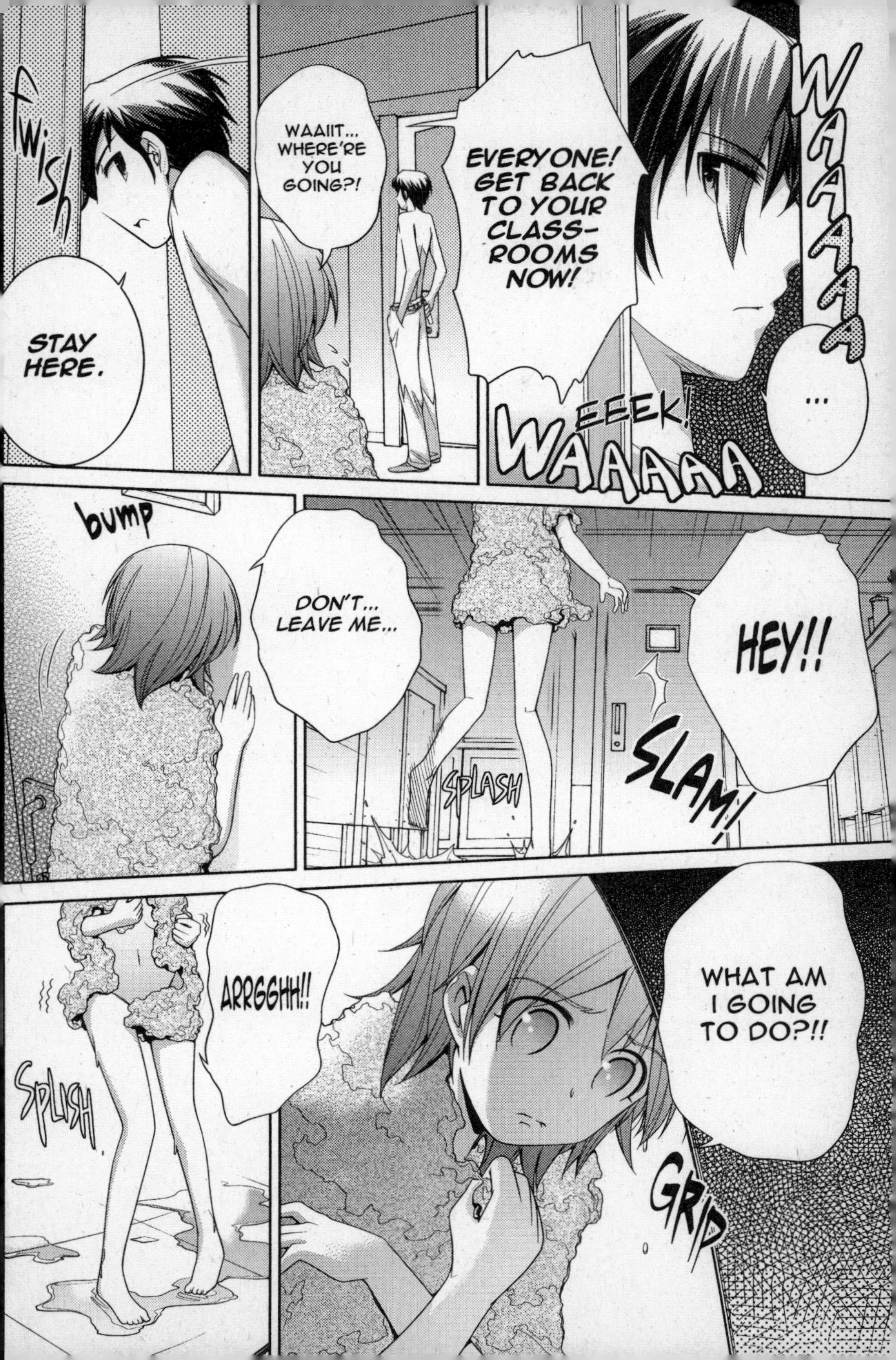
WAAAAAA
...
EVERYONE! GET BACK TO YOUR CLASS-ROOMS NOW!
EEEK!
WAAAAAA
WAAIIT... WHERE'RE YOU GOING?!
STAY HERE.
fwish
HEY!!
SLAM!
DON'T... LEAVE ME...
SPLASH
bump
WHAT AM I GOING TO DO?!!
GRIP
ARRGGHH!!
SPLISH

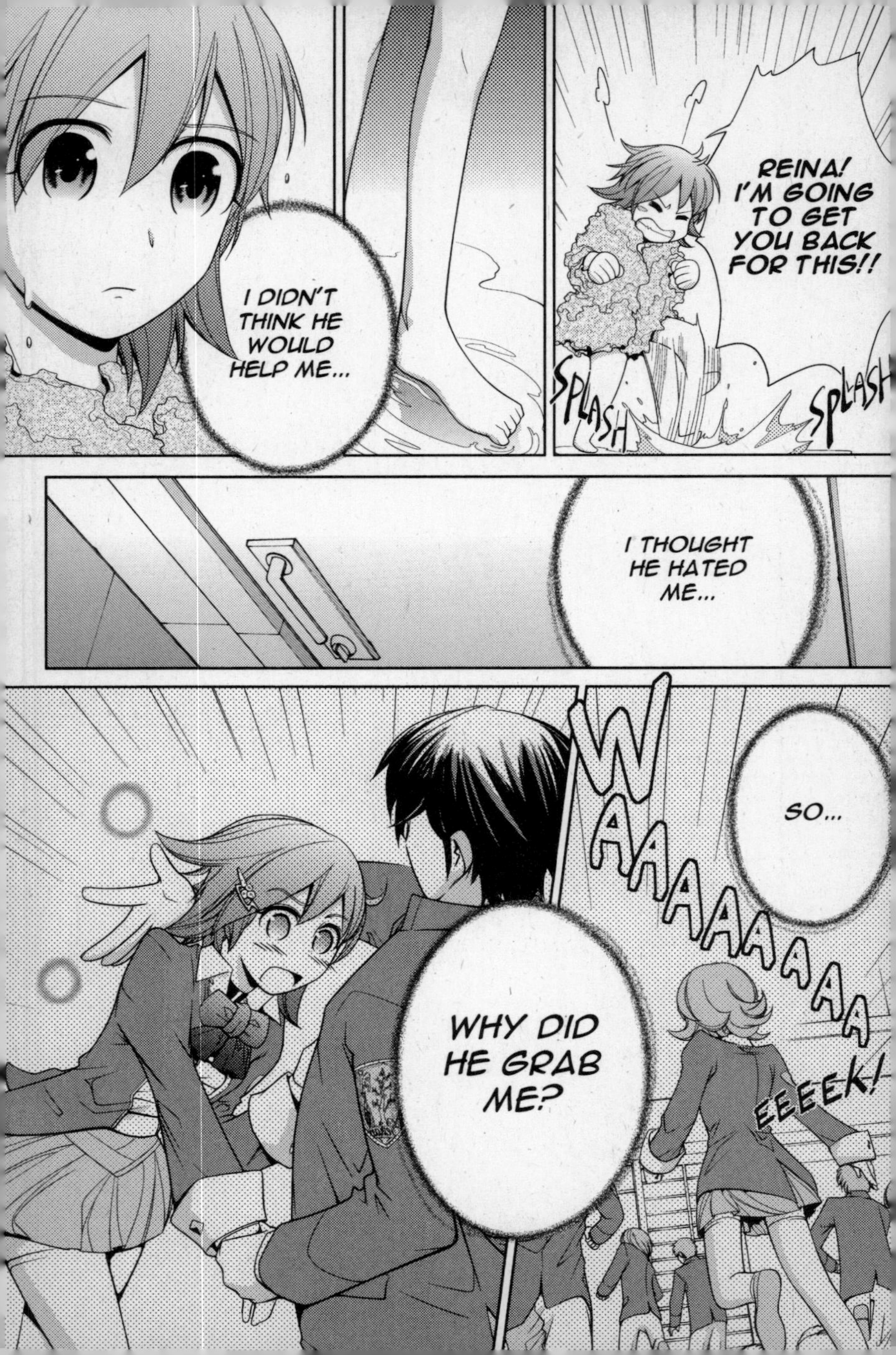
REINA! I'M GOING TO GET YOU BACK FOR THIS!!
SPLASH
SPLASH
I DIDN'T THINK HE WOULD HELP ME...
I THOUGHT HE HATED ME...
SO...
WAAAAAAAAAA
WHY DID HE GRAB ME?
EEEEK!

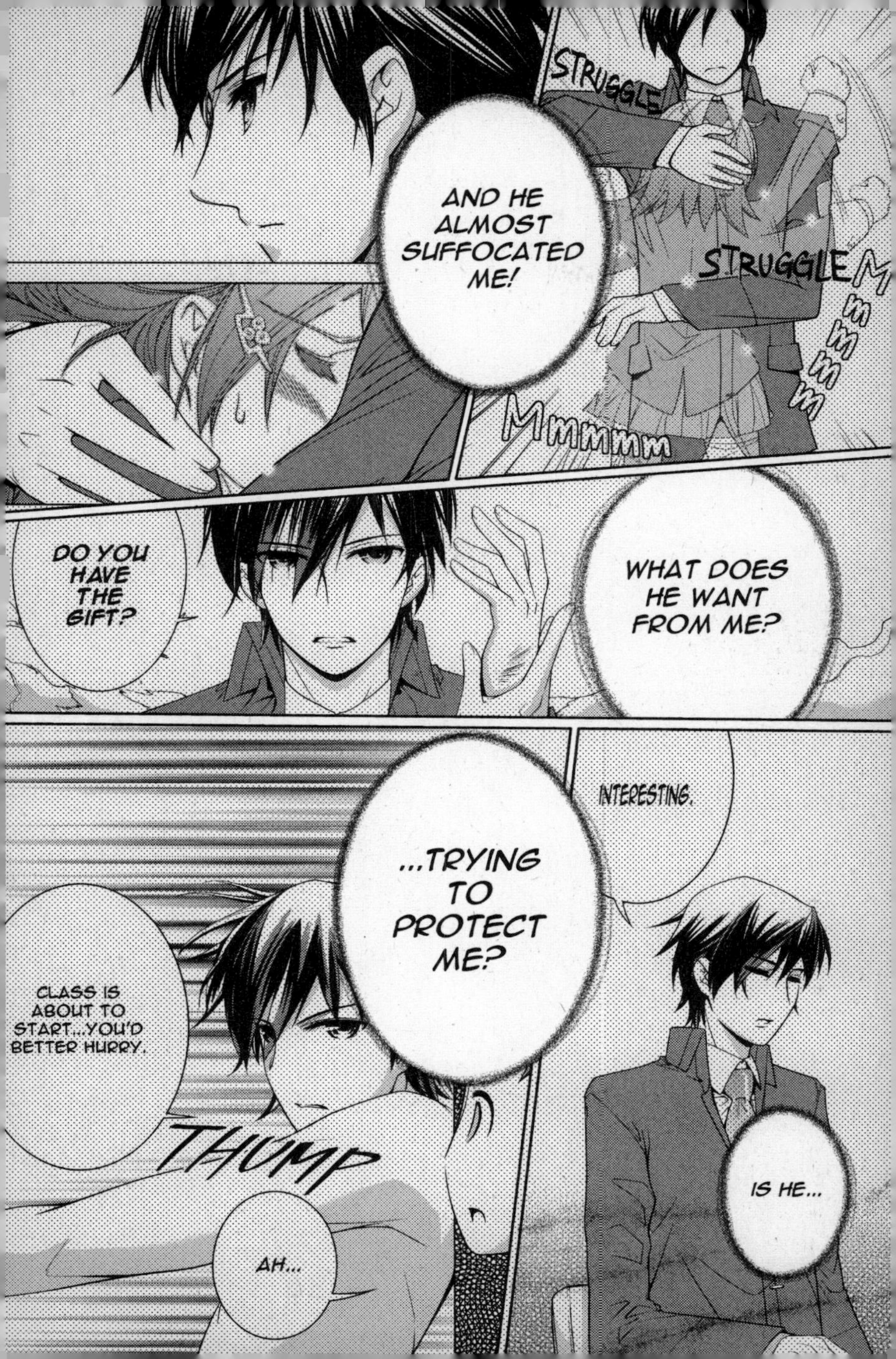
STRUGGLE
STRUGGLE
MMMMM
MMMMMM
AND HE ALMOST SUFFOCATED ME!
WHAT DOES HE WANT FROM ME?
DO YOU HAVE THE GIFT?
INTERESTING.
IS HE...
...TRYING TO PROTECT ME?
CLASS IS ABOUT TO START...YOU'D BETTER HURRY.
THUMP
AH...

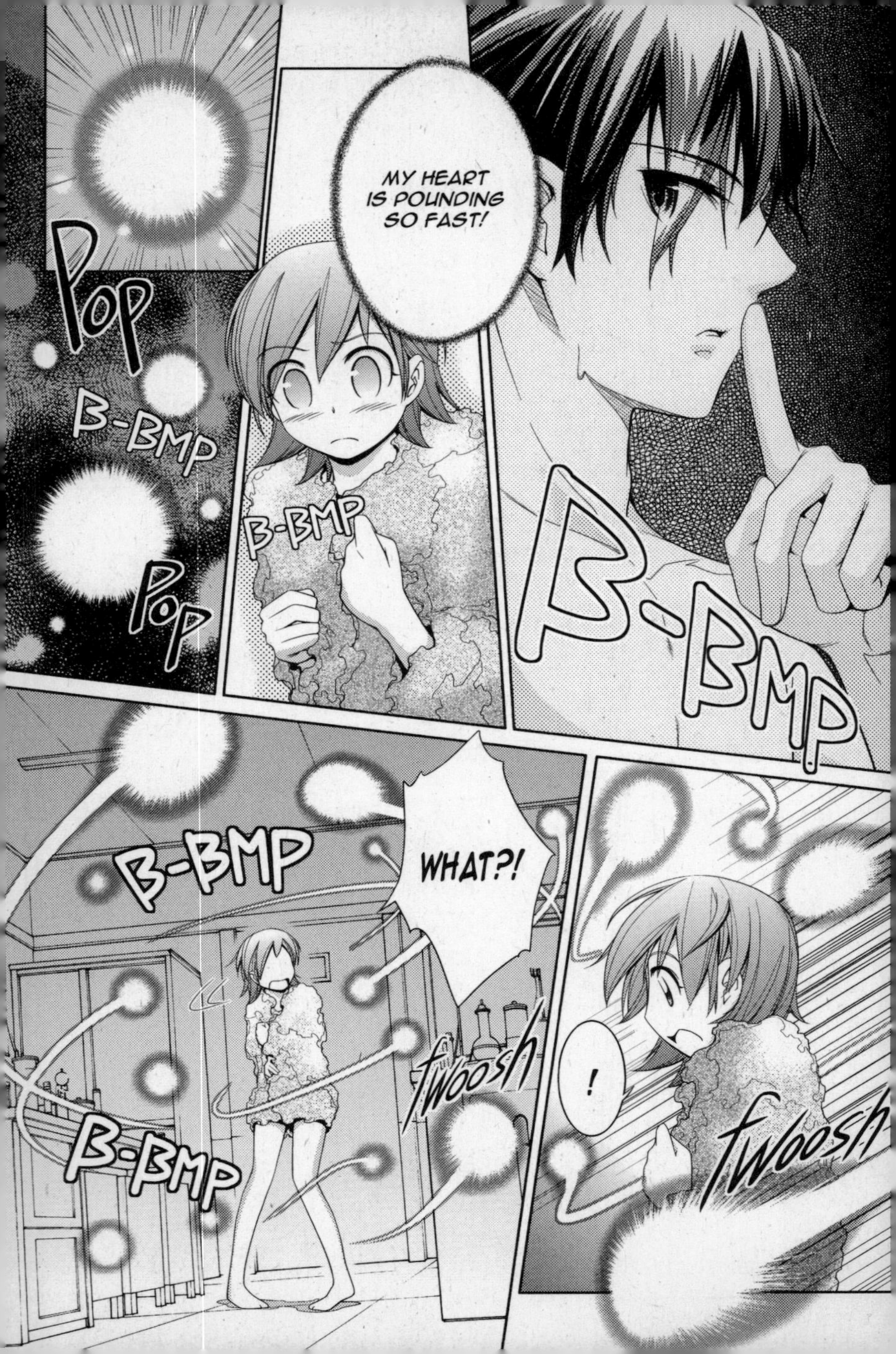
B-BMP
MY HEART IS POUNDING SO FAST!
B-BMP
Pop
B-BMP
Pop
!
twoosh
WHAT?!
B-BMP
twoosh
B-BMP

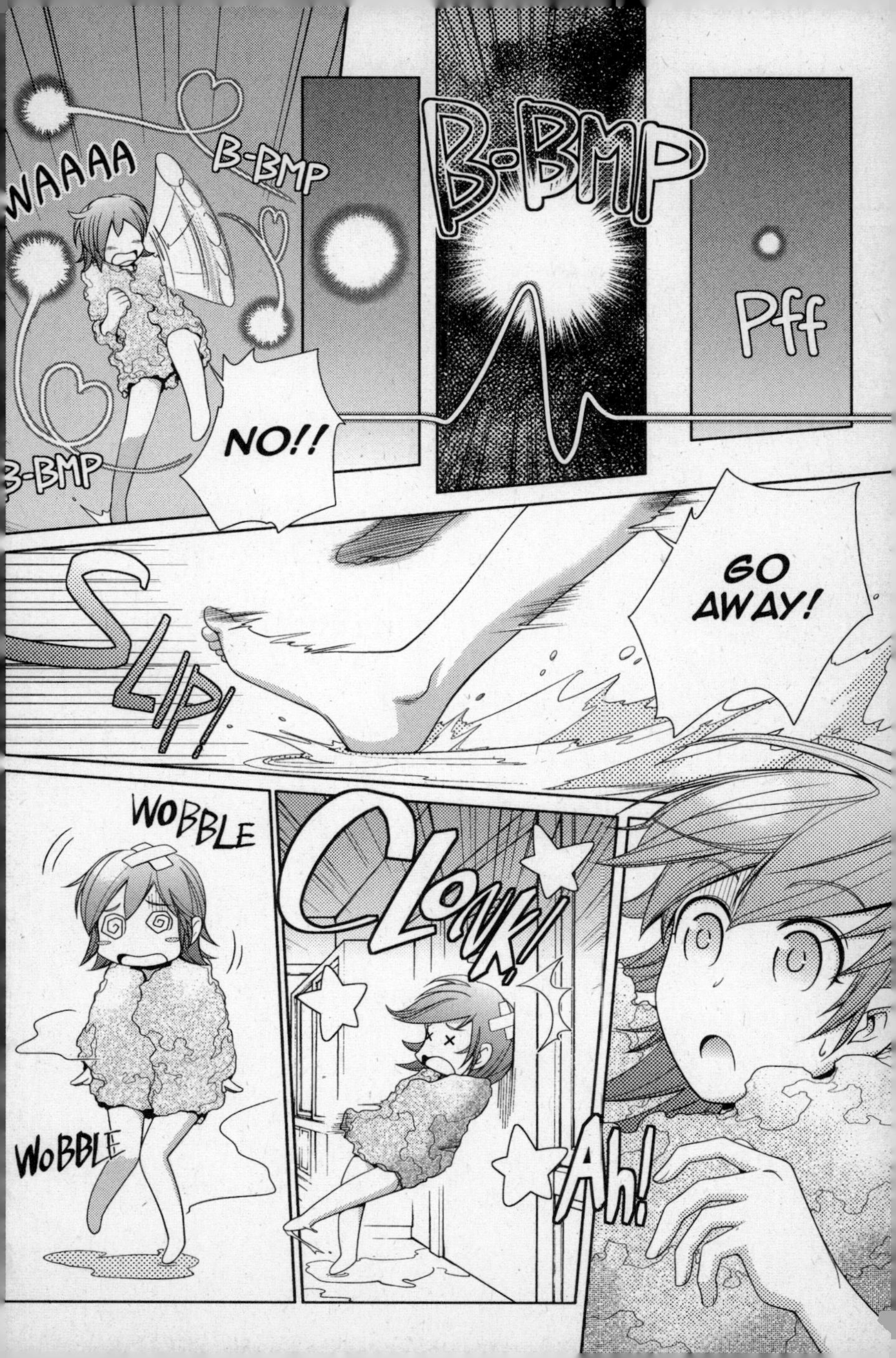
Pff
B-BMP
B-BMP
WAAAA
NO!!
B-BMP
GO AWAY!
SLIP!
Ah!
CLONK!
WOBBLE
WOBBLE

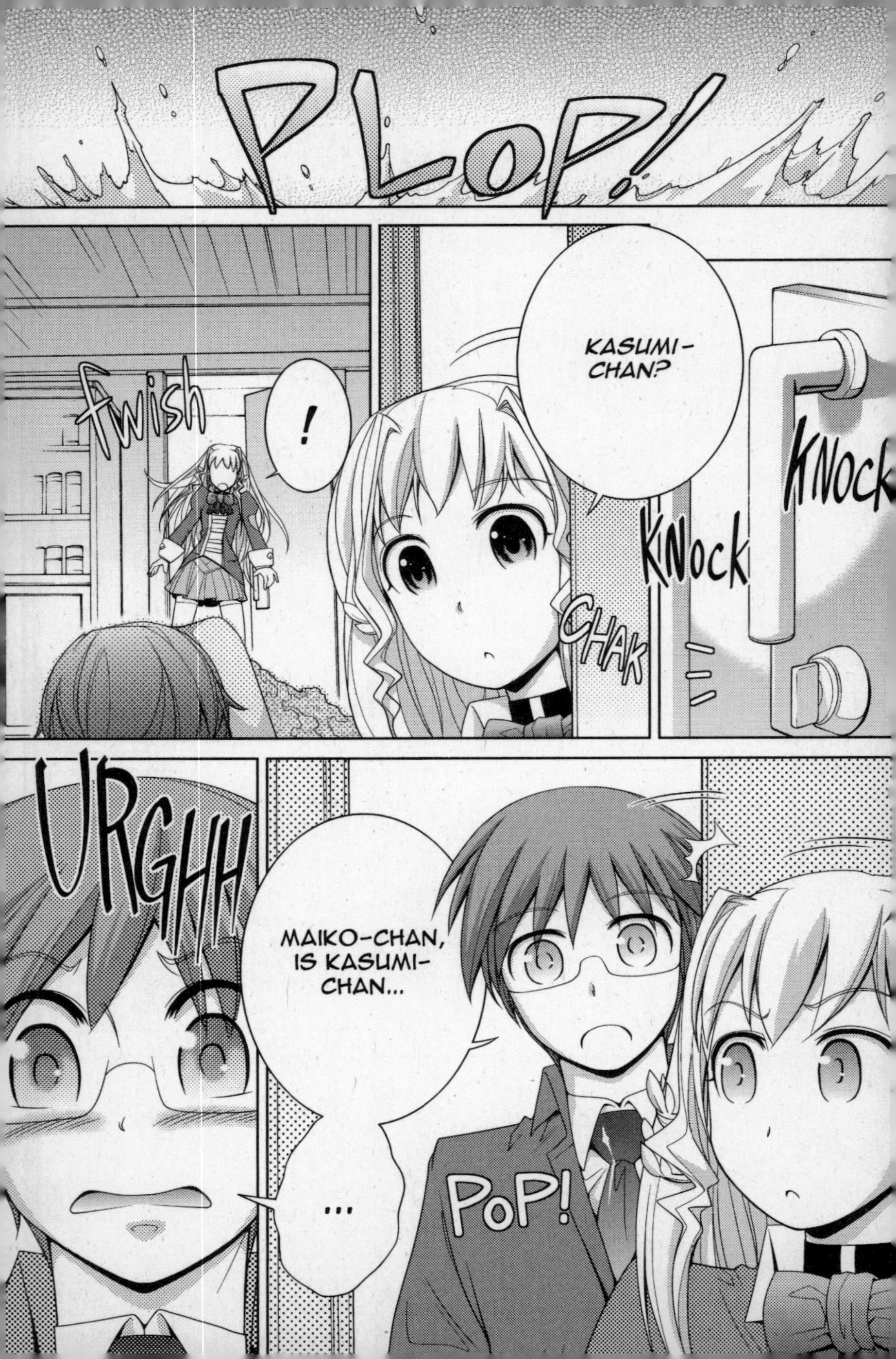
PLOP!
KNOCK
KASUMI-CHAN?
KNOCK
CHAK
!
FWISH
MAIKO-CHAN, IS KASUMI-CHAN...
POP!
URGHH
...

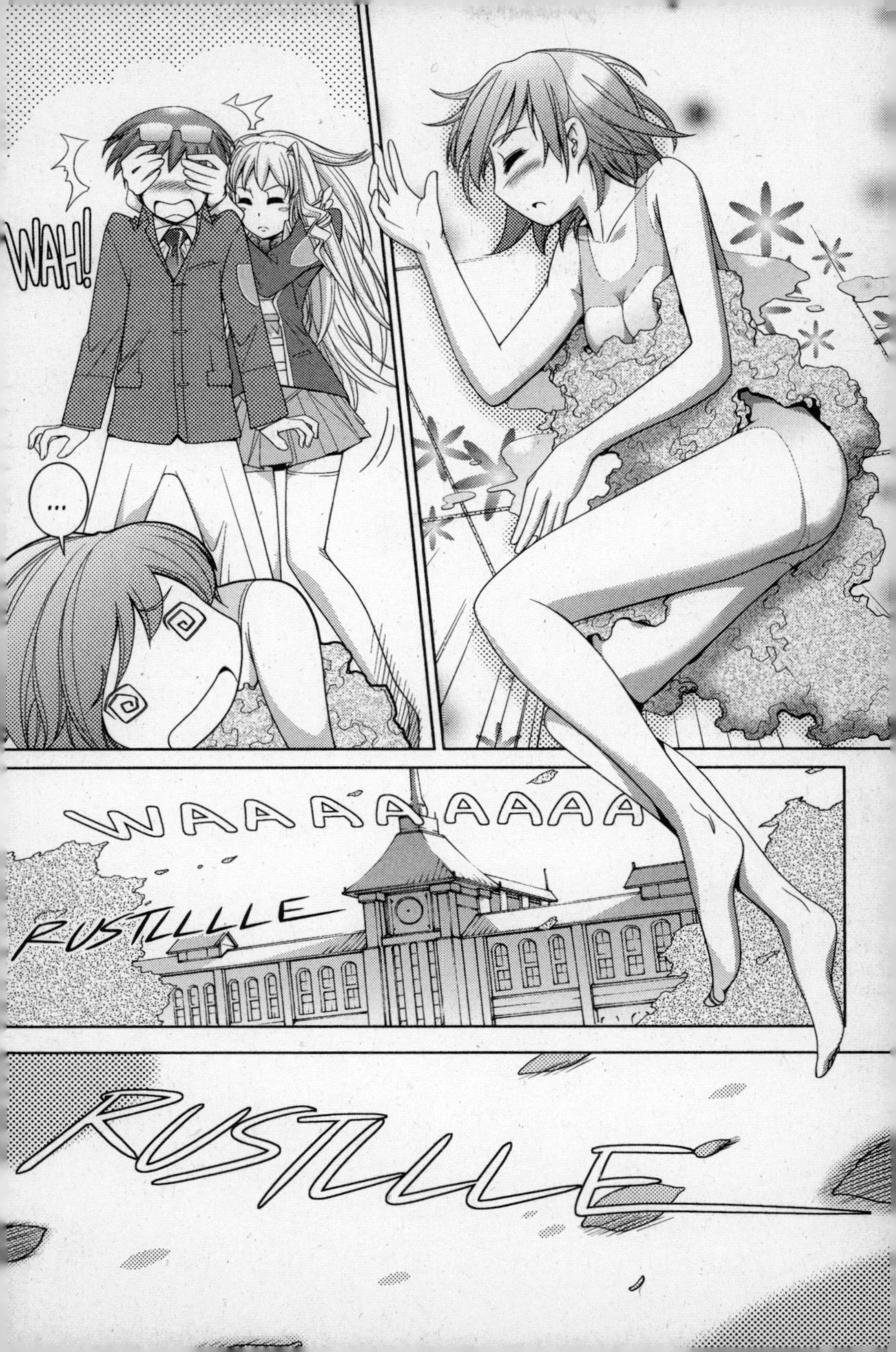
WAH!
...
WAAAAAAAA
RUSTLLLLE
RUSTLLLE

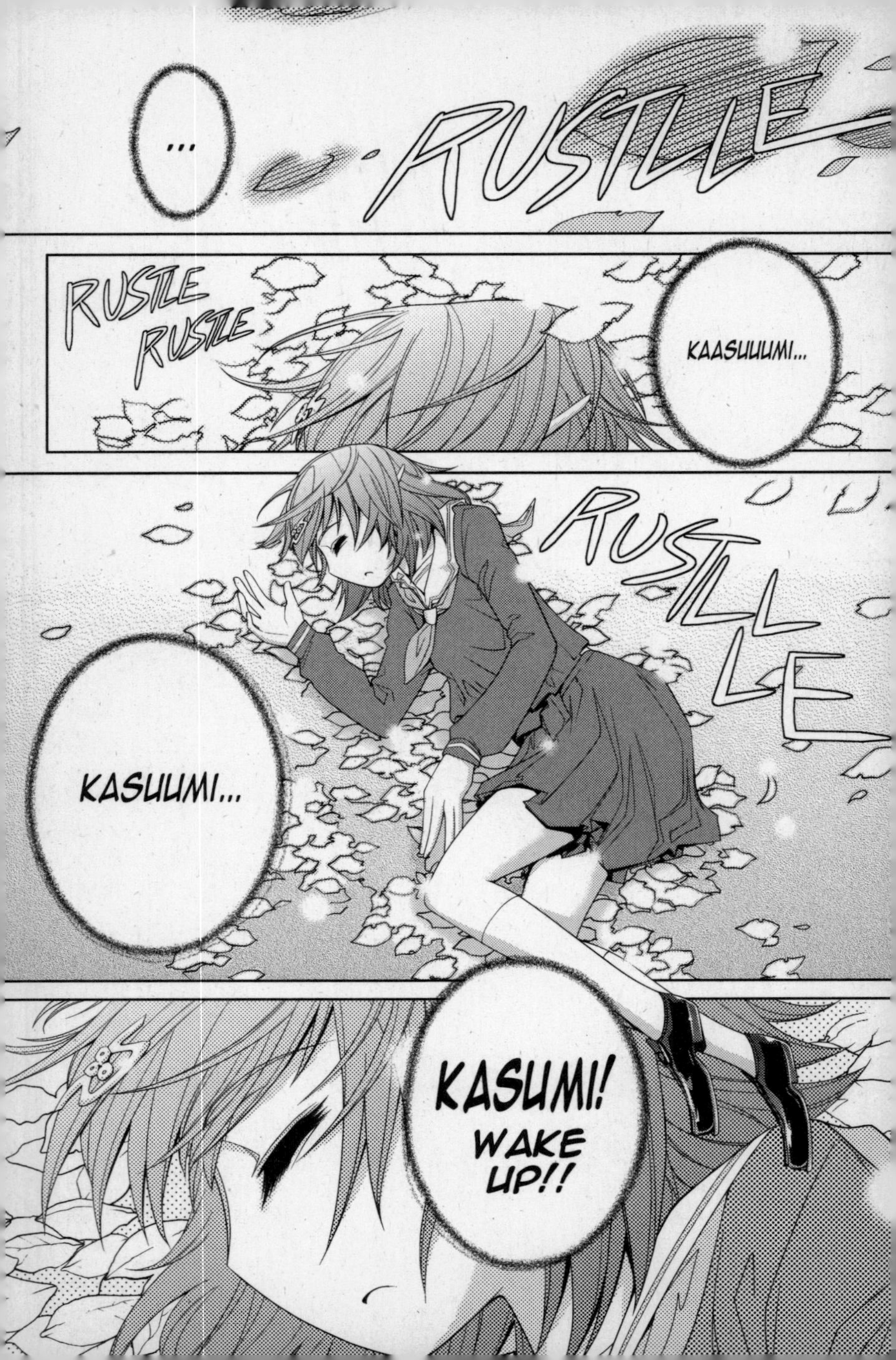
RUSTLLE
...
KAASUUMI...
RUSTLE RUSTLE
RUSTLLE
KASUUMI...
KASUMI! WAKE UP!!

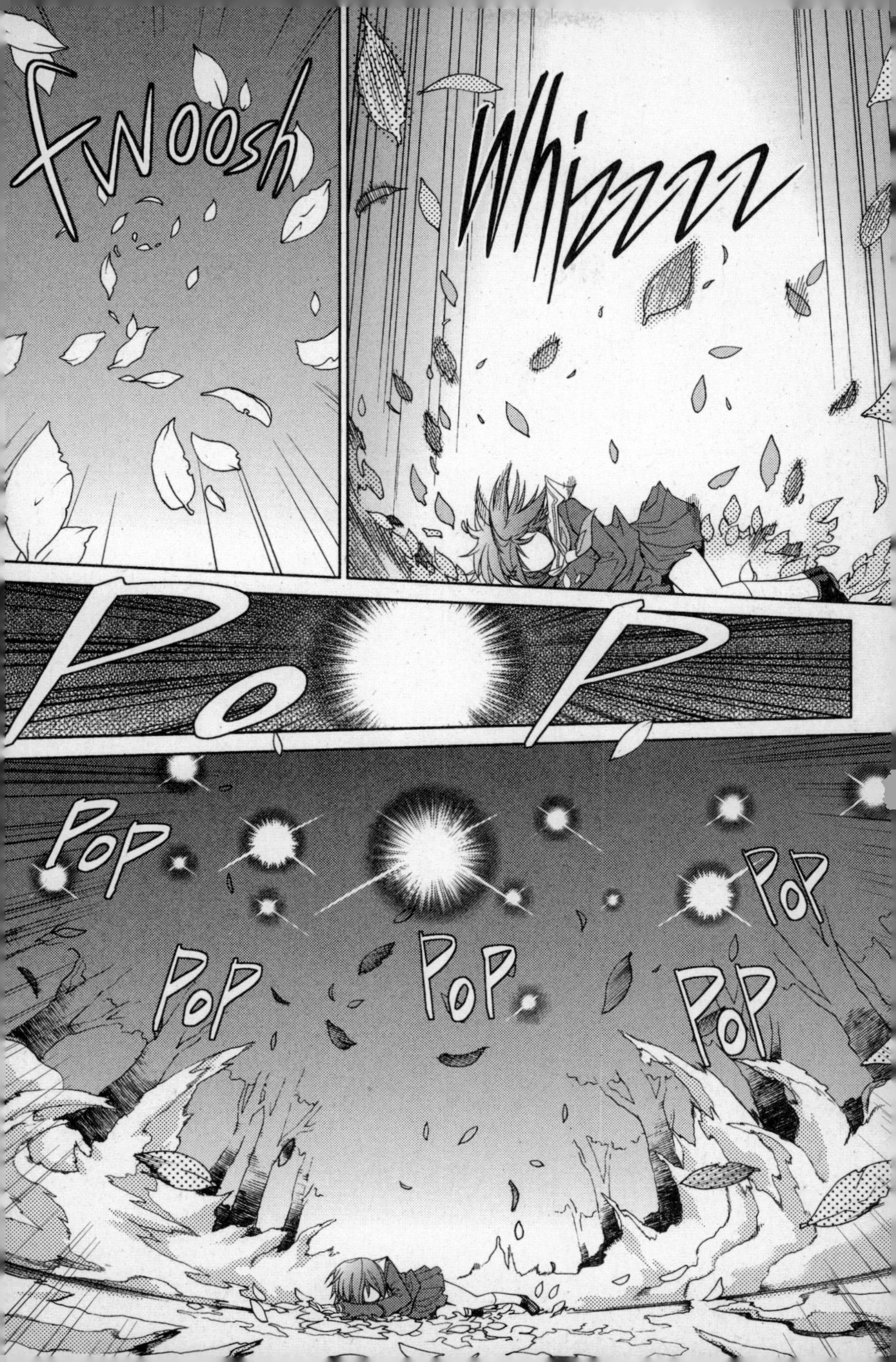

Whizzzz
Fwoosh
POP
POP
POP
POP
POP
POP

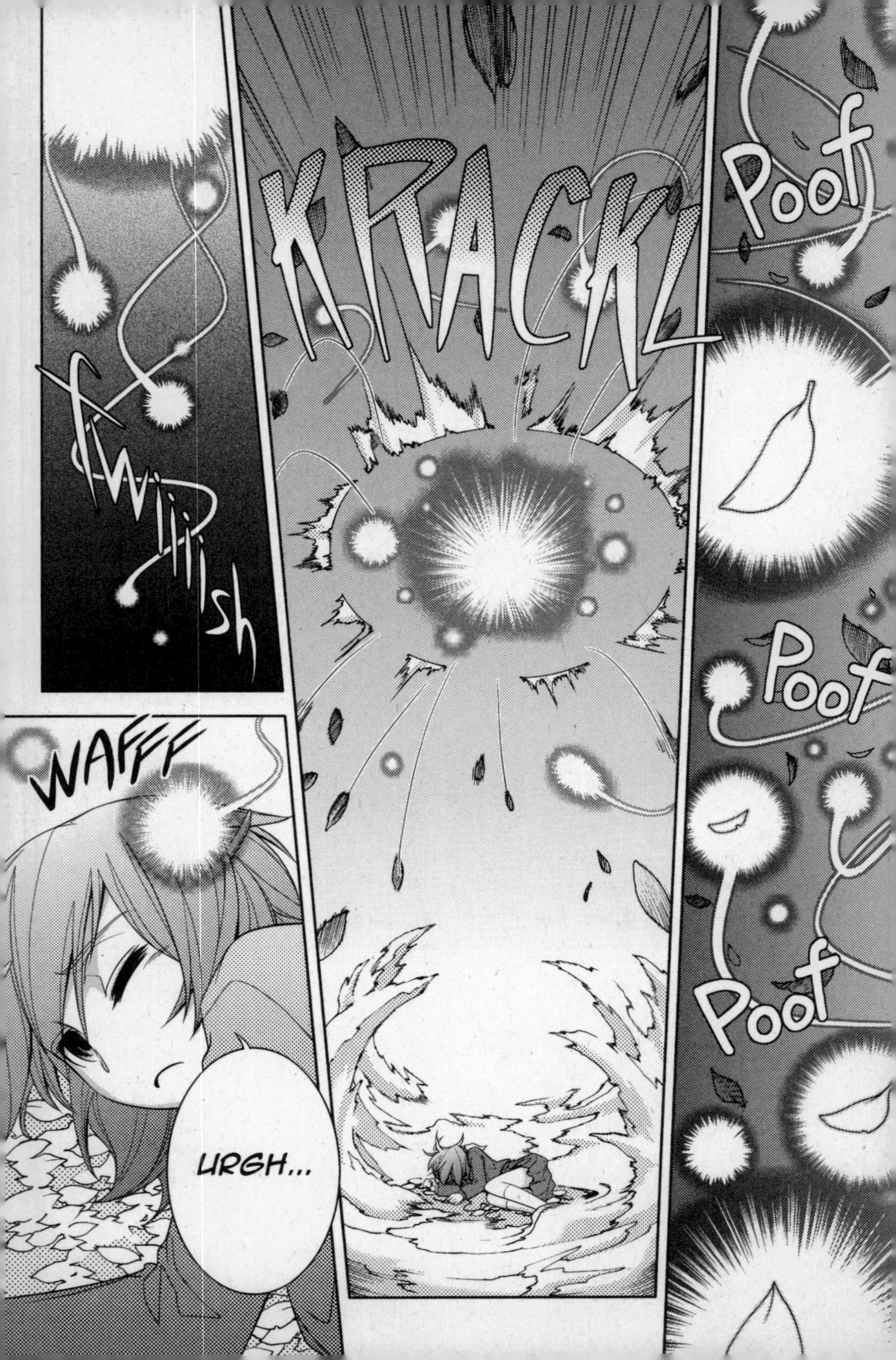
Poof
Poof
Poof
KRACKL
Fwiiiish
WAFFF
URGH...

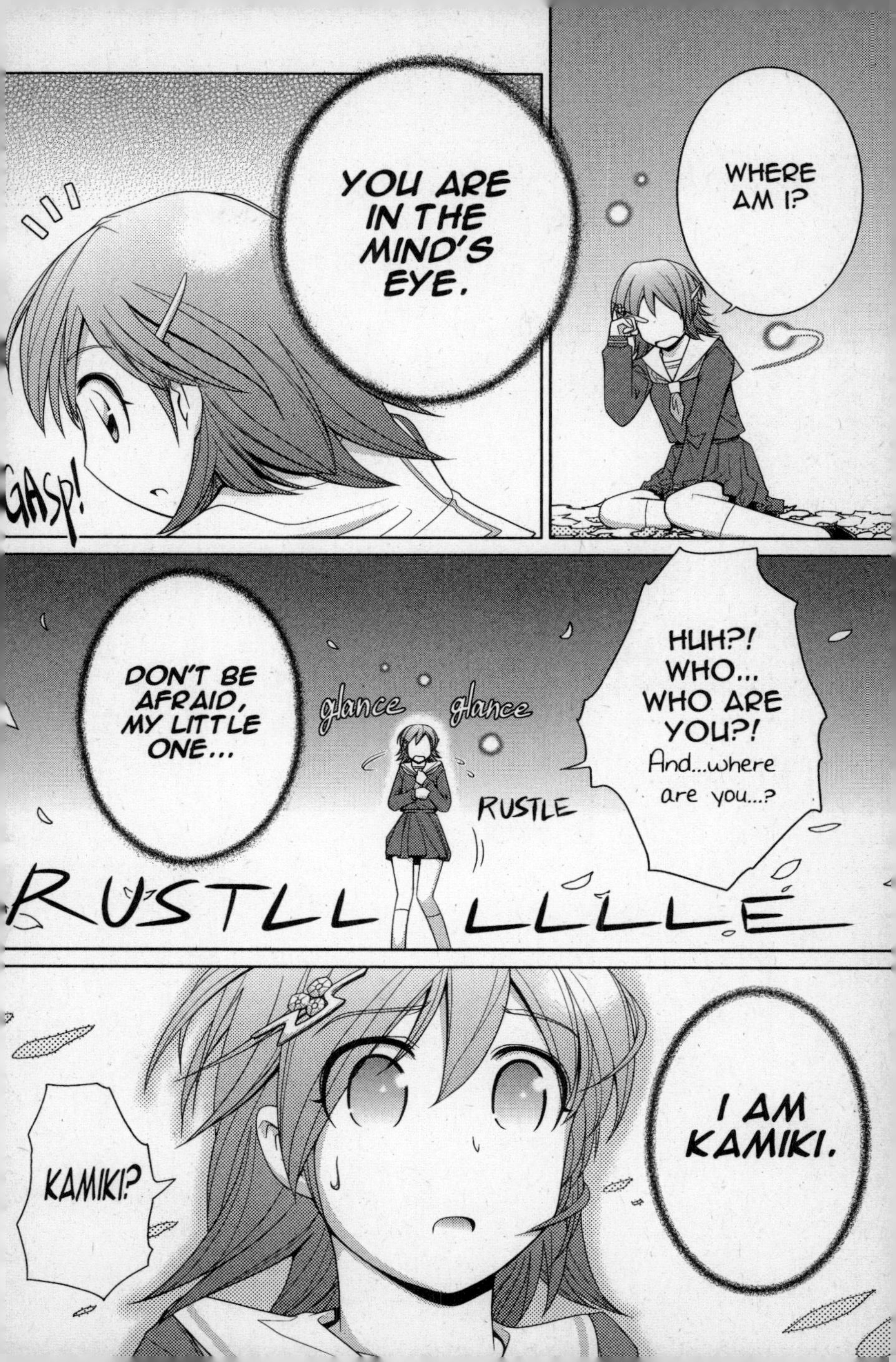
WHERE AM I?
YOU ARE IN THE MIND'S EYE.
GASP!
HUH?! WHO... WHO ARE YOU?! And...where are you...?
glance glance
RUSTLE
DON'T BE AFRAID, MY LITTLE ONE...
RUSTLLLLLLLE
I AM KAMIKI.
KAMIKI?

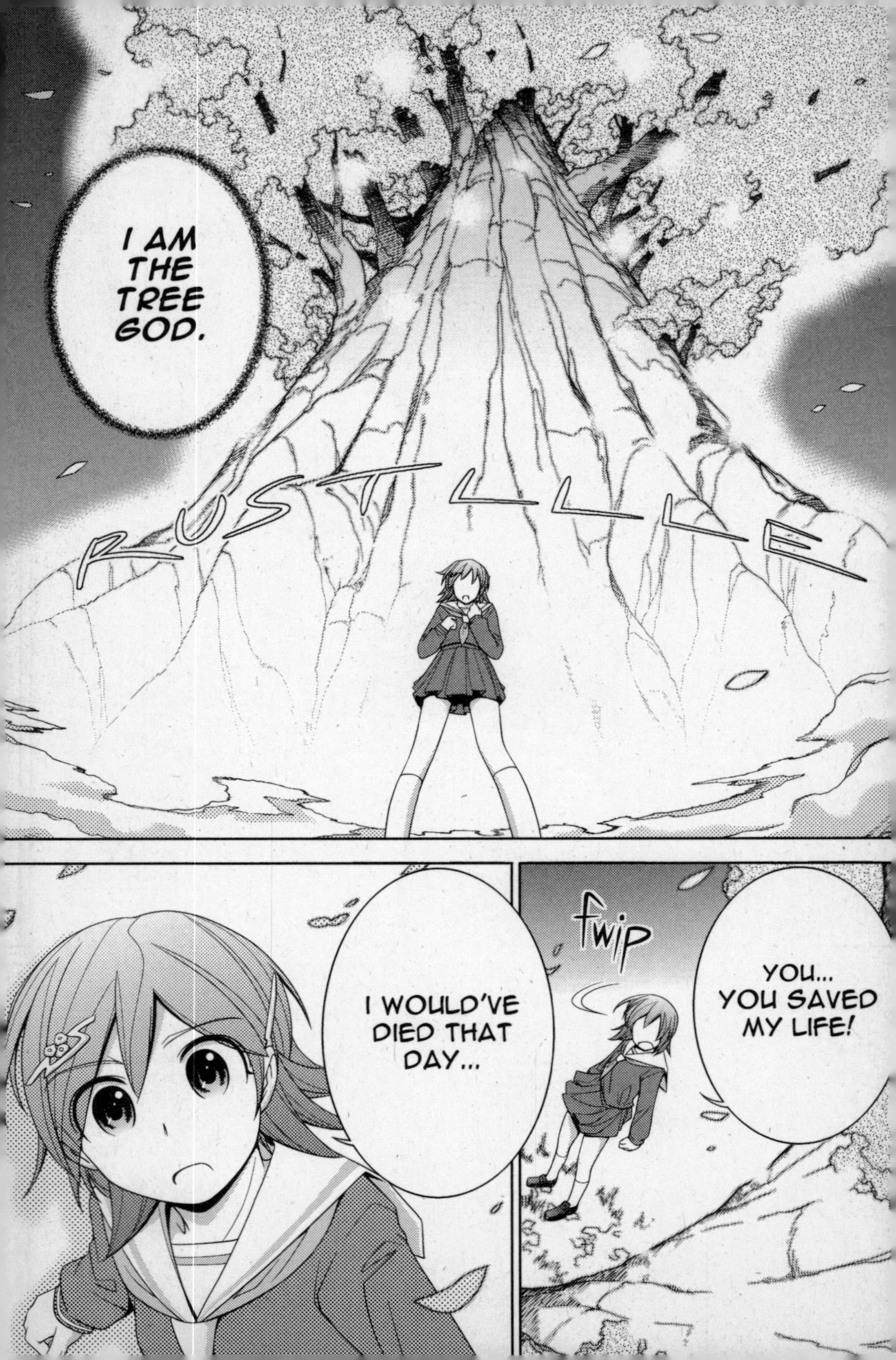
I AM THE TREE GOD.
RUSTLLLE
fwip
YOU... YOU SAVED MY LIFE!
I WOULD'VE DIED THAT DAY...

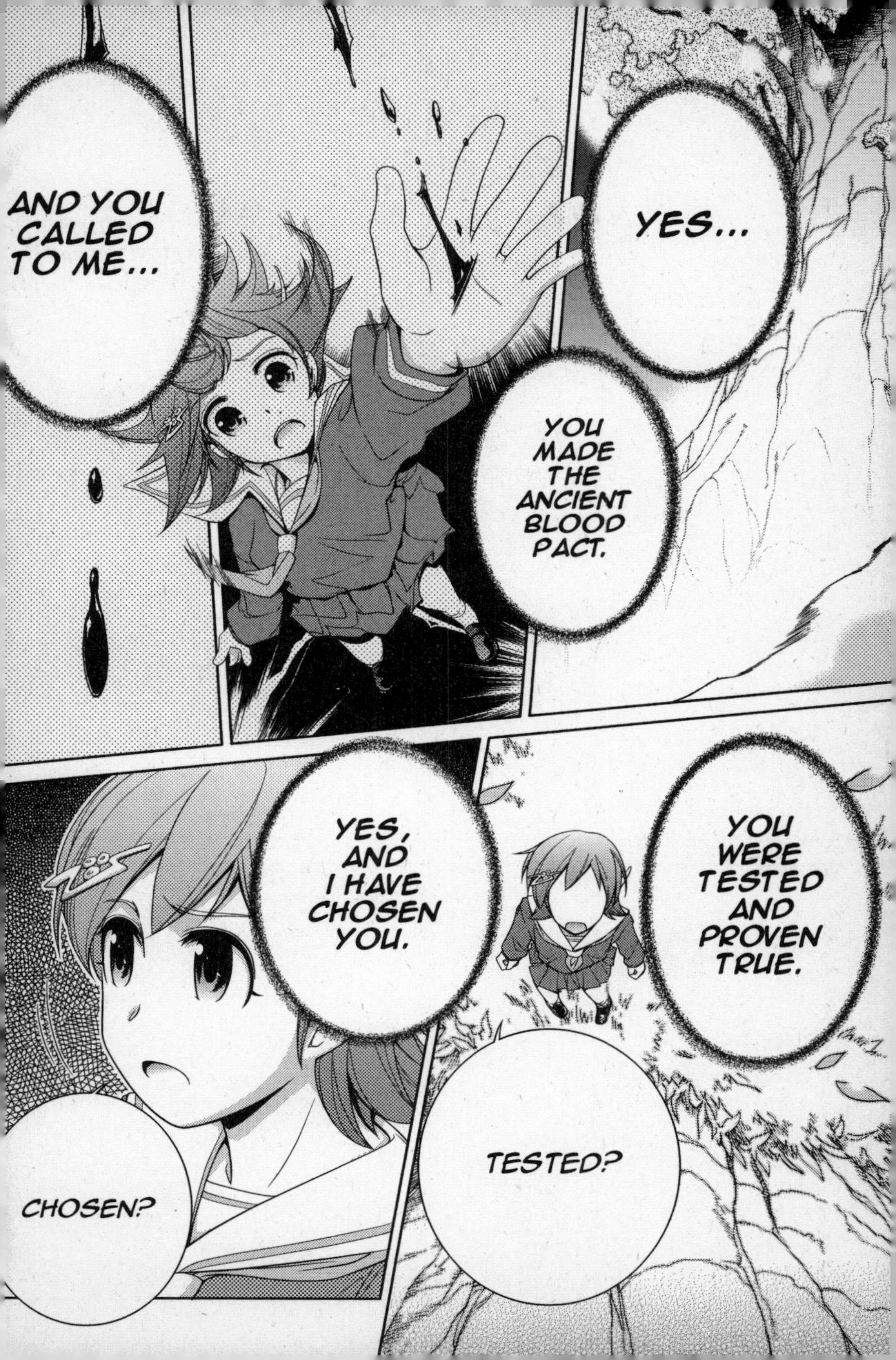
YES...
YOU MADE THE ANCIENT BLOOD PACT.
AND YOU CALLED TO ME...
YOU WERE TESTED AND PROVEN TRUE.
TESTED?
YES, AND I HAVE CHOSEN YOU.
CHOSEN?

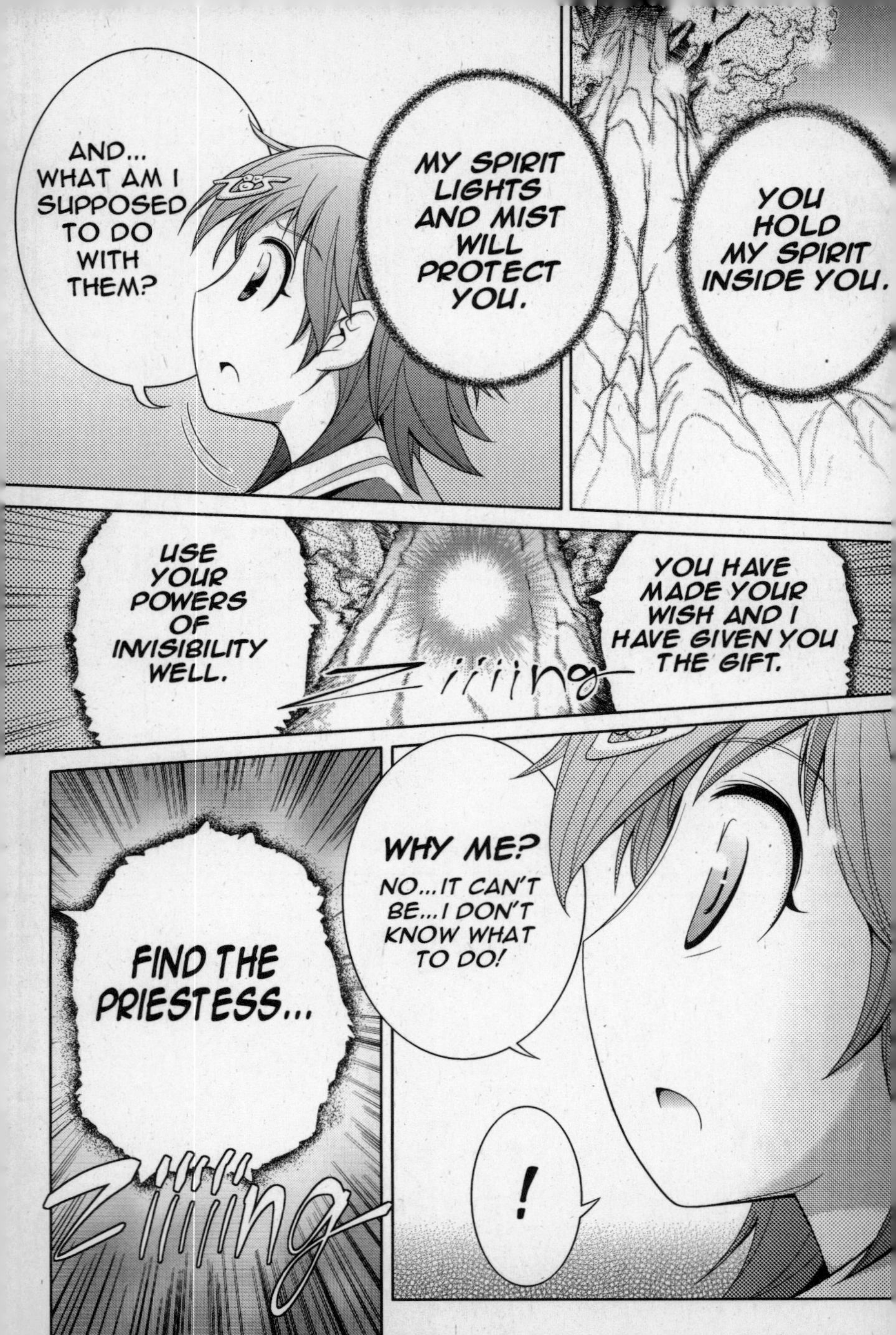
YOU HOLD MY SPIRIT INSIDE YOU.
MY SPIRIT LIGHTS AND MIST WILL PROTECT YOU.
AND... WHAT AM I SUPPOSED TO DO WITH THEM?
YOU HAVE MADE YOUR WISH AND I HAVE GIVEN YOU THE GIFT.
Ziiing
USE YOUR POWERS OF INVISIBILITY WELL.
WHY ME?
NO...IT CAN'T BE...I DON'T KNOW WHAT TO DO!
!
FIND THE PRIESTESS...
Ziiiing

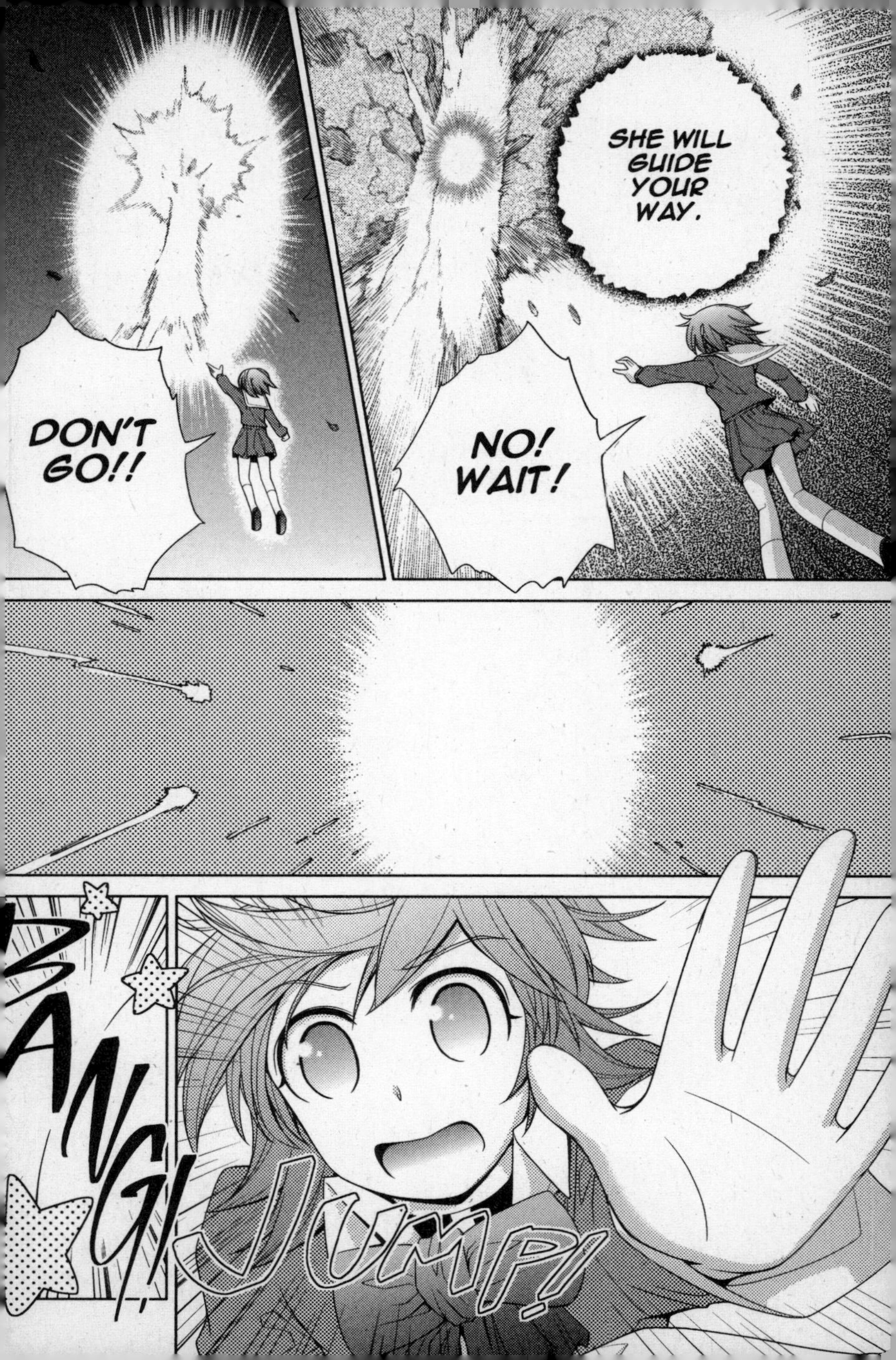
SHE WILL GUIDE YOUR WAY.
NO! WAIT!
DON'T GO!!
JUMP!
BANG!

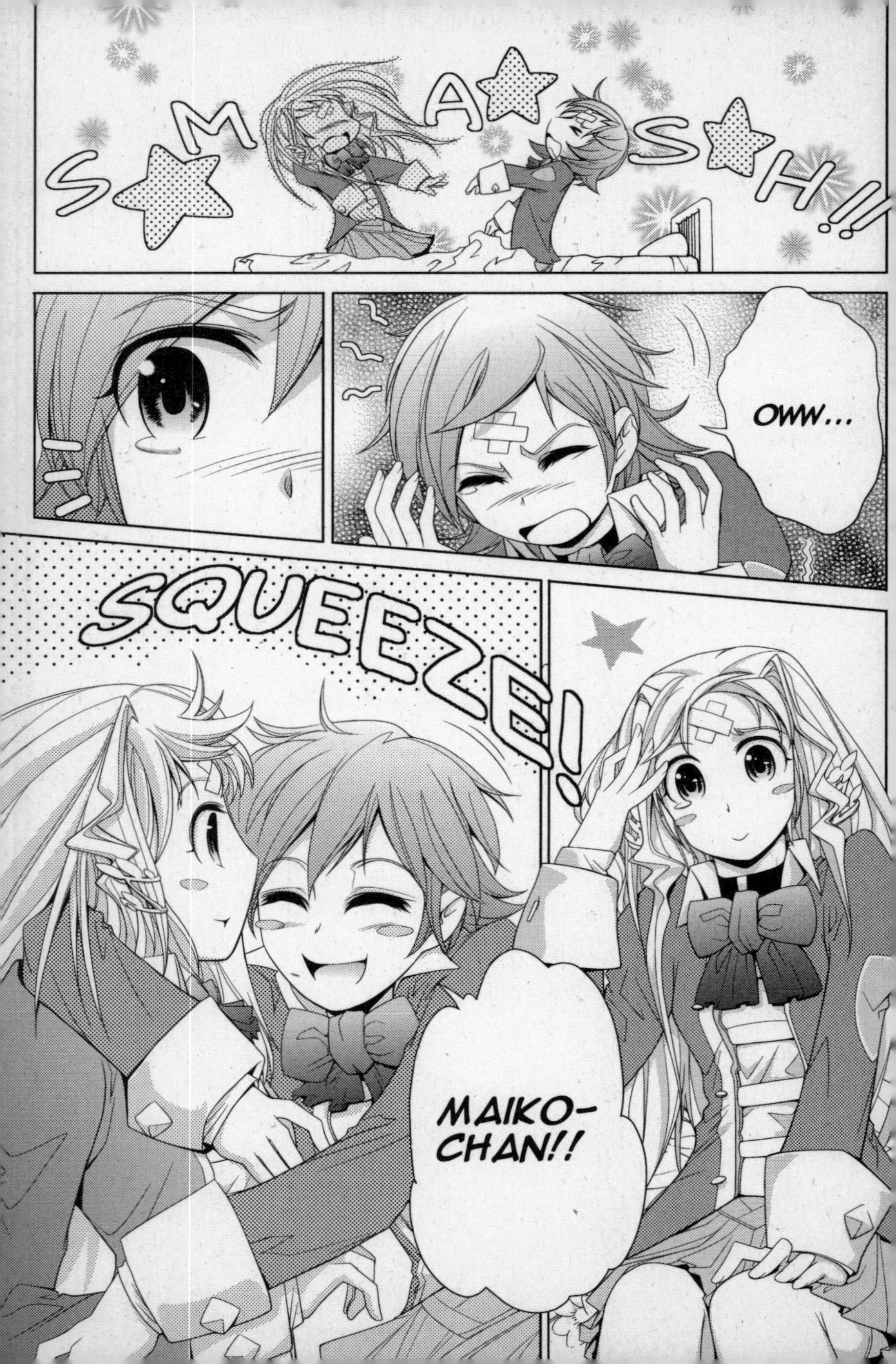
SMASH!!
OWW...
SQUEEZE!
MAIKO-CHAN!!

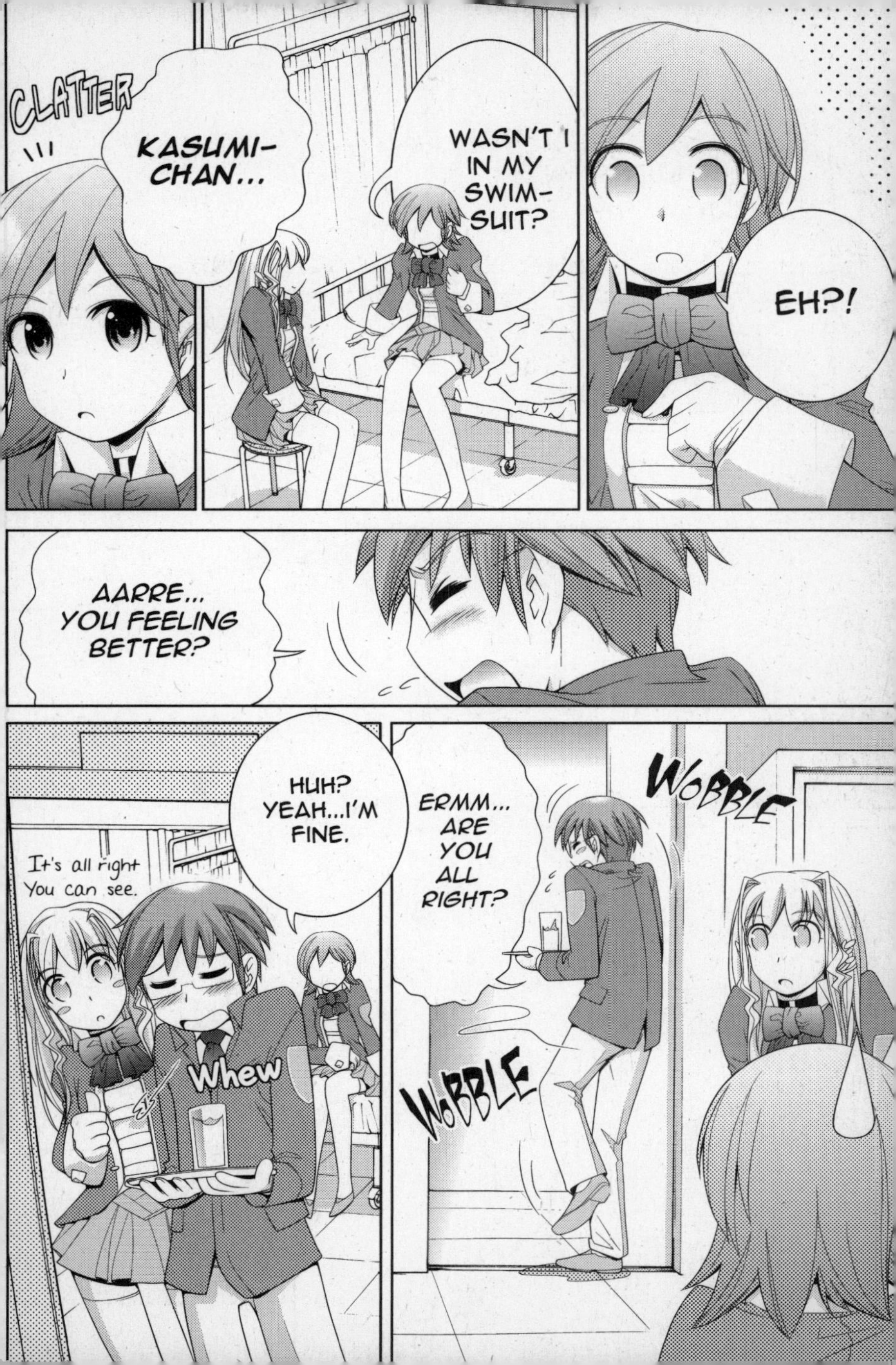
EH?!
WASN'T I IN MY SWIM-SUIT?
CLATTER
KASUMI-CHAN...
AARRE... YOU FEELING BETTER?
WOBBLE
ERMM... ARE YOU ALL RIGHT?
WOBBLE
HUH? YEAH...I'M FINE.
It's all right You can see.
Whew

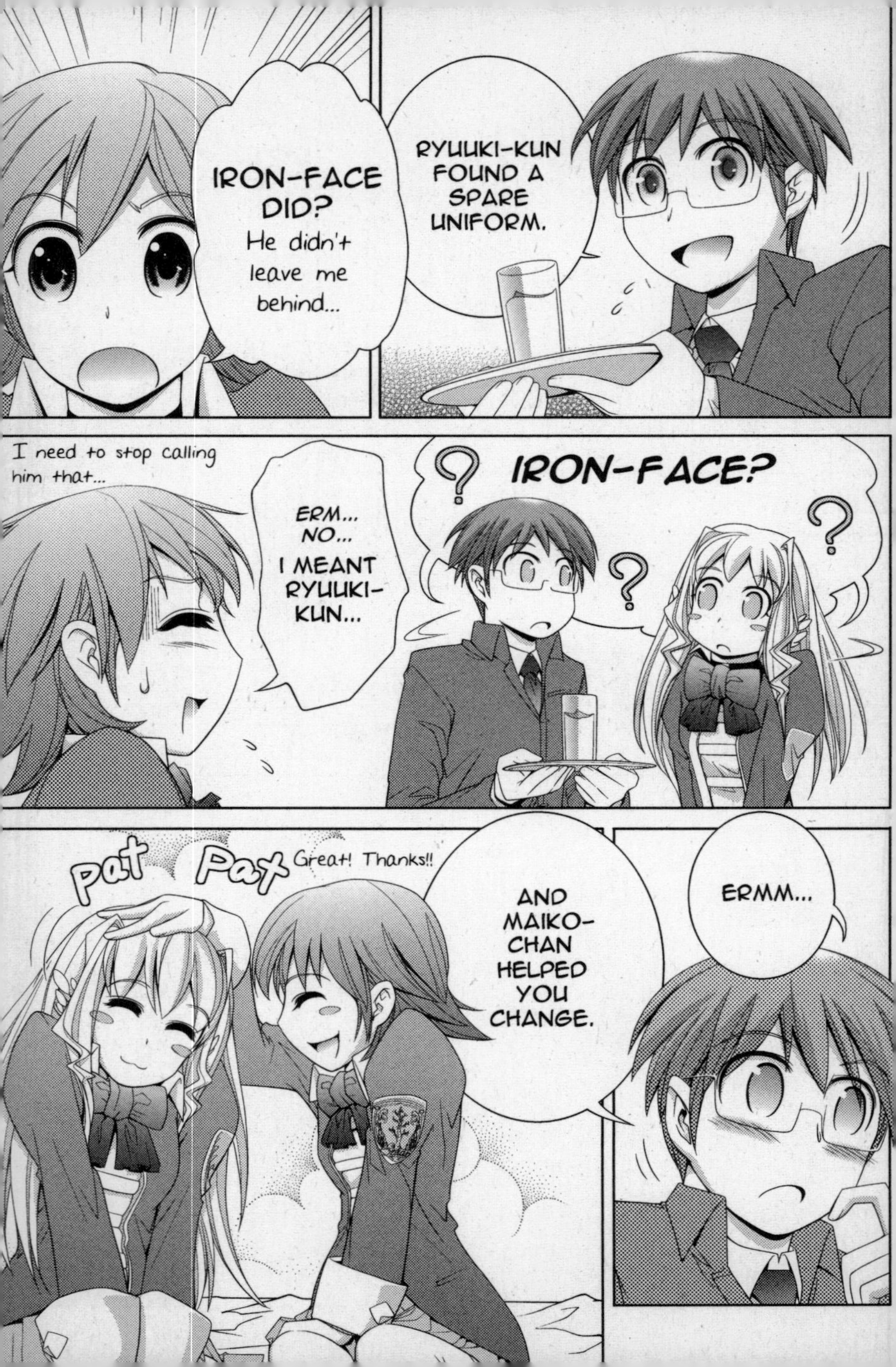
RYUUKI-KUN FOUND A SPARE UNIFORM.
IRON-FACE DID?
He didn't leave me behind...
IRON-FACE?
ERM... NO... I MEANT RYUUKI-KUN...
I need to stop calling him that...
ERMM...
AND MAIKO-CHAN HELPED YOU CHANGE.
Great! Thanks!!
pat Pat

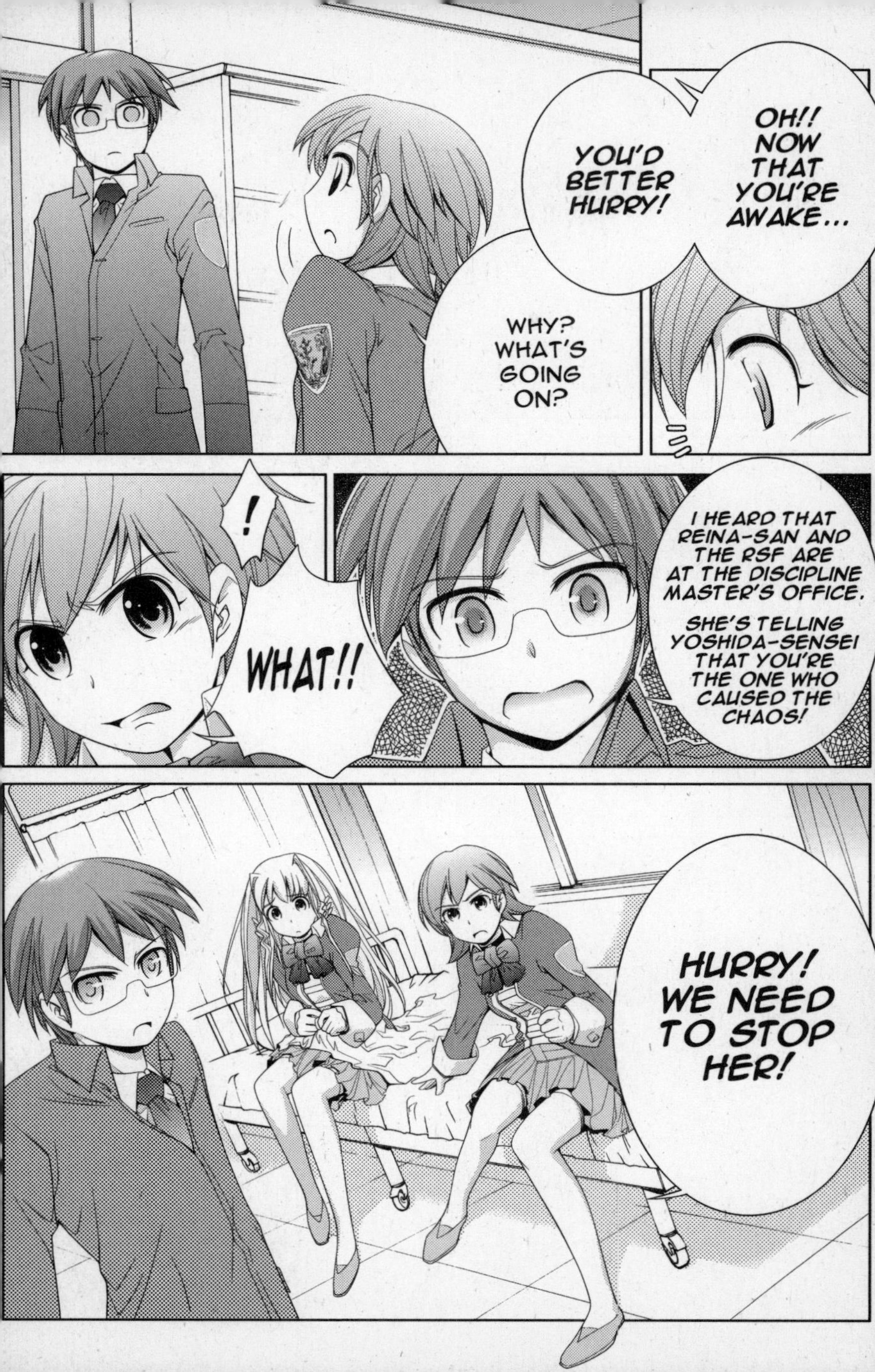
OH!! NOW THAT YOU'RE AWAKE...
YOU'D BETTER HURRY!
WHY? WHAT'S GOING ON?
I HEARD THAT REINA-SAN AND THE RSF ARE AT THE DISCIPLINE MASTER'S OFFICE.
SHE'S TELLING YOSHIDA-SENSEI THAT YOU'RE THE ONE WHO CAUSED THE CHAOS!
!
WHAT!!
HURRY! WE NEED TO STOP HER!

CHAPTER 2

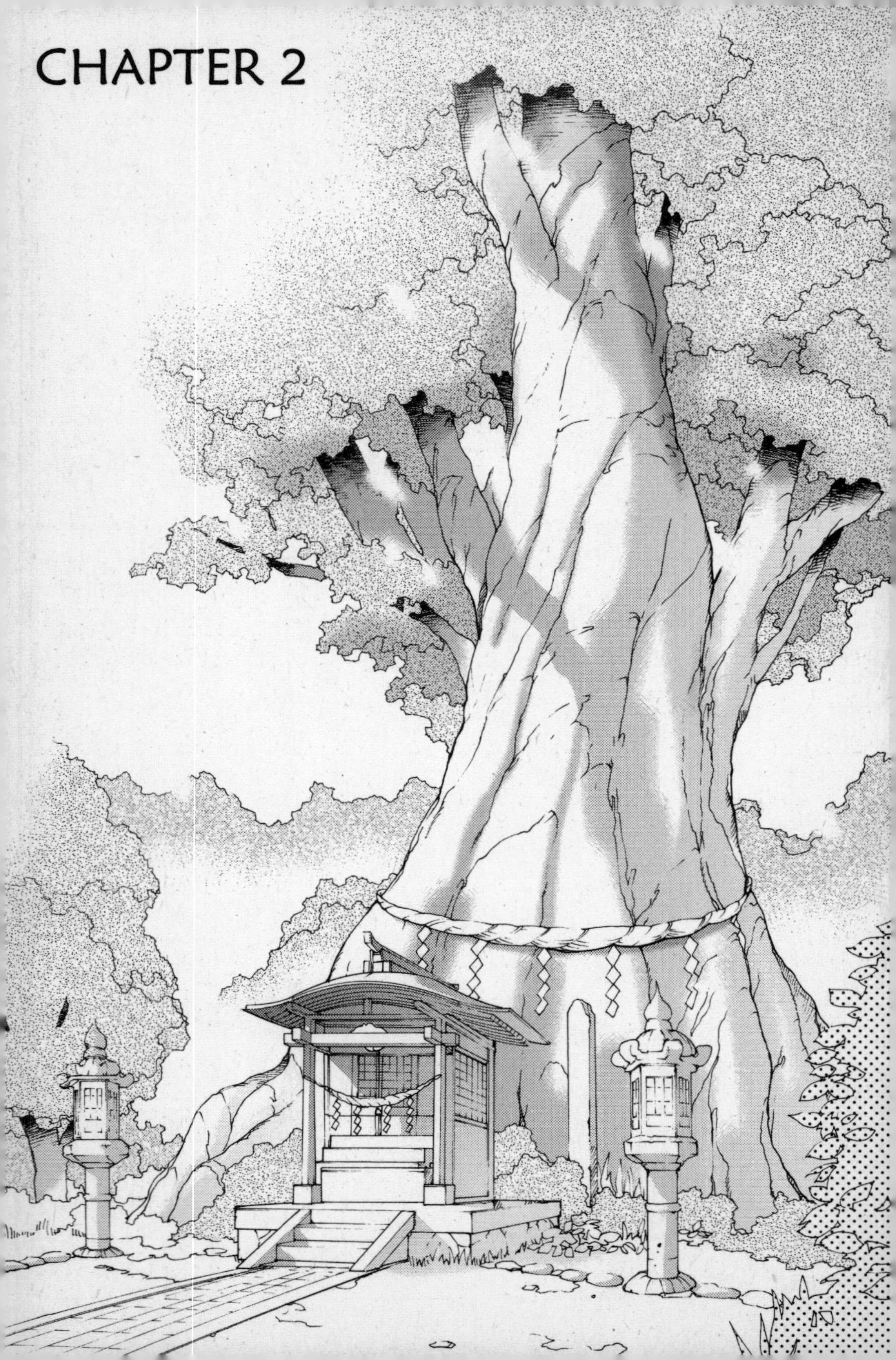

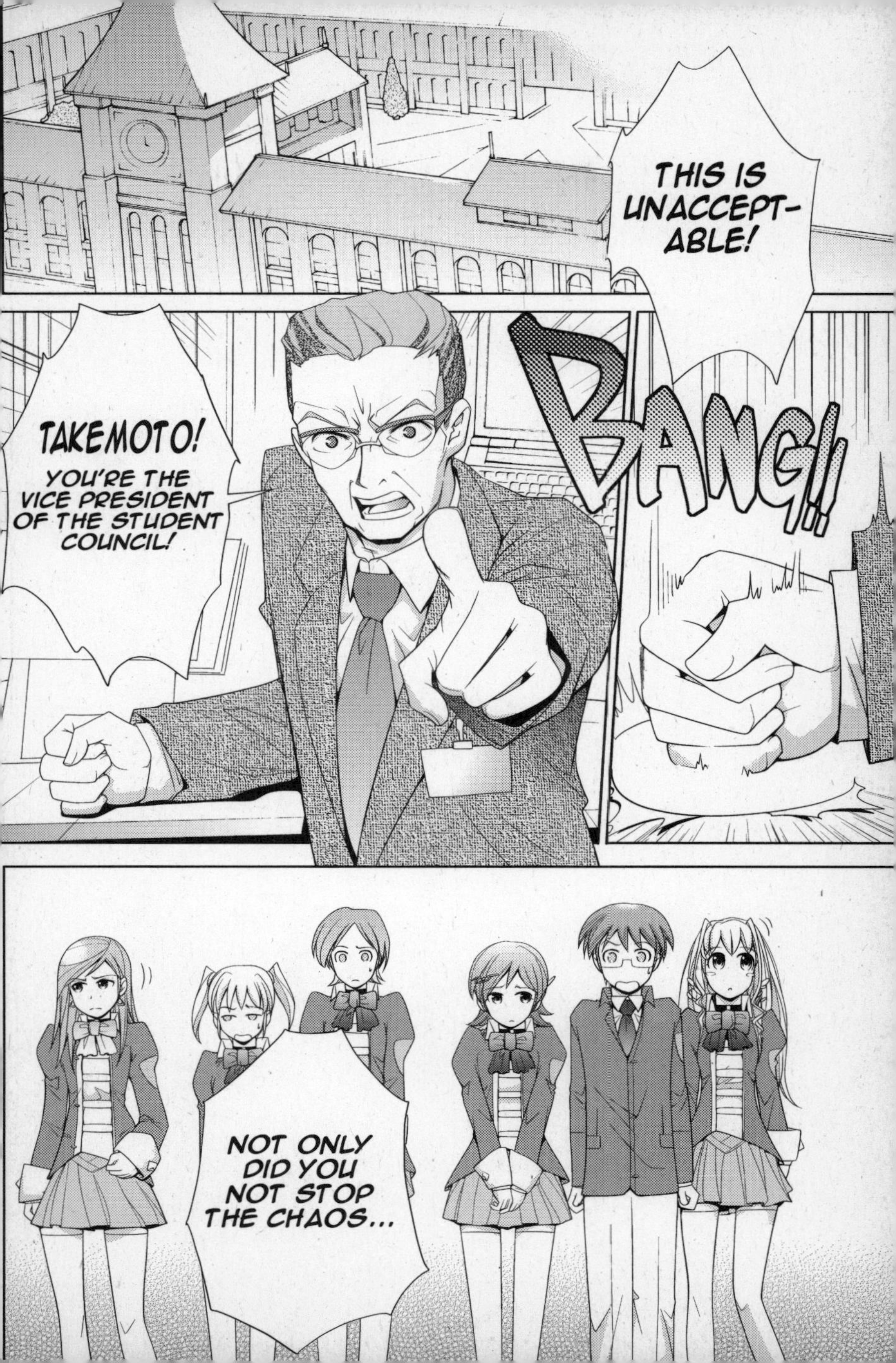
THIS IS UNACCEPT-ABLE!
BANG!!
TAKEMOTO!
YOU'RE THE VICE PRESIDENT OF THE STUDENT COUNCIL!
NOT ONLY DID YOU NOT STOP THE CHAOS...

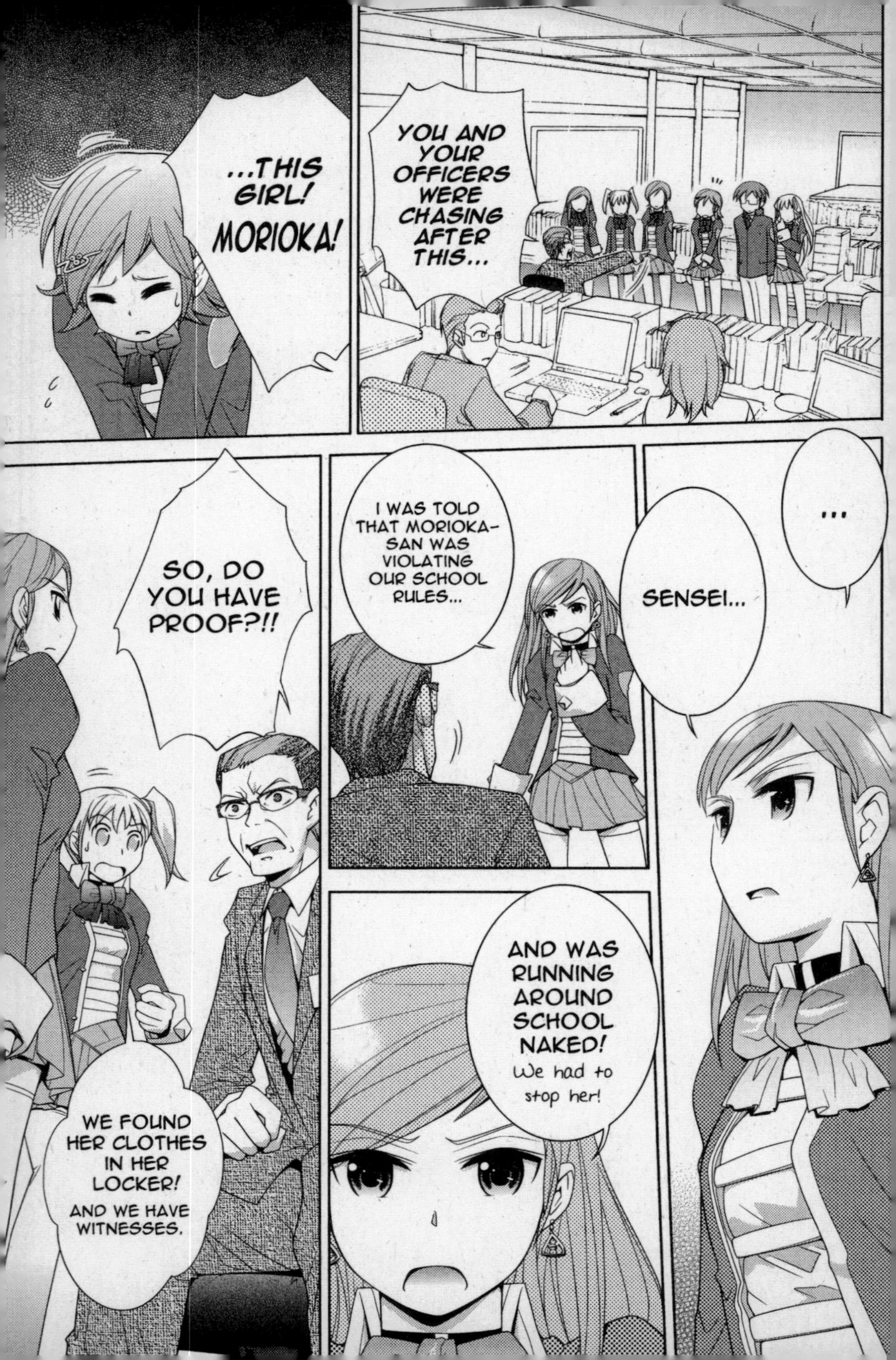
YOU AND YOUR OFFICERS WERE CHASING AFTER THIS...
...THIS GIRL! MORIOKA!
...
SENSEI...
I WAS TOLD THAT MORIOKA-SAN WAS VIOLATING OUR SCHOOL RULES...
AND WAS RUNNING AROUND SCHOOL NAKED! We had to stop her!
SO, DO YOU HAVE PROOF?!!
WE FOUND HER CLOTHES IN HER LOCKER! AND WE HAVE WITNESSES.

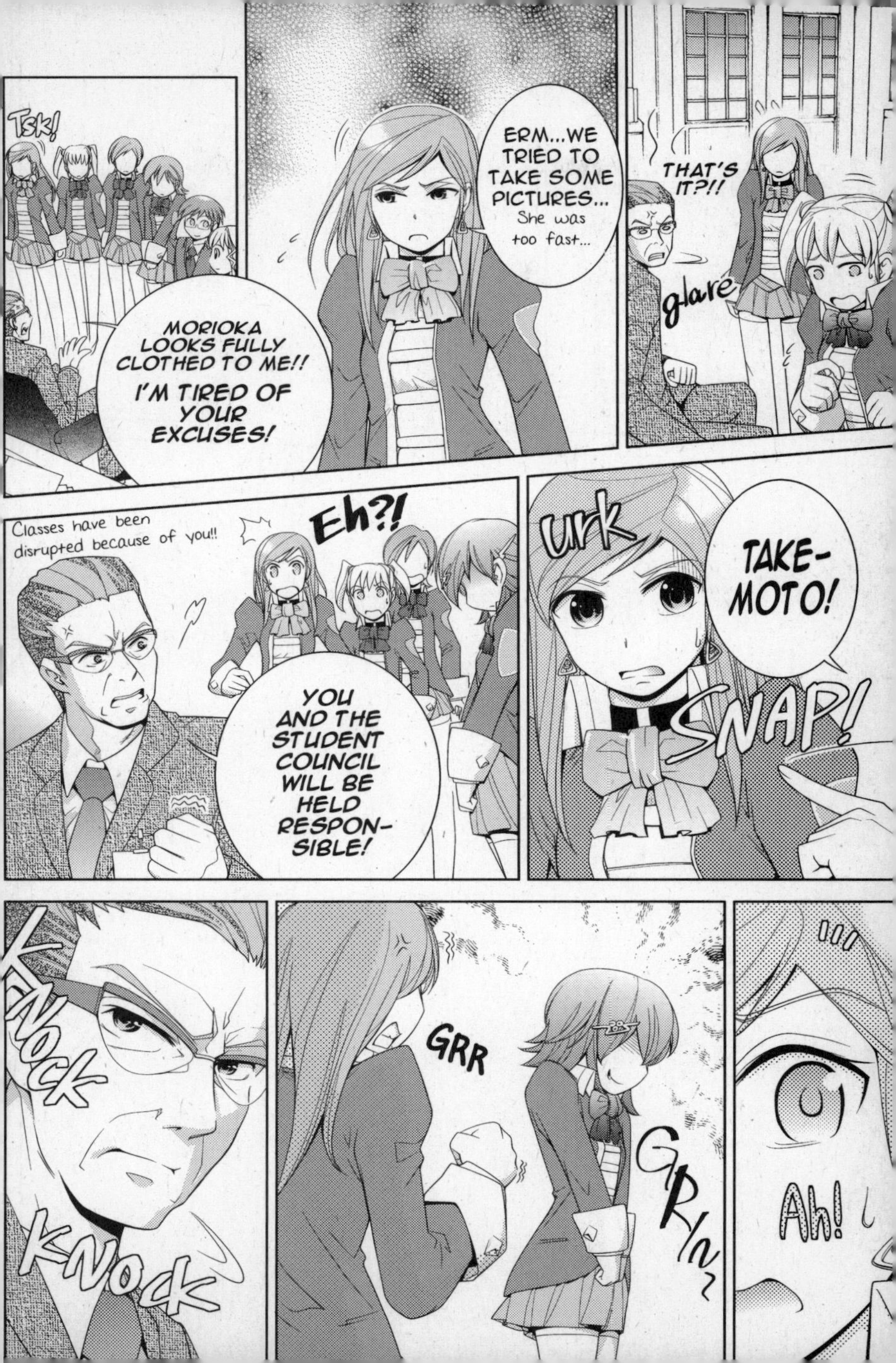

THAT'S IT?!!
glare
ERM...WE TRIED TO TAKE SOME PICTURES...
She was too fast...
Tsk!
MORIOKA LOOKS FULLY CLOTHED TO ME!!
I'M TIRED OF YOUR EXCUSES!
Urk
TAKE-MOTO!
SNAP!
Classes have been disrupted because of you!!
Eh?!
YOU AND THE STUDENT COUNCIL WILL BE HELD RESPON-SIBLE!
!!!
Ah!
GRR
GRIN
KNOCK
KNOCK

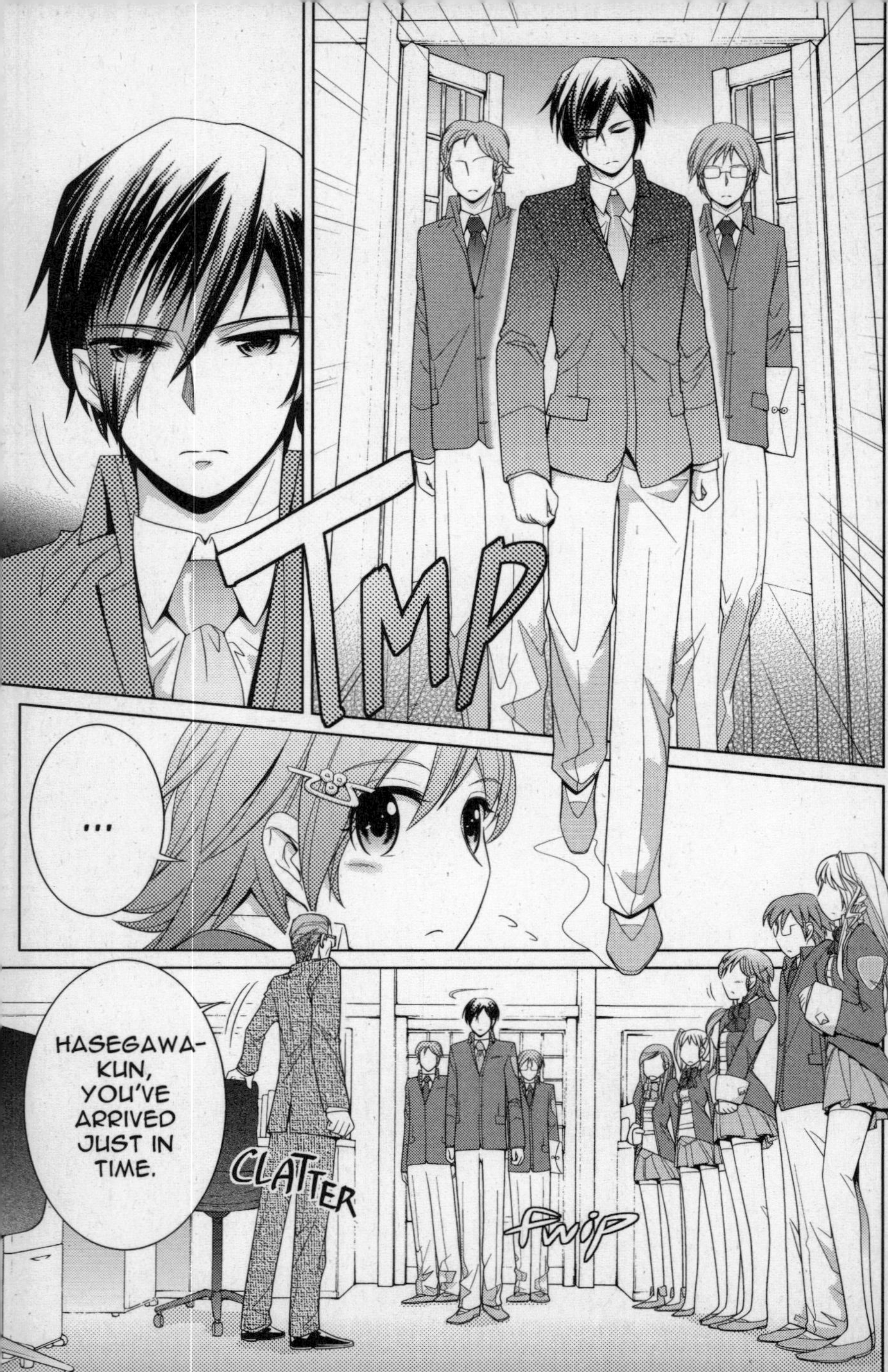
TMP
...
HASEGAWA-KUN, YOU'VE ARRIVED JUST IN TIME.
CLATTER
FWIP

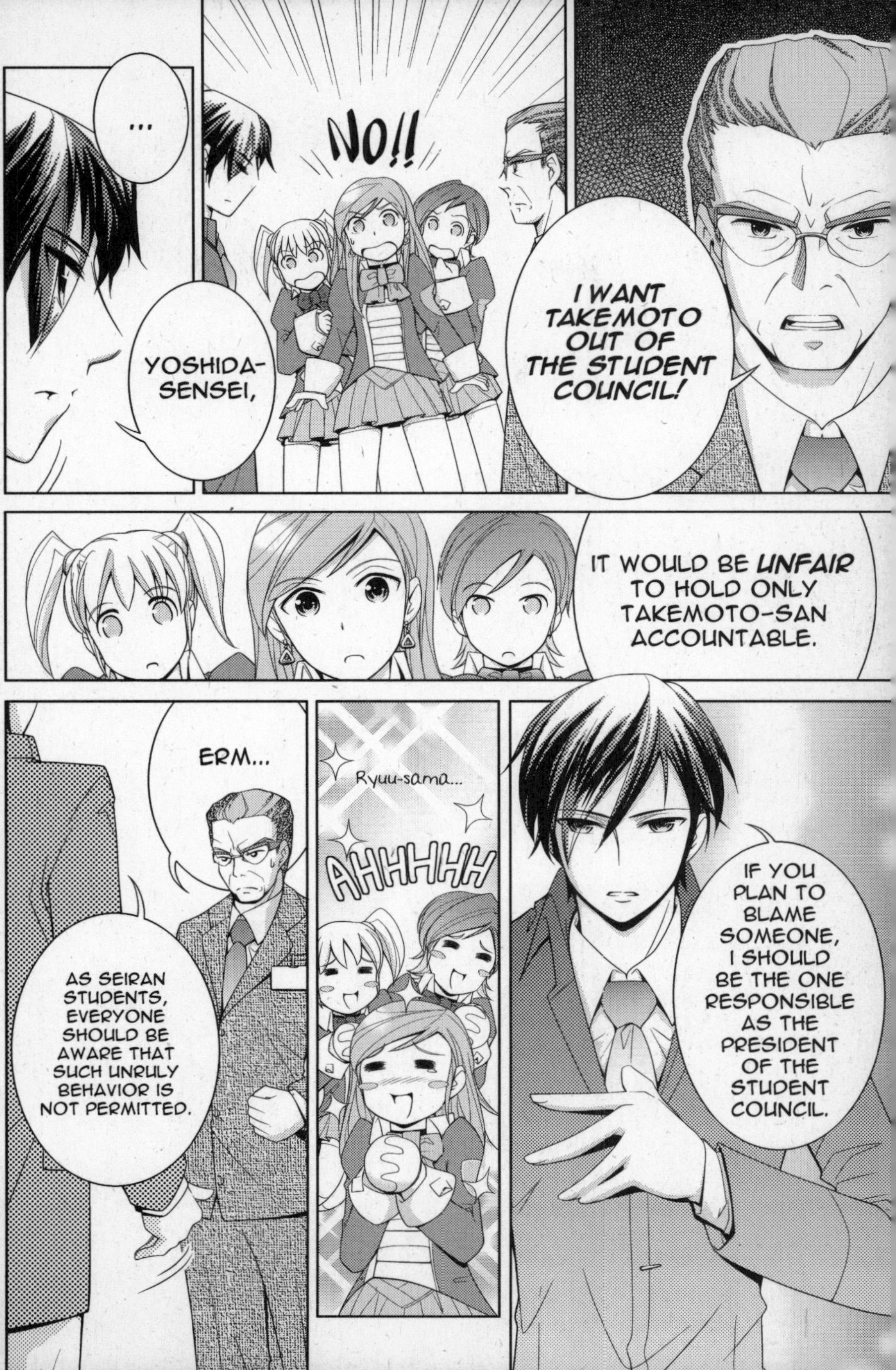
I WANT TAKEMOTO OUT OF THE STUDENT COUNCIL!
NO!!
...
YOSHIDA-SENSEI,
IT WOULD BE *UNFAIR* TO HOLD ONLY TAKEMOTO-SAN ACCOUNTABLE.
IF YOU PLAN TO BLAME SOMEONE, I SHOULD BE THE ONE RESPONSIBLE AS THE PRESIDENT OF THE STUDENT COUNCIL.
Ryuu-sama...
AHHHHH
ERM...
AS SEIRAN STUDENTS, EVERYONE SHOULD BE AWARE THAT SUCH UNRULY BEHAVIOR IS NOT PERMITTED.

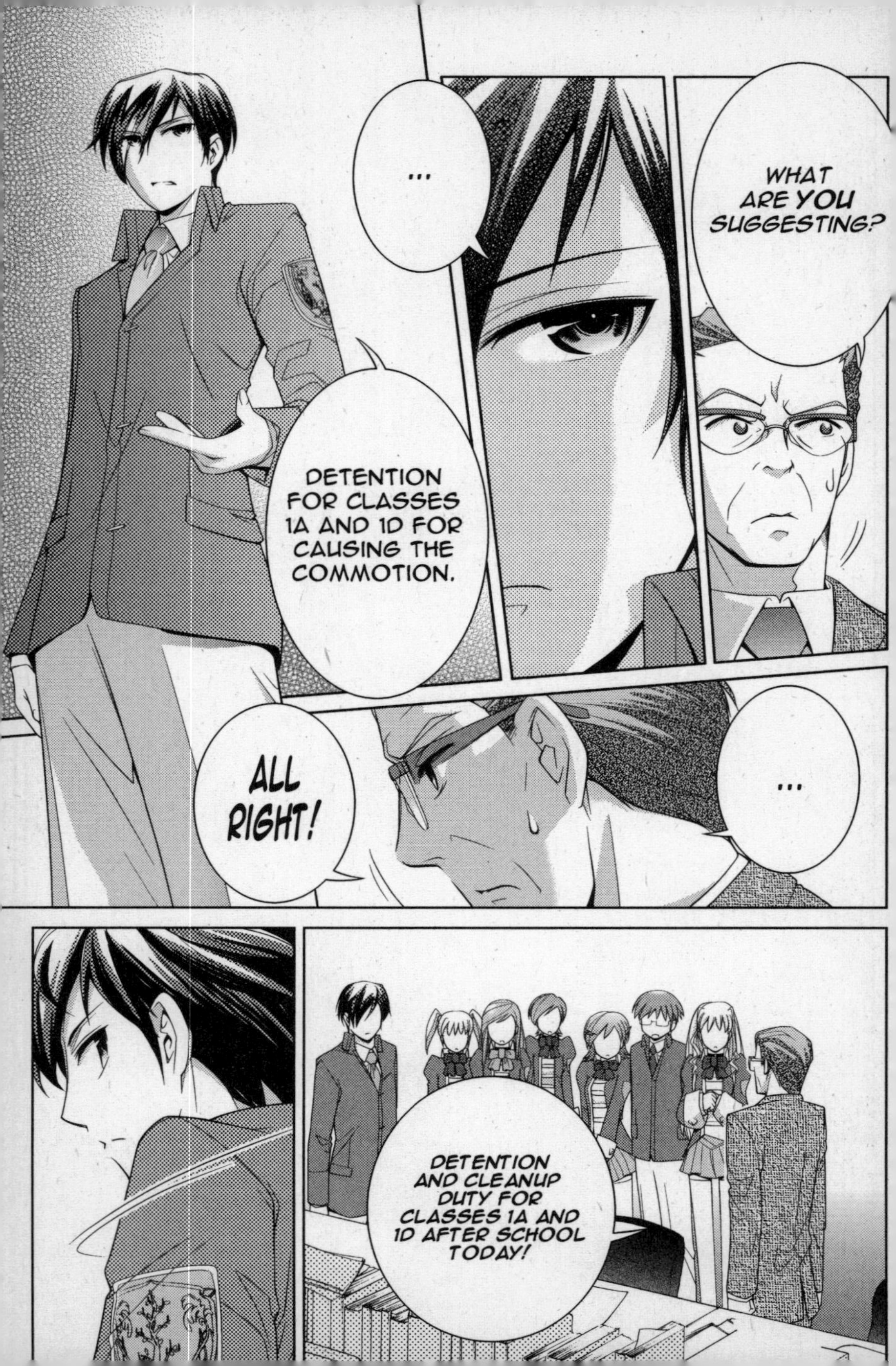

WHAT ARE YOU SUGGESTING?
...
DETENTION FOR CLASSES 1A AND 1D FOR CAUSING THE COMMOTION.
...
ALL RIGHT!
DETENTION AND CLEANUP DUTY FOR CLASSES 1A AND 1D AFTER SCHOOL TODAY!

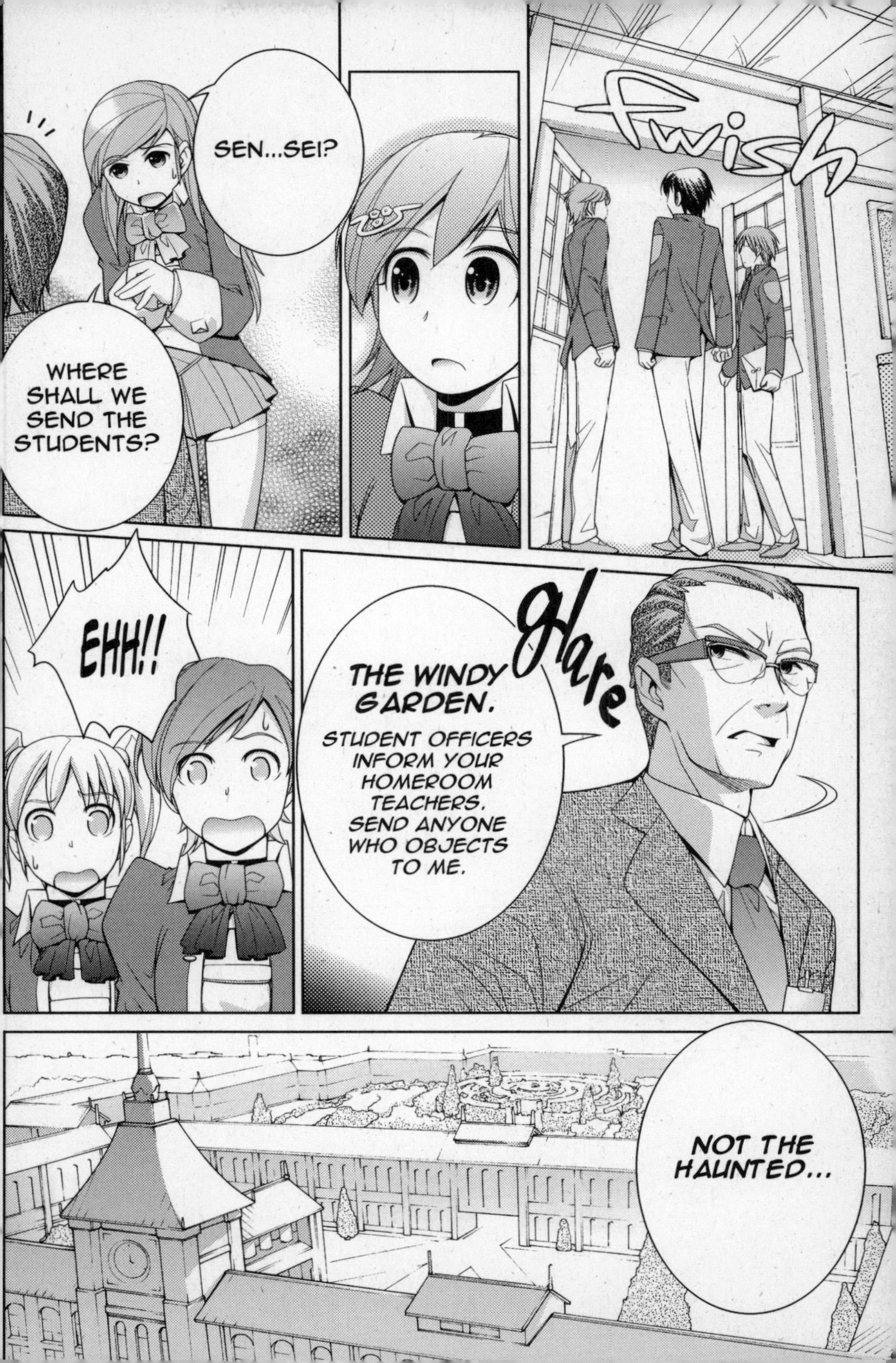
Fwish
SEN...SEI?
WHERE SHALL WE SEND THE STUDENTS?
glare
THE WINDY GARDEN.
STUDENT OFFICERS INFORM YOUR HOMEROOM TEACHERS. SEND ANYONE WHO OBJECTS TO ME.
EHH!!
NOT THE HAUNTED...

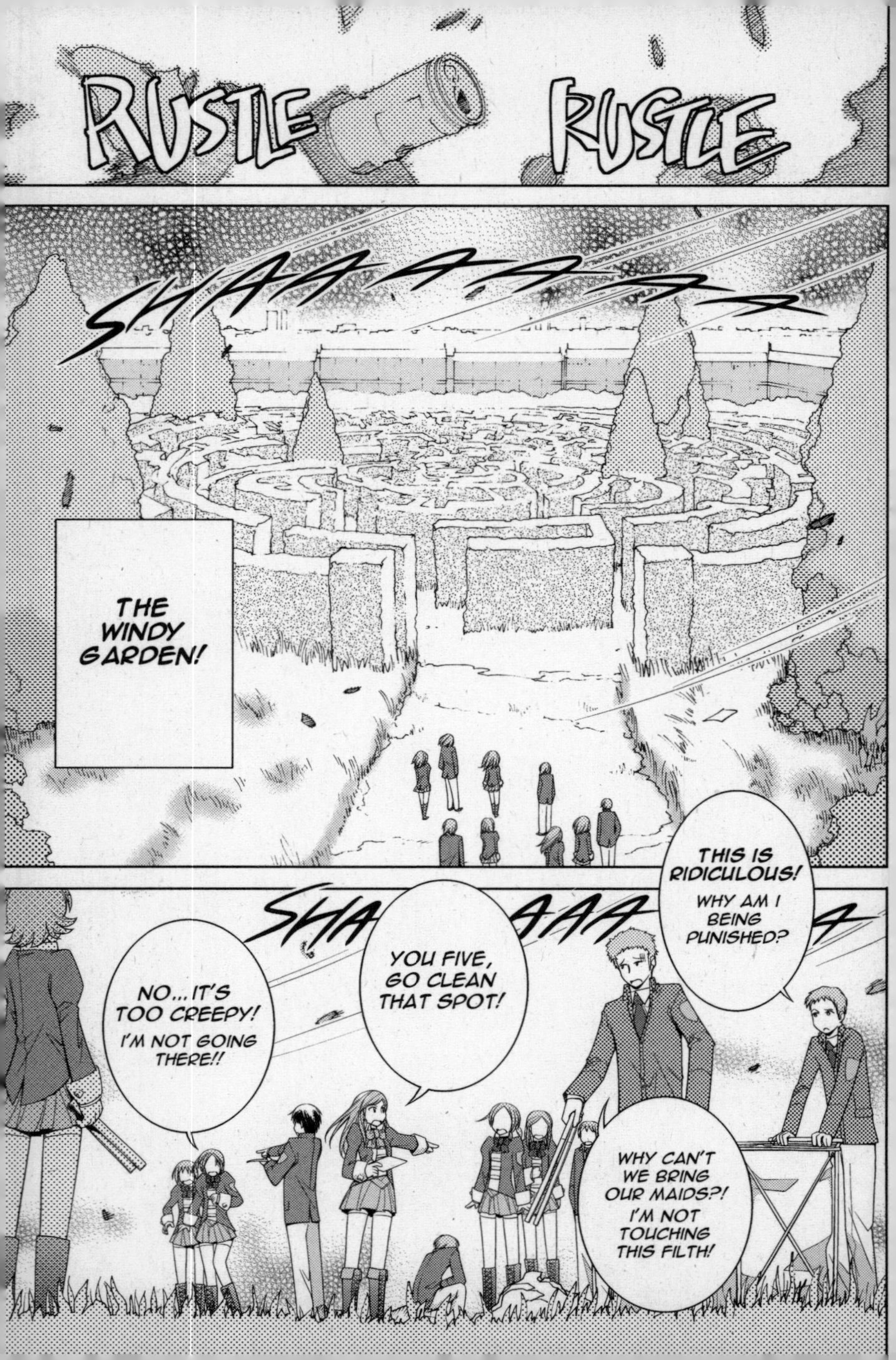
RUSTLE
RUSTLE
SHAAAAAAA
THE WINDY GARDEN!
SHAAAAAAA
THIS IS RIDICULOUS! WHY AM I BEING PUNISHED?
WHY CAN'T WE BRING OUR MAIDS?! I'M NOT TOUCHING THIS FILTH!
YOU FIVE, GO CLEAN THAT SPOT!
NO... IT'S TOO CREEPY! I'M NOT GOING THERE!!

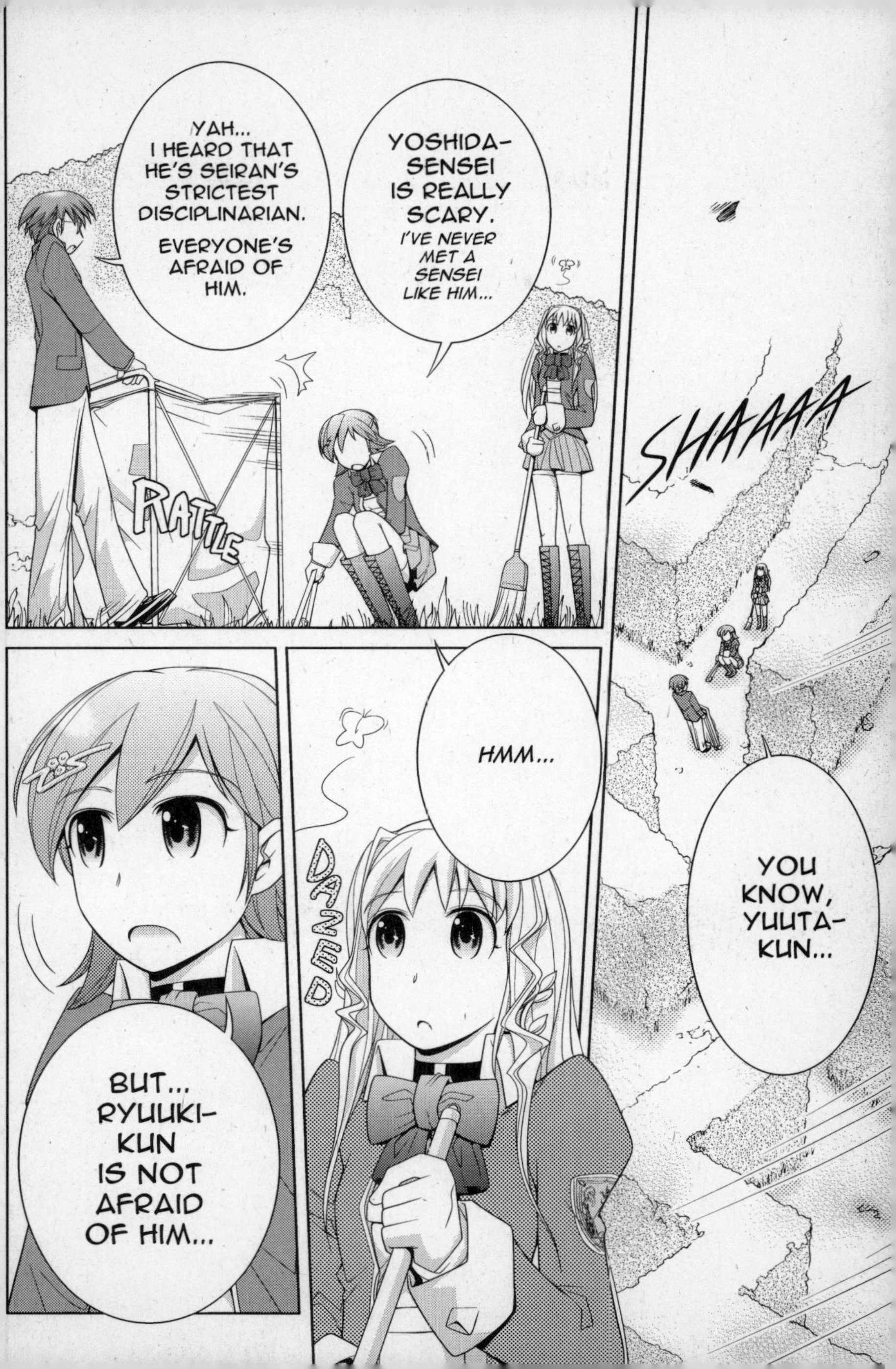
SHAAAA
YOU KNOW, YUUTA-KUN...
YOSHIDA-SENSEI IS REALLY SCARY.
I'VE NEVER MET A SENSEI LIKE HIM...
YAH... I HEARD THAT HE'S SEIRAN'S STRICTEST DISCIPLINARIAN.
EVERYONE'S AFRAID OF HIM.
RATTLE
HMM...
DAZED
BUT... RYUUKI-KUN IS NOT AFRAID OF HIM...

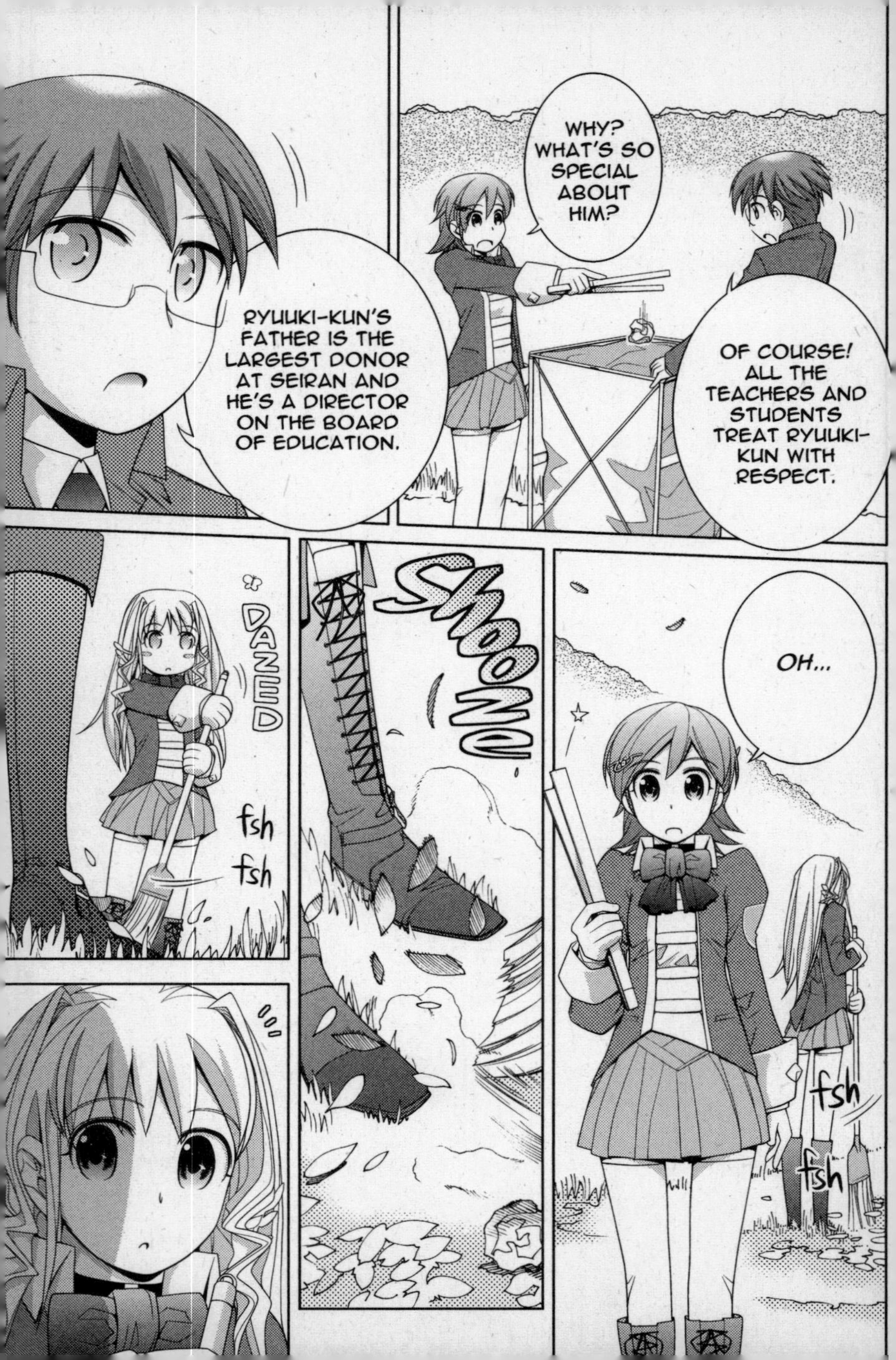
WHY? WHAT'S SO SPECIAL ABOUT HIM?
OF COURSE! ALL THE TEACHERS AND STUDENTS TREAT RYUUKI-KUN WITH RESPECT.
RYUUKI-KUN'S FATHER IS THE LARGEST DONOR AT SEIRAN AND HE'S A DIRECTOR ON THE BOARD OF EDUCATION.
OH...
fsh
fsh
SHOOOM
DAZED
fsh
fsh

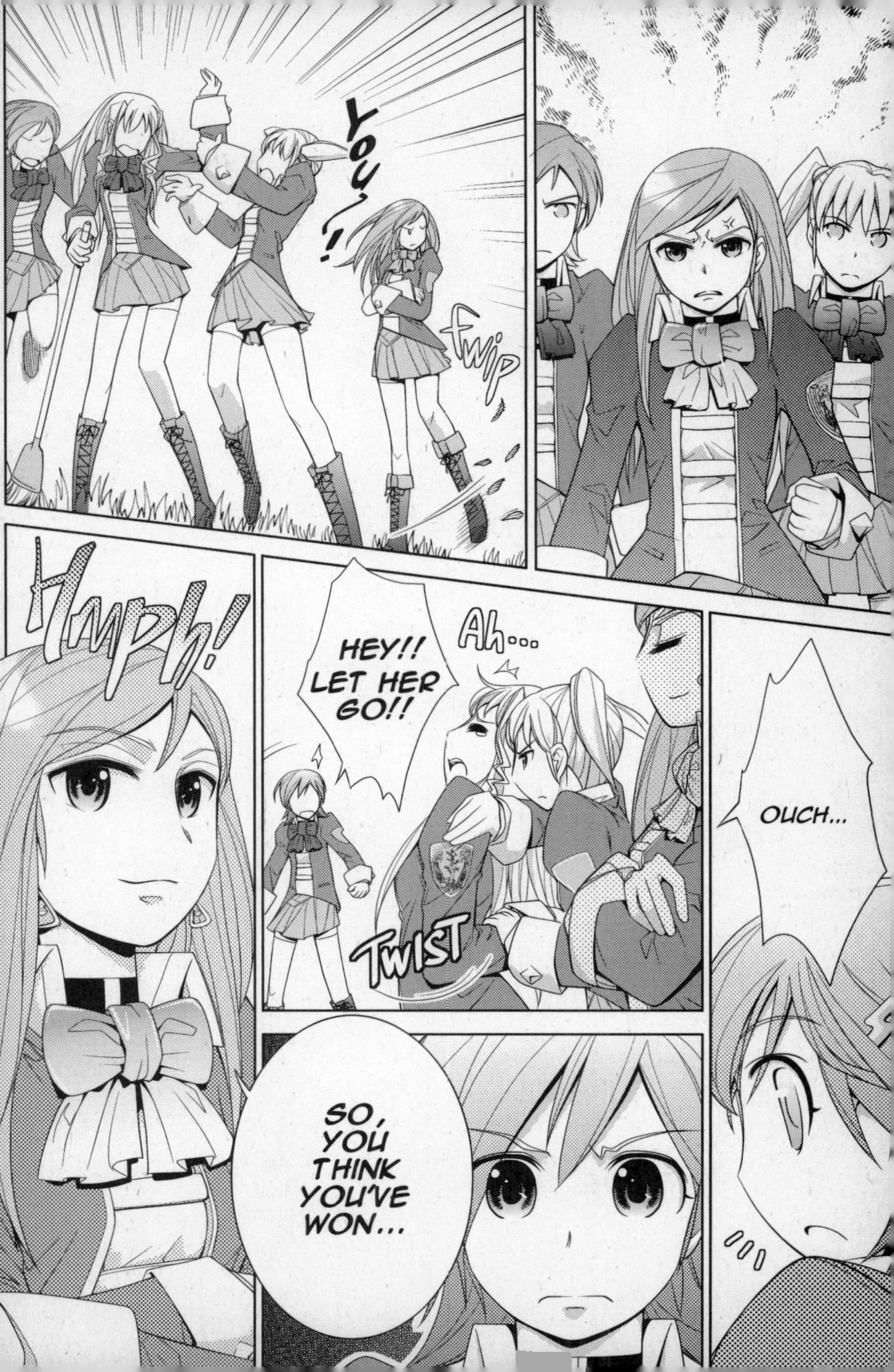
YOU~!!
fwip
OUCH...
Ah...
HEY!! LET HER GO!!
TWIST
SO, YOU THINK YOU'VE WON...
Hmph!

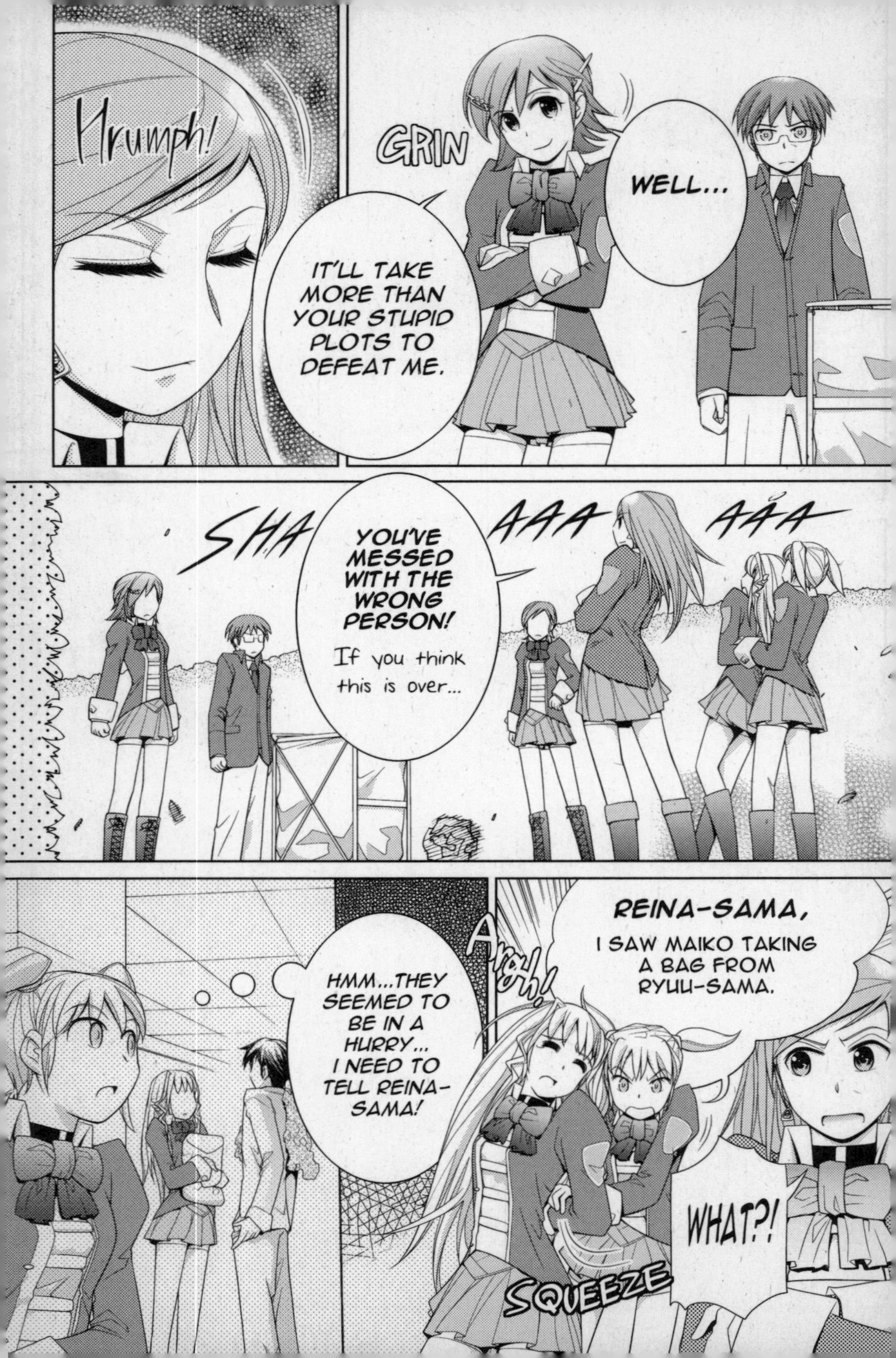
GRIN
WELL...
IT'LL TAKE MORE THAN YOUR STUPID PLOTS TO DEFEAT ME.
Hrumph!
SHAAAAAAA
YOU'VE MESSED WITH THE WRONG PERSON!
If you think this is over...
REINA-SAMA, I SAW MAIKO TAKING A BAG FROM RYUU-SAMA.
Argh!
WHAT?!
SQUEEZE
HMM...THEY SEEMED TO BE IN A HURRY... I NEED TO TELL REINA-SAMA!

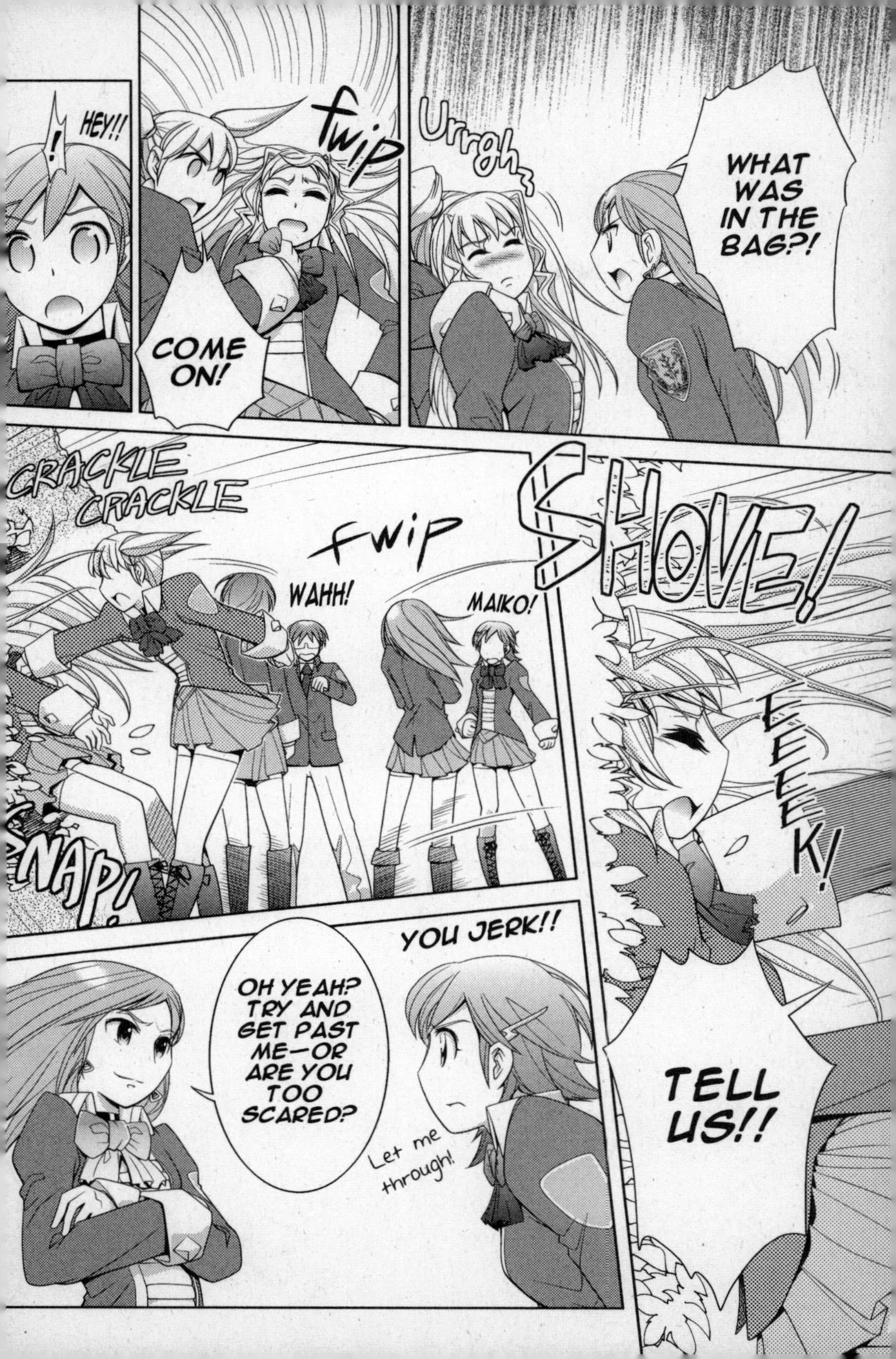
WHAT WAS IN THE BAG?!
Urrrghz
fwip
COME ON!
HEY!!
!
SHOVE!
EEEEEK!
TELL US!!
fwip
MAIKO!
WAHH!
CRACKLE CRACKLE
SNAP!
YOU JERK!!
OH YEAH? TRY AND GET PAST ME—OR ARE YOU TOO SCARED?
Let me through!

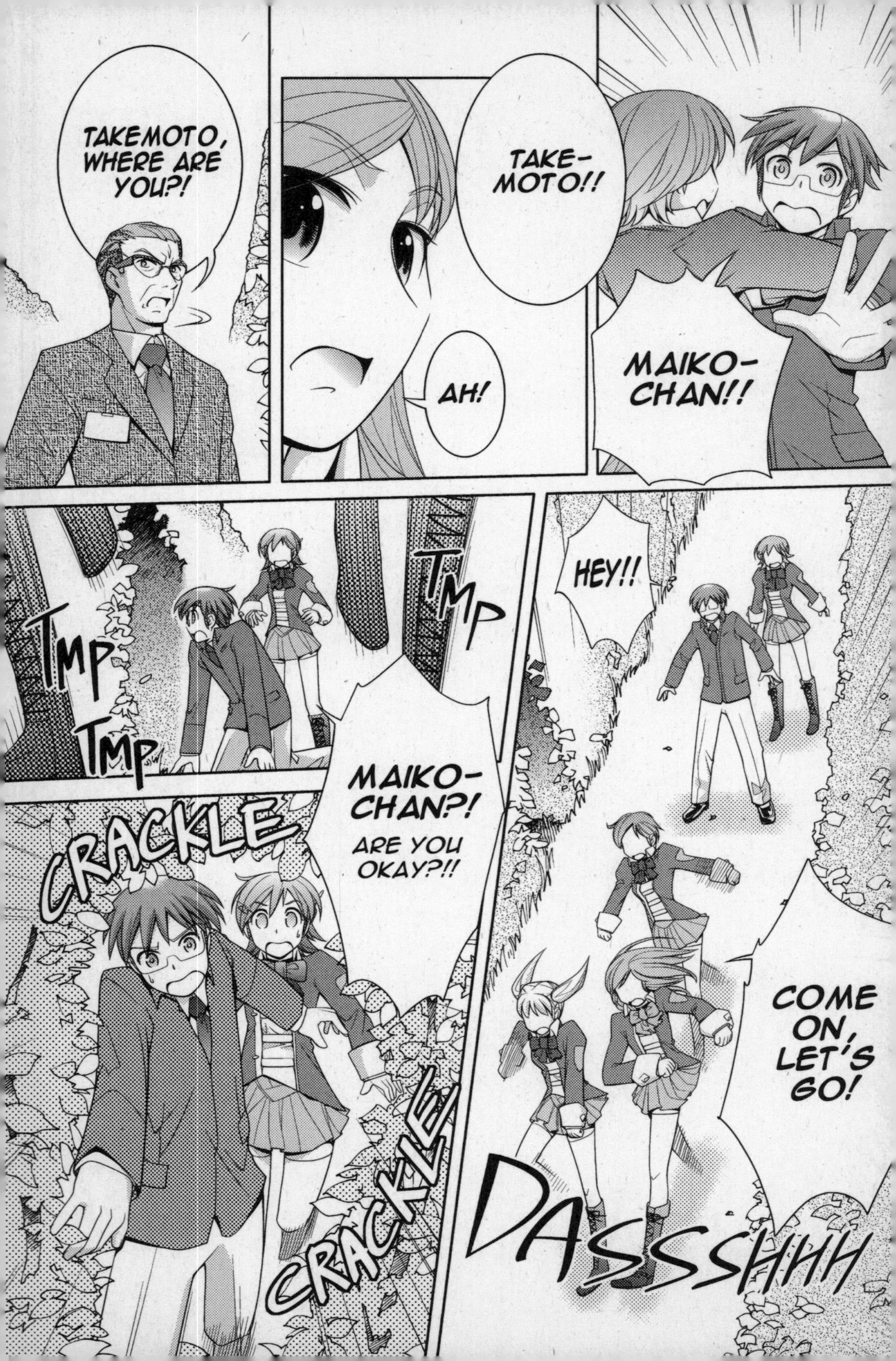
MAIKO-CHAN!!
TAKE-MOTO!!
AH!
TAKEMOTO, WHERE ARE YOU?!
HEY!!
COME ON, LET'S GO!
DASSSHHH
TMP
TMP
TMP
MAIKO-CHAN?!
ARE YOU OKAY?!!
CRACKLE
CRACKLE

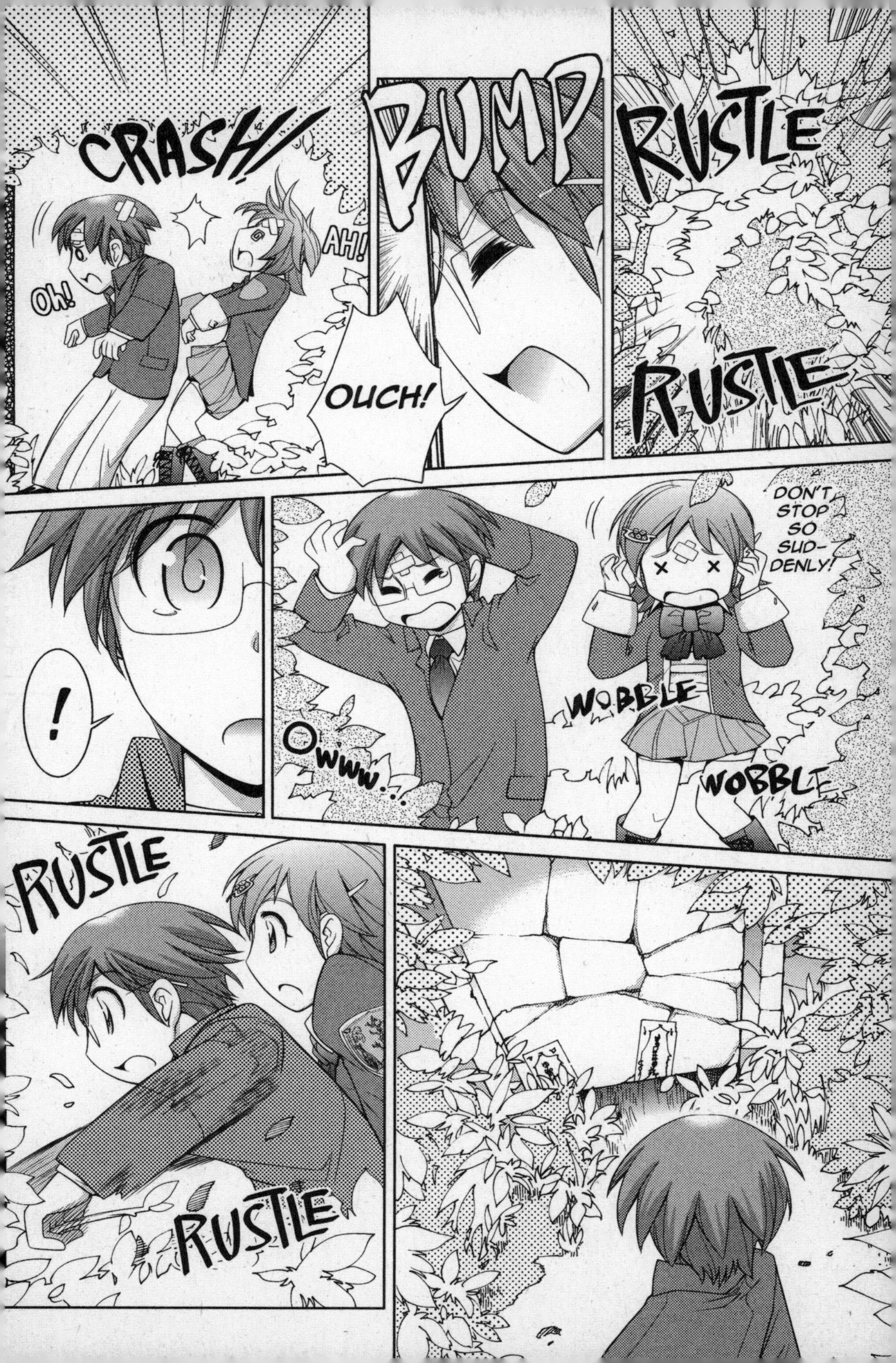
RUSTLE
RUSTLE
BUMP
OUCH!
CRASH!
AH!
Oh!
DON'T STOP SO SUD-DENLY!
WOBBLE
WOBBLE
OWWW...
!
RUSTLE
RUSTLE

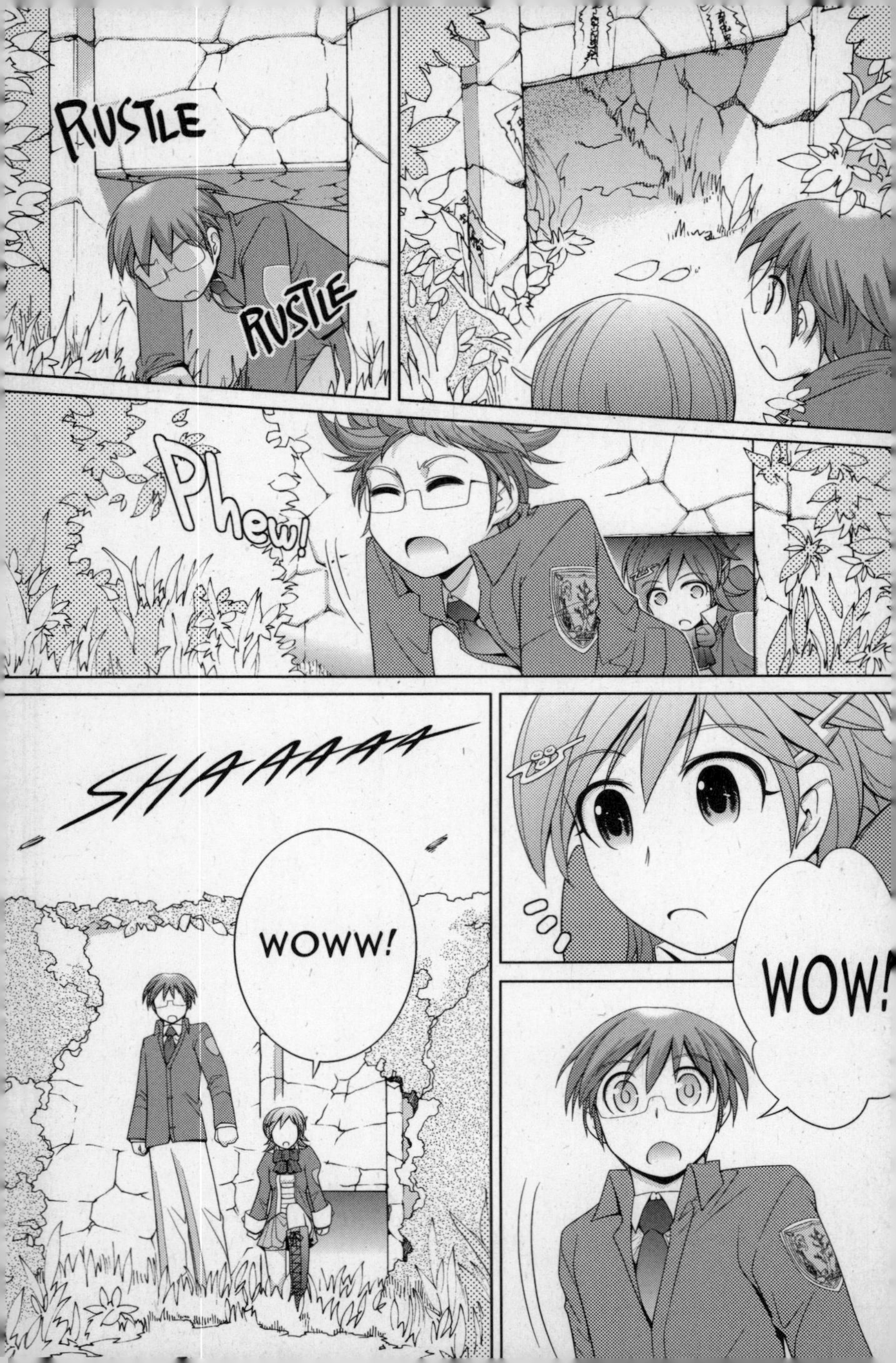
RUSTLE
RUSTLE
Phew!
WOW!
SHAAAAAA
WOWW!

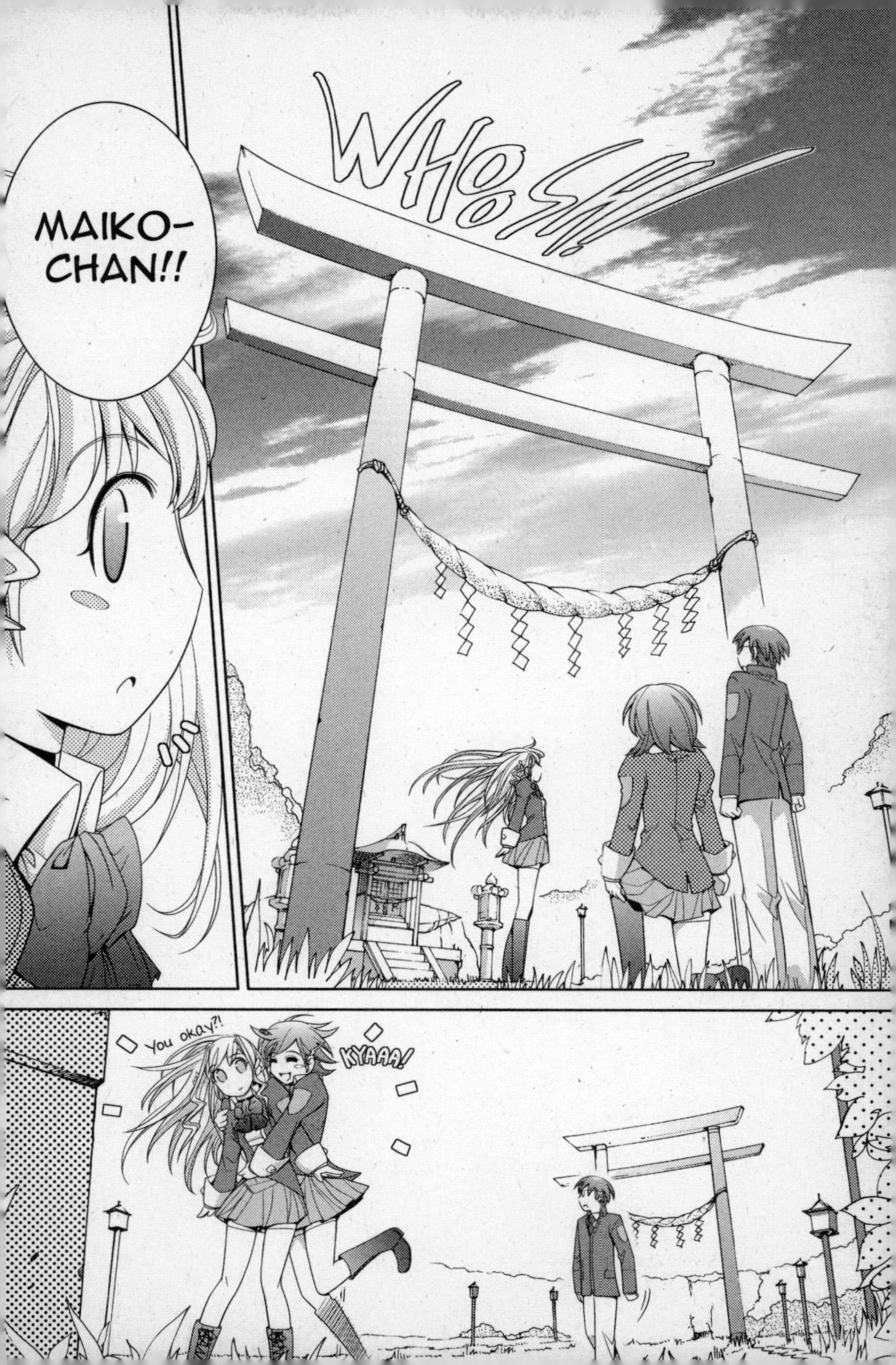
WHOOSH!!
MAIKO-CHAN!!
KYAAA!
You okay?!

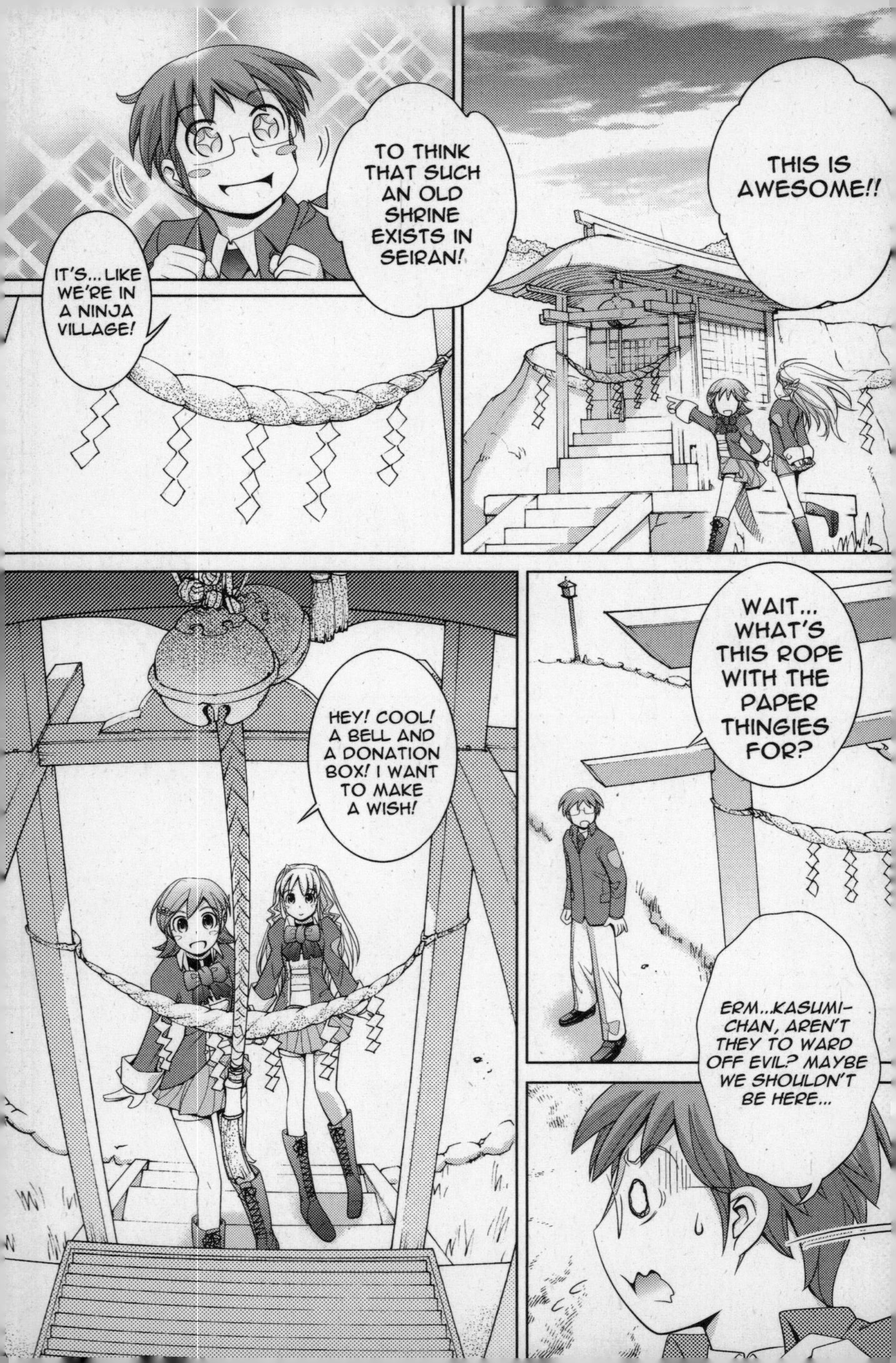
THIS IS AWESOME!!
TO THINK THAT SUCH AN OLD SHRINE EXISTS IN SEIRAN!
IT'S... LIKE WE'RE IN A NINJA VILLAGE!
WAIT... WHAT'S THIS ROPE WITH THE PAPER THINGIES FOR?
ERM...KASUMI-CHAN, AREN'T THEY TO WARD OFF EVIL? MAYBE WE SHOULDN'T BE HERE...
HEY! COOL! A BELL AND A DONATION BOX! I WANT TO MAKE A WISH!

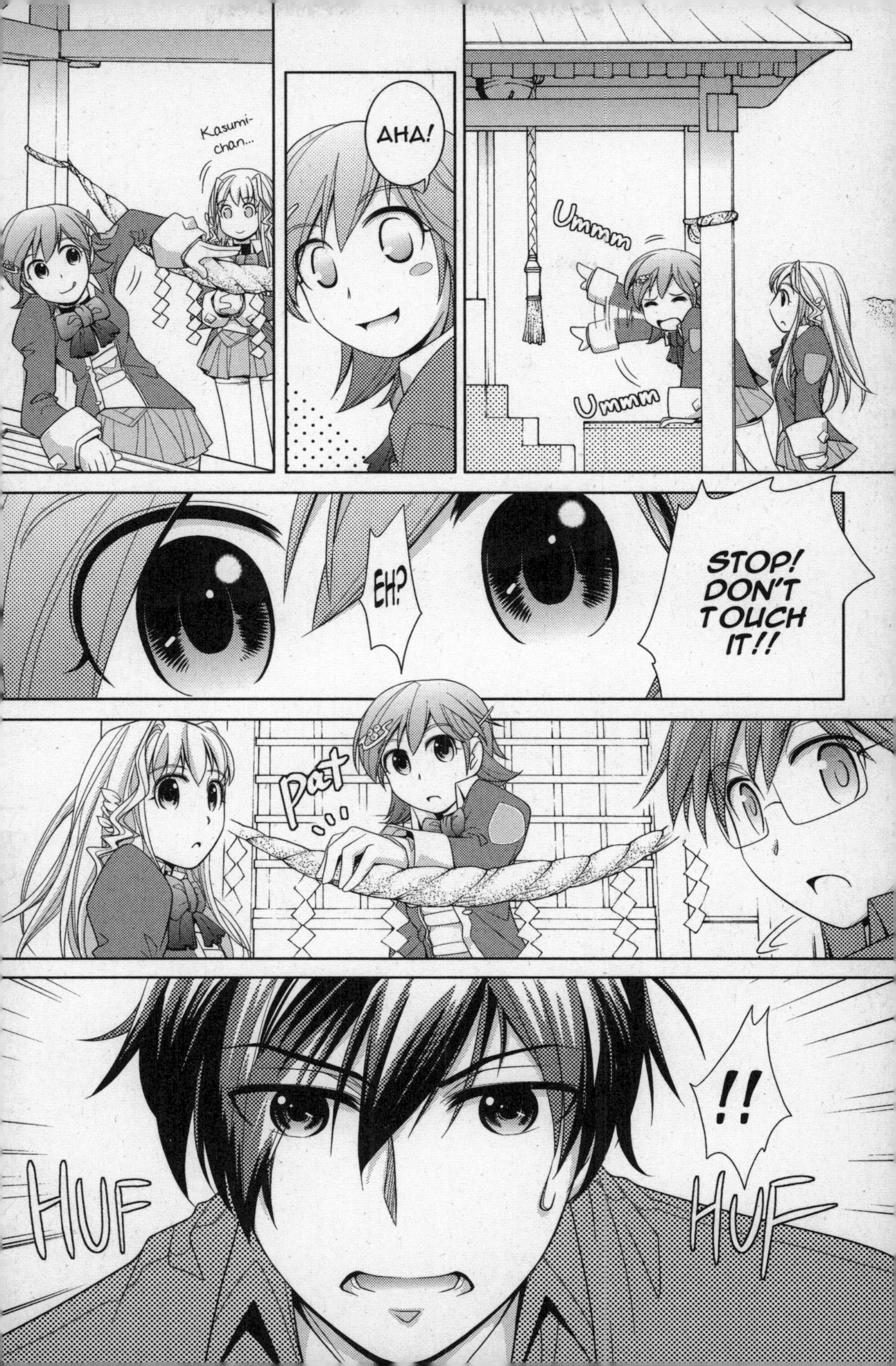
Ummmm
Ummmm
AHA!
Kasumi-chan...
STOP! DON'T TOUCH IT!!
EH?
pat...
!!
HUF
HUF

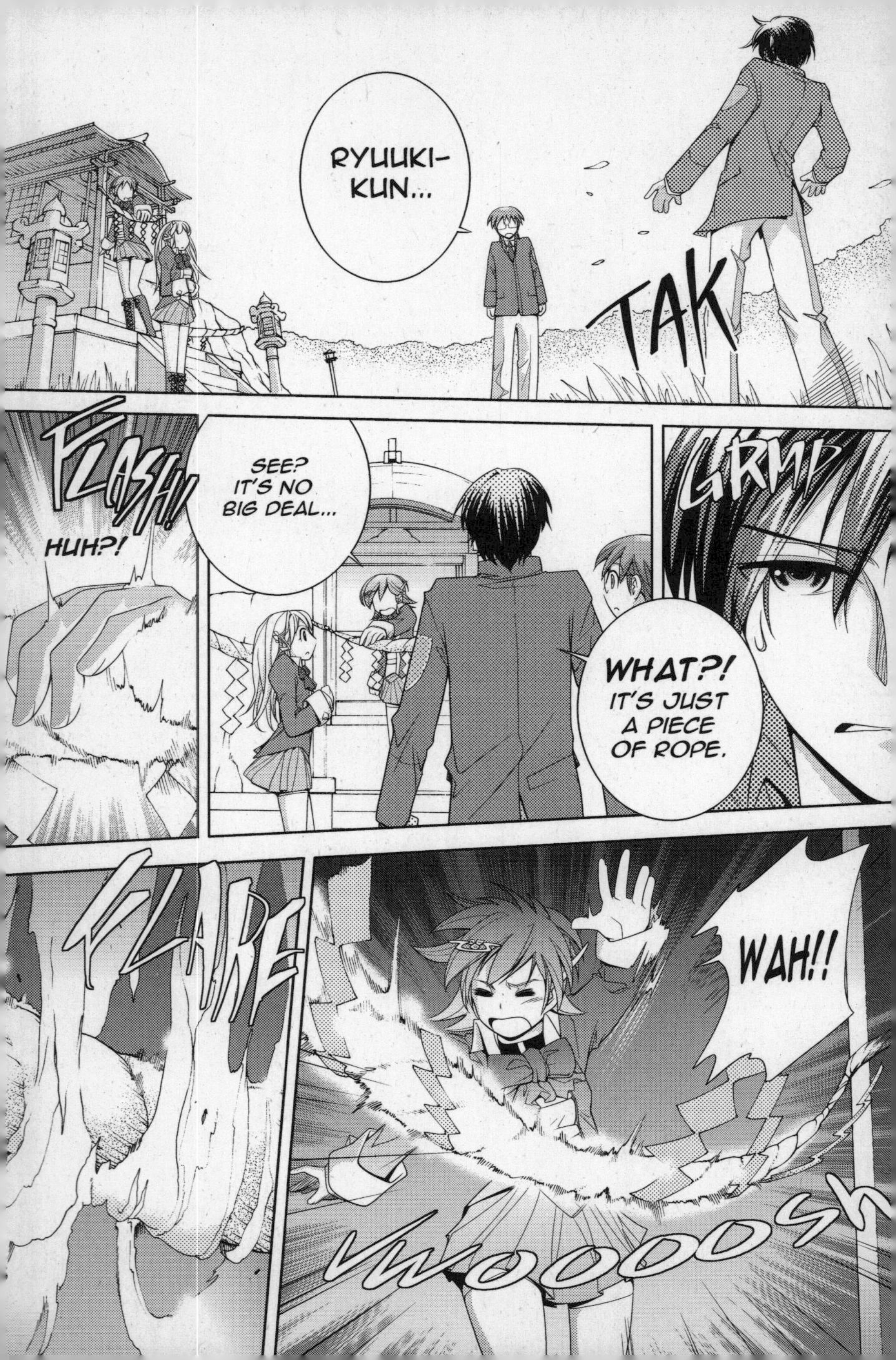
RYUUKI-KUN...
TAK
GRMD
WHAT?! IT'S JUST A PIECE OF ROPE.
SEE? IT'S NO BIG DEAL...
FLASH!
HUH?!
WAH!!
VWOOOOSH
FLARE

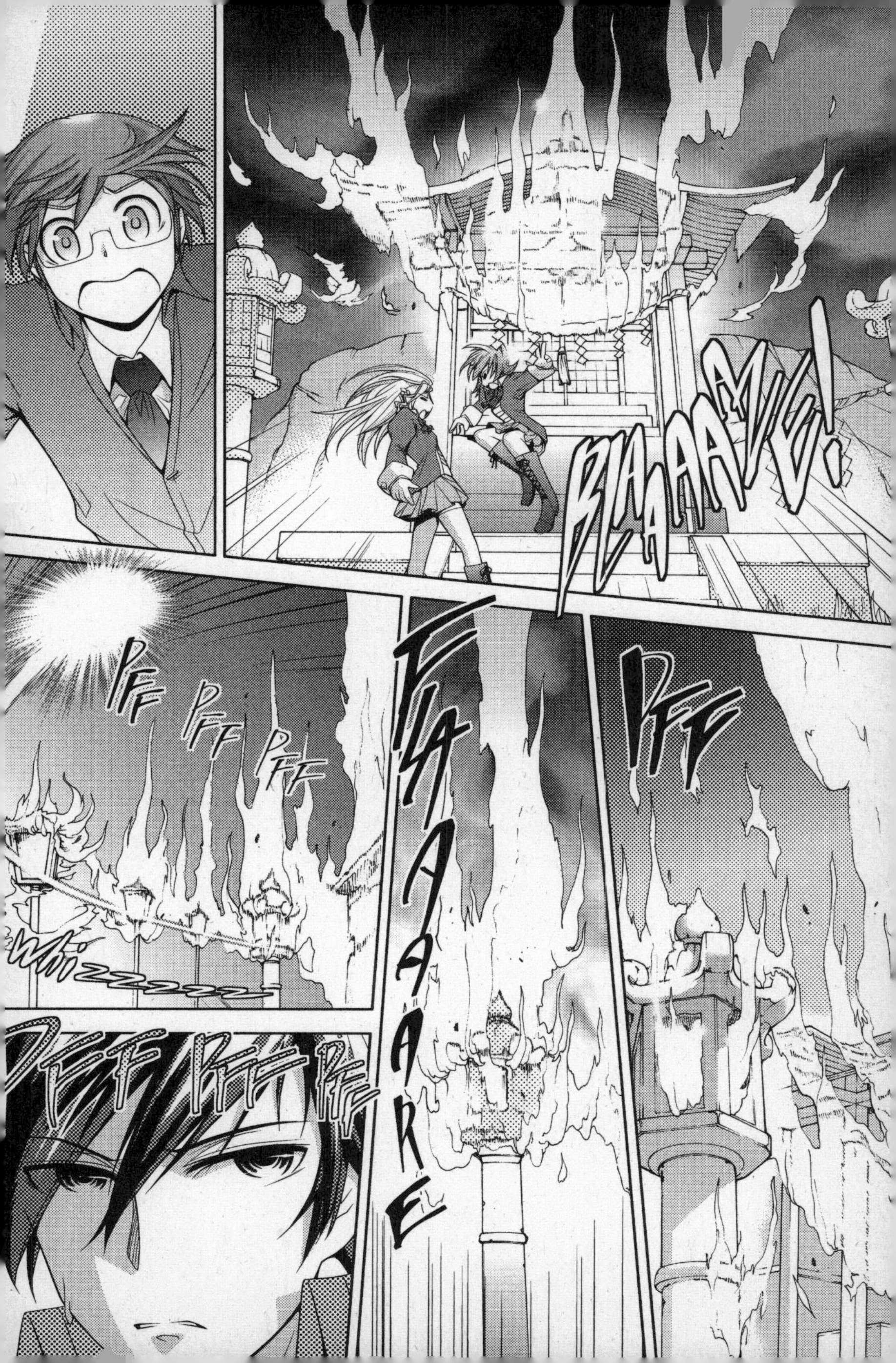
BLAAAAZE!
PFF
FLAAAARE
PFF PFF PFF
Whizzzzzzz
PFF PFFF PFFF

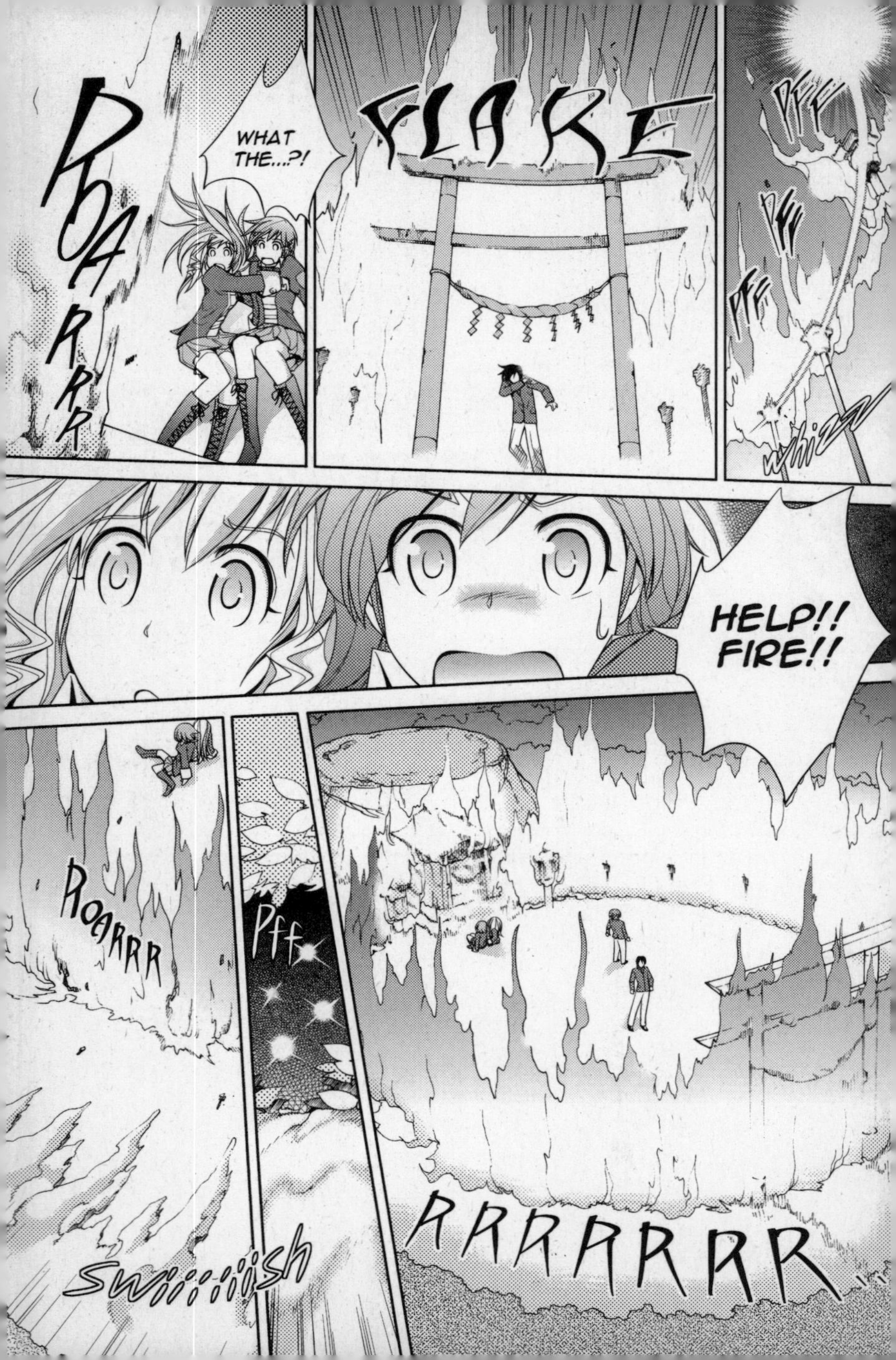
PFF
PFF
PFF
whizz
FLARE
WHAT THE...?!
ROARRRR
HELP!! FIRE!!
RRRRRRRR
Pff
Roarrrr
Swiiiiiiish

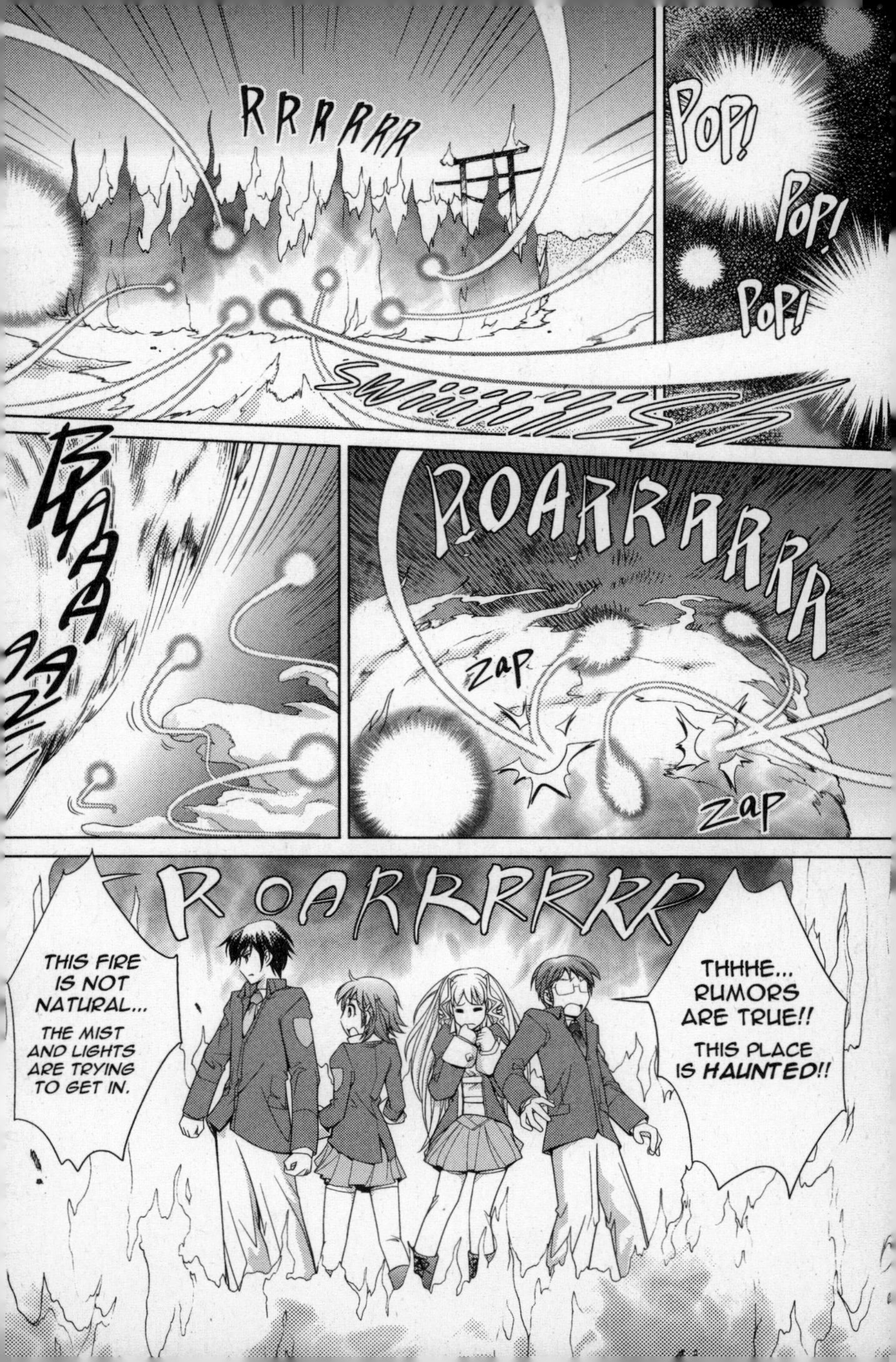
POP!
POP!
POP!
RRRRRR
SWIIIIIISH
ROARRRRRR
ZAP
ZAP
ROARRRRRR
THHHE... RUMORS ARE TRUE!!
THIS PLACE IS **HAUNTED**!!
THIS FIRE IS NOT NATURAL...
THE MIST AND LIGHTS ARE TRYING TO GET IN.

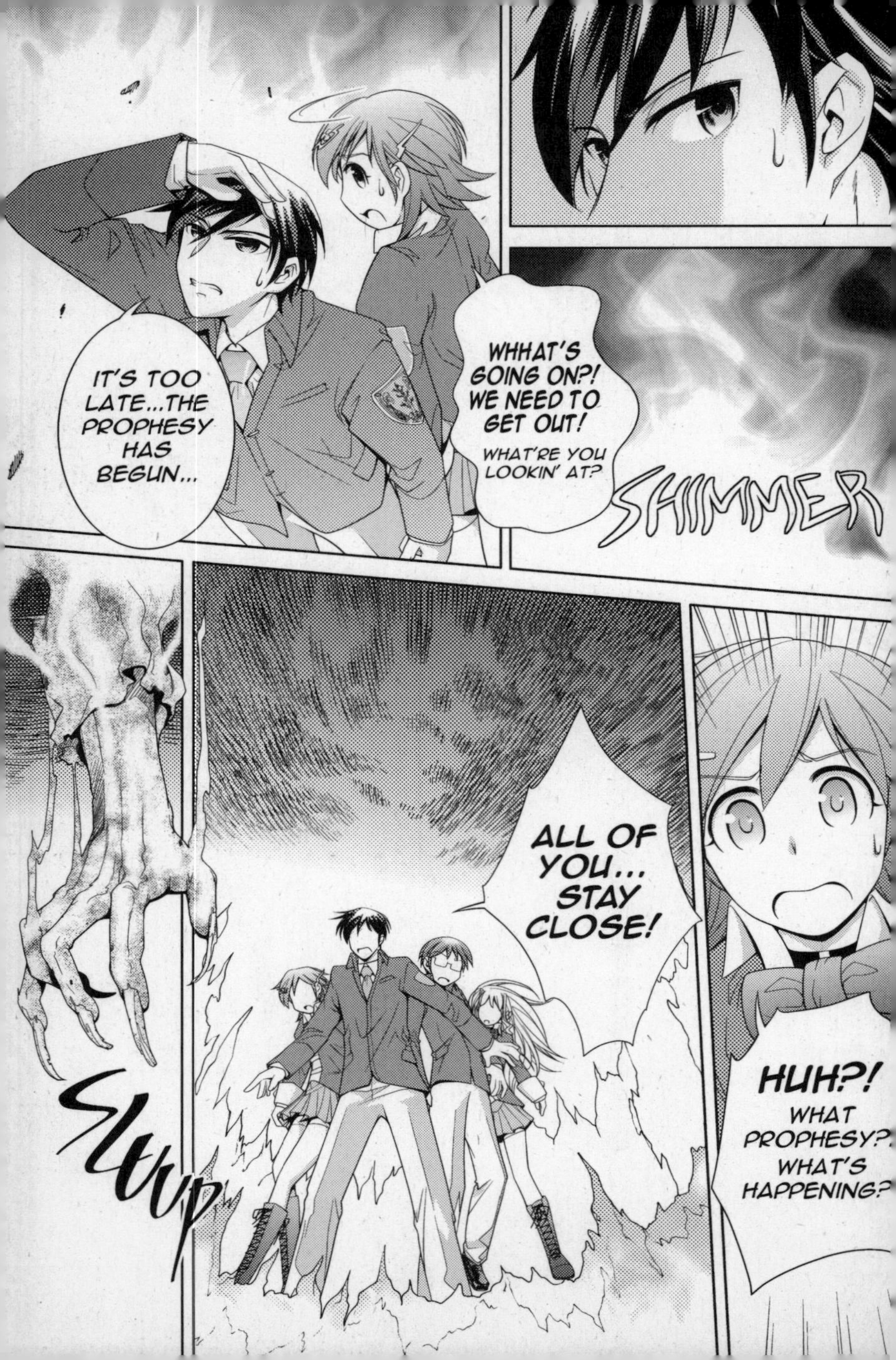
SHIMMER
WHHAT'S GOING ON?! WE NEED TO GET OUT!
WHAT'RE YOU LOOKIN' AT?
IT'S TOO LATE...THE PROPHESY HAS BEGUN...
HUH?!
WHAT PROPHESY?! WHAT'S HAPPENING?
ALL OF YOU... STAY CLOSE!
SLUUP

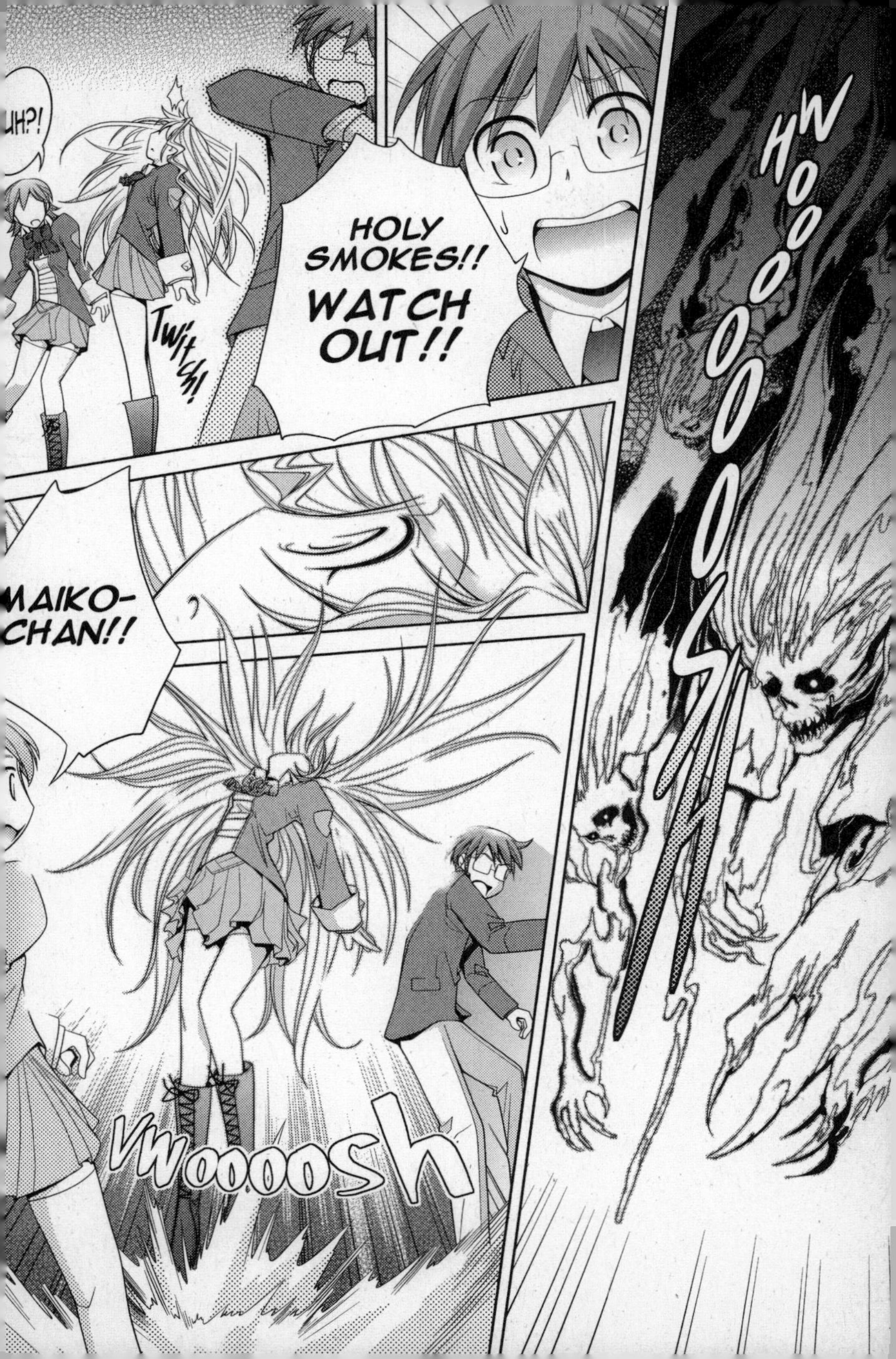
WHOOOOOOSH
HOLY SMOKES!! WATCH OUT!!
UH?!
Twitch!
MAIKO-CHAN!!
Vwoooosh

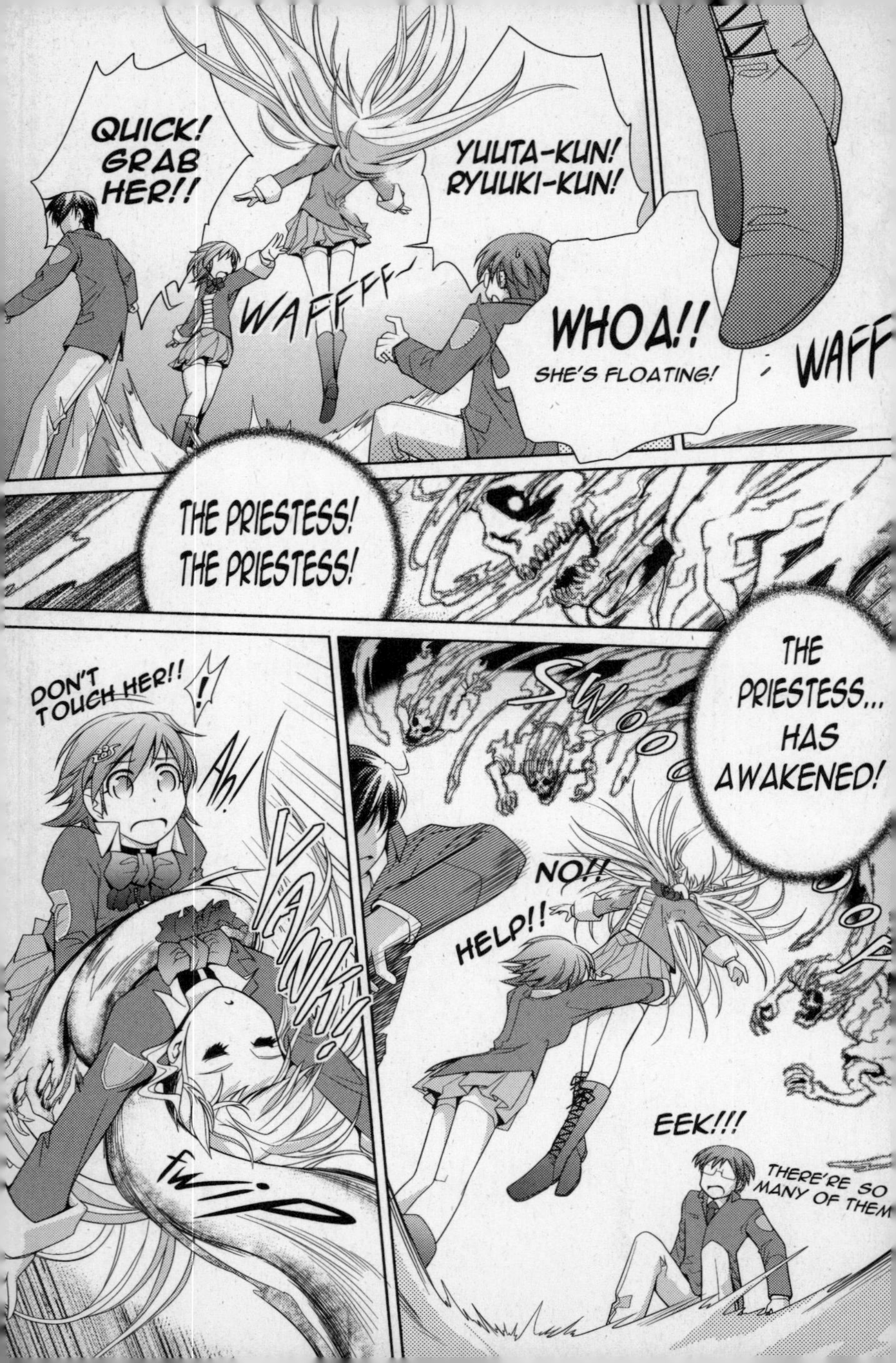
WAFF
YUUTA-KUN! RYUUKI-KUN!
QUICK! GRAB HER!!
WHOA!!
SHE'S FLOATING!
WAFFFF
THE PRIESTESS! THE PRIESTESS!
THE PRIESTESS... HAS AWAKENED!
NO!!
HELP!!
EEK!!!
THERE'RE SO MANY OF THEM
DON'T TOUCH HER!!
!
AH!
YANK!!

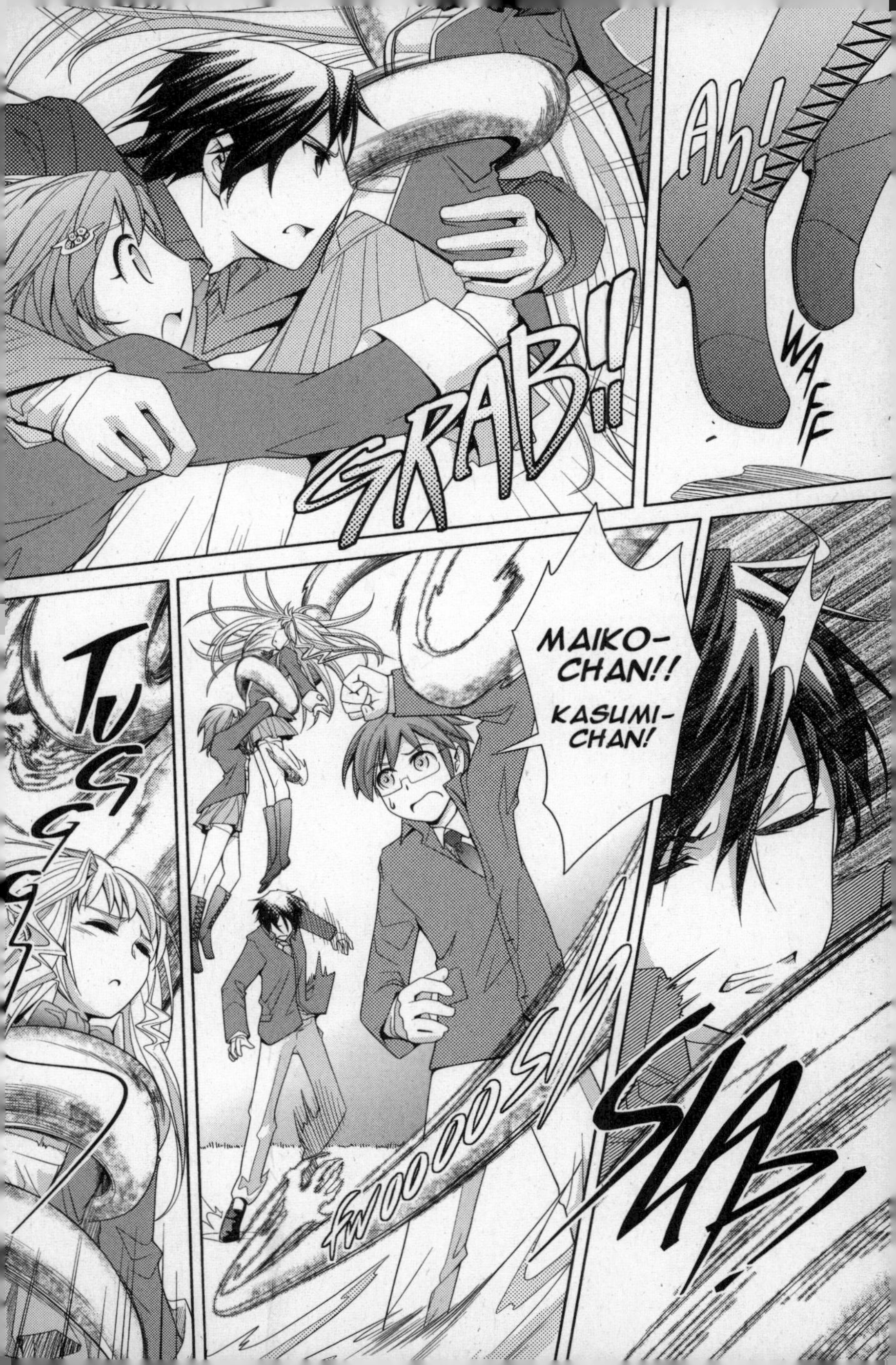
Ah!
WAFF
GRAB!!
MAIKO-CHAN!!
KASUMI-CHAN!
TUGGGG
SHA!
fwooooSH

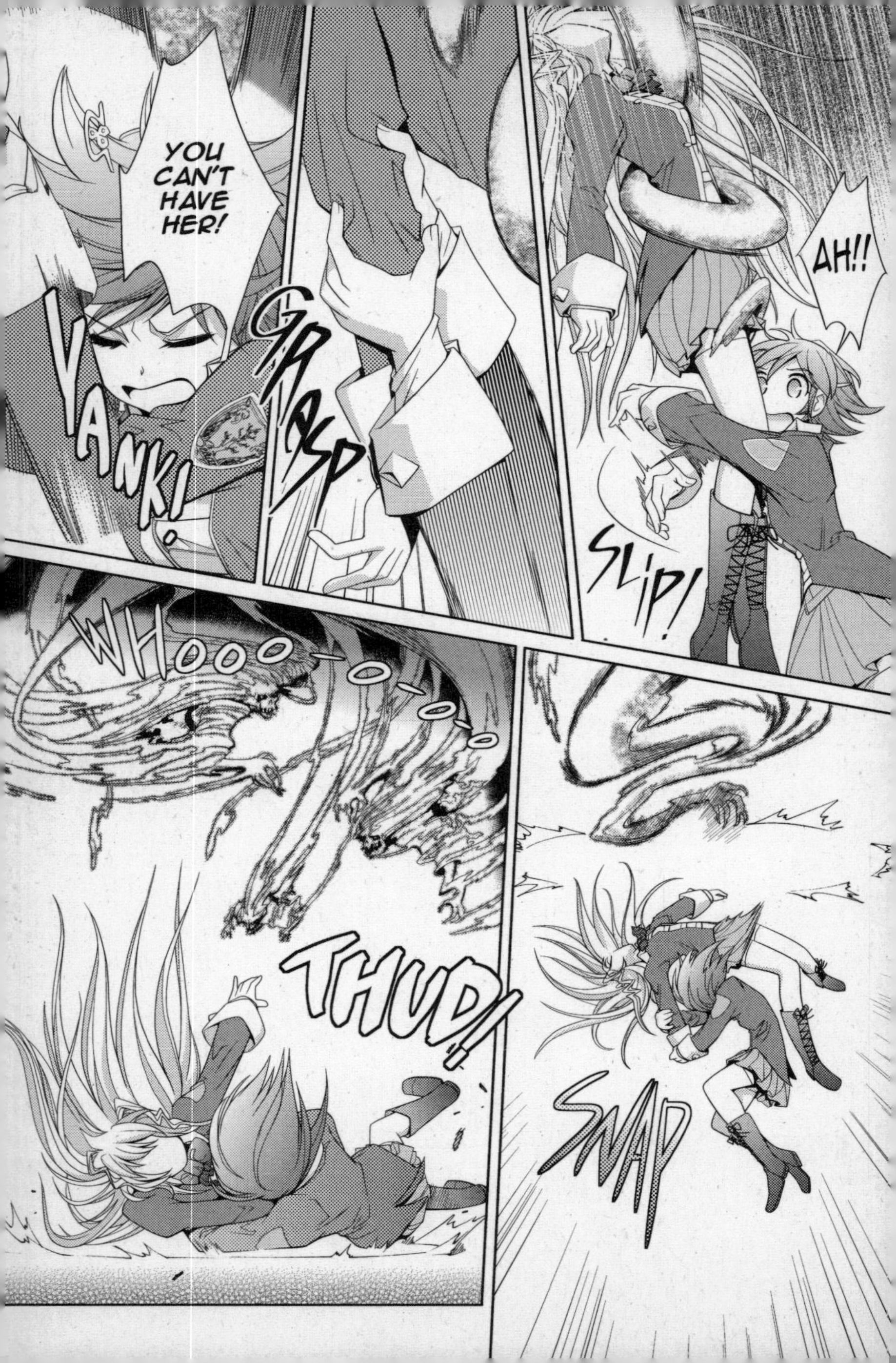
AH!!
SLIP!
GRASP
YOU CAN'T HAVE HER!
YANK!
SNAP
WHOOOO-O-O-O-O
THUD!

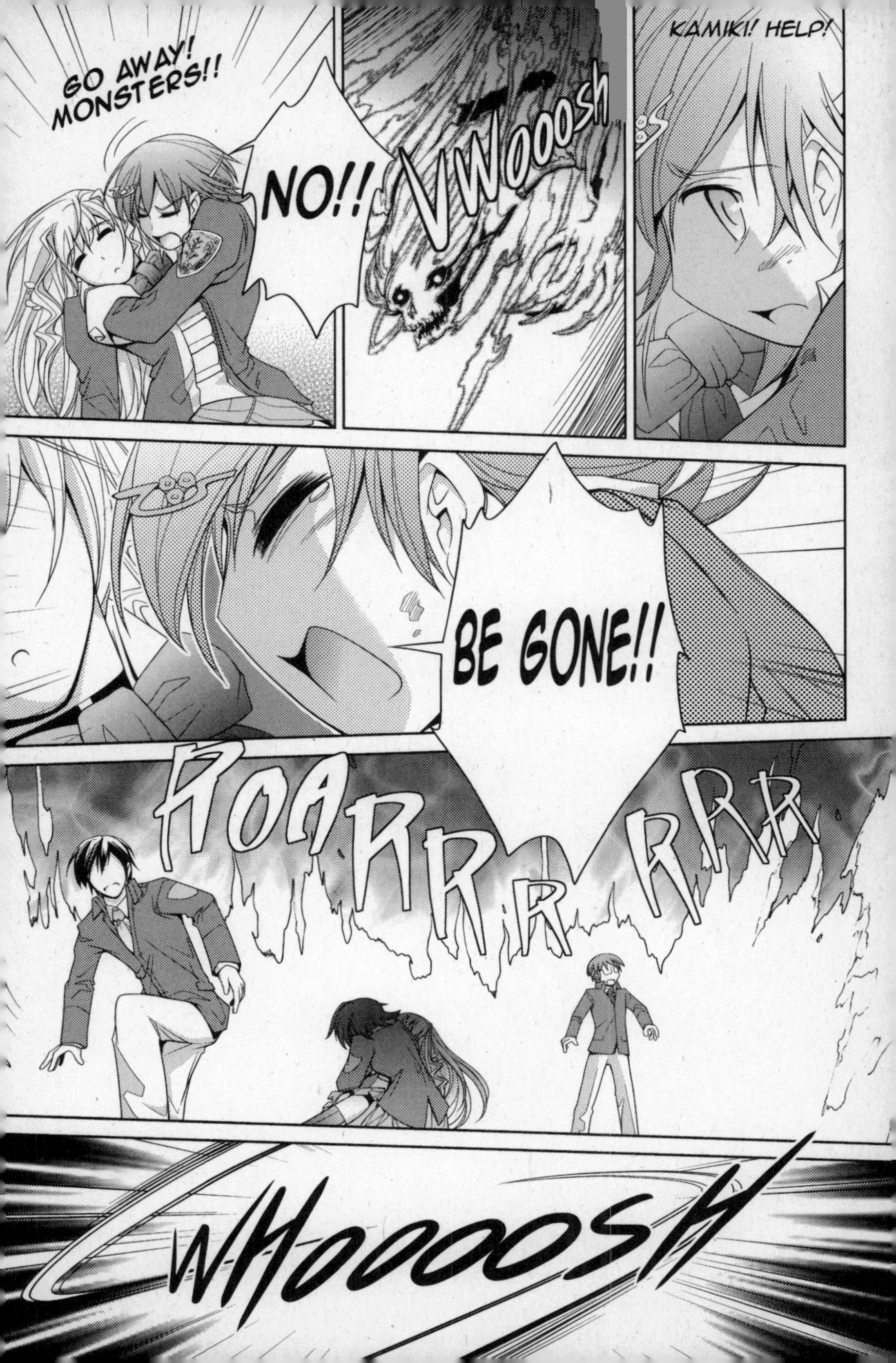

KAMIKI! HELP!
VWooosh
GO AWAY! MONSTERS!!
NO!!
BE GONE!!
ROARRR RRR
WHOOOSH

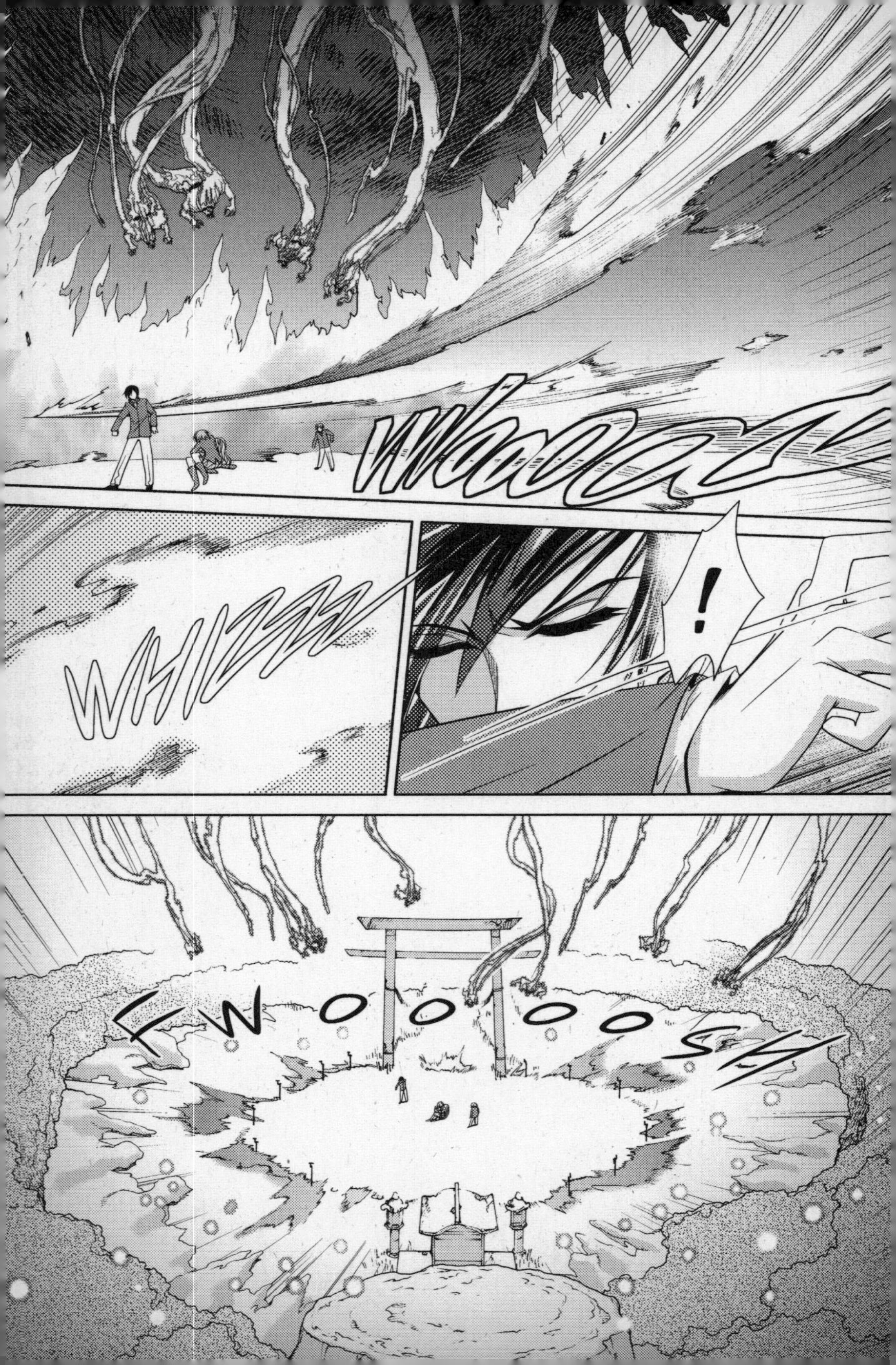
Whaaa!
!
WHUMM
FWOOOOOSH

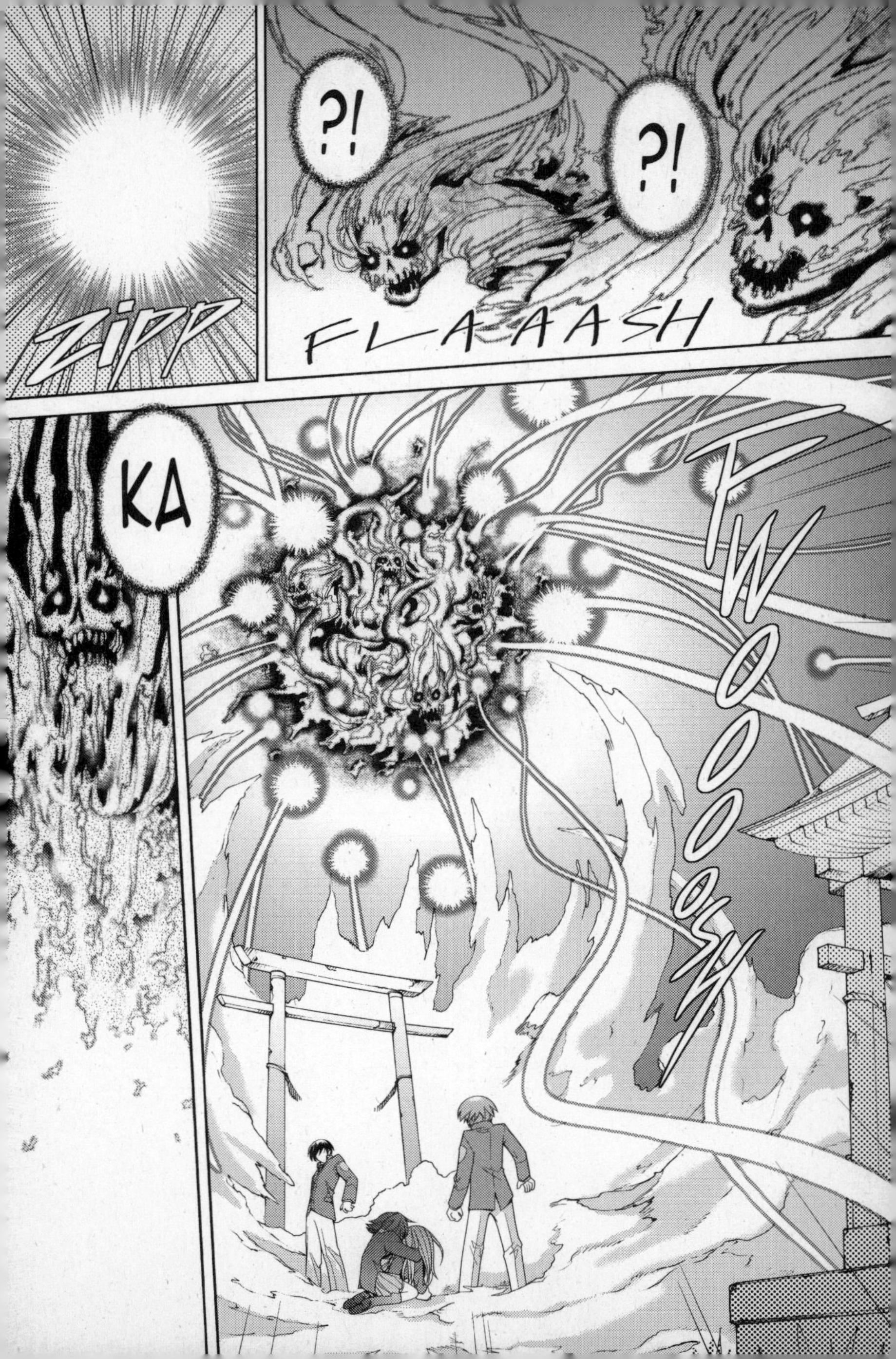
?!
?!
FLAAASH
ZIPP
FWOOOOOSH
KA

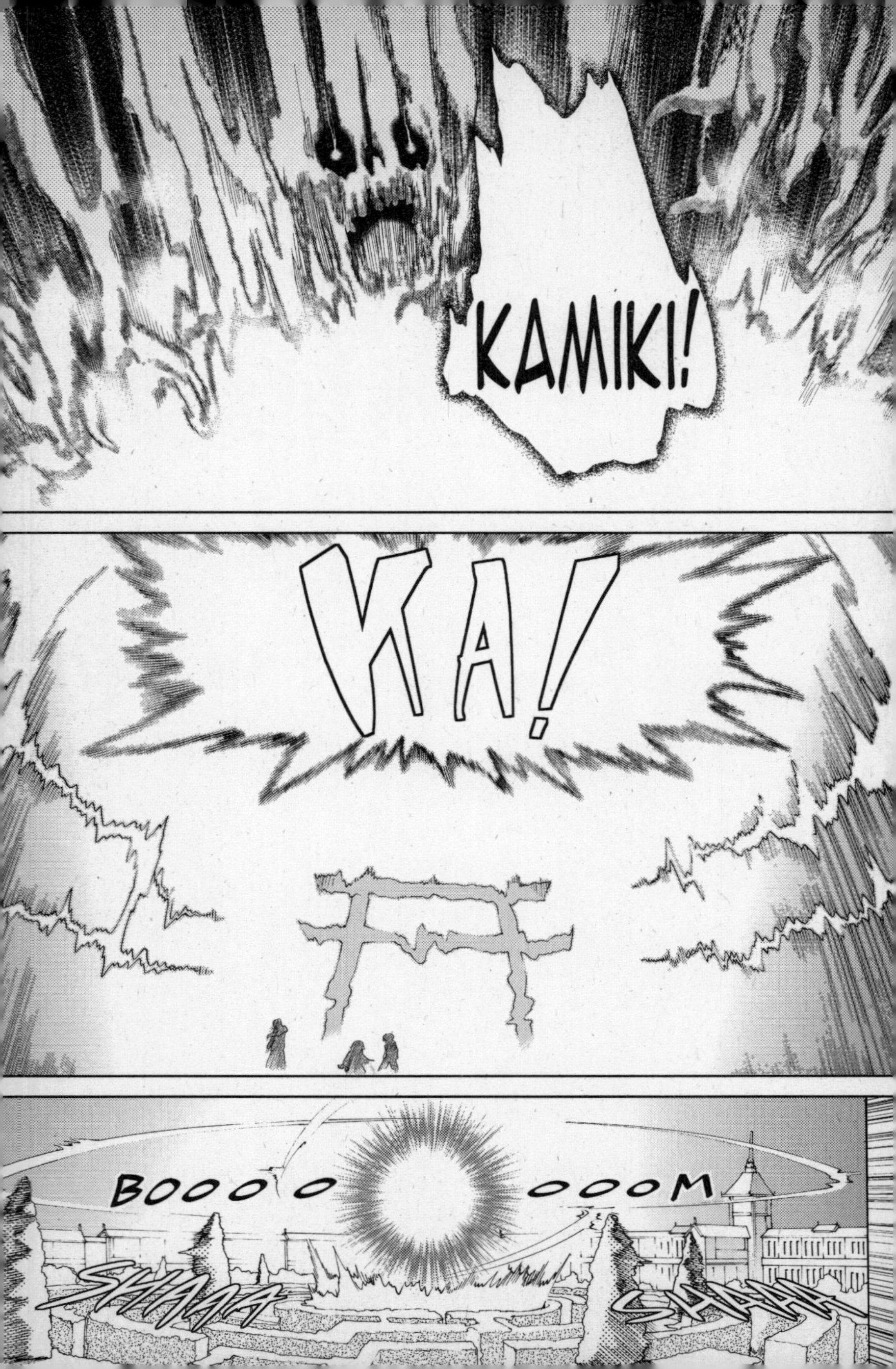
KAMIKI!
KA!
BOOOO OOOOM
SHAAA
SHAAAA

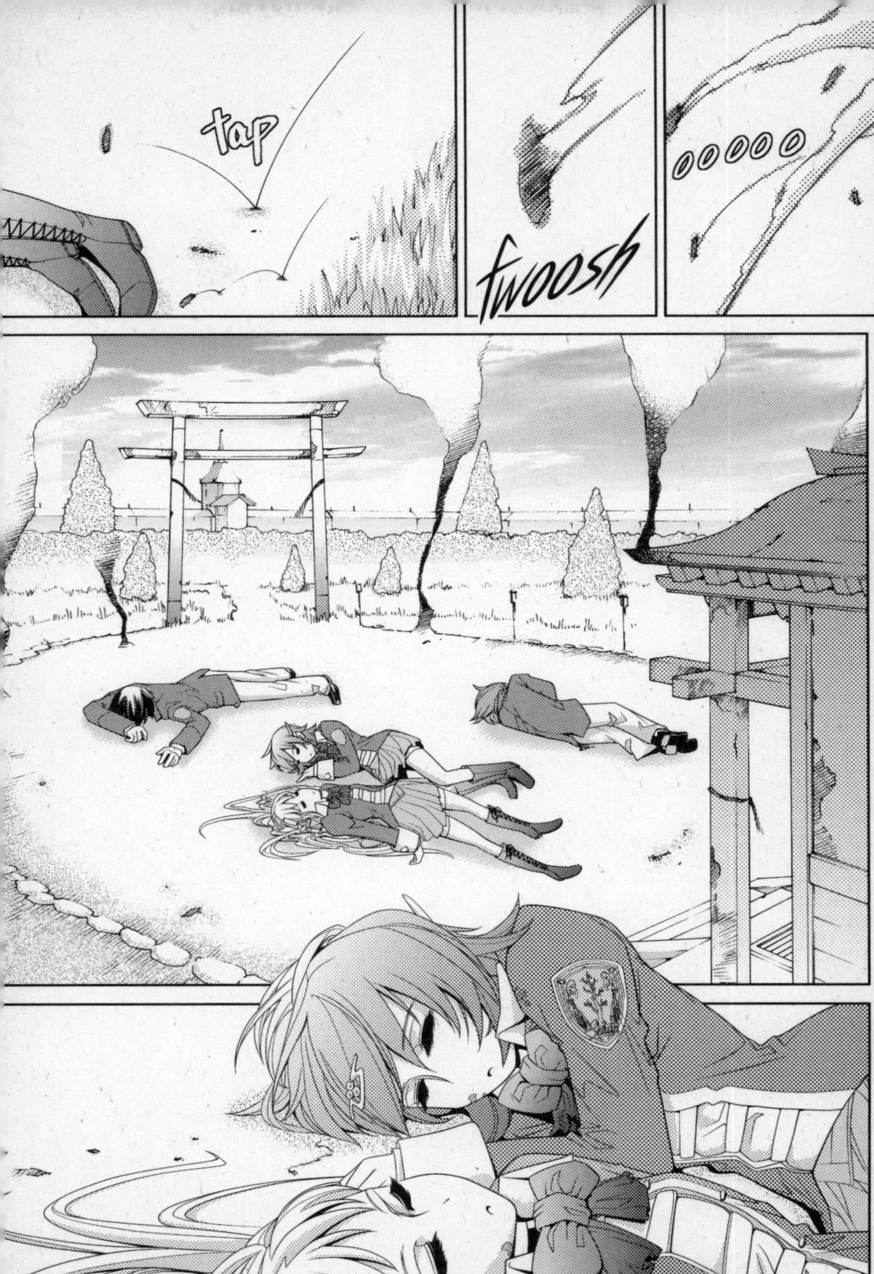
ooooo
fwoosh
tap

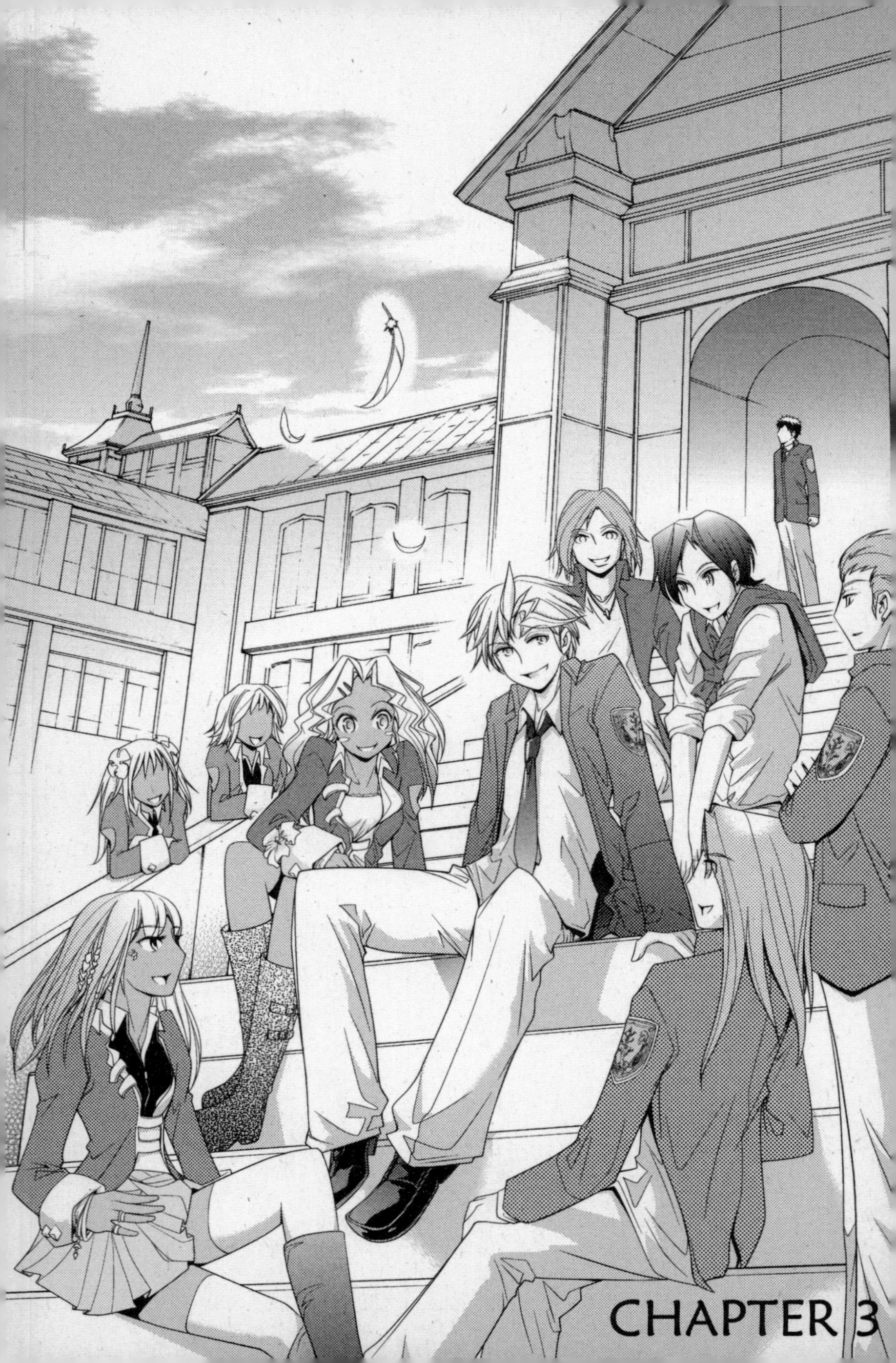

CHAPTER 3

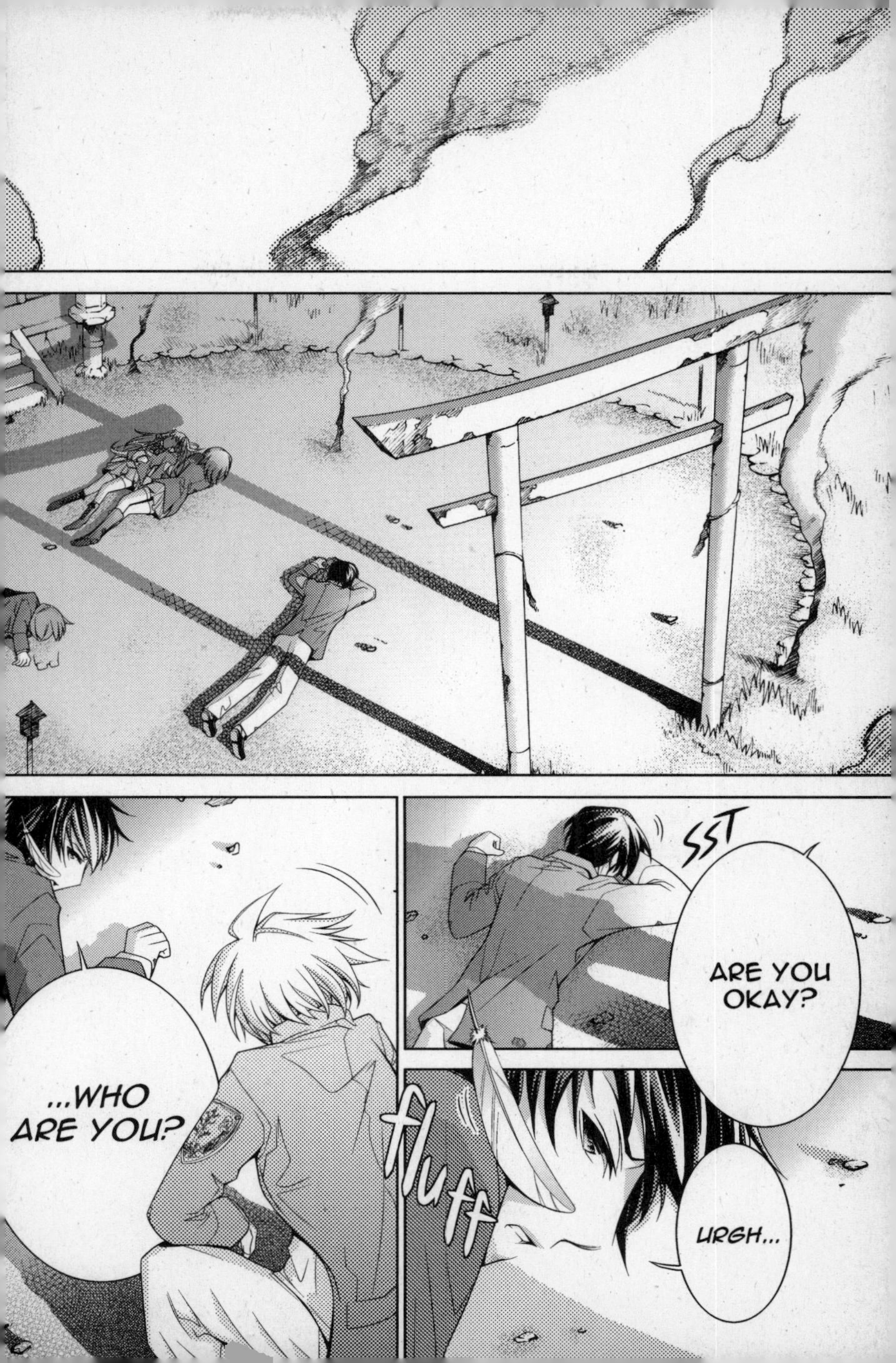
SST
ARE YOU OKAY?
fluff
URGH...
...WHO ARE YOU?

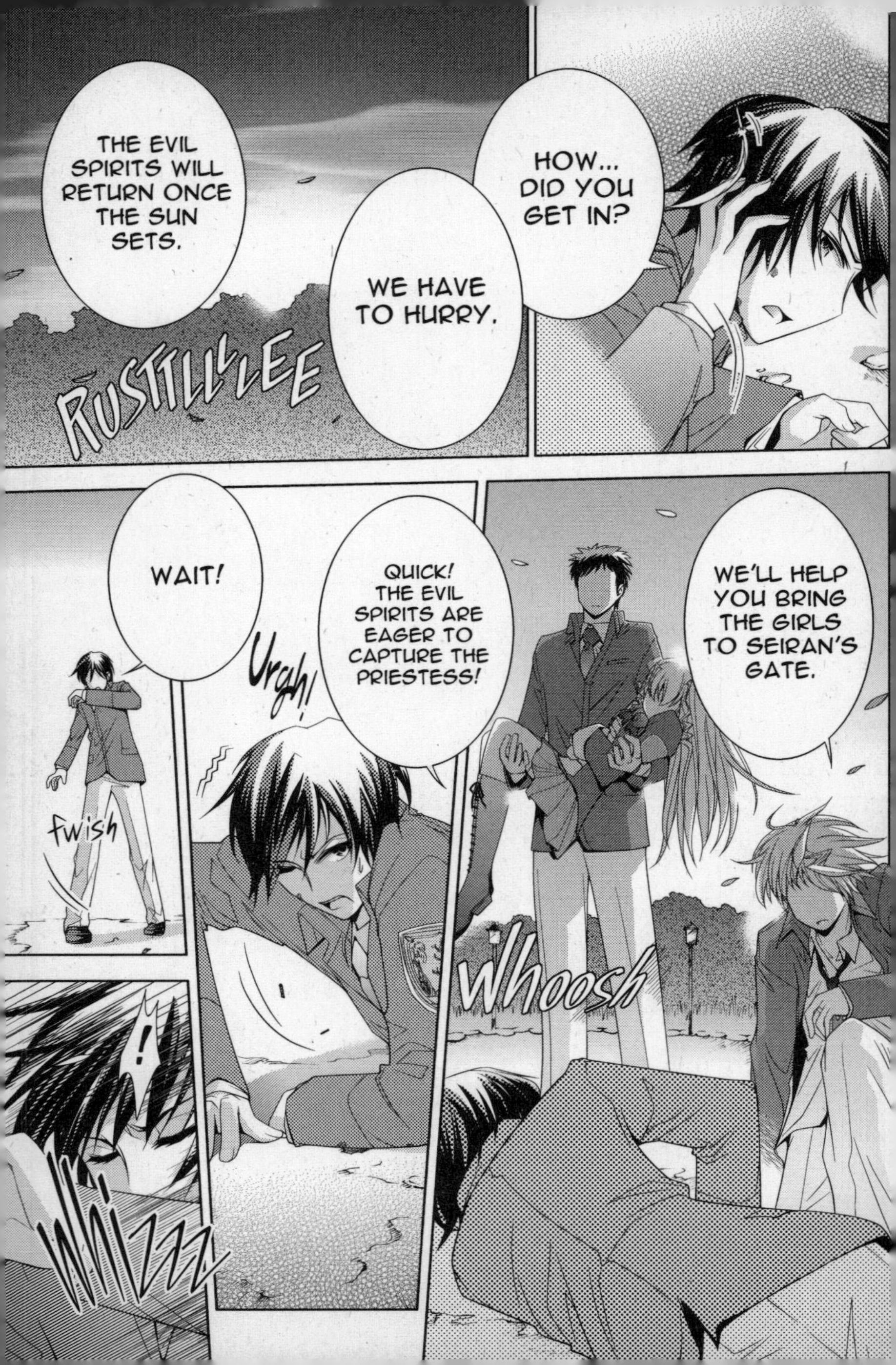
HOW... DID YOU GET IN?
THE EVIL SPIRITS WILL RETURN ONCE THE SUN SETS.
WE HAVE TO HURRY.
RUSTTLLLLEE
WE'LL HELP YOU BRING THE GIRLS TO SEIRAN'S GATE.
Whoosh
QUICK! THE EVIL SPIRITS ARE EAGER TO CAPTURE THE PRIESTESS!
Urgh!
WAIT!
fwish
!
Whizzz

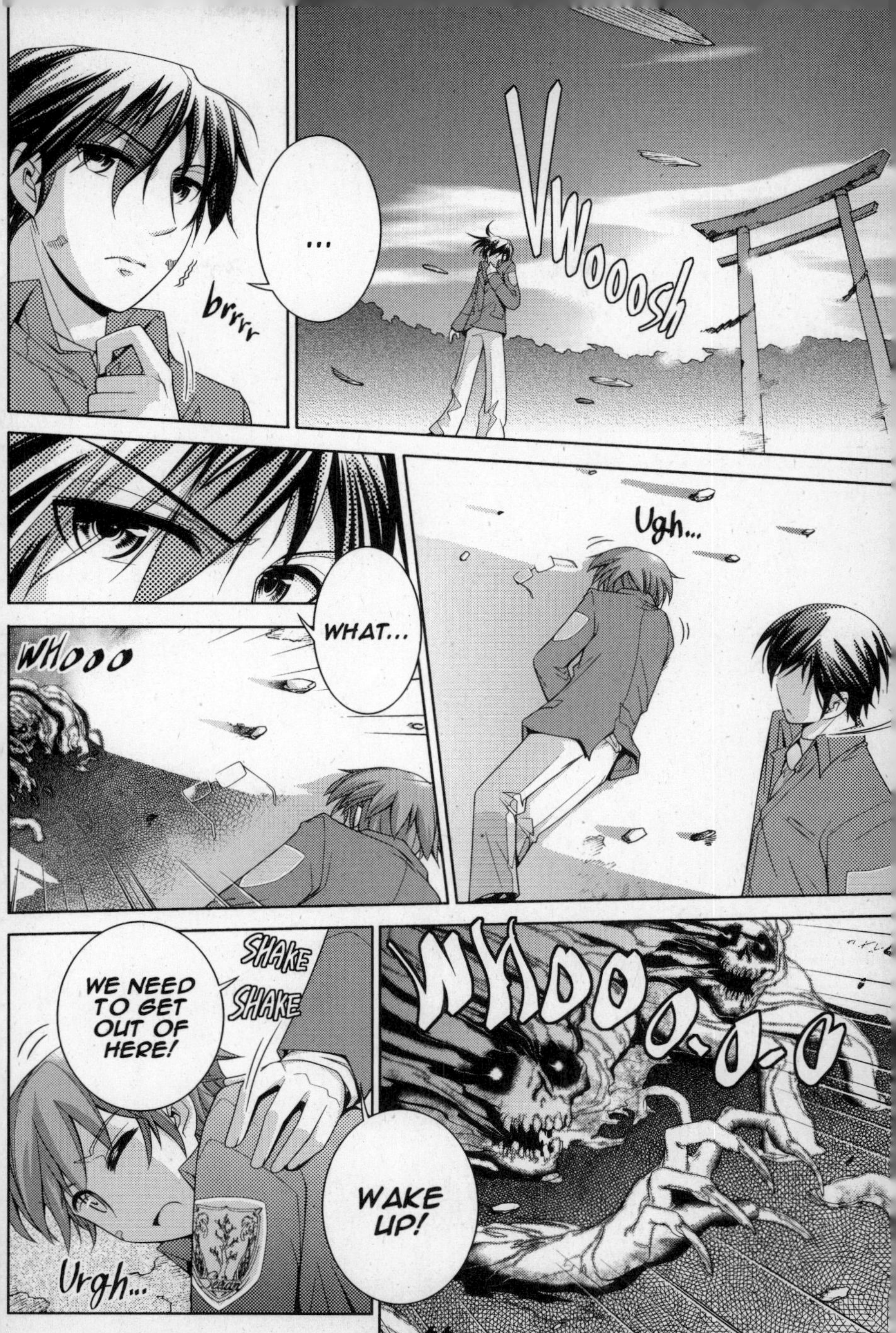
VWooosh
...
brrrr
Ugh...
WHAT...
WHOOO
WHOOO-O-O
WE NEED TO GET OUT OF HERE!
SHAKE
SHAKE
WAKE UP!
Urgh...

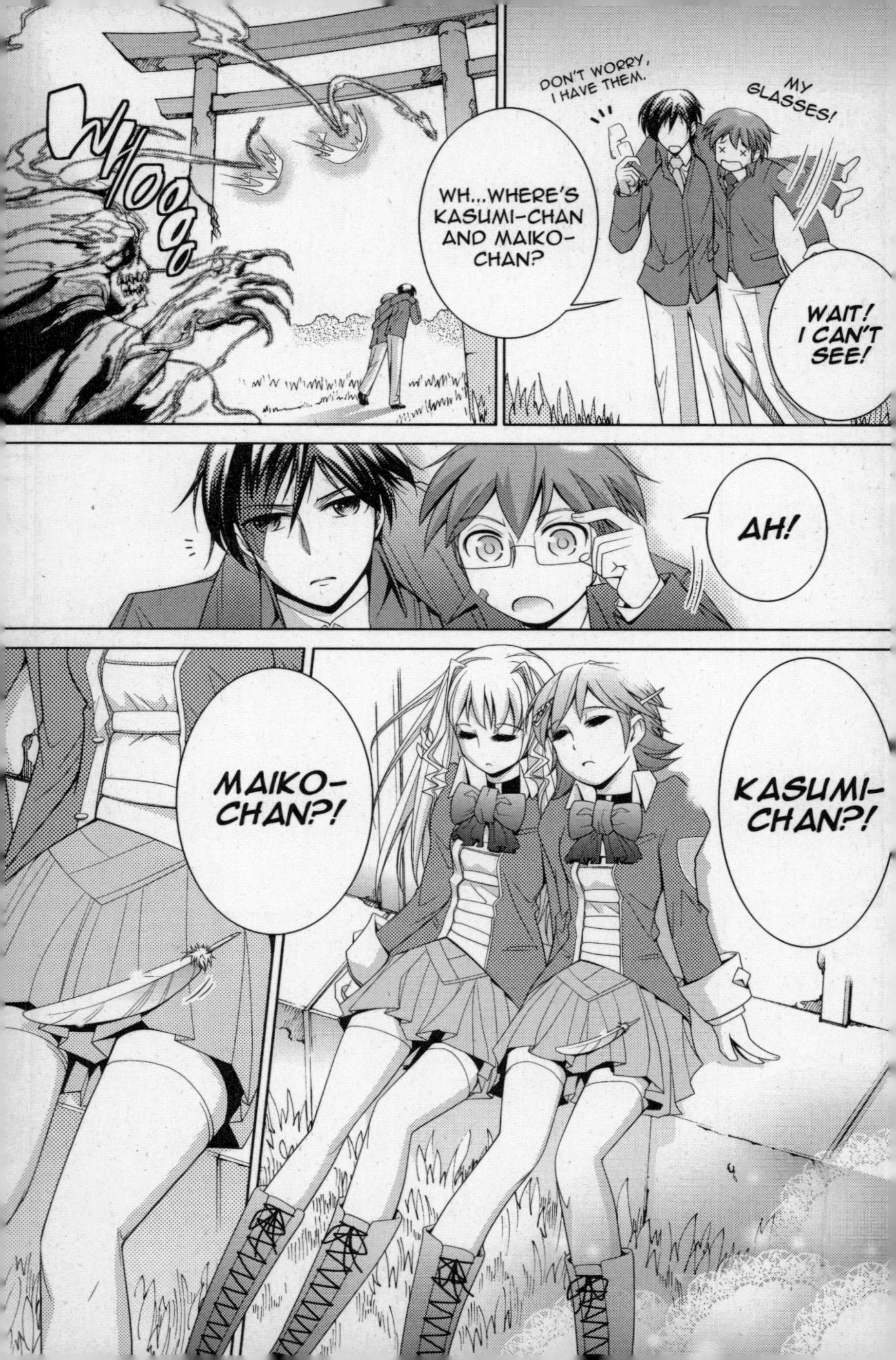

MY GLASSES!
DON'T WORRY, I HAVE THEM.
WAIT! I CAN'T SEE!
WH...WHERE'S KASUMI-CHAN AND MAIKO-CHAN?
WHOOOO
AH!
KASUMI-CHAN?!
MAIKO-CHAN?!

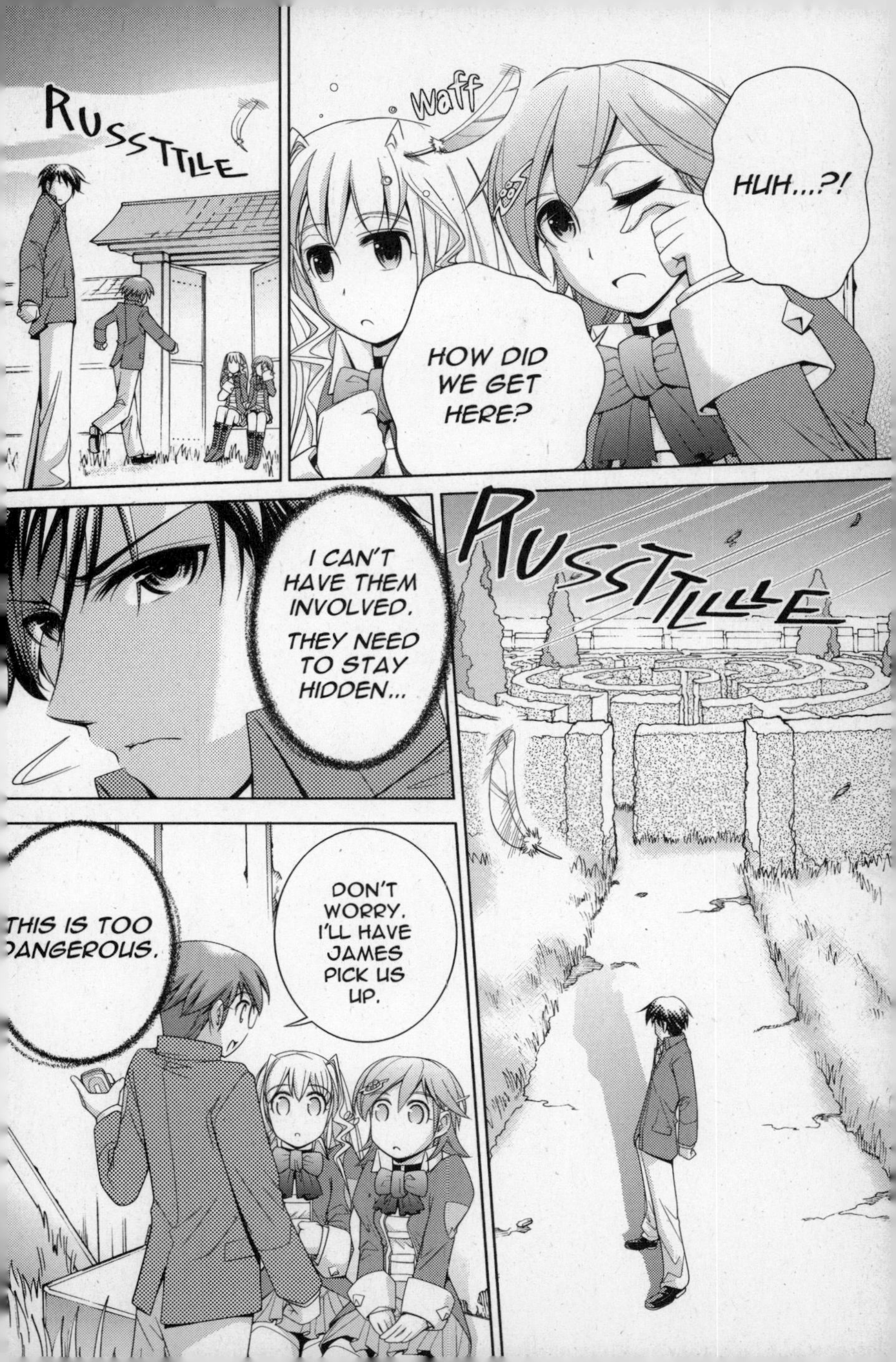
HUH...?!
Waff
HOW DID WE GET HERE?
RUSSTTILLE
RUSSTTILLLLE
I CAN'T HAVE THEM INVOLVED.
THEY NEED TO STAY HIDDEN...
DON'T WORRY. I'LL HAVE JAMES PICK US UP.
THIS IS TOO DANGEROUS.

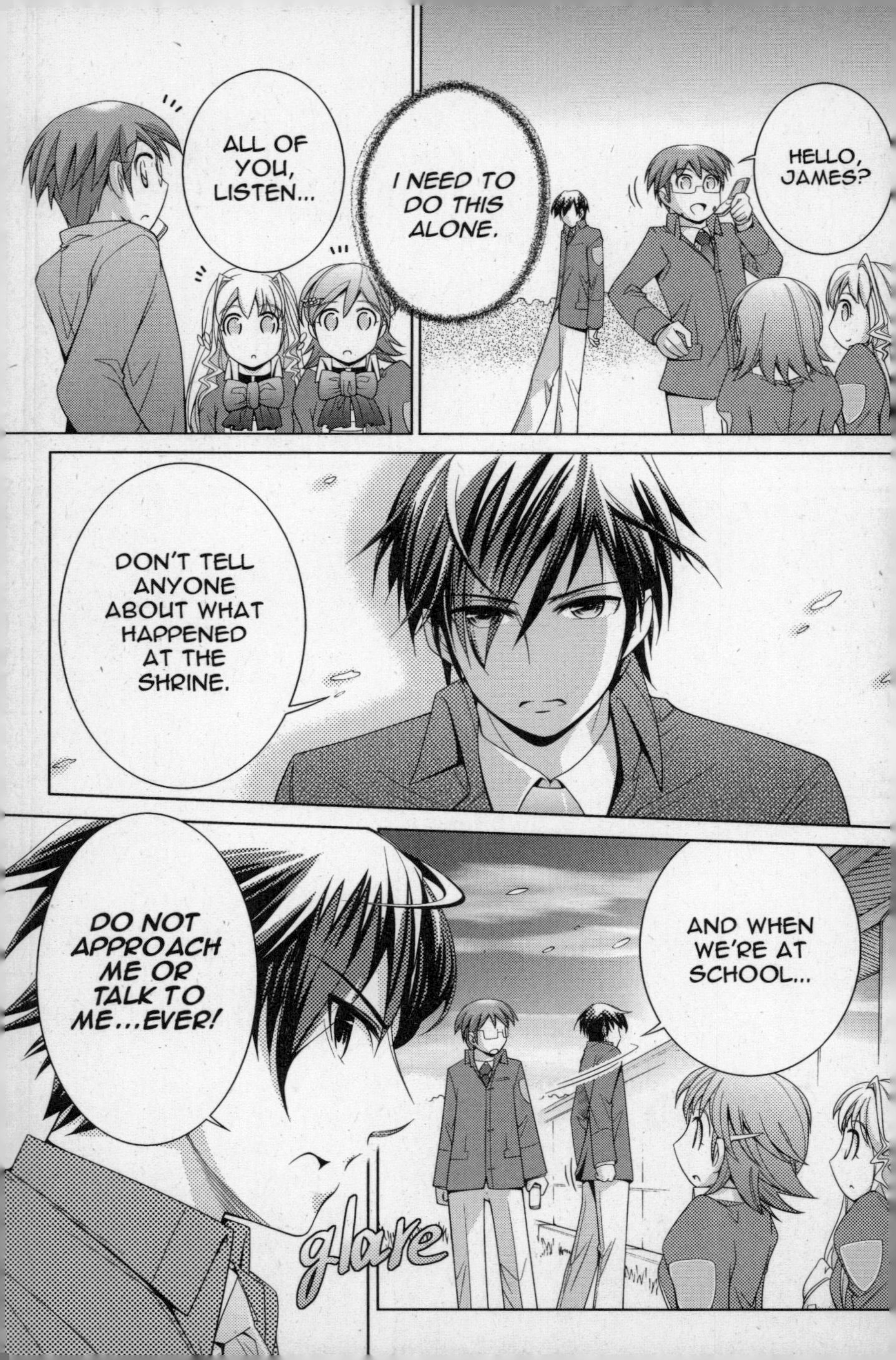
HELLO, JAMES?
ALL OF YOU, LISTEN...
I NEED TO DO THIS ALONE.
DON'T TELL ANYONE ABOUT WHAT HAPPENED AT THE SHRINE.
AND WHEN WE'RE AT SCHOOL...
DO NOT APPROACH ME OR TALK TO ME...EVER!
glare

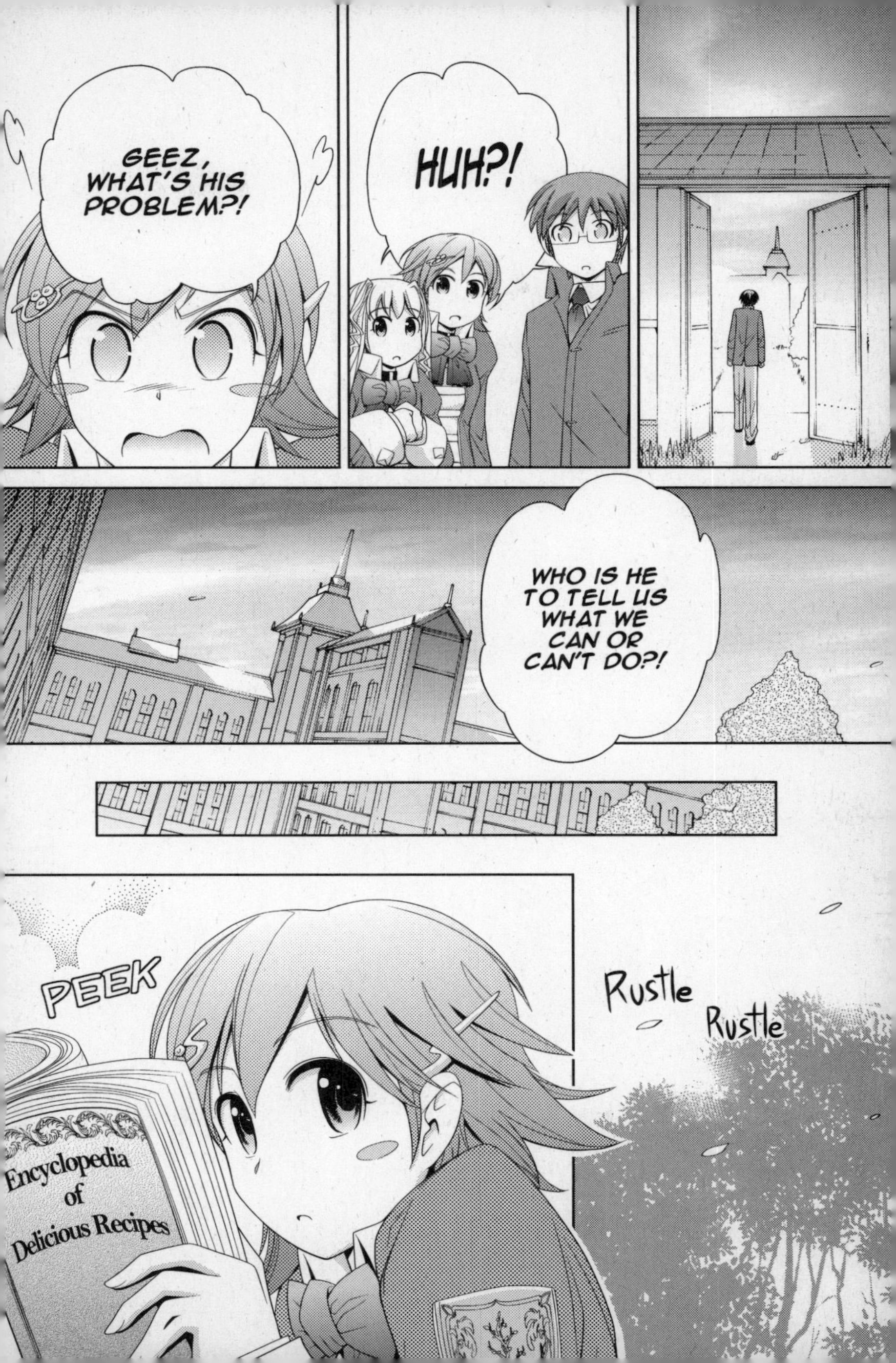
HUH?!
GEEZ, WHAT'S HIS PROBLEM?!
WHO IS HE TO TELL US WHAT WE CAN OR CAN'T DO?!
Rustle
Rustle
PEEK
Encyclopedia of Delicious Recipes

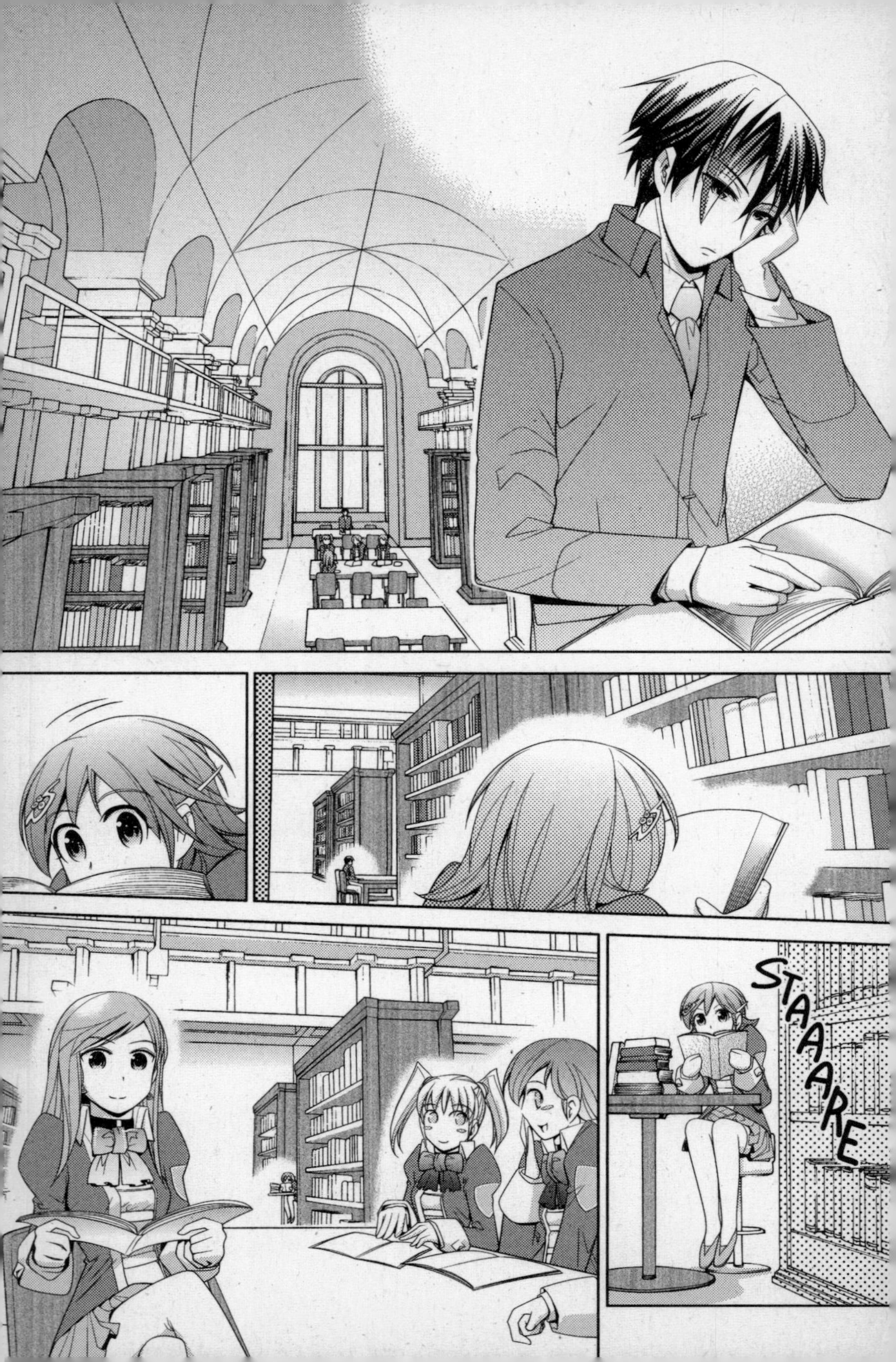
STAAARE

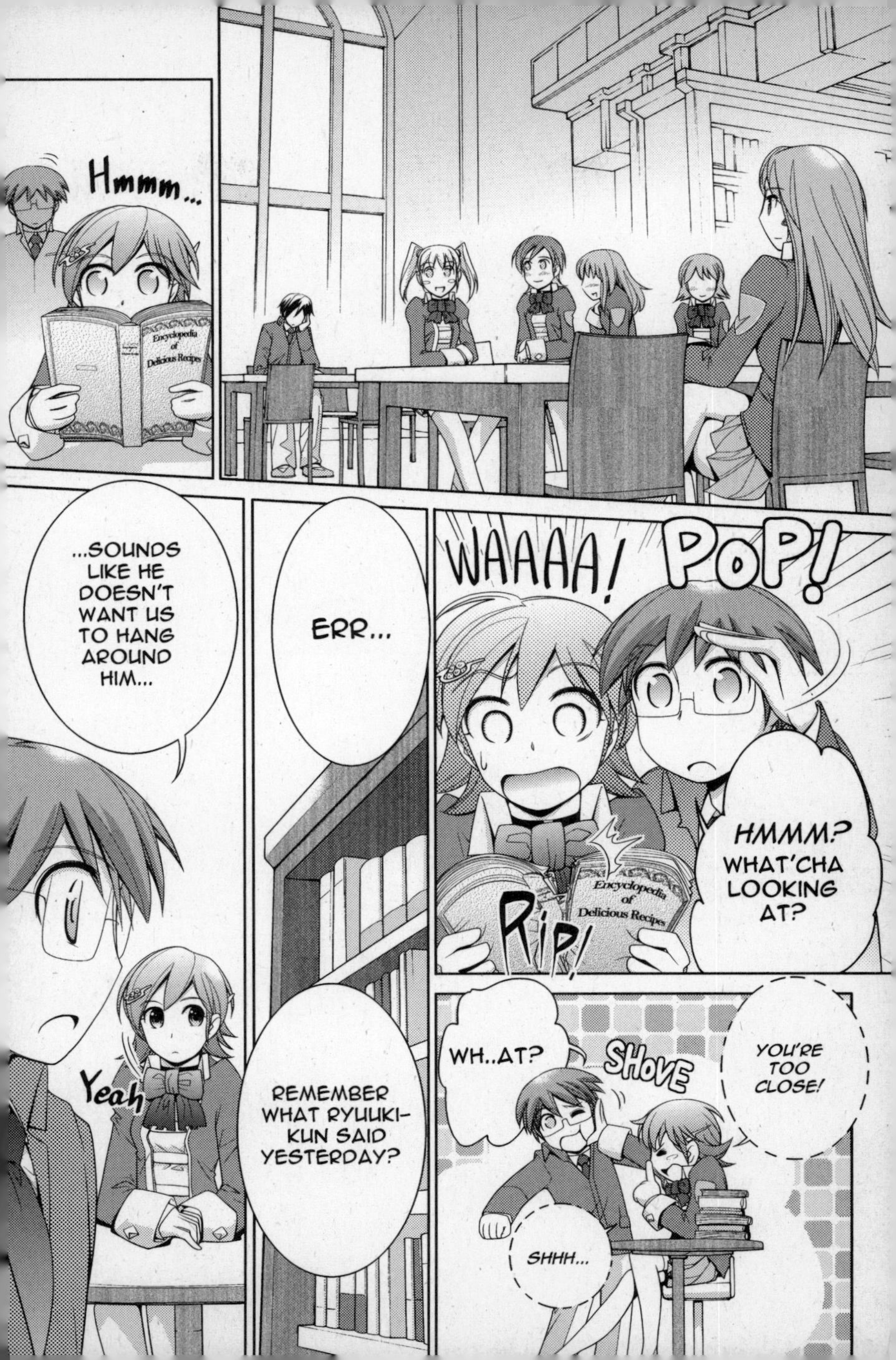
Hmmm...
Encyclopedia of Delicious Recipes
PoP!
WAAAA!
HMMM? WHAT'CHA LOOKING AT?
Encyclopedia of Delicious Recipes
Rip!
YOU'RE TOO CLOSE!
SHOVE
WH..AT?
SHHH...
ERR...
REMEMBER WHAT RYUUKI-KUN SAID YESTERDAY?
Yeah
...SOUNDS LIKE HE DOESN'T WANT US TO HANG AROUND HIM...

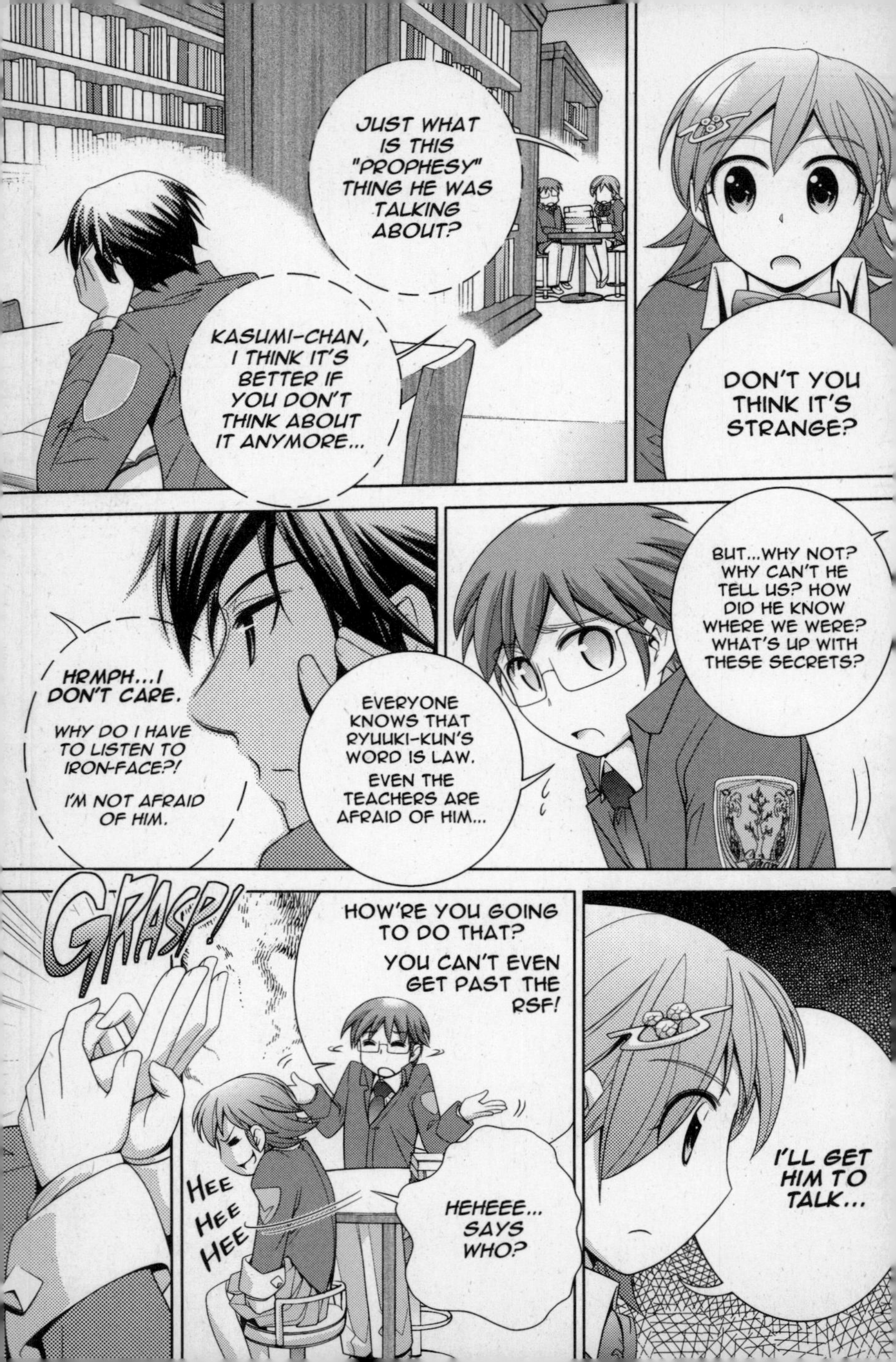
DON'T YOU THINK IT'S STRANGE?
JUST WHAT IS THIS "PROPHESY" THING HE WAS TALKING ABOUT?
KASUMI-CHAN, I THINK IT'S BETTER IF YOU DON'T THINK ABOUT IT ANYMORE...
BUT...WHY NOT? WHY CAN'T HE TELL US? HOW DID HE KNOW WHERE WE WERE? WHAT'S UP WITH THESE SECRETS?
EVERYONE KNOWS THAT RYUUKI-KUN'S WORD IS LAW.
EVEN THE TEACHERS ARE AFRAID OF HIM...
HRMPH...I DON'T CARE.
WHY DO I HAVE TO LISTEN TO IRON-FACE?!
I'M NOT AFRAID OF HIM.
I'LL GET HIM TO TALK...
HOW'RE YOU GOING TO DO THAT?
YOU CAN'T EVEN GET PAST THE RSF!
GRASP!
HEHEEE... SAYS WHO?
HEE HEE HEE

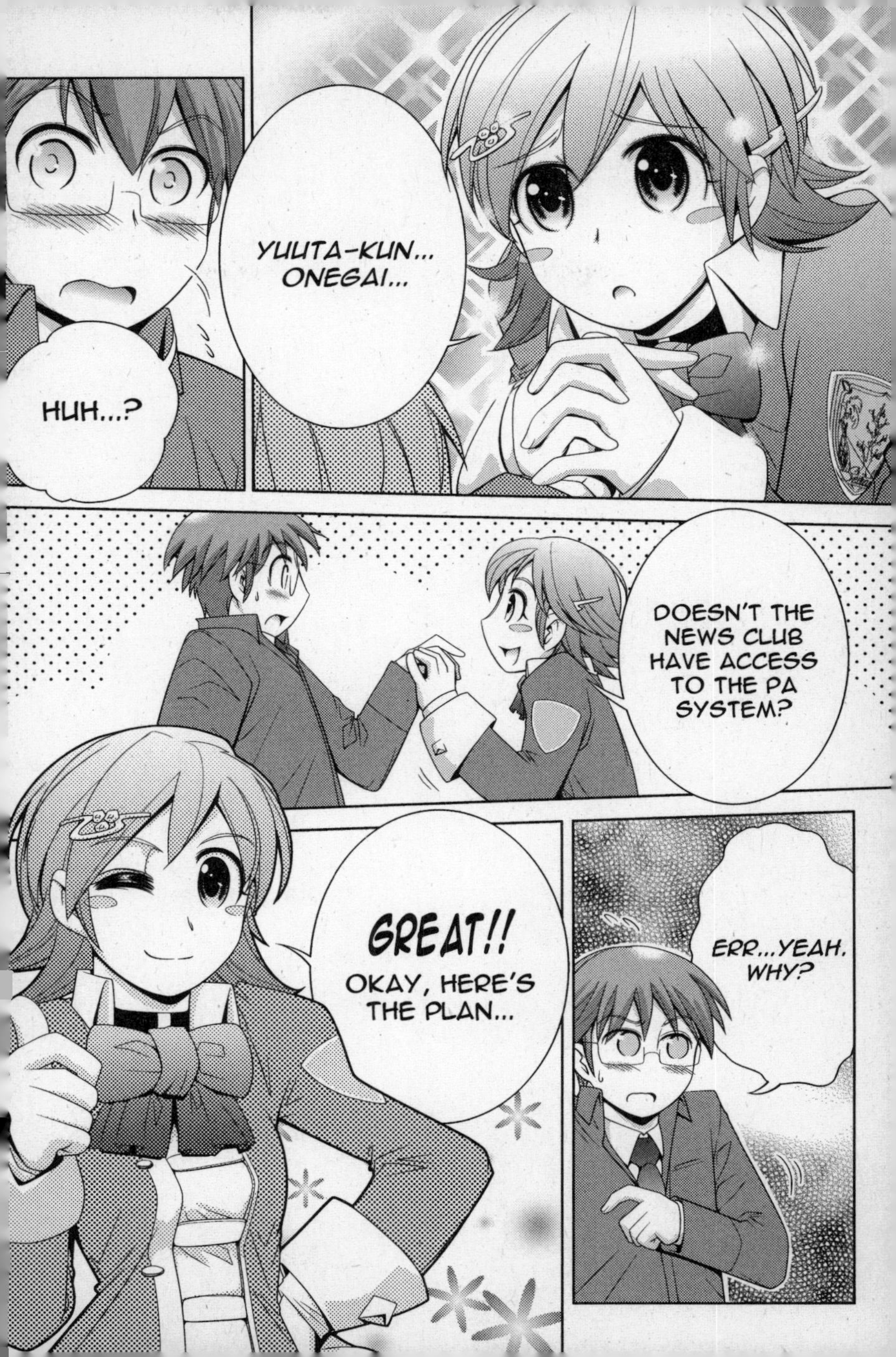
YUUTA-KUN... ONEGAI...
HUH...?
DOESN'T THE NEWS CLUB HAVE ACCESS TO THE PA SYSTEM?
ERR...YEAH. WHY?
GREAT!!
OKAY, HERE'S THE PLAN...

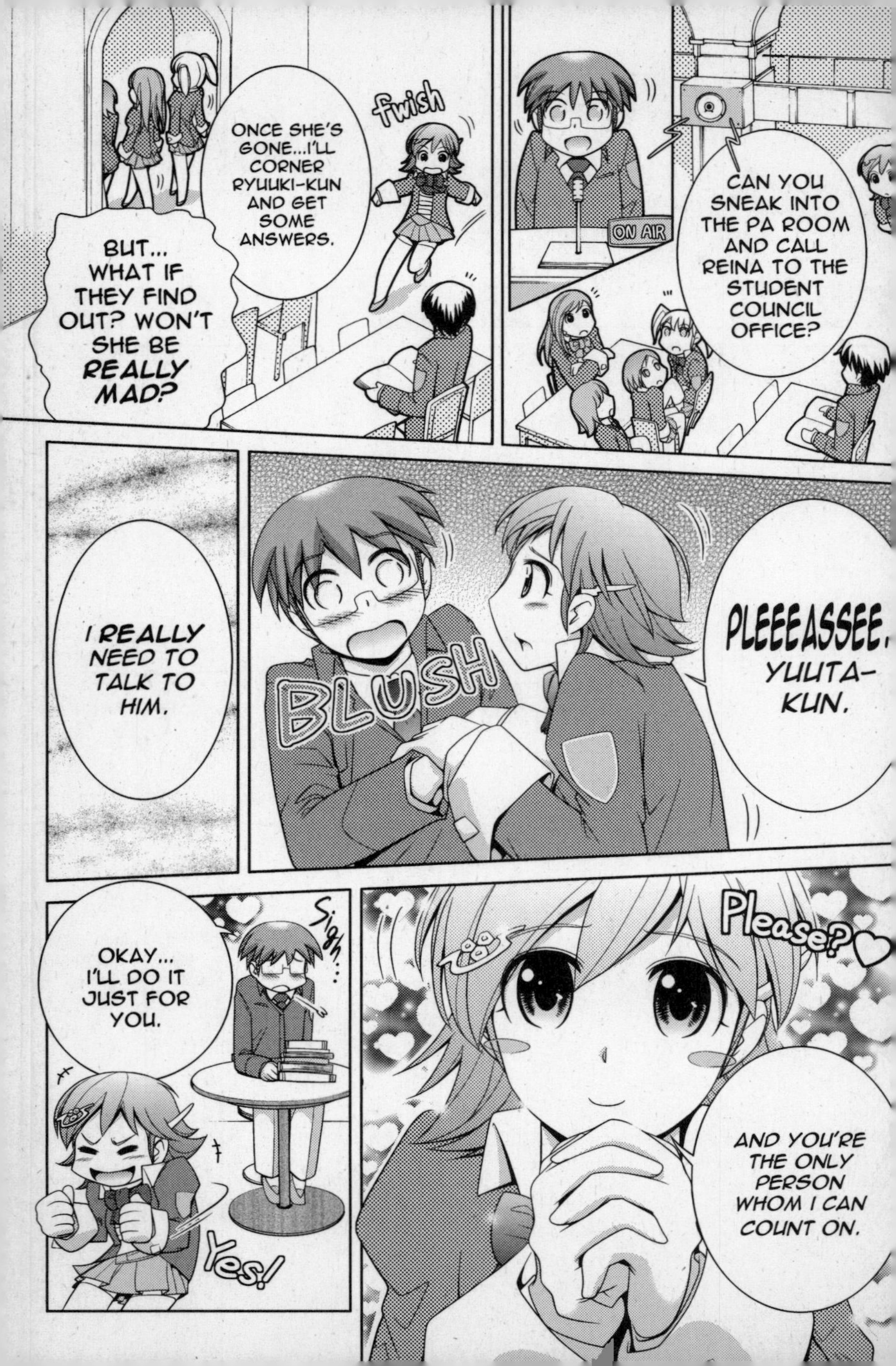
ON AIR
CAN YOU SNEAK INTO THE PA ROOM AND CALL REINA TO THE STUDENT COUNCIL OFFICE?
fwish
ONCE SHE'S GONE...I'LL CORNER RYUUKI-KUN AND GET SOME ANSWERS.
BUT... WHAT IF THEY FIND OUT? WON'T SHE BE **REALLY MAD?**
PLEEEASSEE, YUUTA-KUN.
BLUSH
I **REALLY** NEED TO TALK TO HIM.
Please?♡
AND YOU'RE THE ONLY PERSON WHOM I CAN COUNT ON.
Sigh...
OKAY... I'LL DO IT JUST FOR YOU.
Yes!

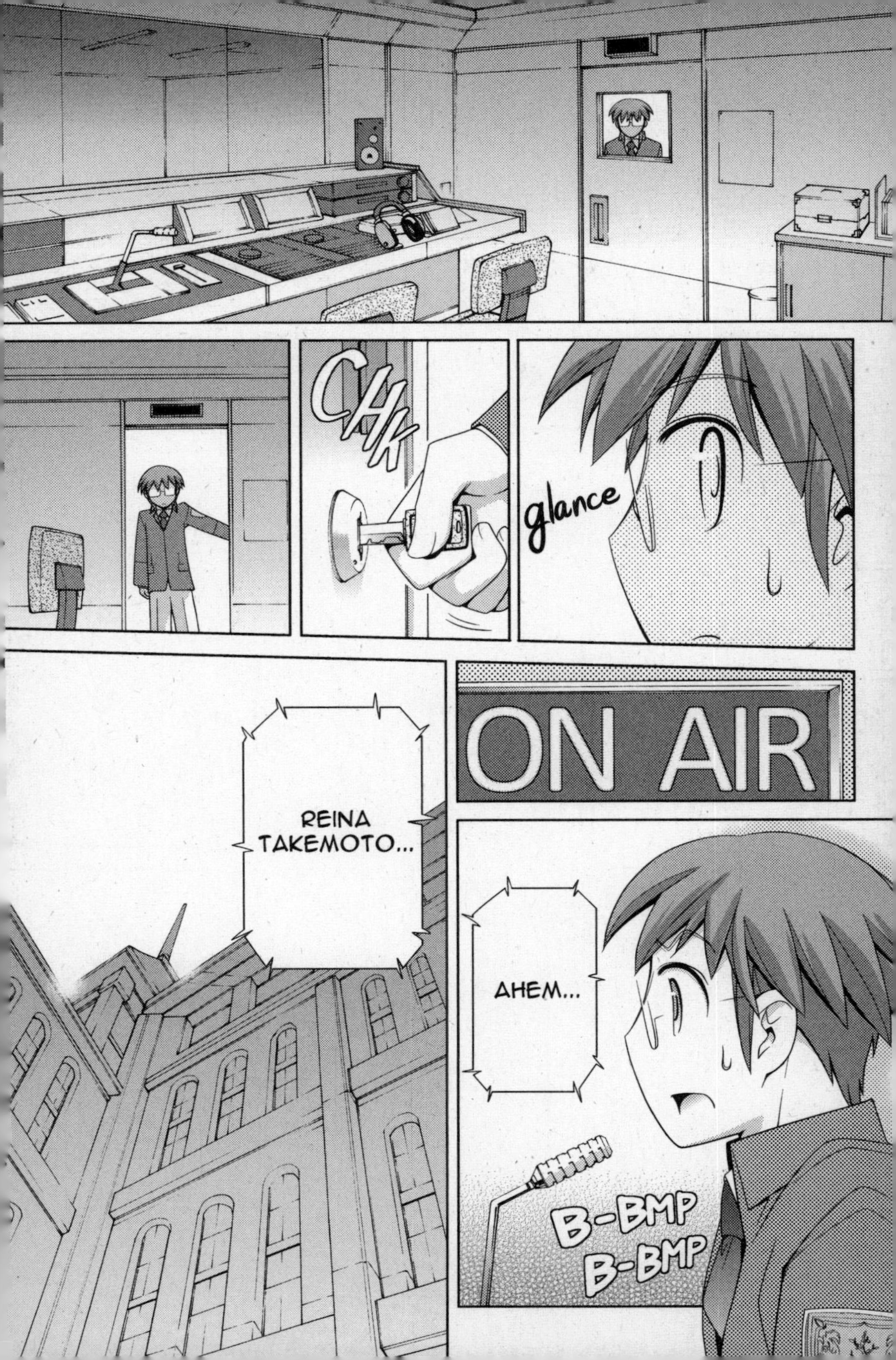

glance
CHK
ON AIR
AHEM...
B-BMP B-BMP
REINA TAKEMOTO...

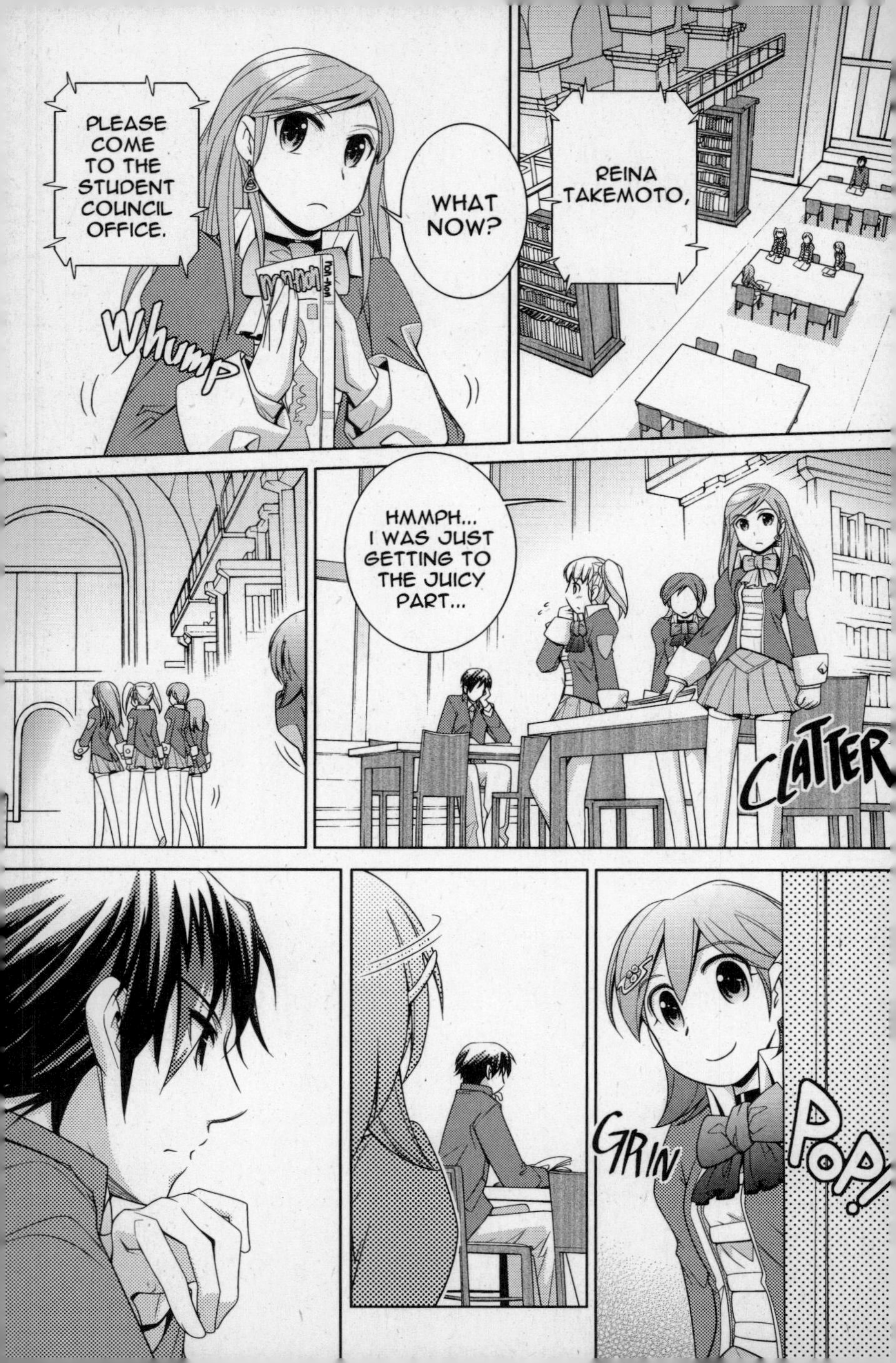
REINA TAKEMOTO,
PLEASE COME TO THE STUDENT COUNCIL OFFICE.
WHAT NOW?
Whump
HMMPH... I WAS JUST GETTING TO THE JUICY PART...
CLATTER
POP!
GRIN

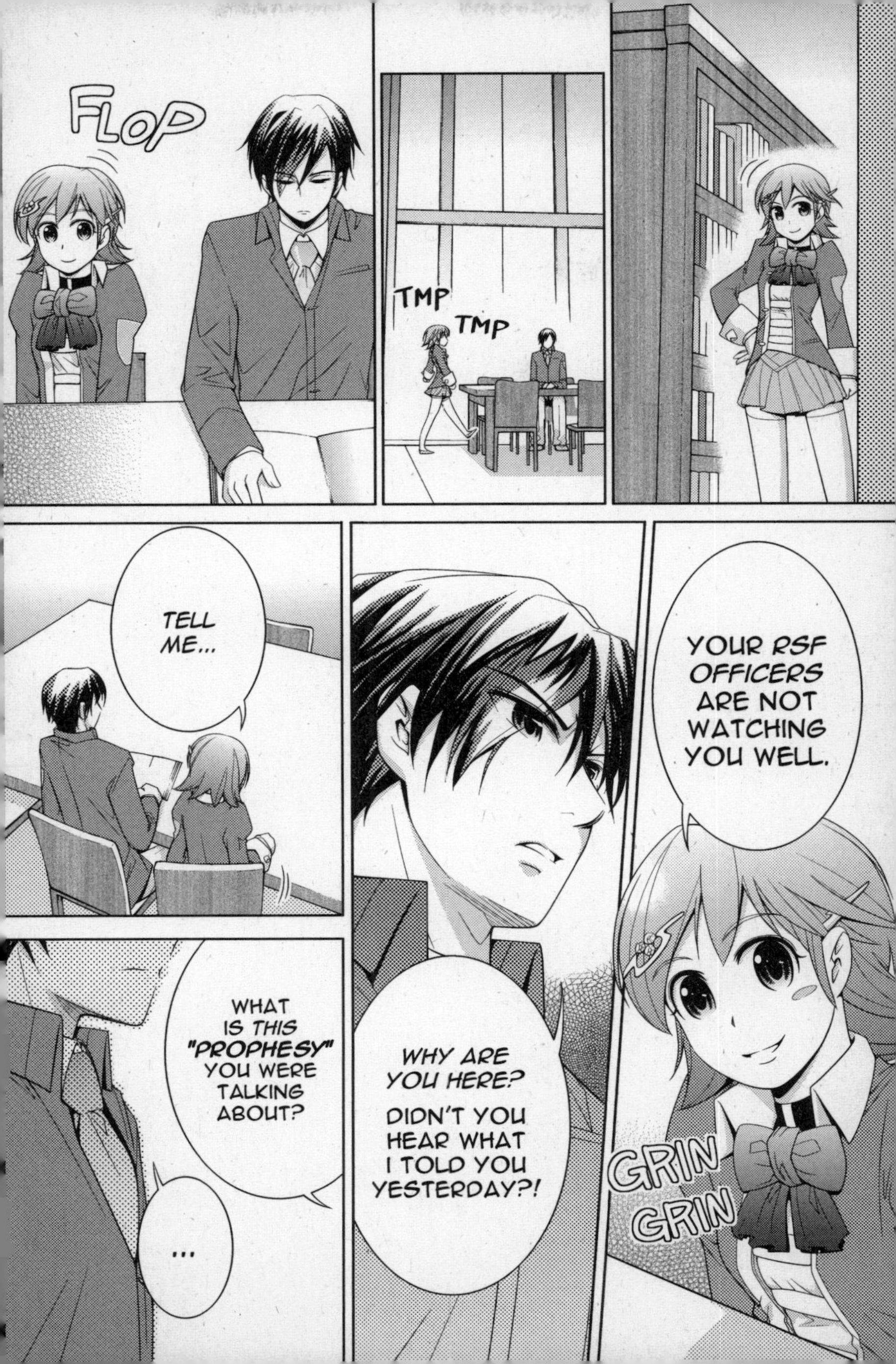
TMP
TMP
FLOP
YOUR RSF OFFICERS ARE NOT WATCHING YOU WELL.
GRIN GRIN
WHY ARE YOU HERE?
DIDN'T YOU HEAR WHAT I TOLD YOU YESTERDAY?!
TELL ME...
WHAT IS THIS "PROPHESY" YOU WERE TALKING ABOUT?
...

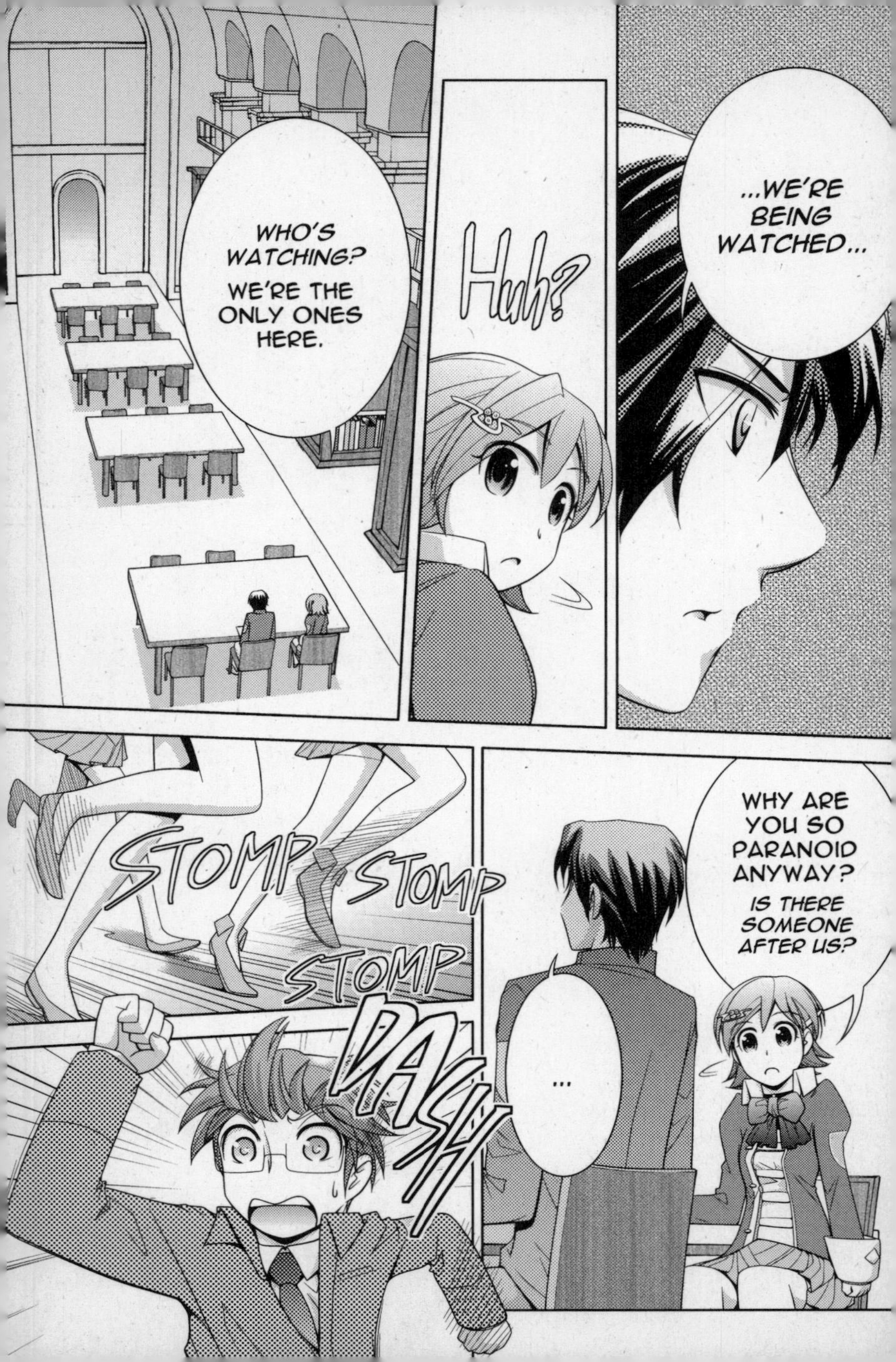
...WE'RE BEING WATCHED...
Huh?
WHO'S WATCHING?
WE'RE THE ONLY ONES HERE.
WHY ARE YOU SO PARANOID ANYWAY?
IS THERE SOMEONE AFTER US?
...
STOMP
STOMP
STOMP
DASH

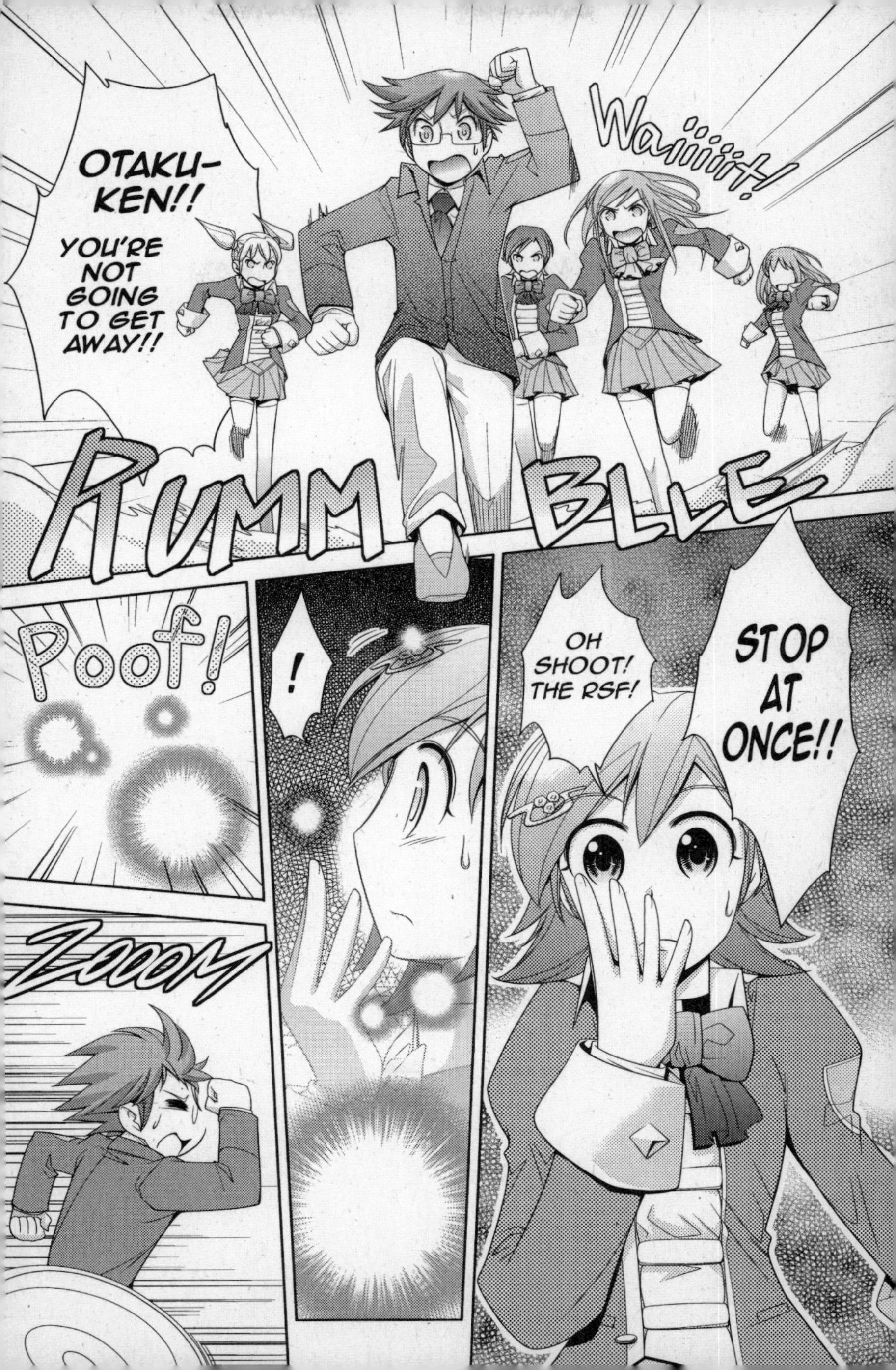
Waiiiit!
OTAKU-KEN!!
YOU'RE NOT GOING TO GET AWAY!!
RUMM BLLE
STOP AT ONCE!!
OH SHOOT! THE RSF!
!
Poof!
Zooom

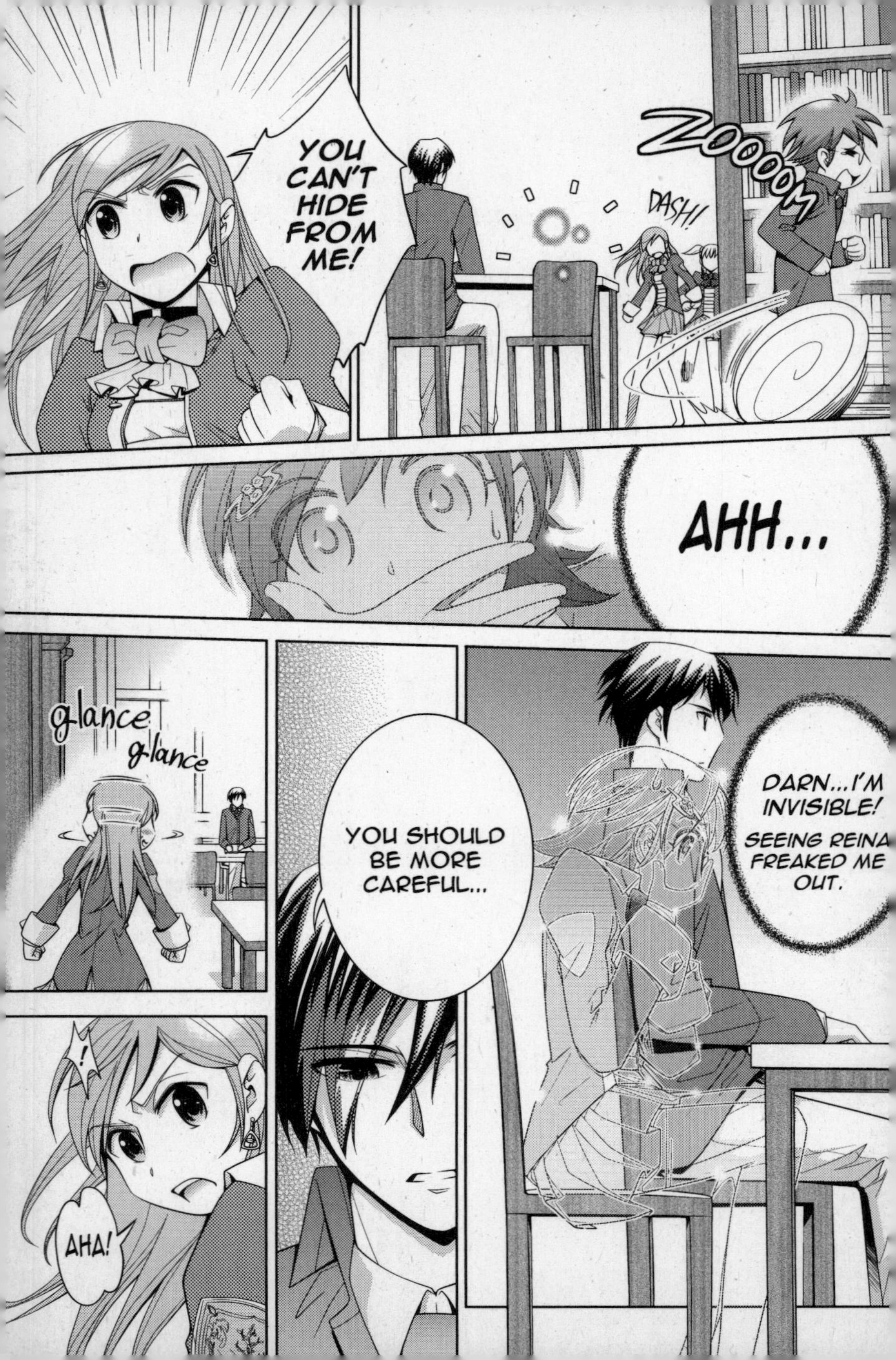
ZOOOOM
DASH!
YOU CAN'T HIDE FROM ME!
AHH...
DARN...I'M INVISIBLE!
SEEING REINA FREAKED ME OUT.
YOU SHOULD BE MORE CAREFUL...
glance
glance
!
AHA!

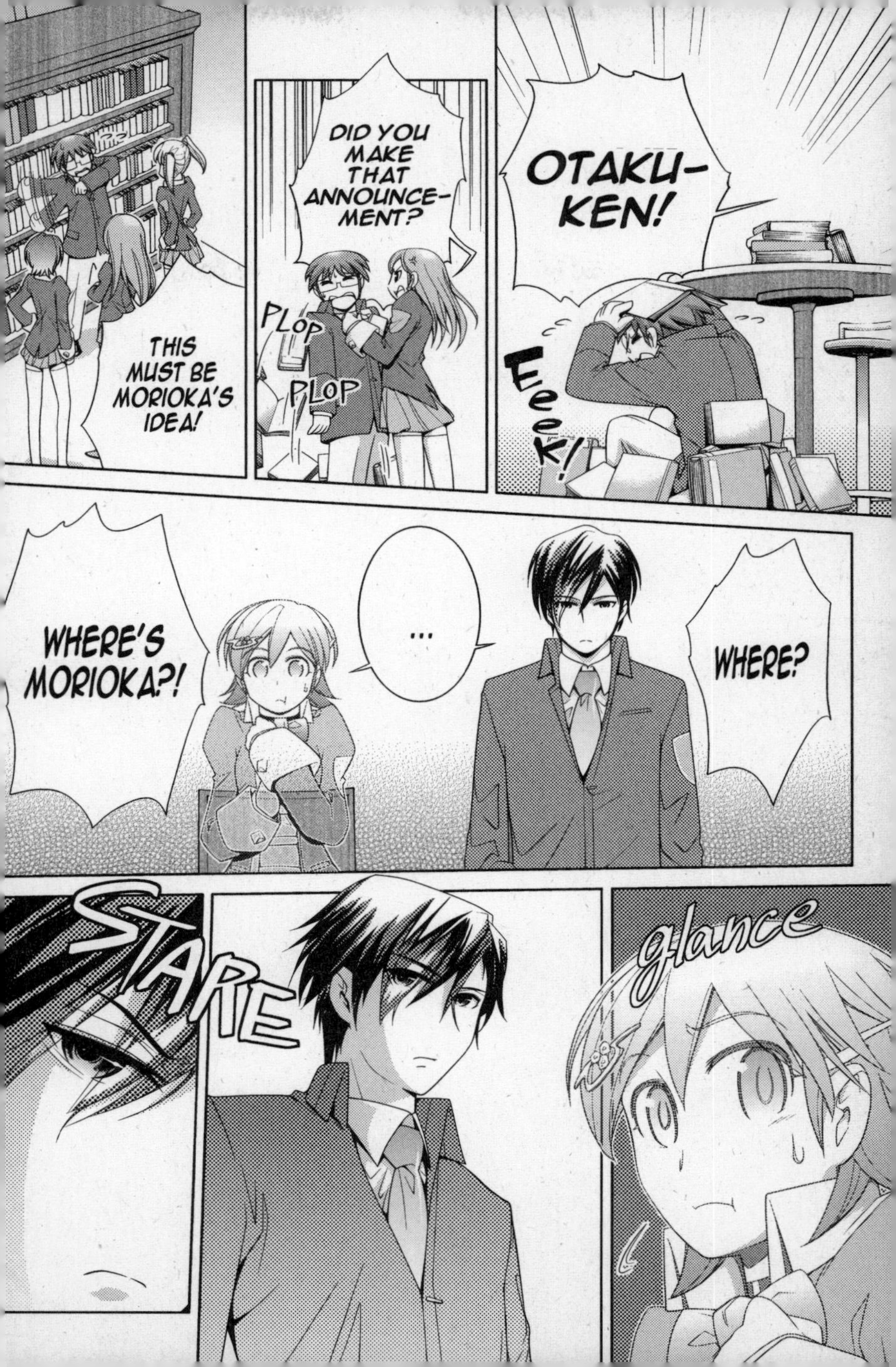
OTAKU-KEN!
Eeek!
DID YOU MAKE THAT ANNOUNCE-MENT?
PLOP
PLOP
THIS MUST BE MORIOKA'S IDEA!
WHERE?
...
WHERE'S MORIOKA?!
glance
STARE

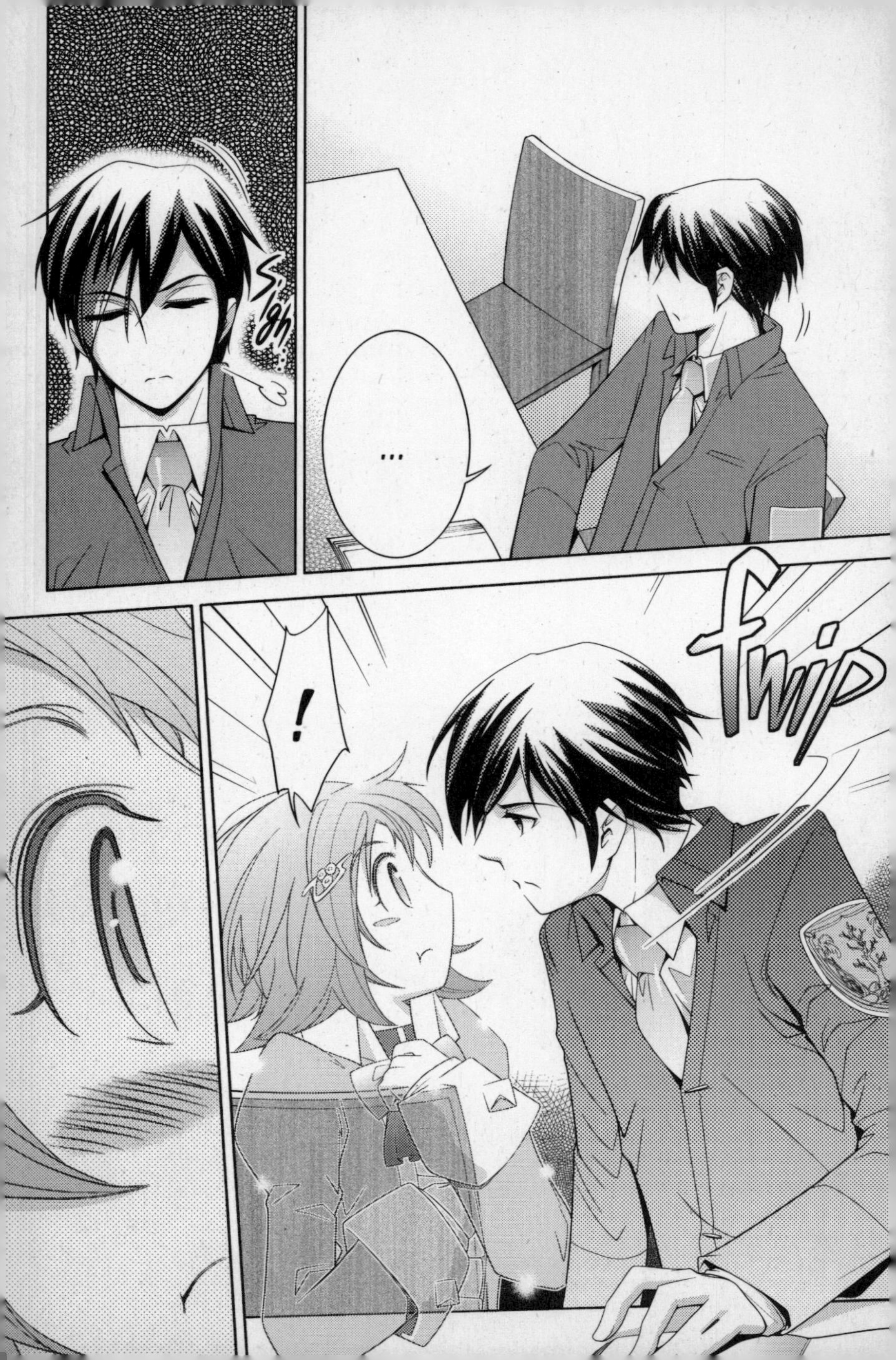
...
sigh
fwip
!

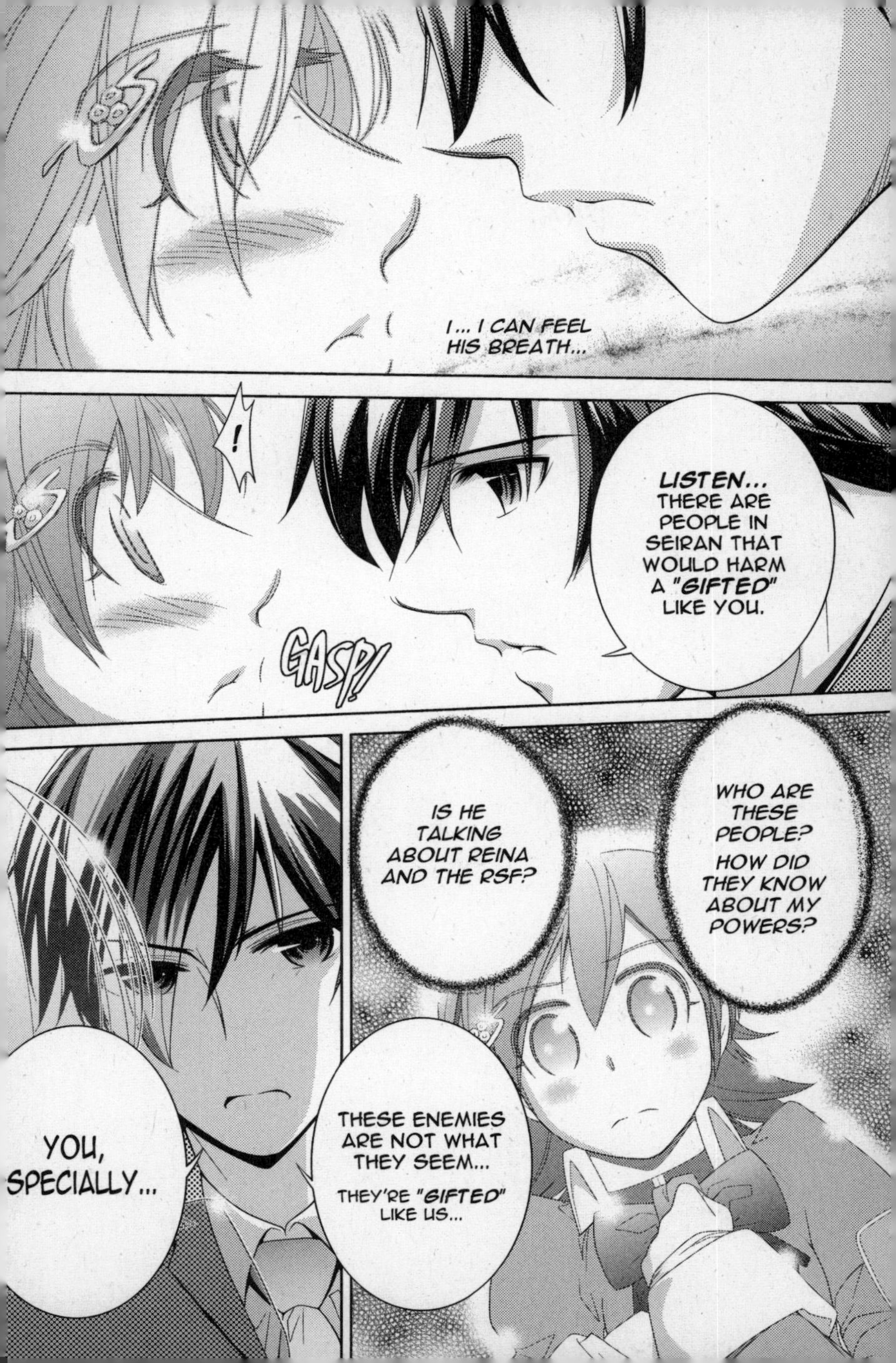
I... I CAN FEEL HIS BREATH...
LISTEN... THERE ARE PEOPLE IN SEIRAN THAT WOULD HARM A "GIFTED" LIKE YOU.
!
GASP!
WHO ARE THESE PEOPLE? HOW DID THEY KNOW ABOUT MY POWERS?
IS HE TALKING ABOUT REINA AND THE RSF?
YOU, SPECIALLY...
THESE ENEMIES ARE NOT WHAT THEY SEEM... THEY'RE "GIFTED" LIKE US...

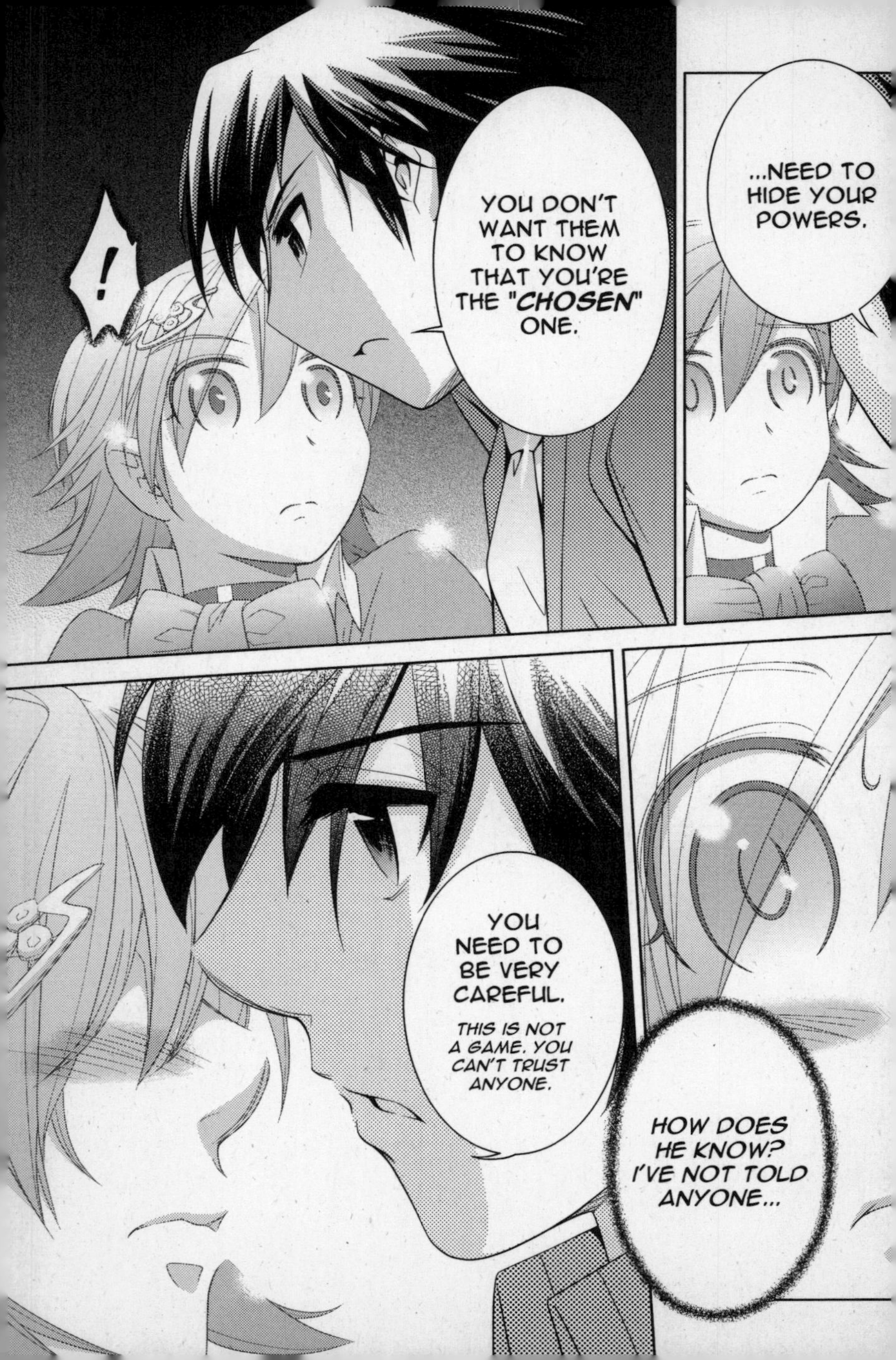
...NEED TO HIDE YOUR POWERS.
!
YOU DON'T WANT THEM TO KNOW THAT YOU'RE THE "*CHOSEN*" ONE.
HOW DOES HE KNOW? I'VE NOT TOLD ANYONE...
YOU NEED TO BE VERY CAREFUL.
THIS IS NOT A GAME. YOU CAN'T TRUST ANYONE.

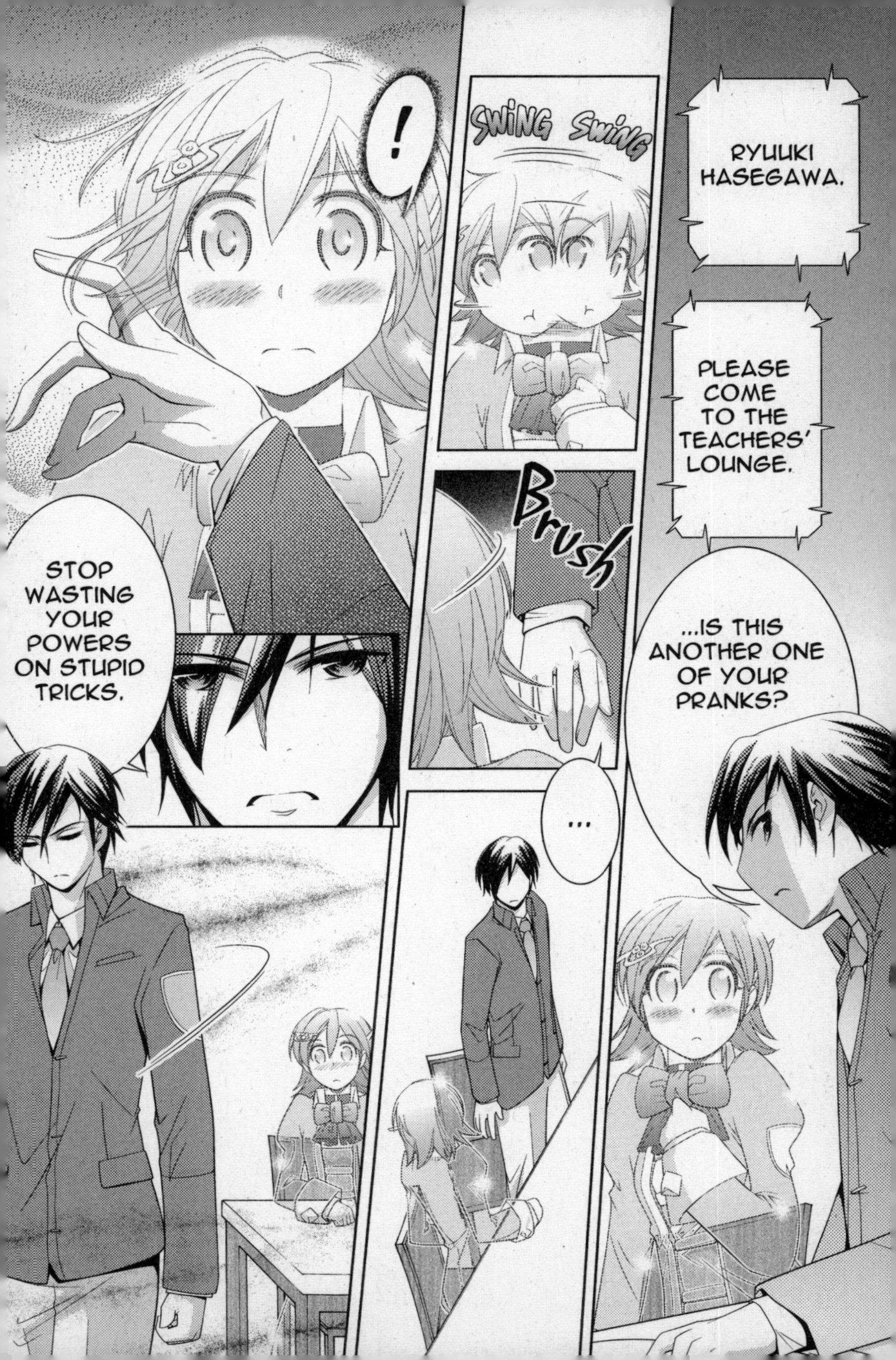
RYUUKI HASEGAWA.
PLEASE COME TO THE TEACHERS' LOUNGE.
...IS THIS ANOTHER ONE OF YOUR PRANKS?
SWING SWING
Brush
...
!
STOP WASTING YOUR POWERS ON STUPID TRICKS.

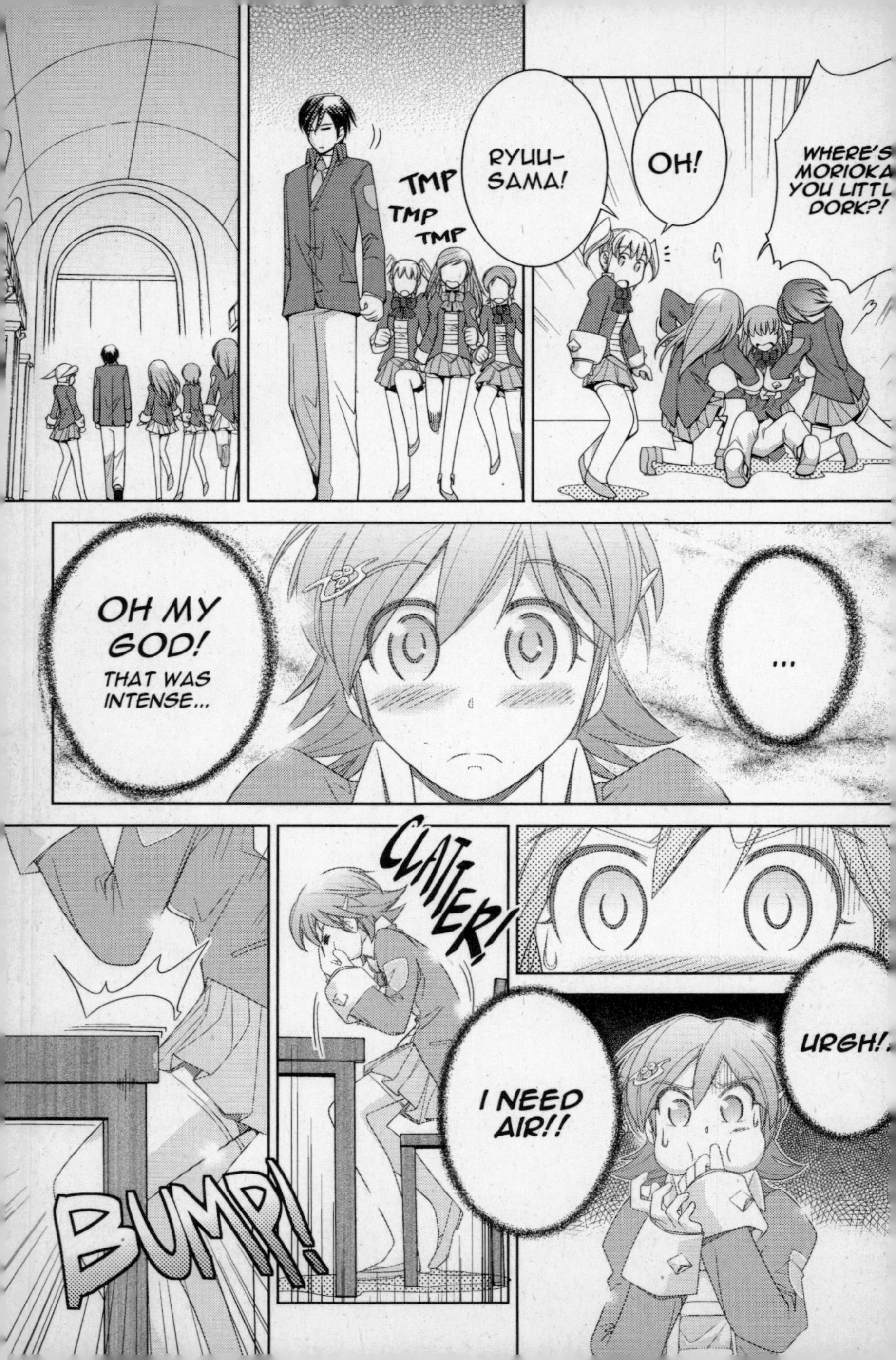
WHERE'S MORIOKA YOU LITTL DORK?!
OH!
RYUU-SAMA!
TMP
TMP
TMP
...
OH MY GOD! THAT WAS INTENSE...
URGH!.
I NEED AIR!!
CLATTER!
BUMP!

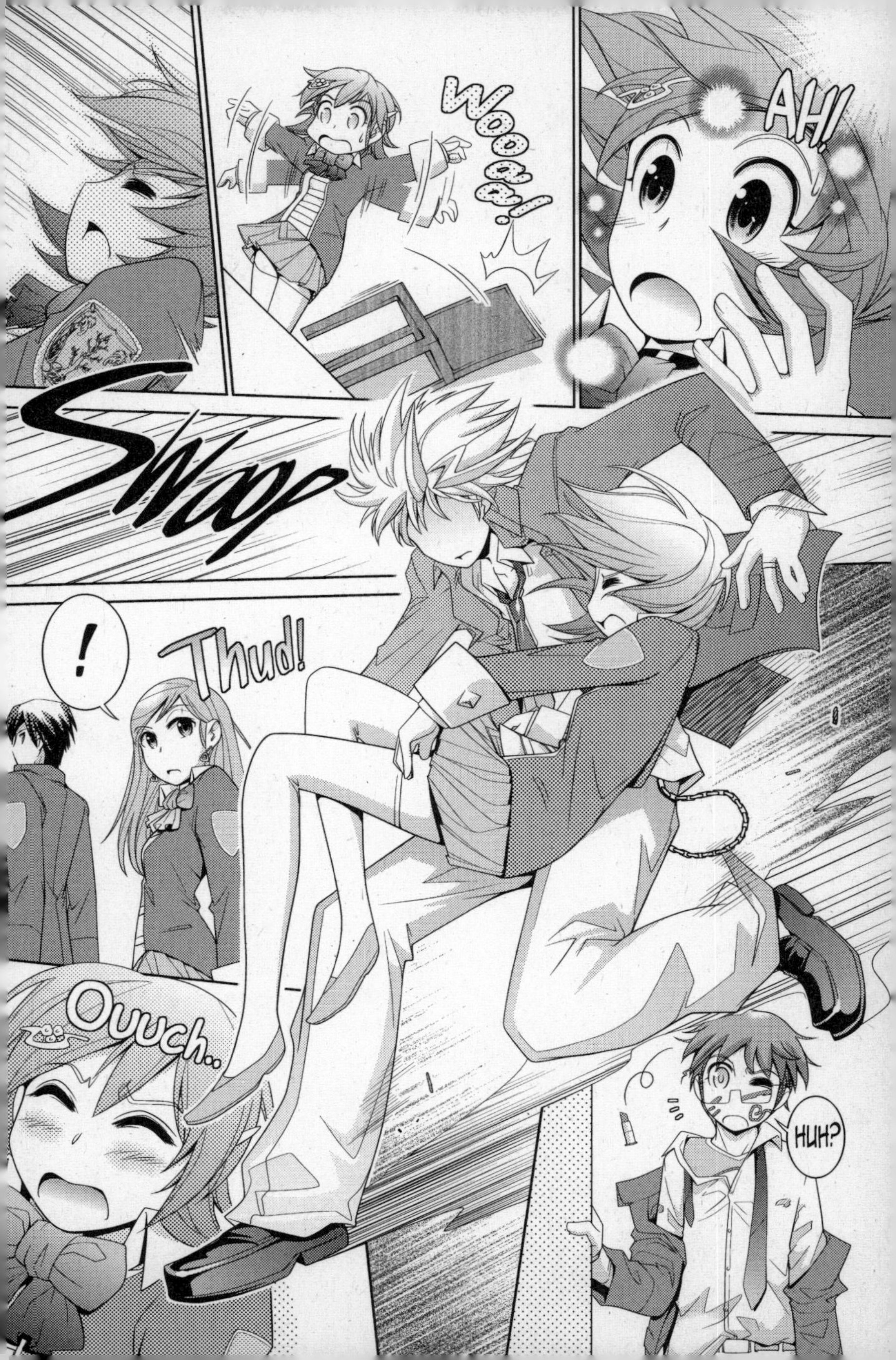
AH!
Wooaa!
Swap
!
Thud!
HUH?
Ouuch..

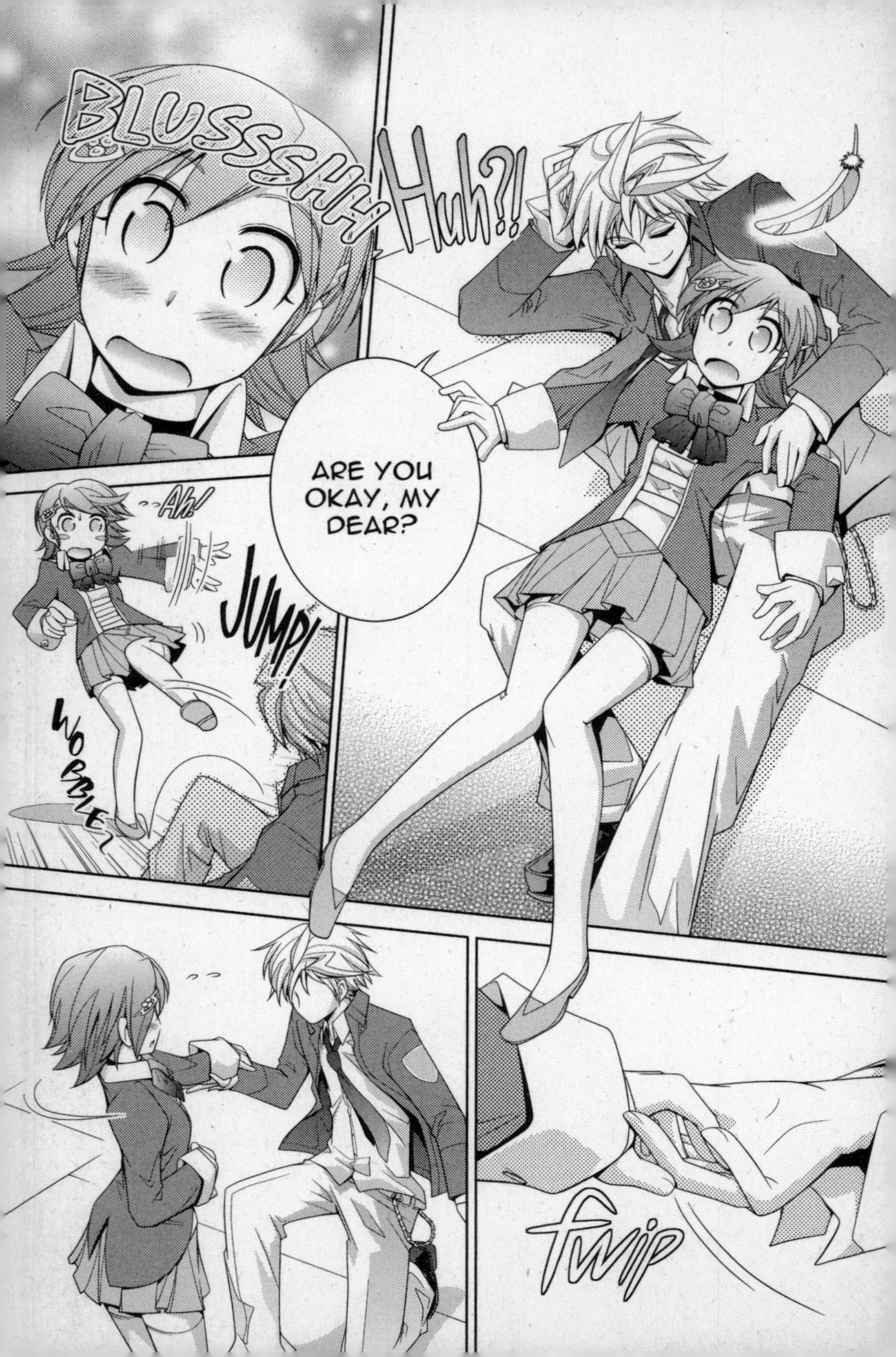
Huh?!
ARE YOU OKAY, MY DEAR?
BLUSSHH
Ah!
JUMP!
WOBBLE
fwip

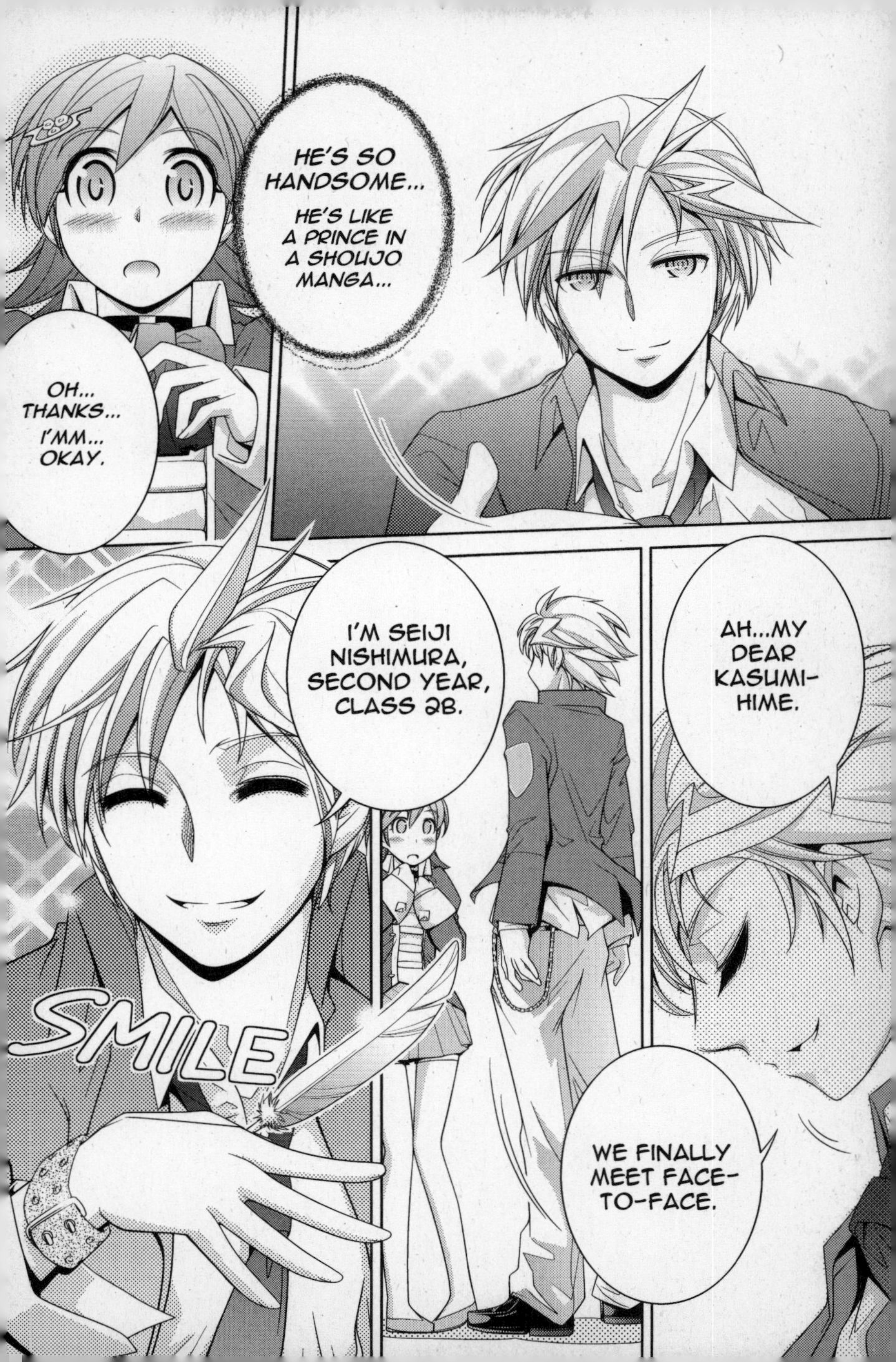
HE'S SO HANDSOME...
HE'S LIKE A PRINCE IN A SHOUJO MANGA...
OH... THANKS... I'MM... OKAY.
AH...MY DEAR KASUMI-HIME.
WE FINALLY MEET FACE-TO-FACE.
I'M SEIJI NISHIMURA, SECOND YEAR, CLASS 2B.
SMILE

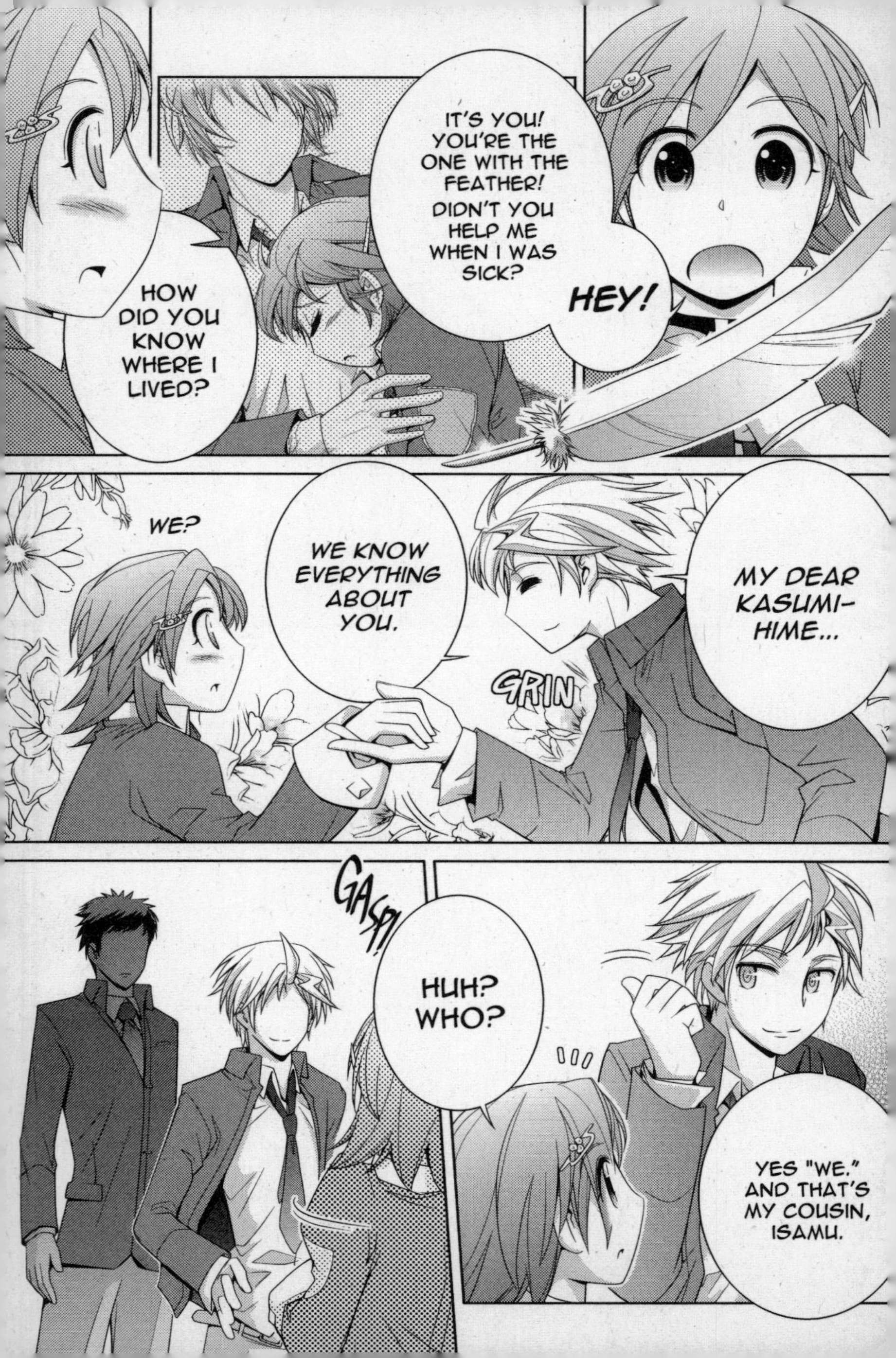
HEY!
IT'S YOU! YOU'RE THE ONE WITH THE FEATHER! DIDN'T YOU HELP ME WHEN I WAS SICK?
HOW DID YOU KNOW WHERE I LIVED?
MY DEAR KASUMI-HIME...
GRIN
WE KNOW EVERYTHING ABOUT YOU.
WE?
HUH? WHO?
YES "WE." AND THAT'S MY COUSIN, ISAMU.
GASP!

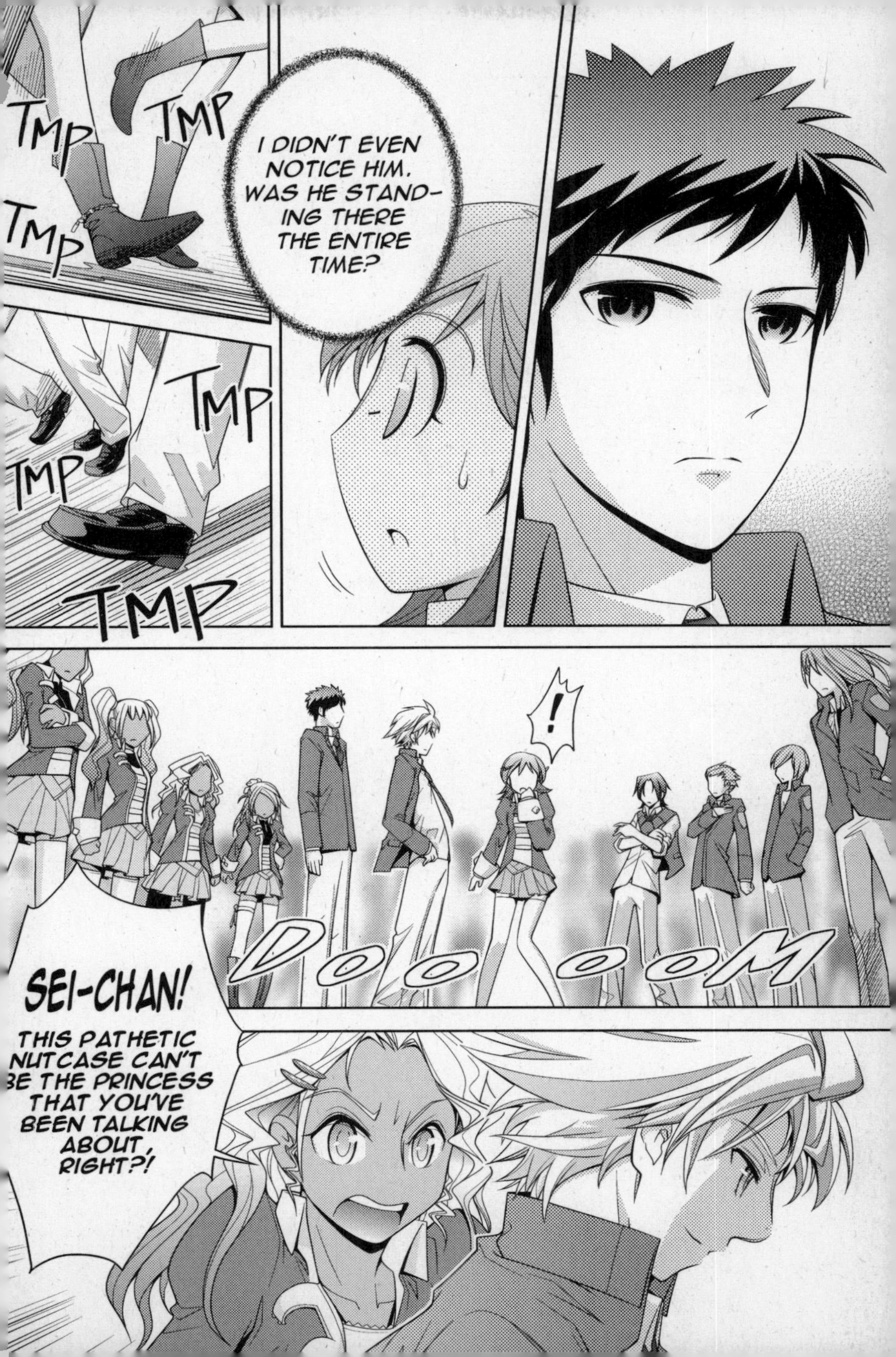
I DIDN'T EVEN NOTICE HIM. WAS HE STANDING THERE THE ENTIRE TIME?
TMP
TMP
TMP
TMP
TMP
TMP
!
DOOOOOM
SEI-CHAN!
THIS PATHETIC NUTCASE CAN'T BE THE PRINCESS THAT YOU'VE BEEN TALKING ABOUT, RIGHT?!

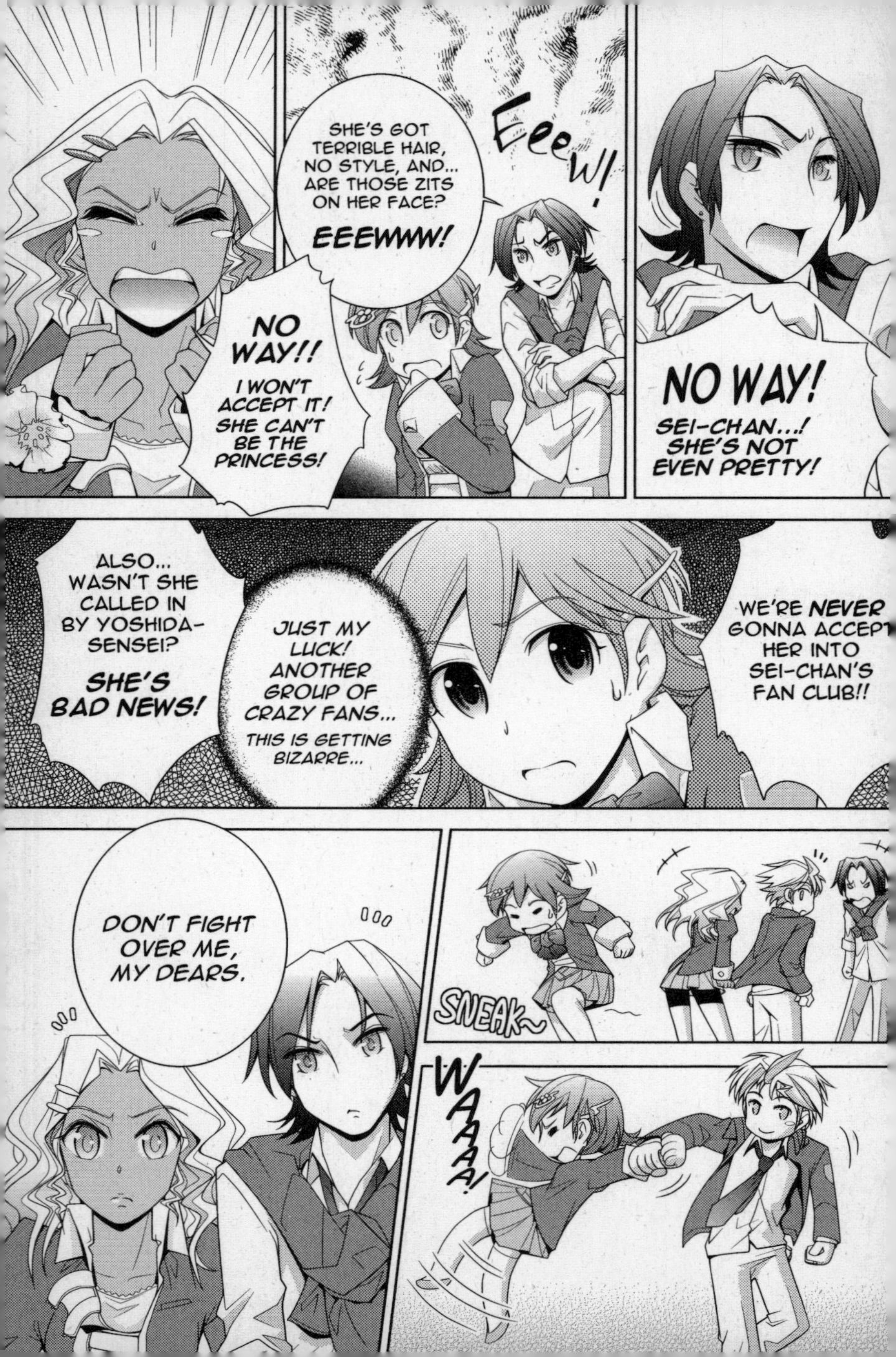
NO WAY!
SEI-CHAN...! SHE'S NOT EVEN PRETTY!
Eeew!
SHE'S GOT TERRIBLE HAIR, NO STYLE, AND... ARE THOSE ZITS ON HER FACE?
EEEWWW!
NO WAY!!
I WON'T ACCEPT IT! SHE CAN'T BE THE PRINCESS!
WE'RE NEVER GONNA ACCEPT HER INTO SEI-CHAN'S FAN CLUB!!
JUST MY LUCK! ANOTHER GROUP OF CRAZY FANS...
THIS IS GETTING BIZARRE...
ALSO... WASN'T SHE CALLED IN BY YOSHIDA-SENSEI?
SHE'S BAD NEWS!
SNEAK~
WAAAAA!
DON'T FIGHT OVER ME, MY DEARS.

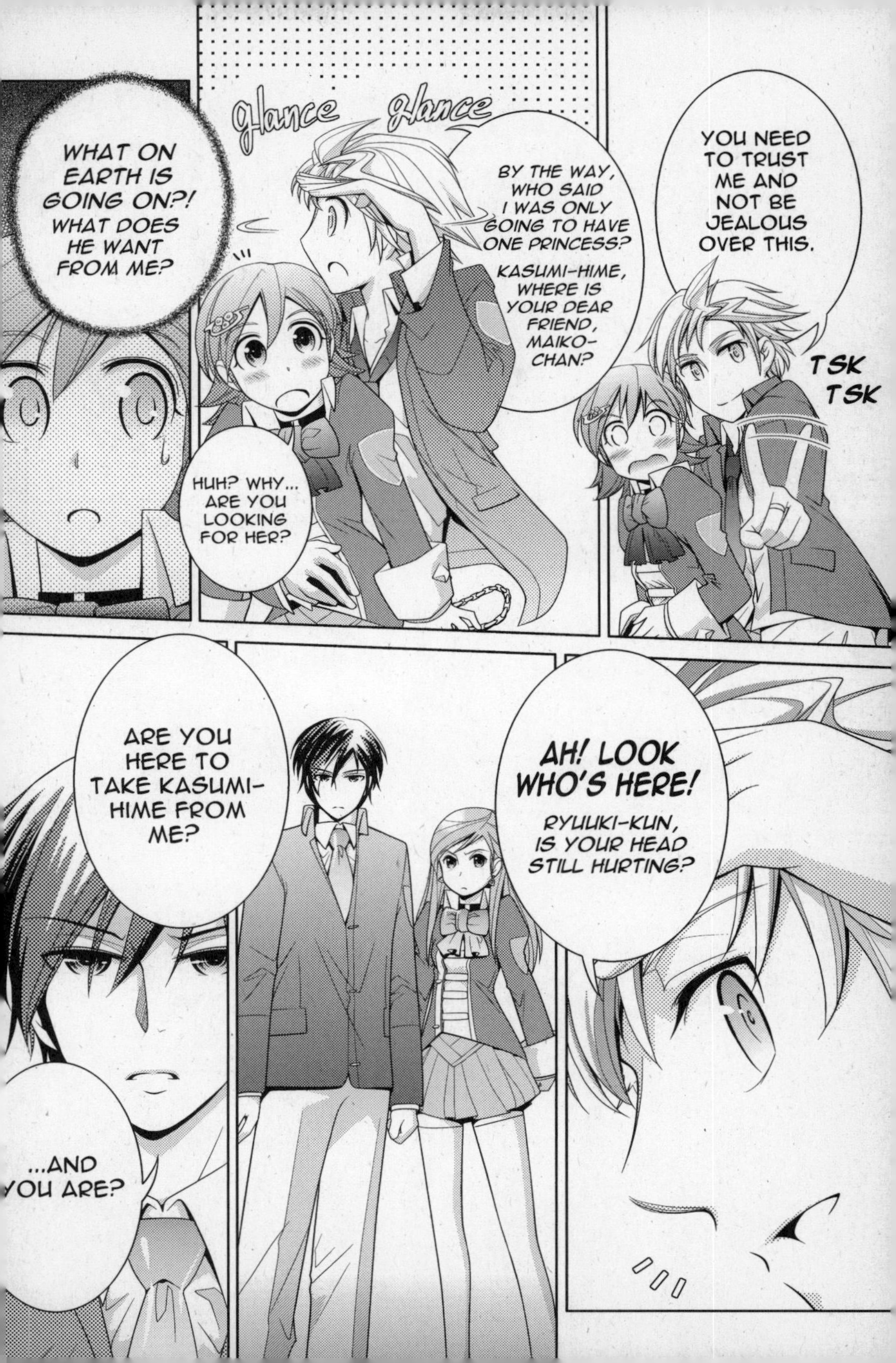
YOU NEED TO TRUST ME AND NOT BE JEALOUS OVER THIS.
TSK TSK
glance glance
BY THE WAY, WHO SAID I WAS ONLY GOING TO HAVE ONE PRINCESS?
KASUMI-HIME, WHERE IS YOUR DEAR FRIEND, MAIKO-CHAN?
HUH? WHY... ARE YOU LOOKING FOR HER?
WHAT ON EARTH IS GOING ON?! WHAT DOES HE WANT FROM ME?
AH! LOOK WHO'S HERE!
RYUUKI-KUN, IS YOUR HEAD STILL HURTING?
ARE YOU HERE TO TAKE KASUMI-HIME FROM ME?
...AND YOU ARE?

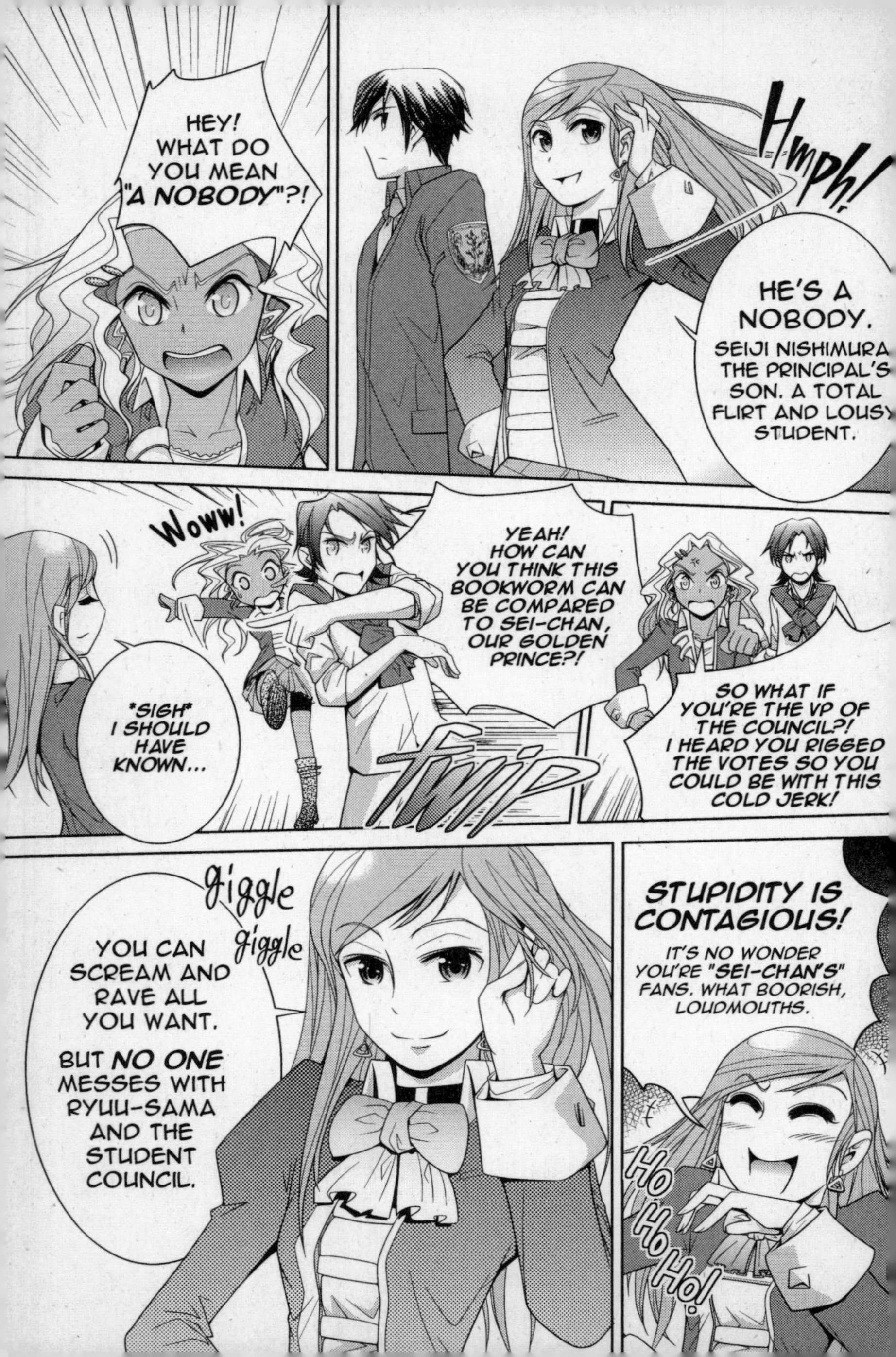
Hmph!
HE'S A NOBODY. SEIJI NISHIMURA THE PRINCIPAL'S SON. A TOTAL FLIRT AND LOUSY STUDENT.
HEY! WHAT DO YOU MEAN "A NOBODY"?!
SO WHAT IF YOU'RE THE VP OF THE COUNCIL?! I HEARD YOU RIGGED THE VOTES SO YOU COULD BE WITH THIS COLD JERK!
YEAH! HOW CAN YOU THINK THIS BOOKWORM CAN BE COMPARED TO SEI-CHAN, OUR GOLDEN PRINCE?!
Woww!
fwip
SIGH I SHOULD HAVE KNOWN...
STUPIDITY IS CONTAGIOUS!
IT'S NO WONDER YOU'RE "SEI-CHAN'S" FANS. WHAT BOORISH, LOUDMOUTHS.
Ho Ho Ho!
giggle
giggle
YOU CAN SCREAM AND RAVE ALL YOU WANT.
BUT NO ONE MESSES WITH RYUU-SAMA AND THE STUDENT COUNCIL.

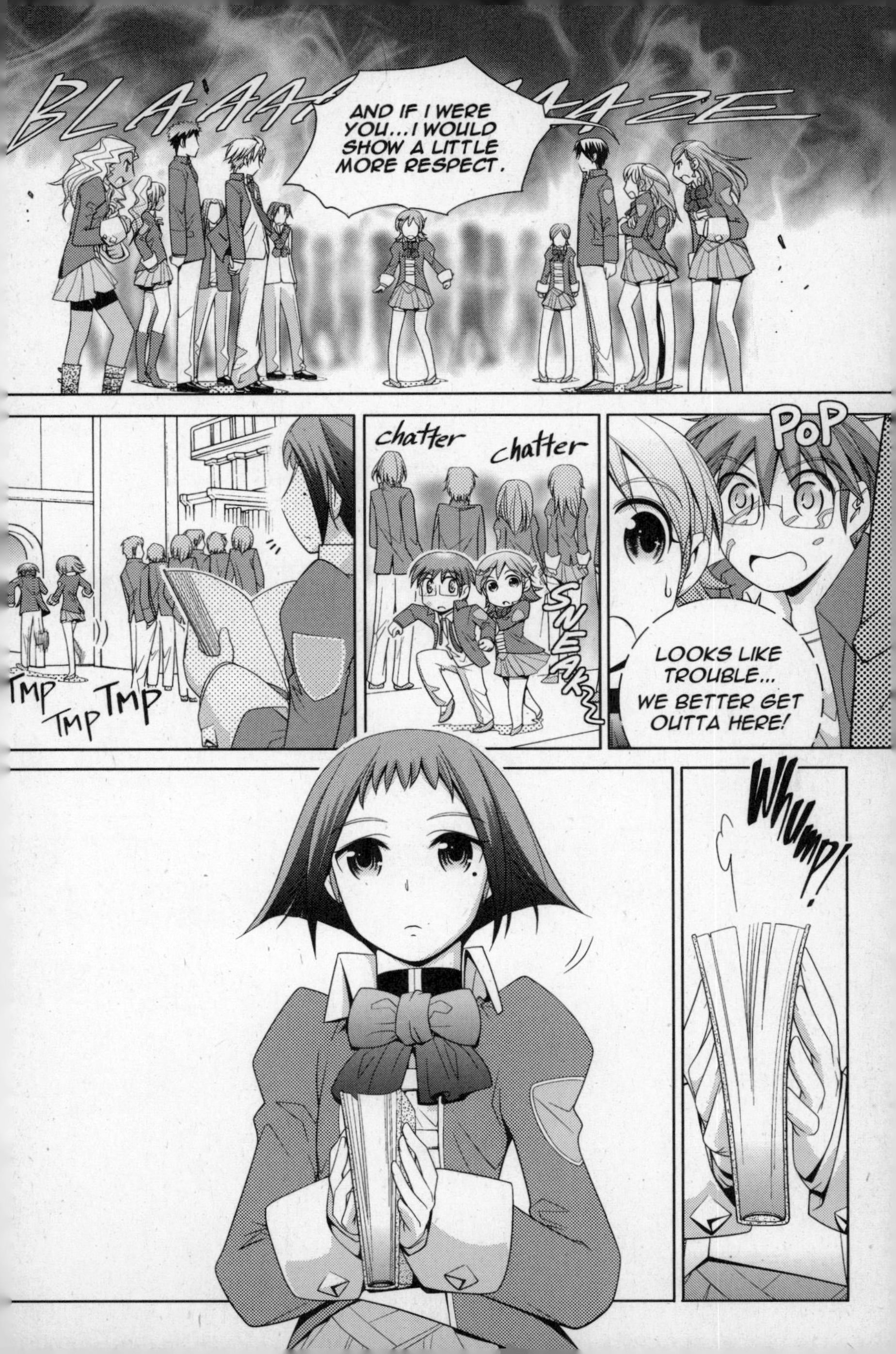
AND IF I WERE YOU...I WOULD SHOW A LITTLE MORE RESPECT.
POP
LOOKS LIKE TROUBLE... WE BETTER GET OUTTA HERE!
chatter
chatter
SNEAK
TMP
TMP TMP
Whump!

CHAPTER 4

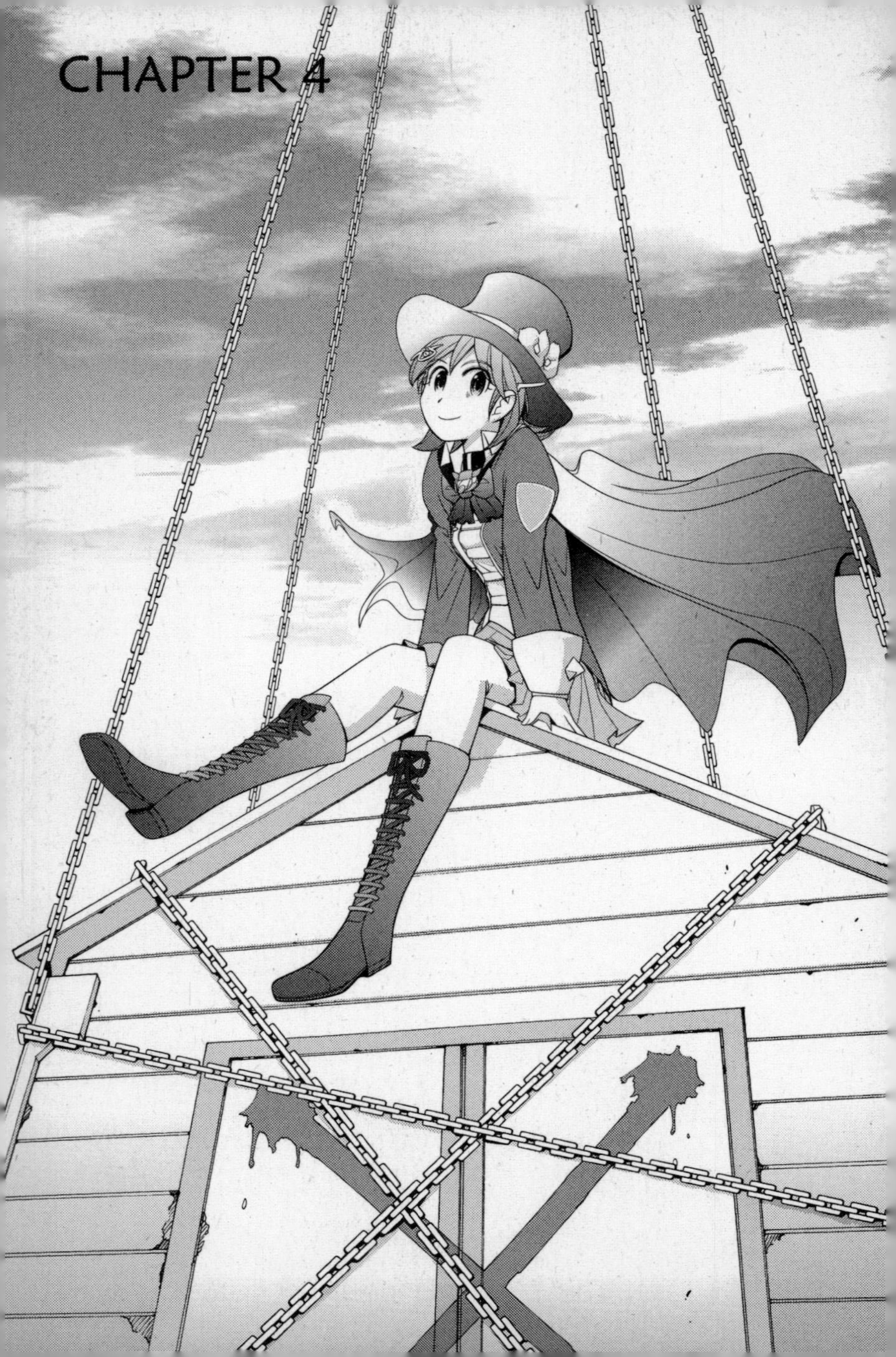

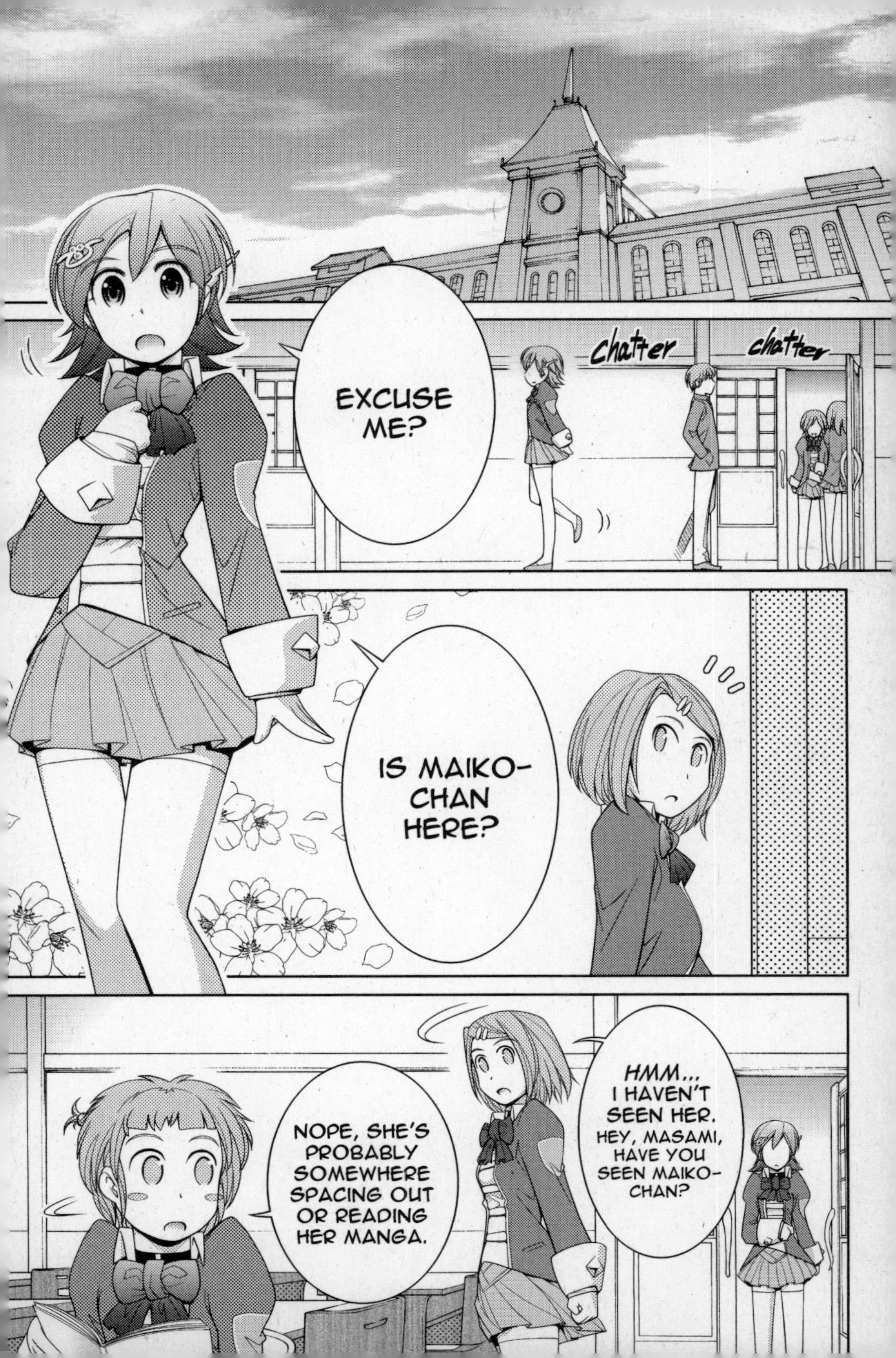
chatter
chatter
EXCUSE ME?
IS MAIKO-CHAN HERE?
HMM... I HAVEN'T SEEN HER. HEY, MASAMI, HAVE YOU SEEN MAIKO-CHAN?
NOPE, SHE'S PROBABLY SOMEWHERE SPACING OUT OR READING HER MANGA.

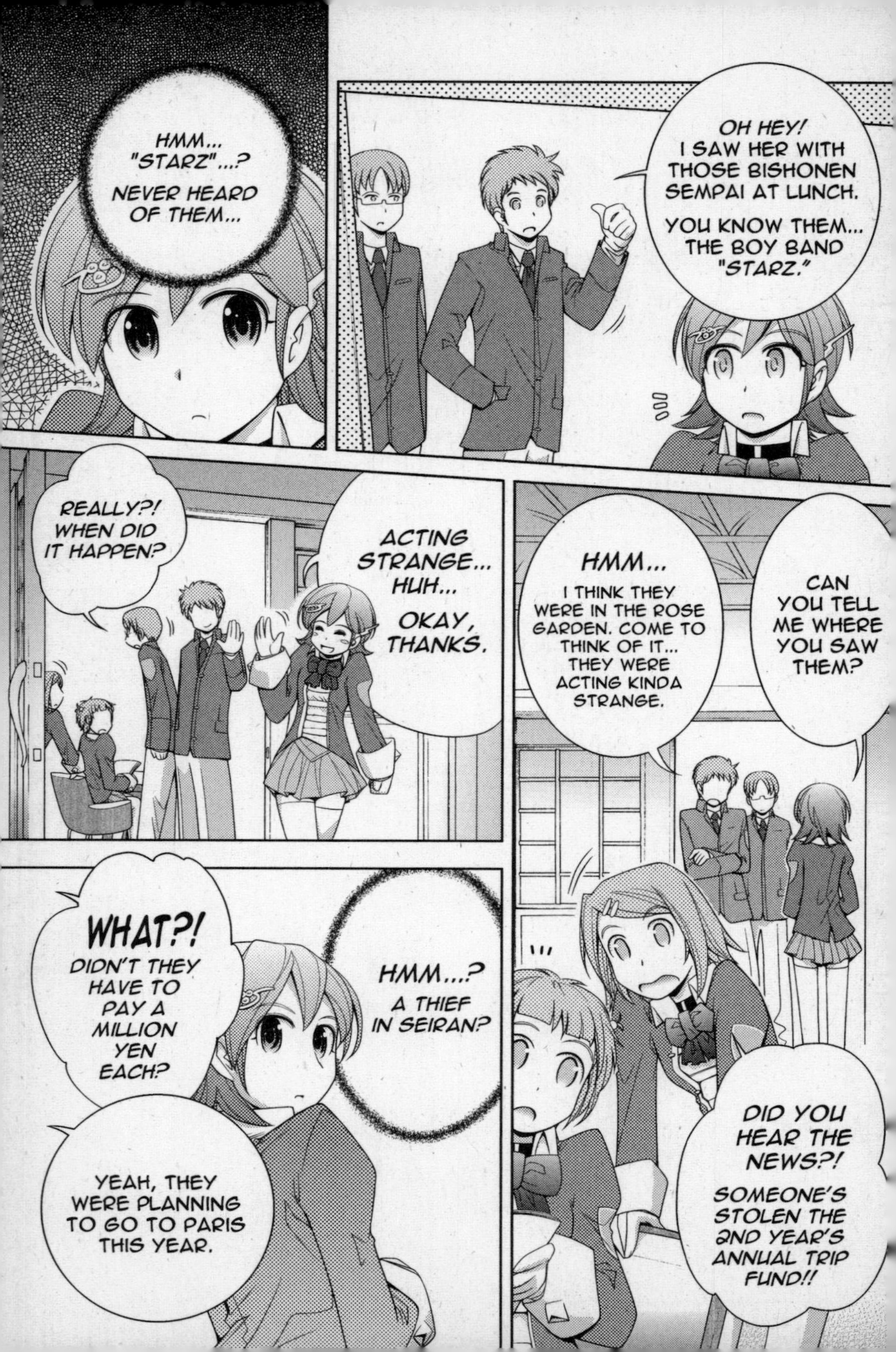
OH HEY! I SAW HER WITH THOSE BISHONEN SEMPAI AT LUNCH.
YOU KNOW THEM... THE BOY BAND "STARZ."
HMM... "STARZ"...?
NEVER HEARD OF THEM...
CAN YOU TELL ME WHERE YOU SAW THEM?
HMM...
I THINK THEY WERE IN THE ROSE GARDEN. COME TO THINK OF IT... THEY WERE ACTING KINDA STRANGE.
ACTING STRANGE... HUH...
OKAY, THANKS.
REALLY?! WHEN DID IT HAPPEN?
DID YOU HEAR THE NEWS?!
SOMEONE'S STOLEN THE 2ND YEAR'S ANNUAL TRIP FUND!!
HMM...?
A THIEF IN SEIRAN?
WHAT?!
DIDN'T THEY HAVE TO PAY A MILLION YEN EACH?
YEAH, THEY WERE PLANNING TO GO TO PARIS THIS YEAR.

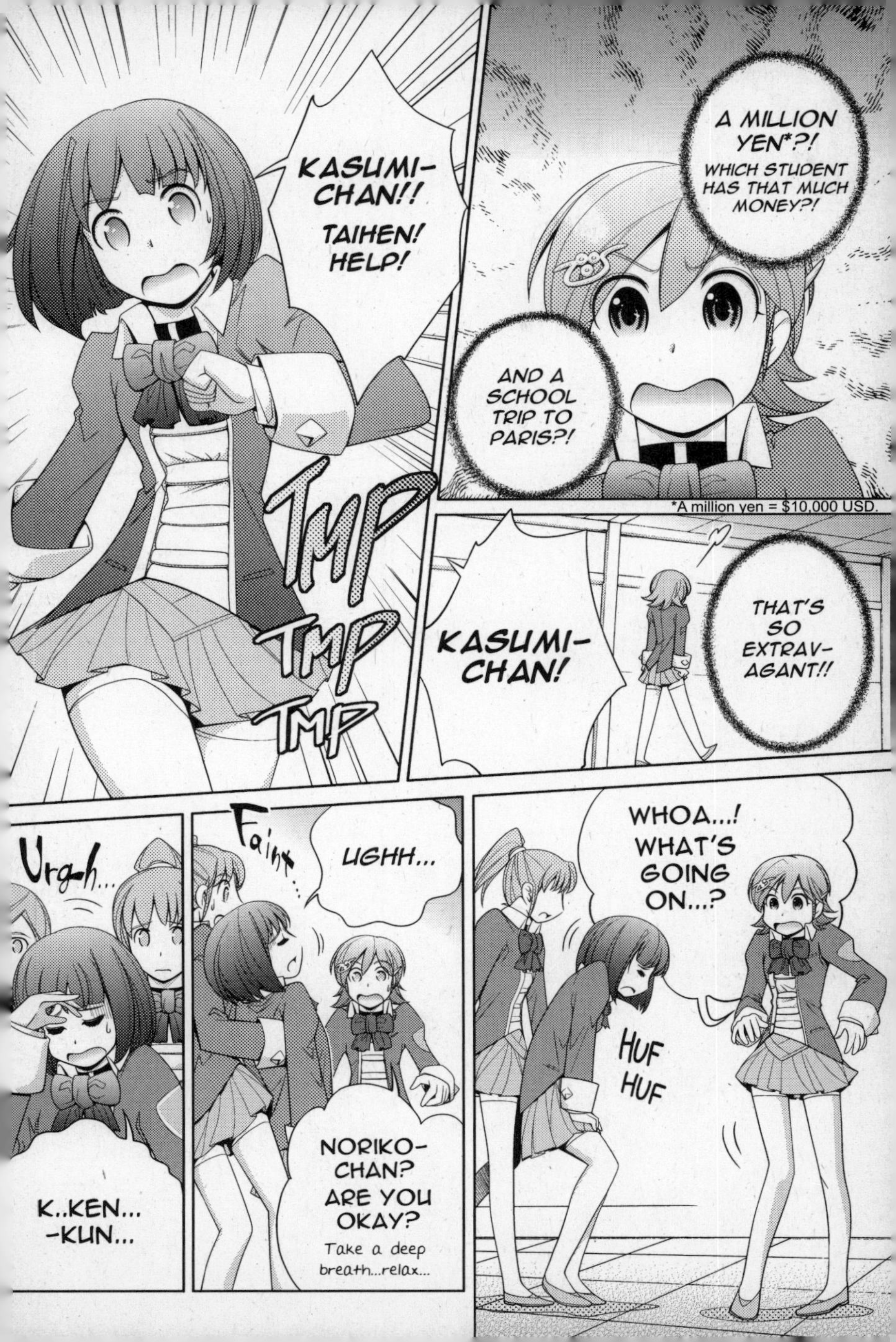
A MILLION YEN*?! WHICH STUDENT HAS THAT MUCH MONEY?!
AND A SCHOOL TRIP TO PARIS?!
*A million yen = $10,000 USD.
THAT'S SO EXTRAVAGANT!!
KASUMI-CHAN!
KASUMI-CHAN!! TAIHEN! HELP!
TMP TMP TMP
WHOA...! WHAT'S GOING ON...?
HUF HUF
UGHH...
Faint...
NORIKO-CHAN? ARE YOU OKAY?
Take a deep breath...relax...
Urgh...
K..KEN... -KUN...

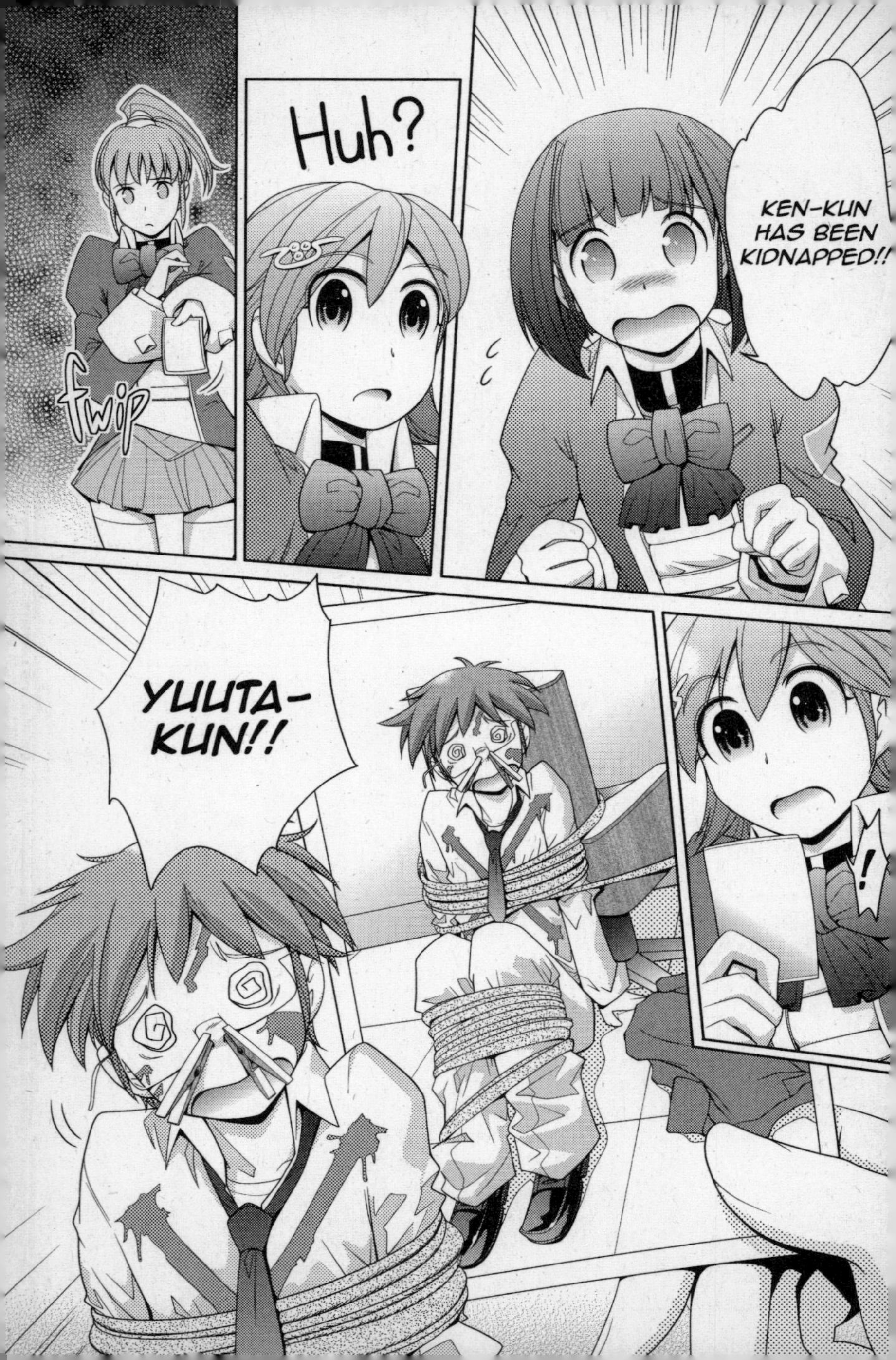
KEN-KUN HAS BEEN KIDNAPPED!!
Huh?
fwip
!
YUUTA-KUN!!

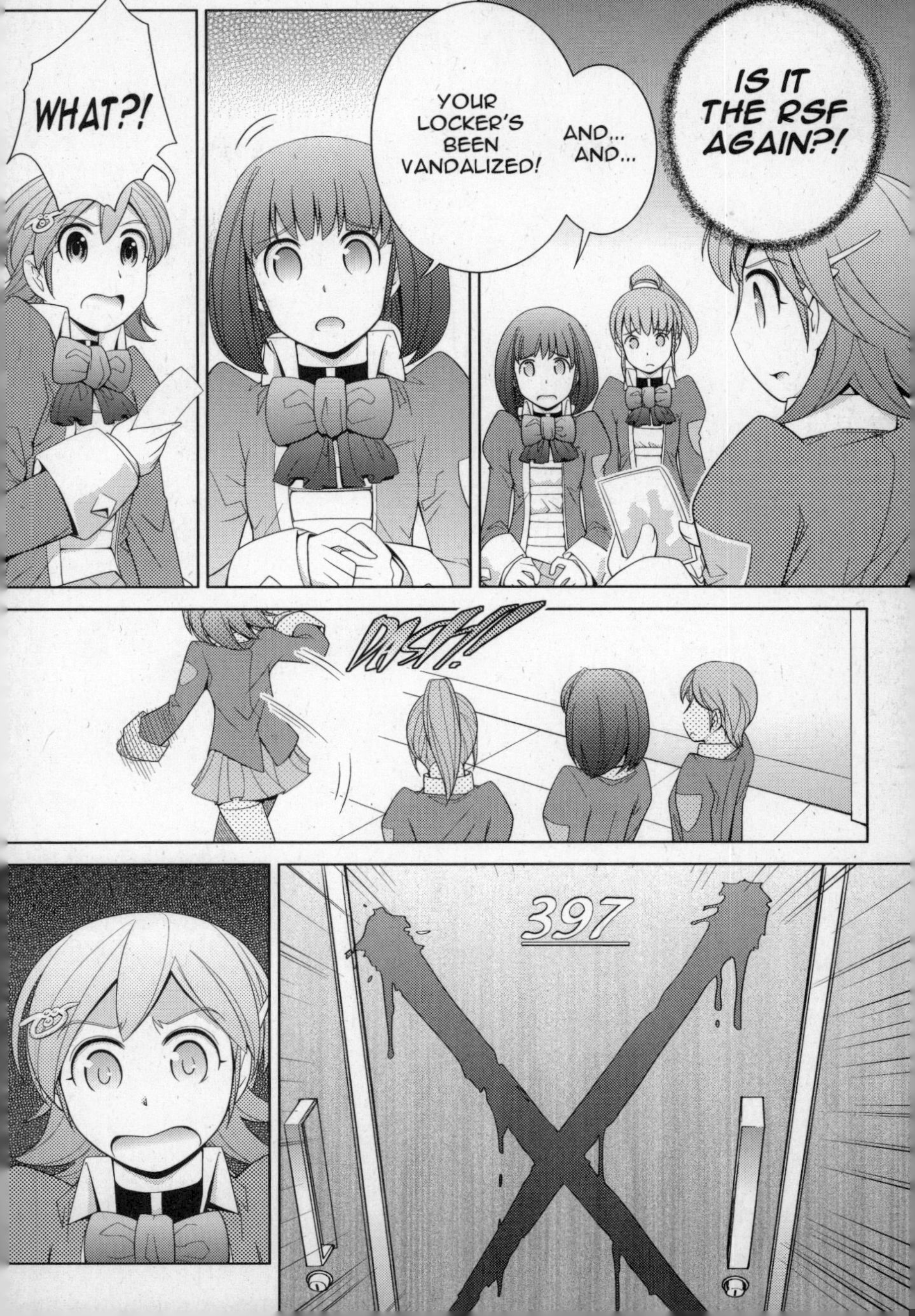
IS IT THE RSF AGAIN?!
YOUR LOCKER'S BEEN VANDALIZED!
AND... AND...
WHAT?!
DASH!!
397

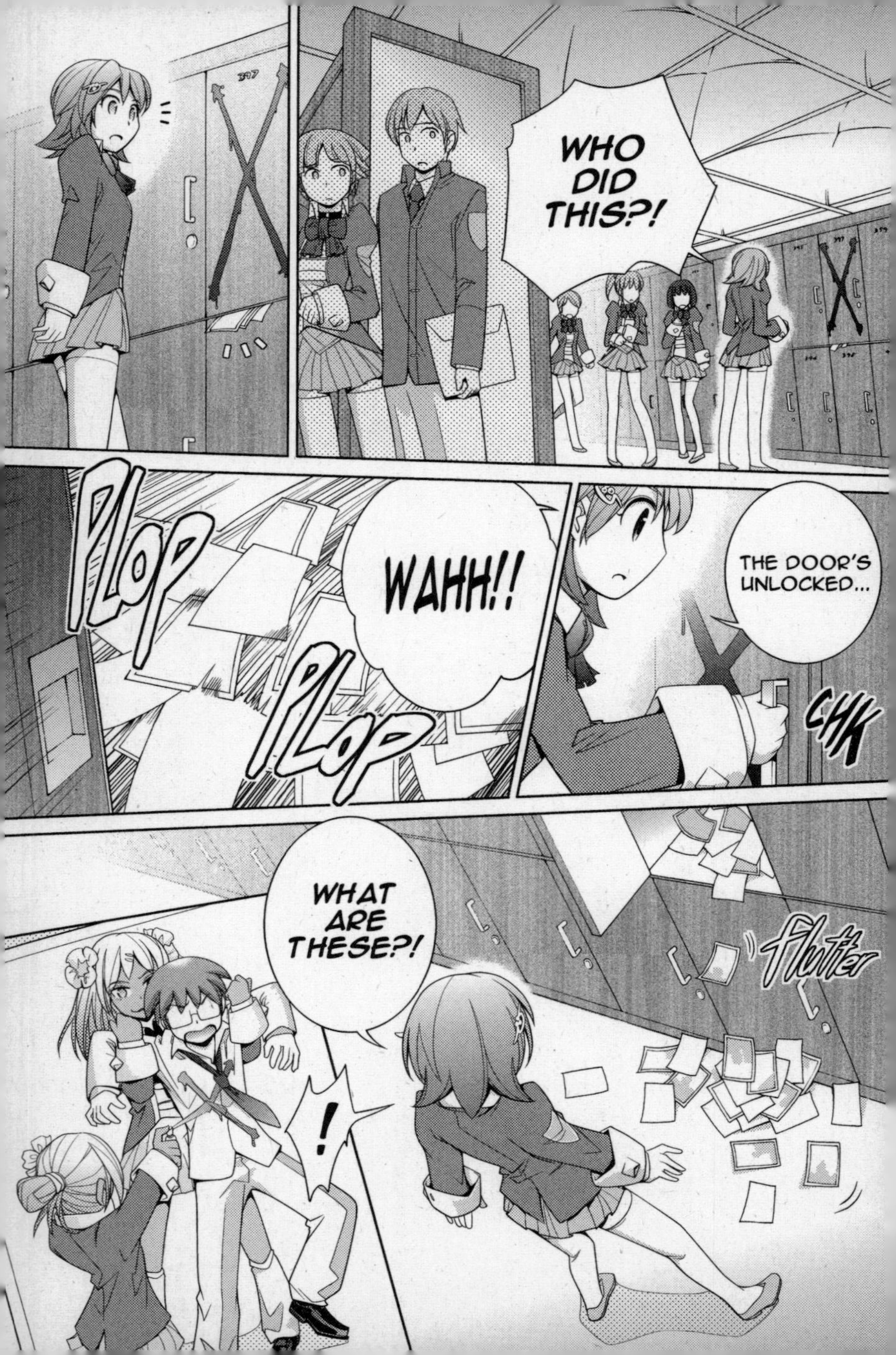

WHO DID THIS?!
THE DOOR'S UNLOCKED...
CHK
WAHH!!
PLOP
PLOP
WHAT ARE THESE?!
Flutter
!

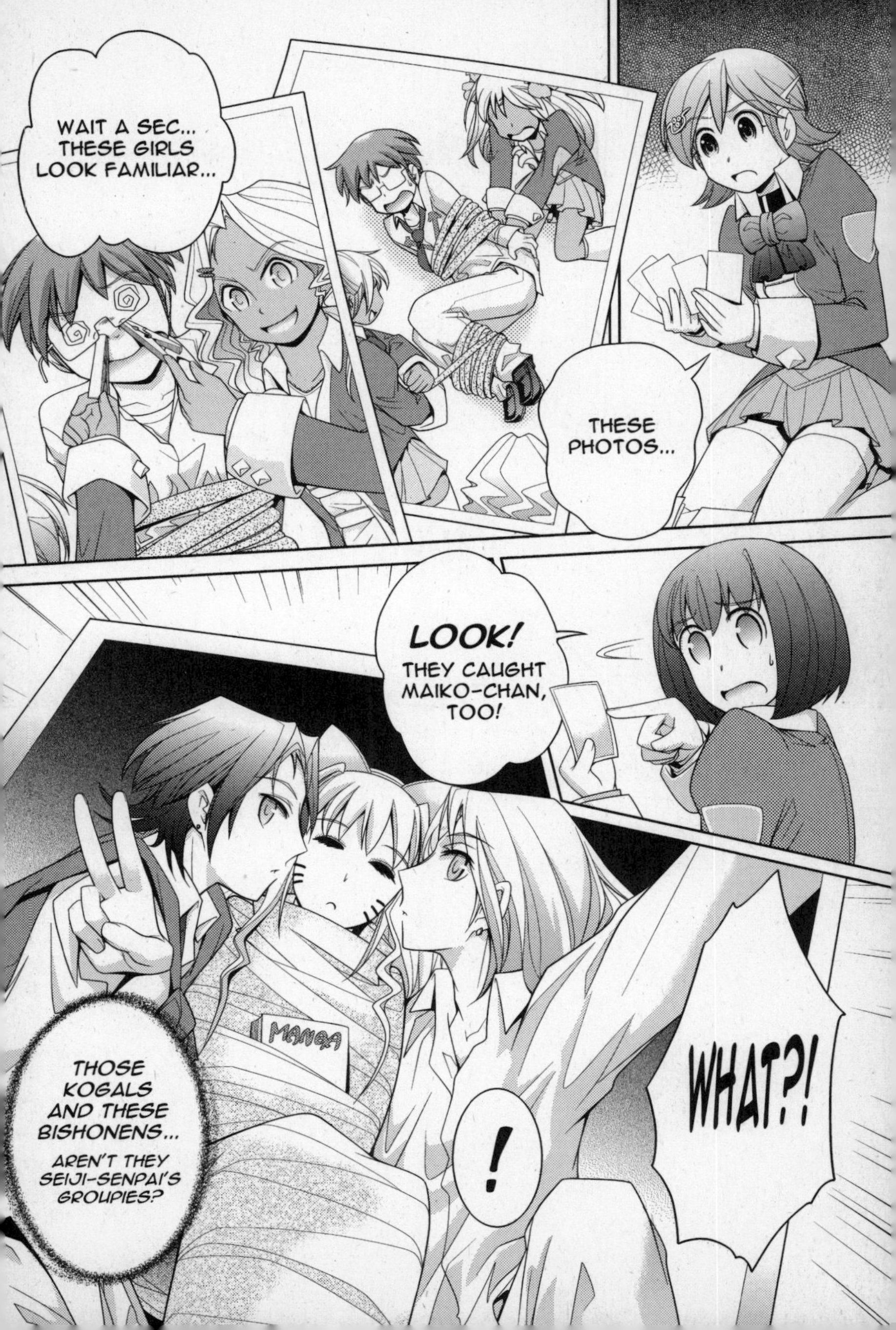
THESE PHOTOS...
WAIT A SEC... THESE GIRLS LOOK FAMILIAR...
LOOK! THEY CAUGHT MAIKO-CHAN, TOO!
WHAT?!
!
THOSE KOGALS AND THESE BISHONENS... AREN'T THEY SEIJI-SENPAI'S GROUPIES?
MANGA

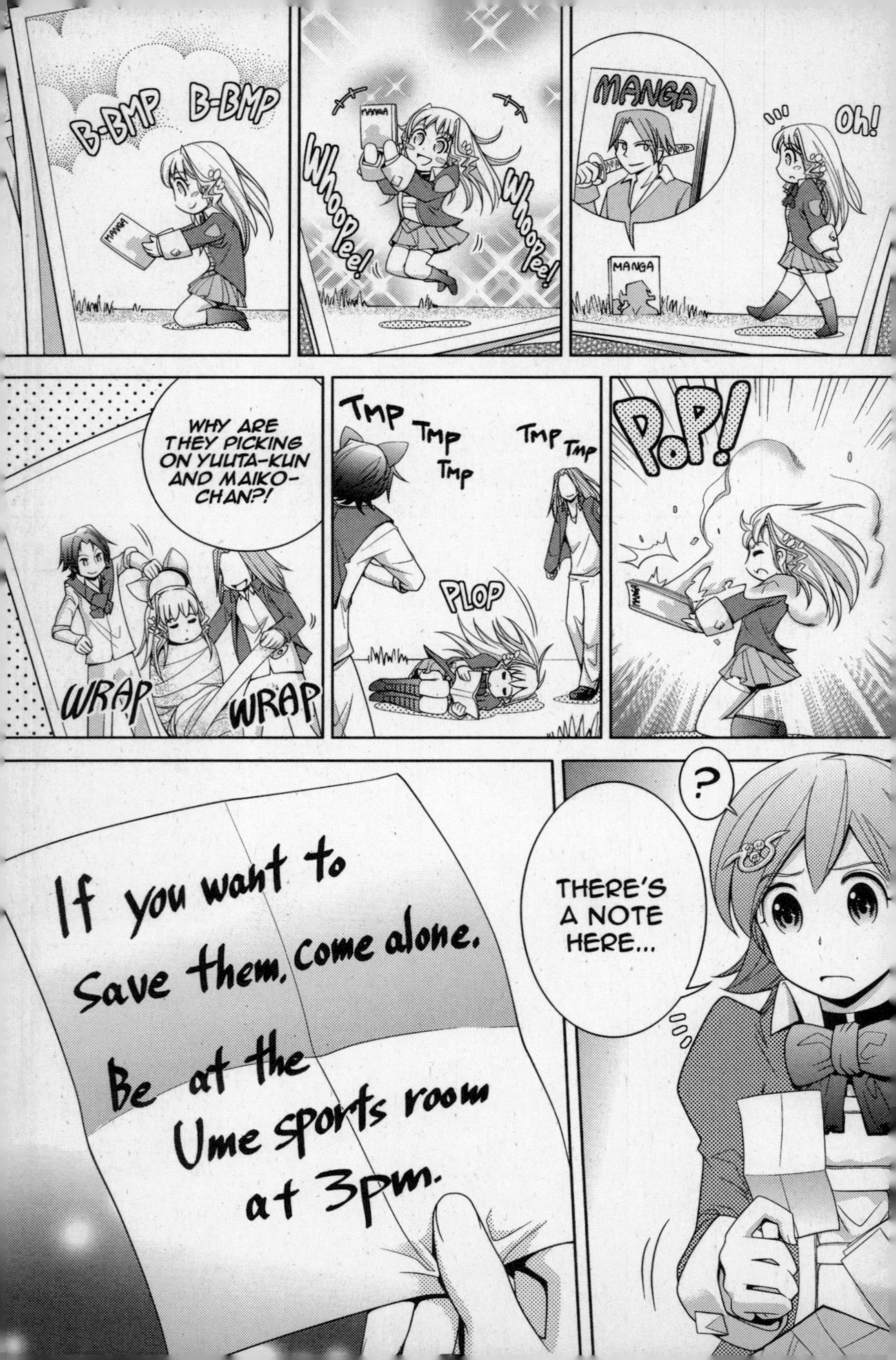

Oh!
MANGA
MANGA
Whoopee!
Whoopee!
MANGA
B-BMP
B-BMP
MANGA
POP!
TMP
TMP
TMP
TMP
TMP
PLOP
WHY ARE THEY PICKING ON YUUTA-KUN AND MAIKO-CHAN?!
WRAP
WRAP
?
THERE'S A NOTE HERE...
If you want to Save them, come alone. Be at the Ume sports room at 3pm.

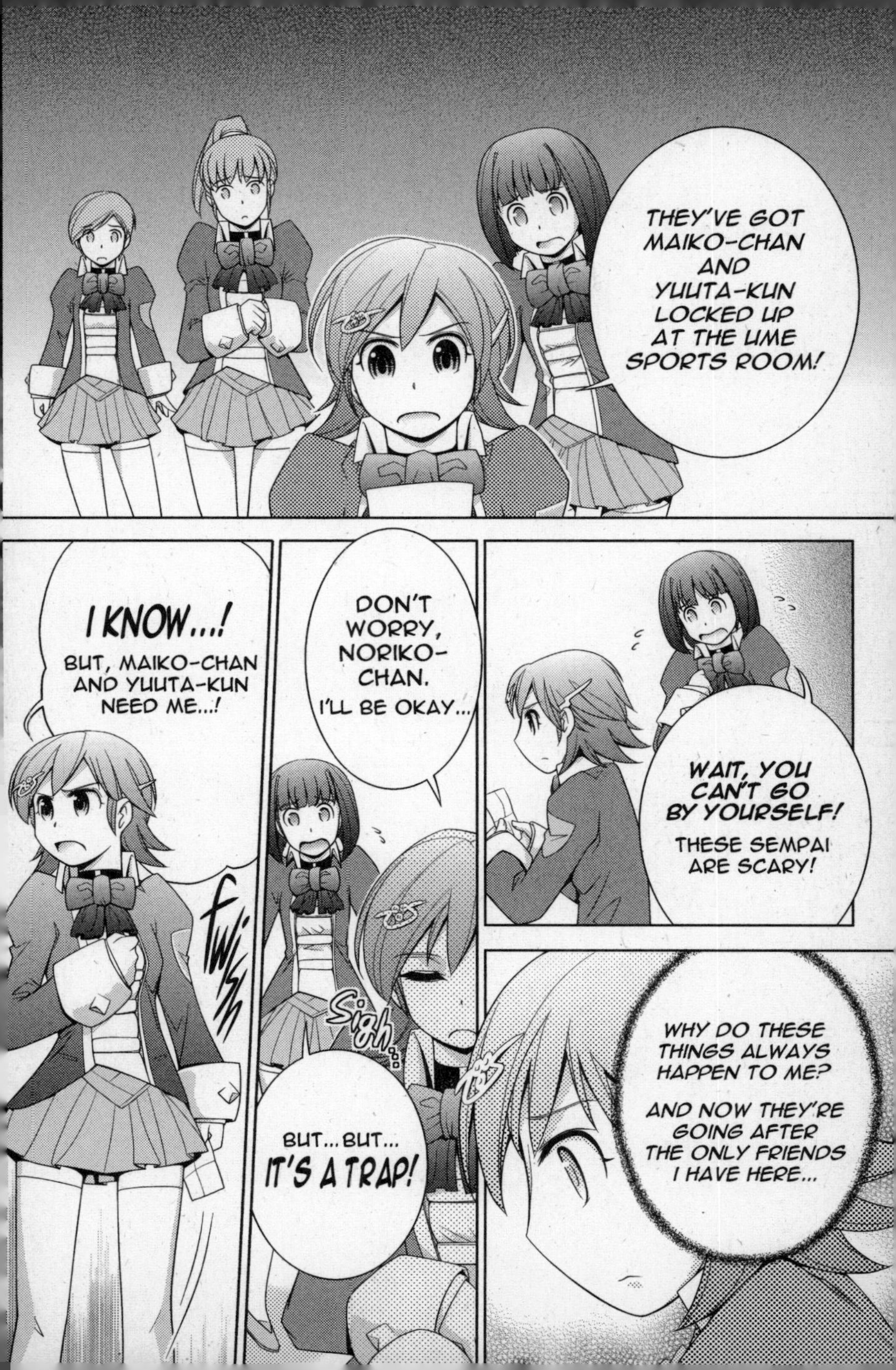
THEY'VE GOT MAIKO-CHAN AND YUUTA-KUN LOCKED UP AT THE UME SPORTS ROOM!
WAIT, YOU CAN'T GO BY YOURSELF!
THESE SEMPAI ARE SCARY!
WHY DO THESE THINGS ALWAYS HAPPEN TO ME?
AND NOW THEY'RE GOING AFTER THE ONLY FRIENDS I HAVE HERE...
DON'T WORRY, NORIKO-CHAN.
I'LL BE OKAY...
Sigh...
BUT... BUT...
IT'S A TRAP!
I KNOW...!
BUT, MAIKO-CHAN AND YUUTA-KUN NEED ME...!
fwish

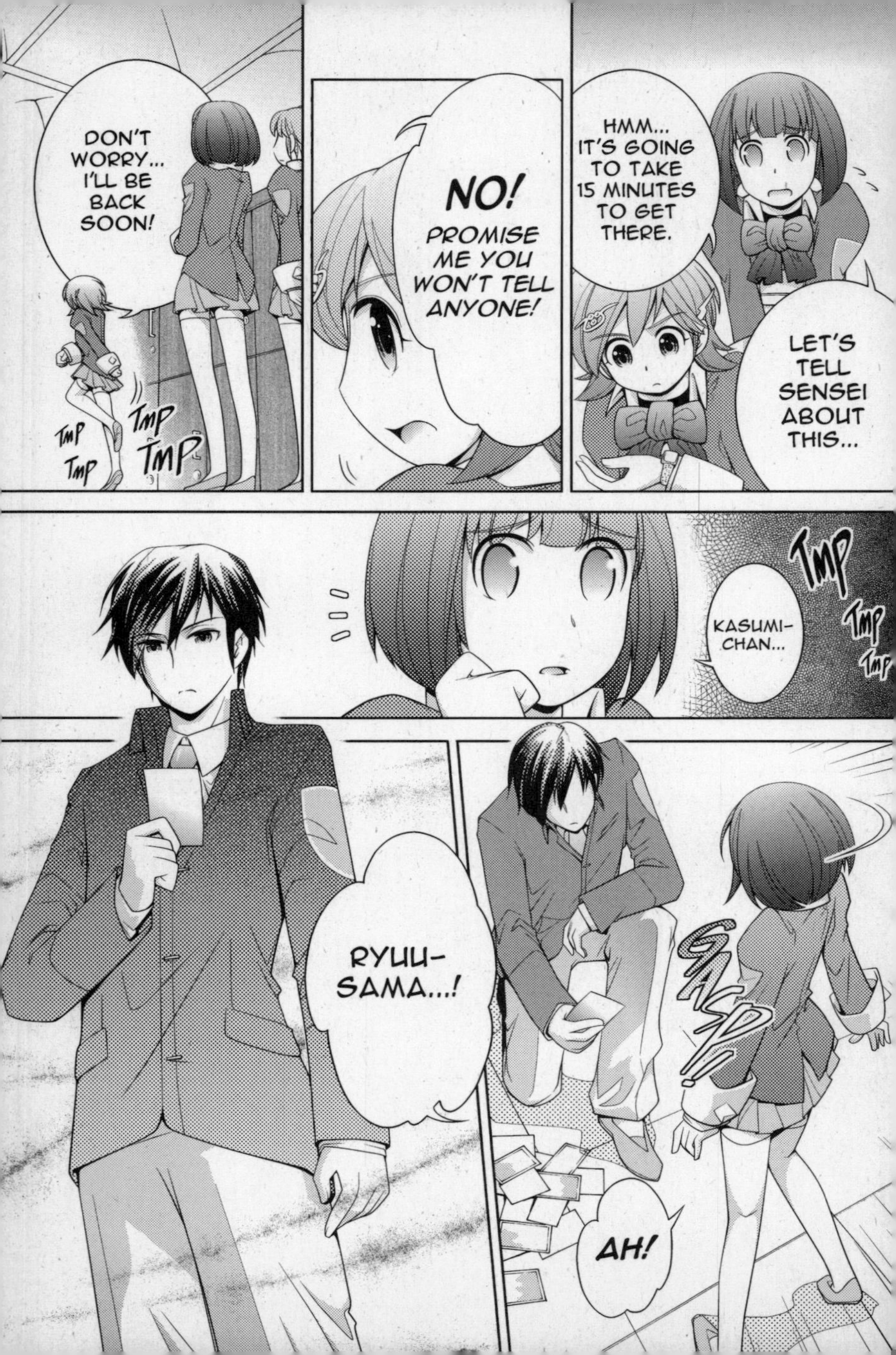
HMM... IT'S GOING TO TAKE 15 MINUTES TO GET THERE.
LET'S TELL SENSEI ABOUT THIS...
NO! PROMISE ME YOU WON'T TELL ANYONE!
DON'T WORRY... I'LL BE BACK SOON!
TMP TMP
TMP TMP
TMP TMP TMP
KASUMI-CHAN...
GASP!
AH!
RYUU-SAMA...!

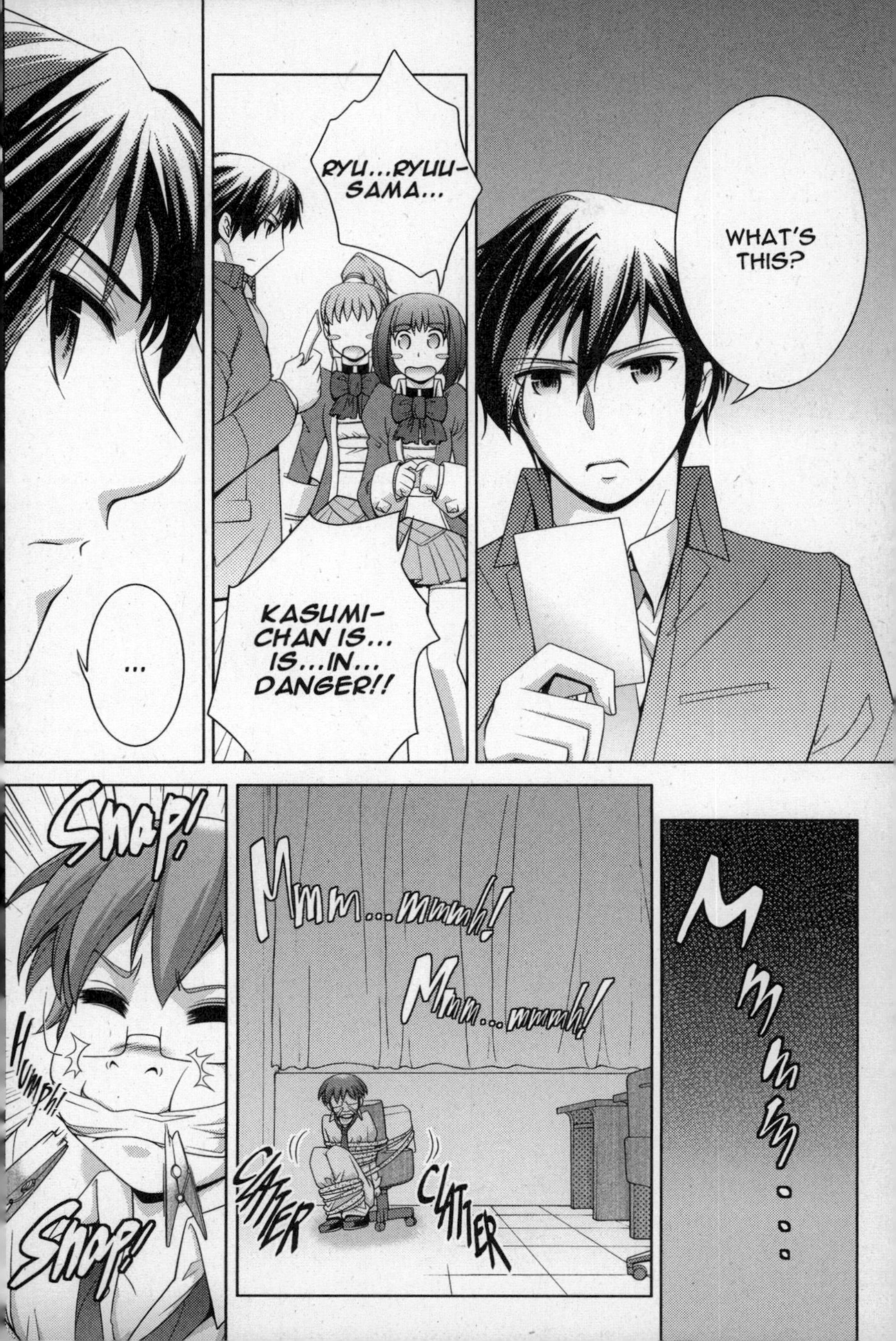
WHAT'S THIS?
RYU...RYUU-SAMA...
KASUMI-CHAN IS... IS...IN... DANGER!!
...
Mmmm...
Mmm...mmmh!
Mmm...mmmh!
CLATTER
CLATTER
Snap!
Humph!
Snap!

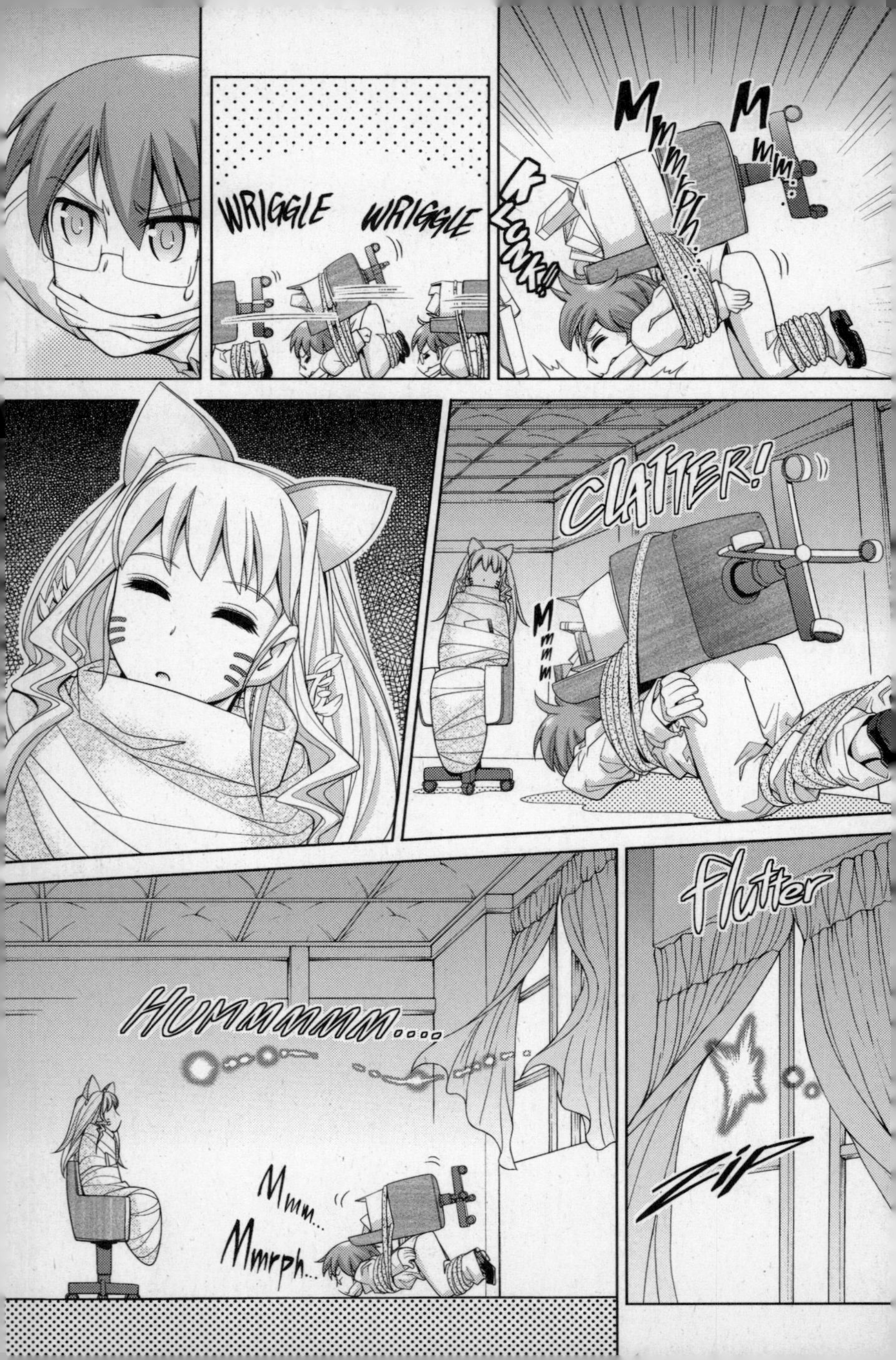
Mmmmrph...
Mmm...
KLONK!!
WRIGGLE
WRIGGLE
CLATTER!
Mmmm
Flutter
Zip
Hummmmm....
Mmm...
Mmrph...

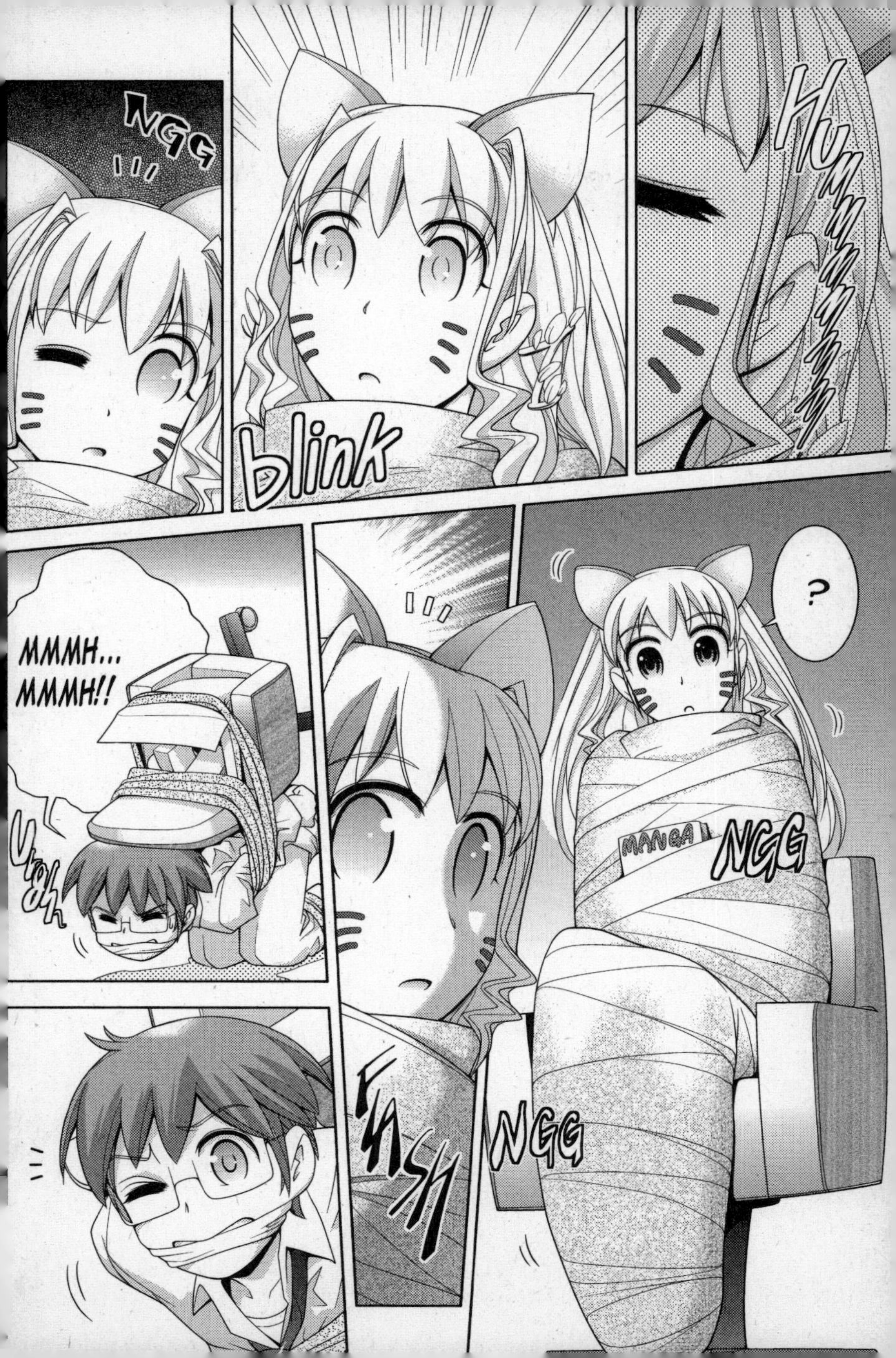
HUMMMMMMMMM
blink
NGG!!!
?
MANGA
NGG
NGG
!!!
FSSH
MMMH...
MMMH!!
Urghh

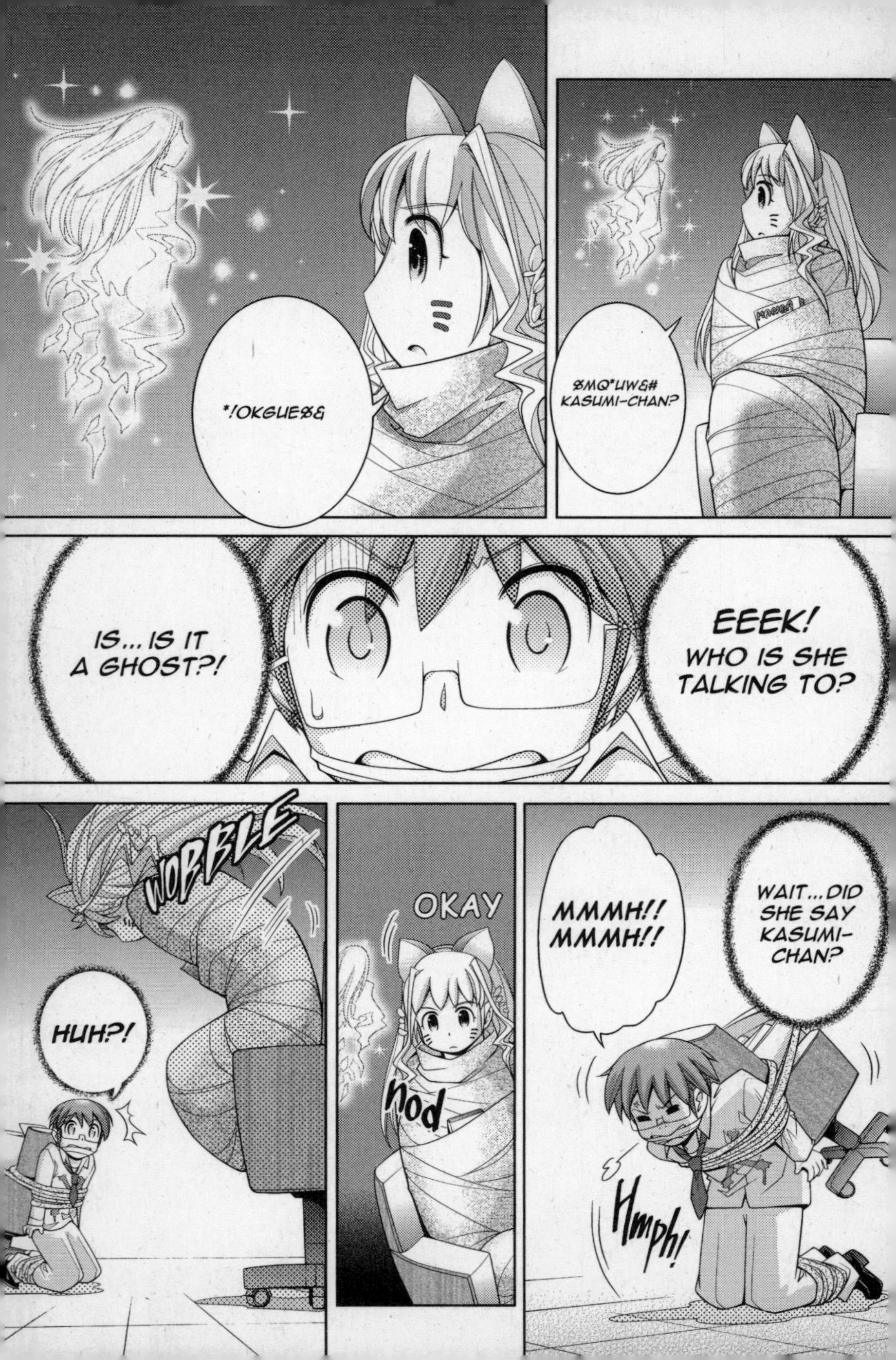
$MQ*UW&#
KASUMI-CHAN?
*!OKGUE$&
EEEK!
WHO IS SHE
TALKING TO?
IS... IS IT
A GHOST?!
WAIT...DID
SHE SAY
KASUMI-
CHAN?
MMMH!!
MMMH!!
Hmph!
OKAY
nod
WOBBLE
HUH?!

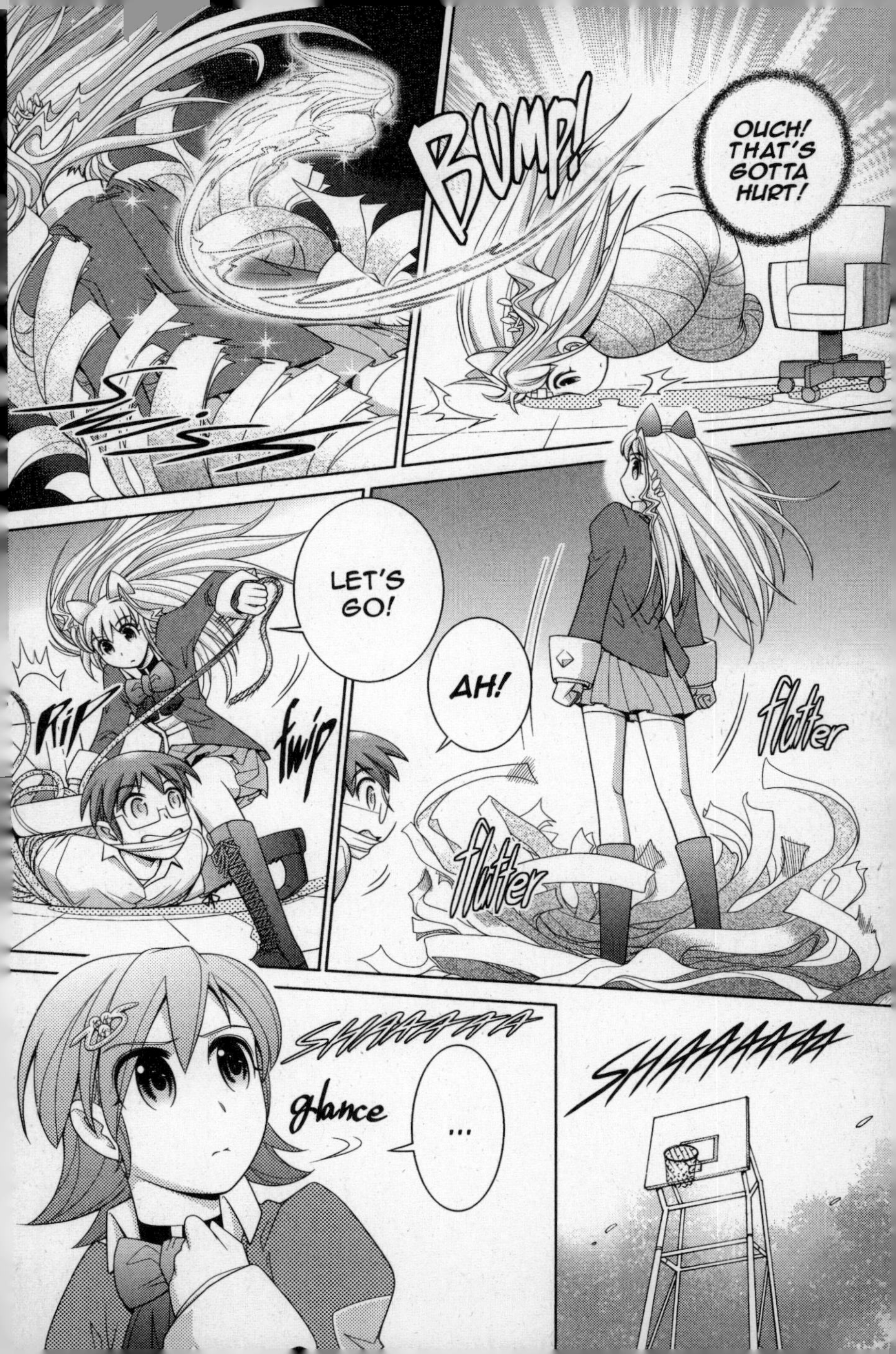
BUMP!
OUCH! THAT'S GOTTA HURT!
SWISS
flutter
flutter
AH!
LET'S GO!
fwip
Rip
SHAAAAAA
SHAAAAAA
glance
...

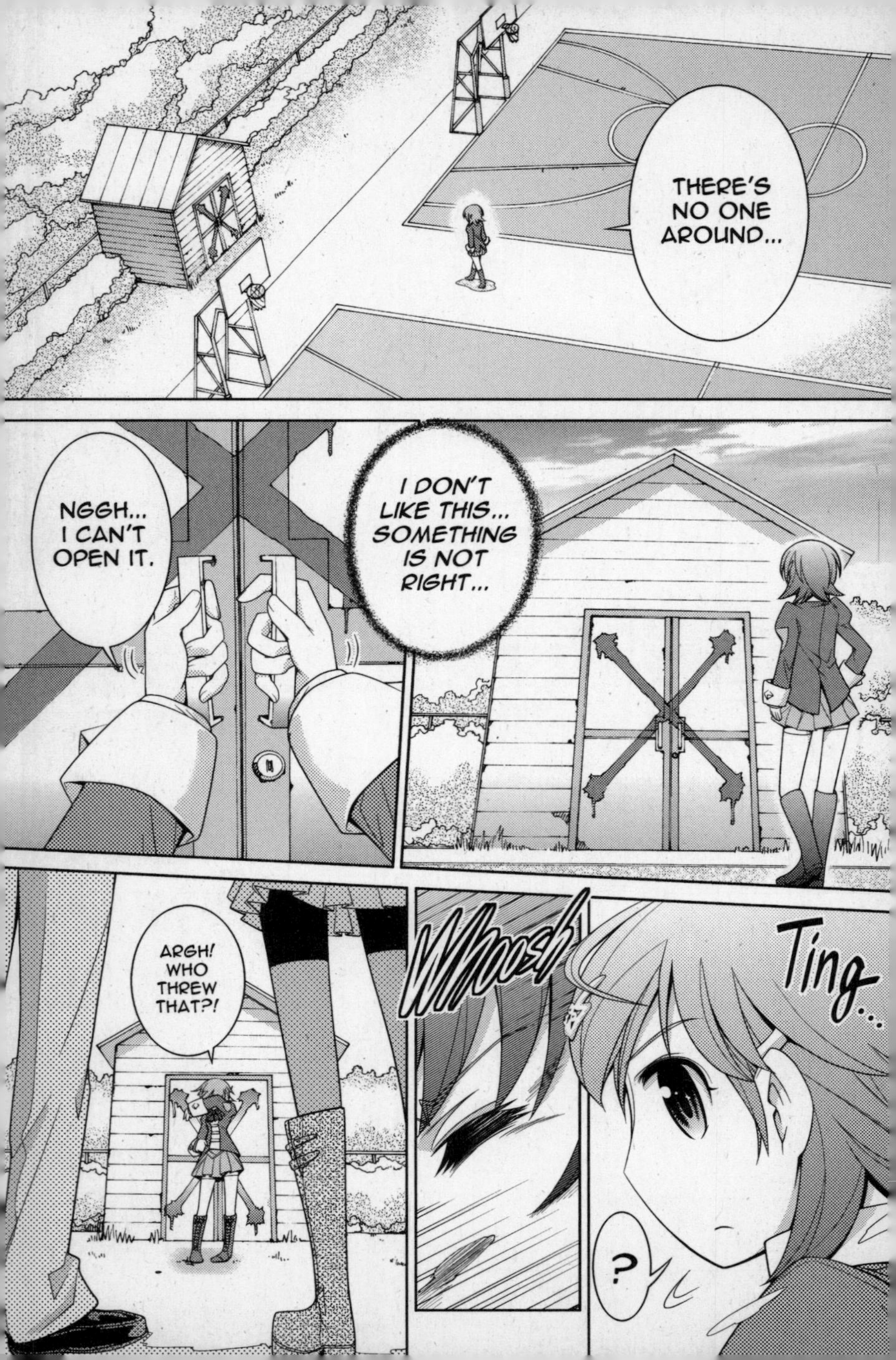
THERE'S NO ONE AROUND...
I DON'T LIKE THIS... SOMETHING IS NOT RIGHT...
NGGH... I CAN'T OPEN IT.
Ting...
Whoosh
?
ARGH! WHO THREW THAT?!

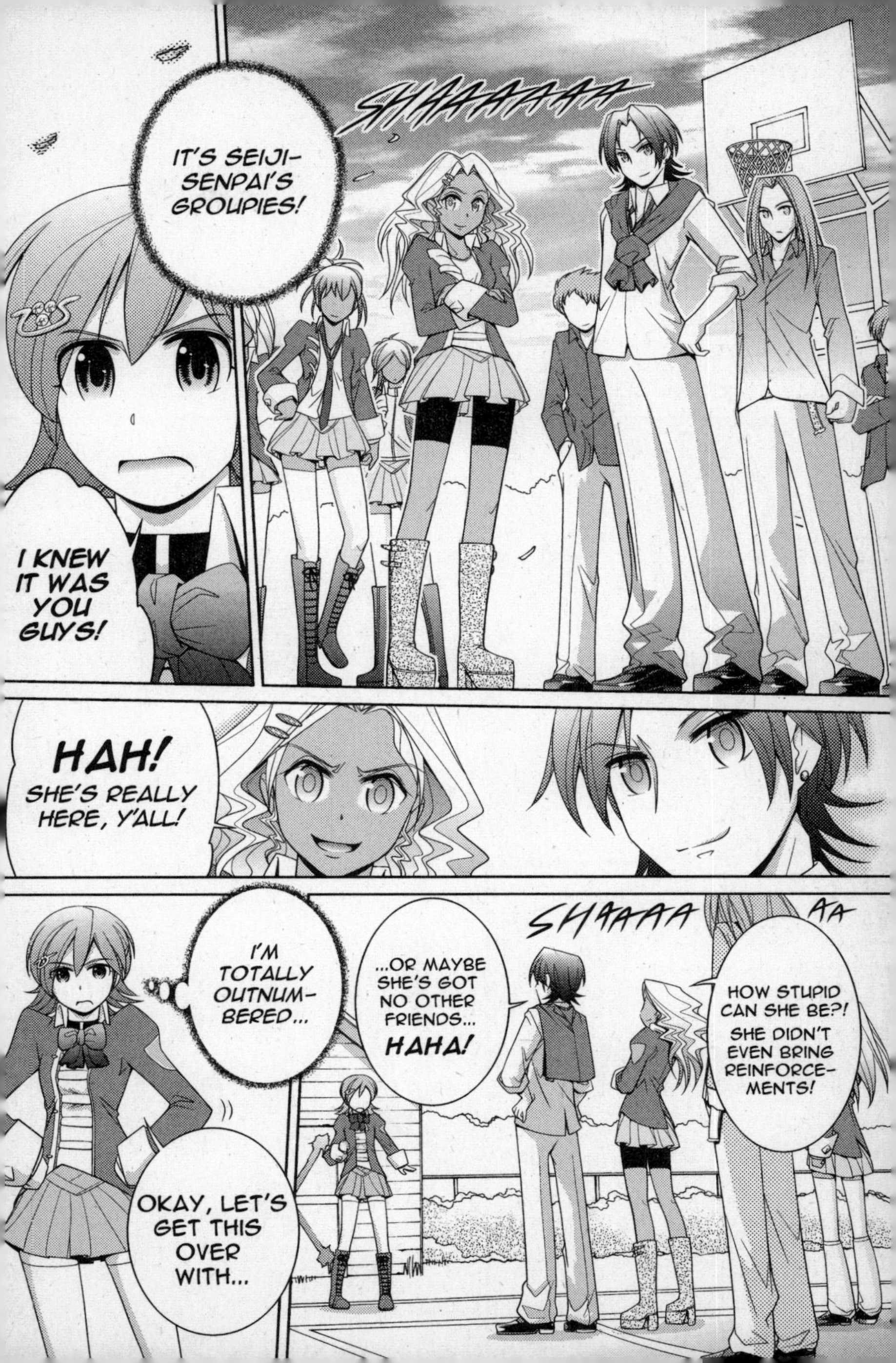
SHAAAAAAAA
IT'S SEIJI-SENPAI'S GROUPIES!
I KNEW IT WAS YOU GUYS!
HAH! SHE'S REALLY HERE, Y'ALL!
SHAAAAA AA
HOW STUPID CAN SHE BE?! SHE DIDN'T EVEN BRING REINFORCEMENTS!
...OR MAYBE SHE'S GOT NO OTHER FRIENDS... HAHA!
I'M TOTALLY OUTNUMBERED...
OKAY, LET'S GET THIS OVER WITH...

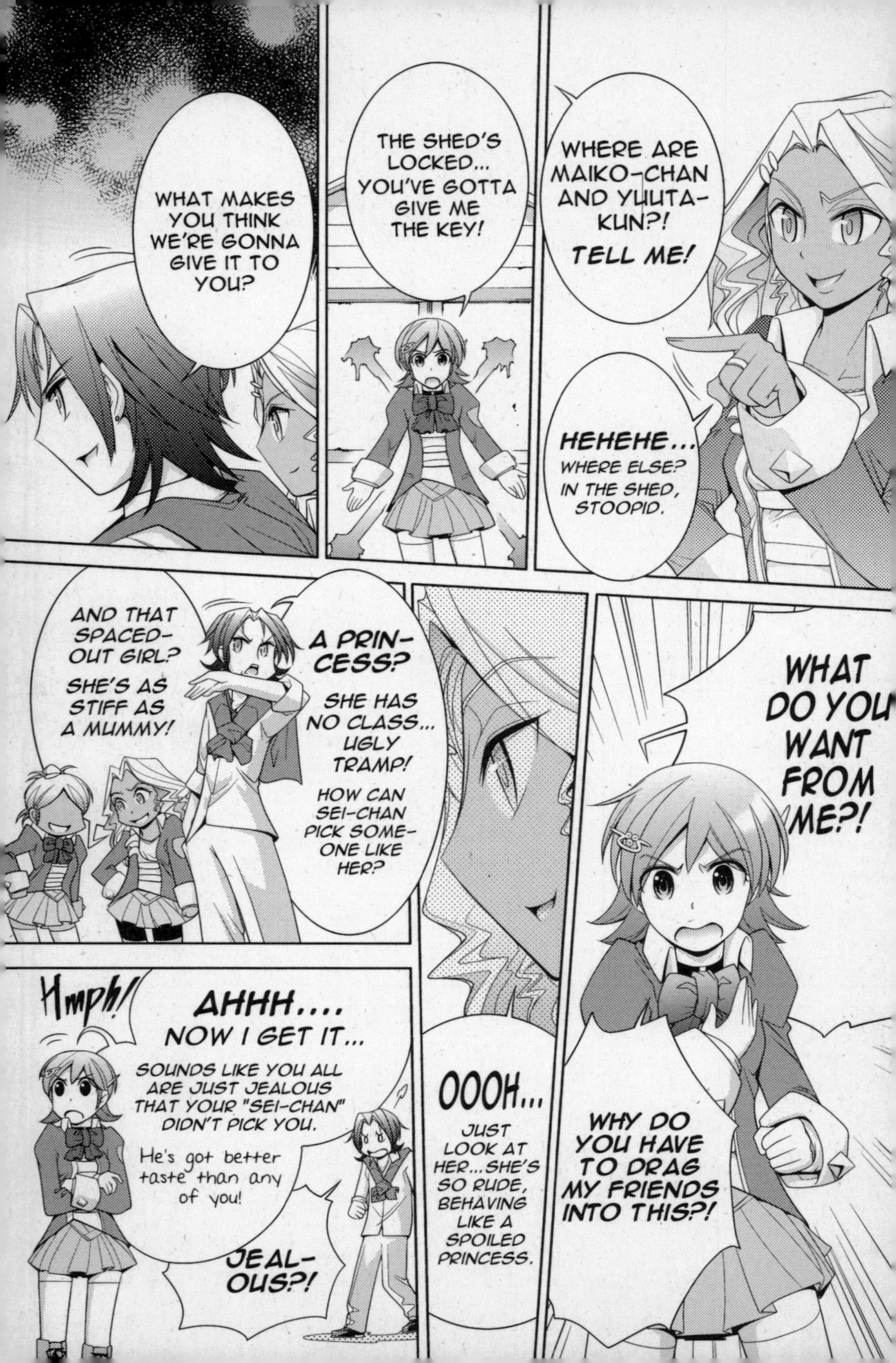
WHERE ARE MAIKO-CHAN AND YUUTA-KUN?! TELL ME!
HEHEHE... WHERE ELSE? IN THE SHED, STOOPID.
THE SHED'S LOCKED... YOU'VE GOTTA GIVE ME THE KEY!
WHAT MAKES YOU THINK WE'RE GONNA GIVE IT TO YOU?
WHAT DO YOU WANT FROM ME?!
WHY DO YOU HAVE TO DRAG MY FRIENDS INTO THIS?!
OOOH... JUST LOOK AT HER...SHE'S SO RUDE, BEHAVING LIKE A SPOILED PRINCESS.
A PRINCESS? SHE HAS NO CLASS... UGLY TRAMP! HOW CAN SEI-CHAN PICK SOMEONE LIKE HER?
AND THAT SPACED-OUT GIRL? SHE'S AS STIFF AS A MUMMY!
AHHH.... NOW I GET IT... SOUNDS LIKE YOU ALL ARE JUST JEALOUS THAT YOUR "SEI-CHAN" DIDN'T PICK YOU. He's got better taste than any of you!
Hmph!
JEALOUS?!

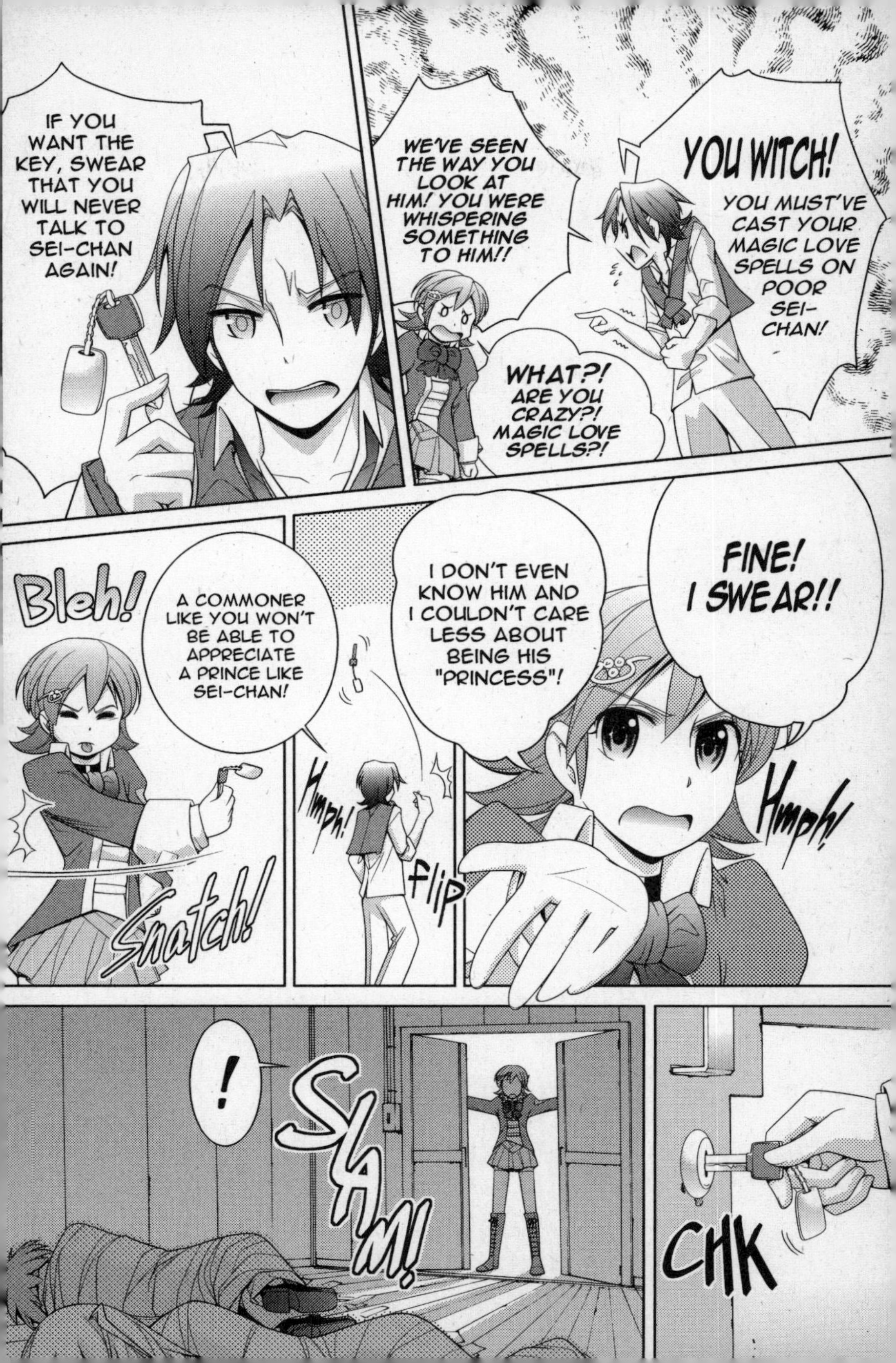

YOU WITCH!
YOU MUST'VE CAST YOUR MAGIC LOVE SPELLS ON POOR SEI-CHAN!
WE'VE SEEN THE WAY YOU LOOK AT HIM! YOU WERE WHISPERING SOMETHING TO HIM!!
WHAT?! ARE YOU CRAZY?! MAGIC LOVE SPELLS?!
IF YOU WANT THE KEY, SWEAR THAT YOU WILL NEVER TALK TO SEI-CHAN AGAIN!
FINE! I SWEAR!!
I DON'T EVEN KNOW HIM AND I COULDN'T CARE LESS ABOUT BEING HIS "PRINCESS"!
Hmph!
Hmph!
flip
A COMMONER LIKE YOU WON'T BE ABLE TO APPRECIATE A PRINCE LIKE SEI-CHAN!
Bleh!
Snatch!
CHK
!
SLAM!

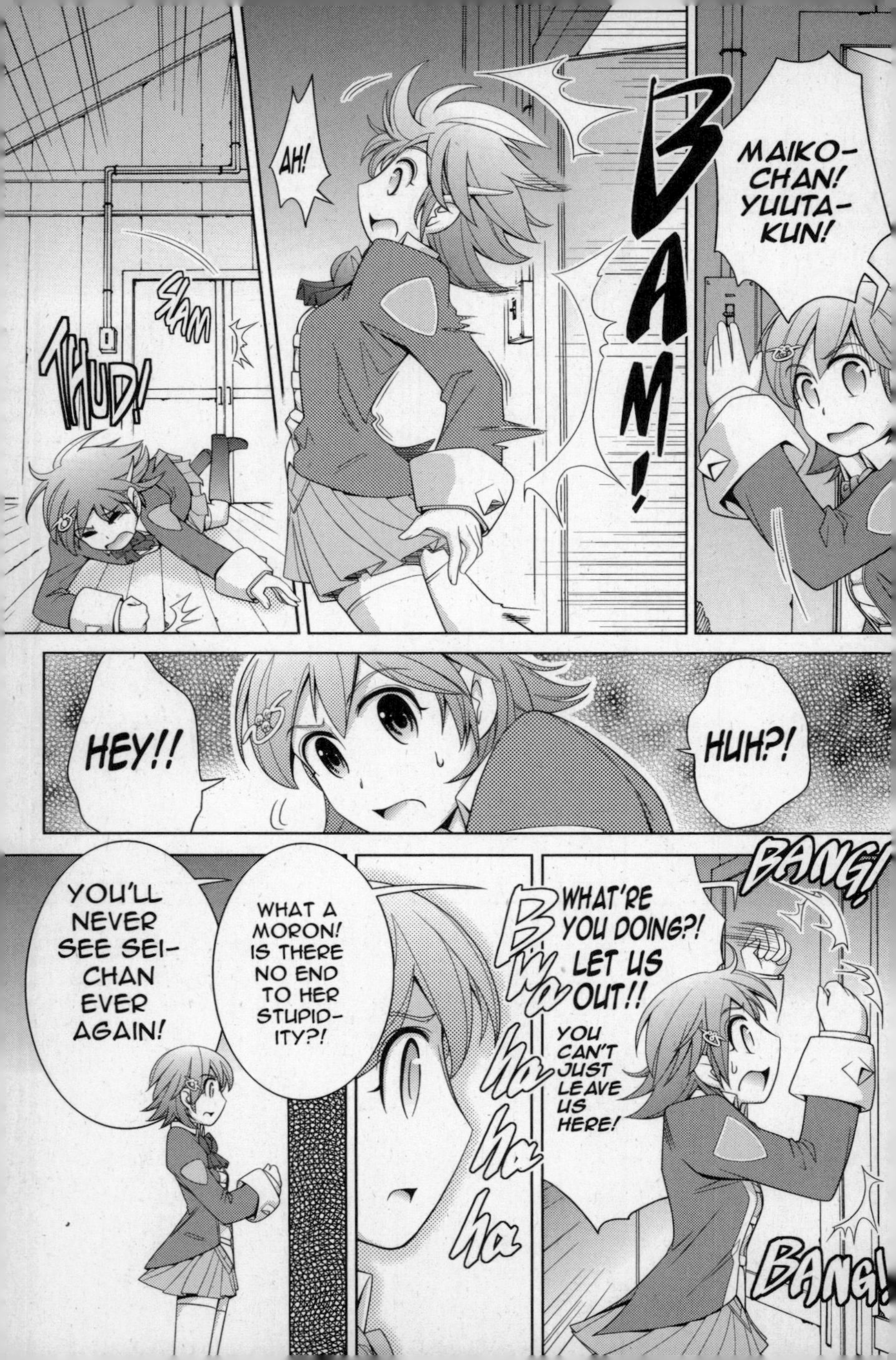
MAIKO-CHAN! YUUTA-KUN!
BAM!
AH!
SLAM
THUD!
HUH?!
HEY!!
BANG!
WHAT'RE YOU DOING?! LET US OUT!!
YOU CAN'T JUST LEAVE US HERE!
BANG!
Bwahahaha
WHAT A MORON! IS THERE NO END TO HER STUPIDITY?!
YOU'LL NEVER SEE SEI-CHAN EVER AGAIN!

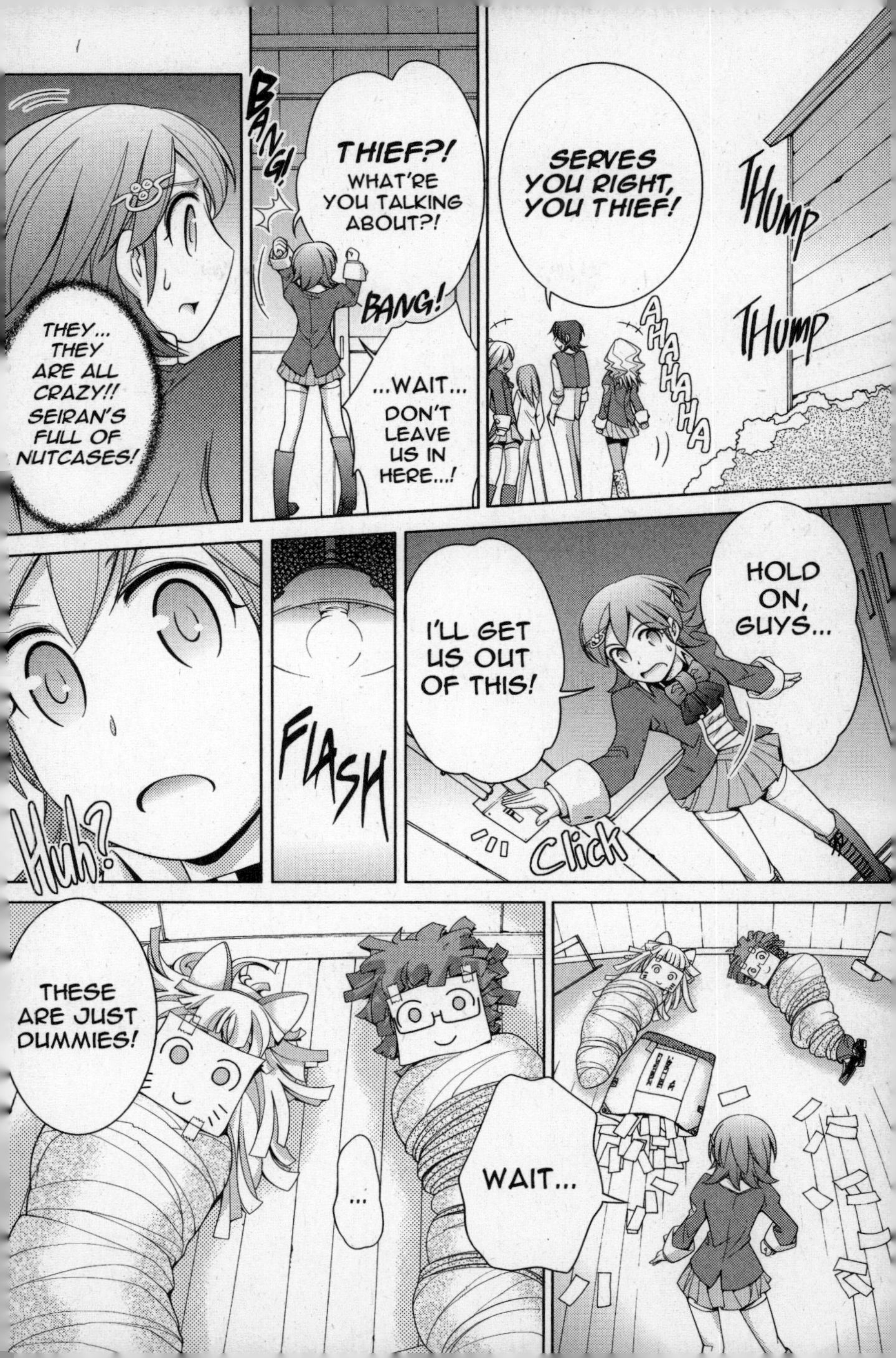
THUMP
THUMP
SERVES YOU RIGHT, YOU THIEF!
AHAHAHAHA
BANG!
THIEF?! WHAT'RE YOU TALKING ABOUT?!
BANG!
...WAIT... DON'T LEAVE US IN HERE...!
THEY... THEY ARE ALL CRAZY!! SEIRAN'S FULL OF NUTCASES!
HOLD ON, GUYS...
I'LL GET US OUT OF THIS!
Click
FLASH
Huh?
WAIT...
THESE ARE JUST DUMMIES!
...

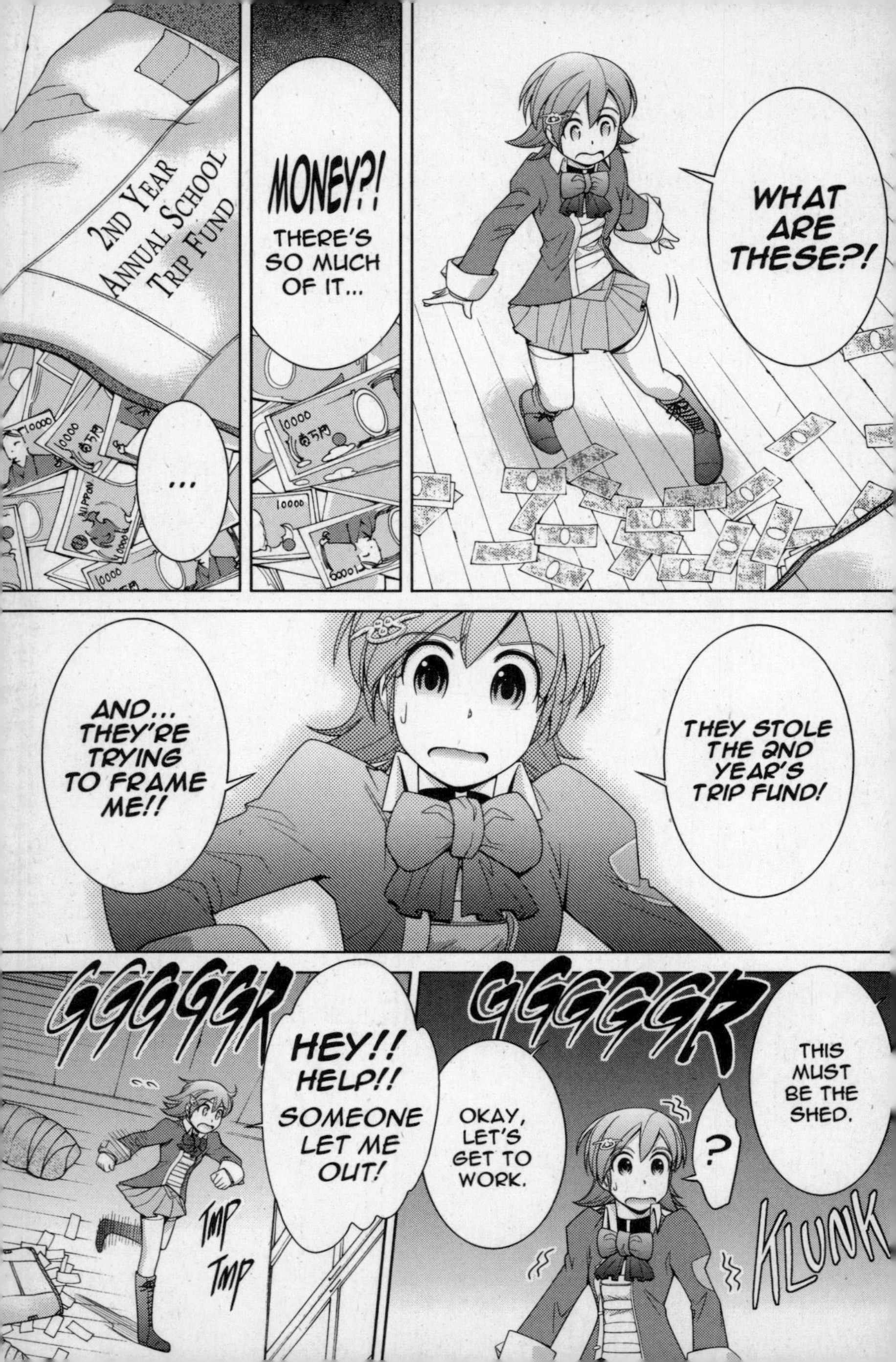
WHAT ARE THESE?!
MONEY?! THERE'S SO MUCH OF IT...
2ND YEAR ANNUAL SCHOOL TRIP FUND
...
THEY STOLE THE 2ND YEAR'S TRIP FUND!
AND... THEY'RE TRYING TO FRAME ME!!
GGGGGR
THIS MUST BE THE SHED.
?
OKAY, LET'S GET TO WORK.
KLUNK
GGGGGR
HEY!! HELP!! SOMEONE LET ME OUT!
TMP
TMP

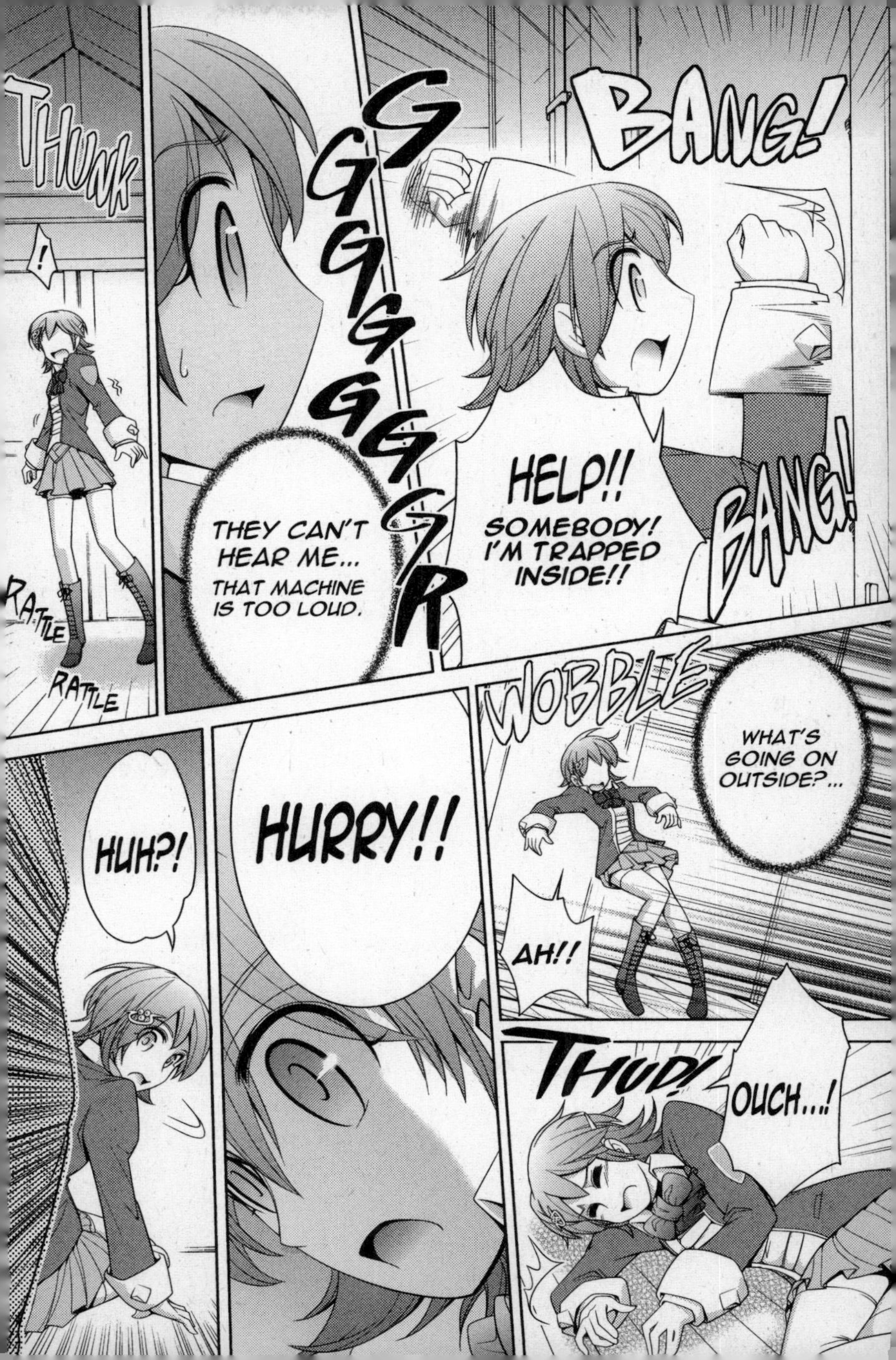
BANG!
HELP!!
SOMEBODY! I'M TRAPPED INSIDE!!
BANG!
GGGGGGGR
THEY CAN'T HEAR ME... THAT MACHINE IS TOO LOUD.
THUNK
!
RATTLE
RATTLE
WOBBLE
WHAT'S GOING ON OUTSIDE?...
AH!!
THUD!
OUCH...!
HURRY!!
HUH?!

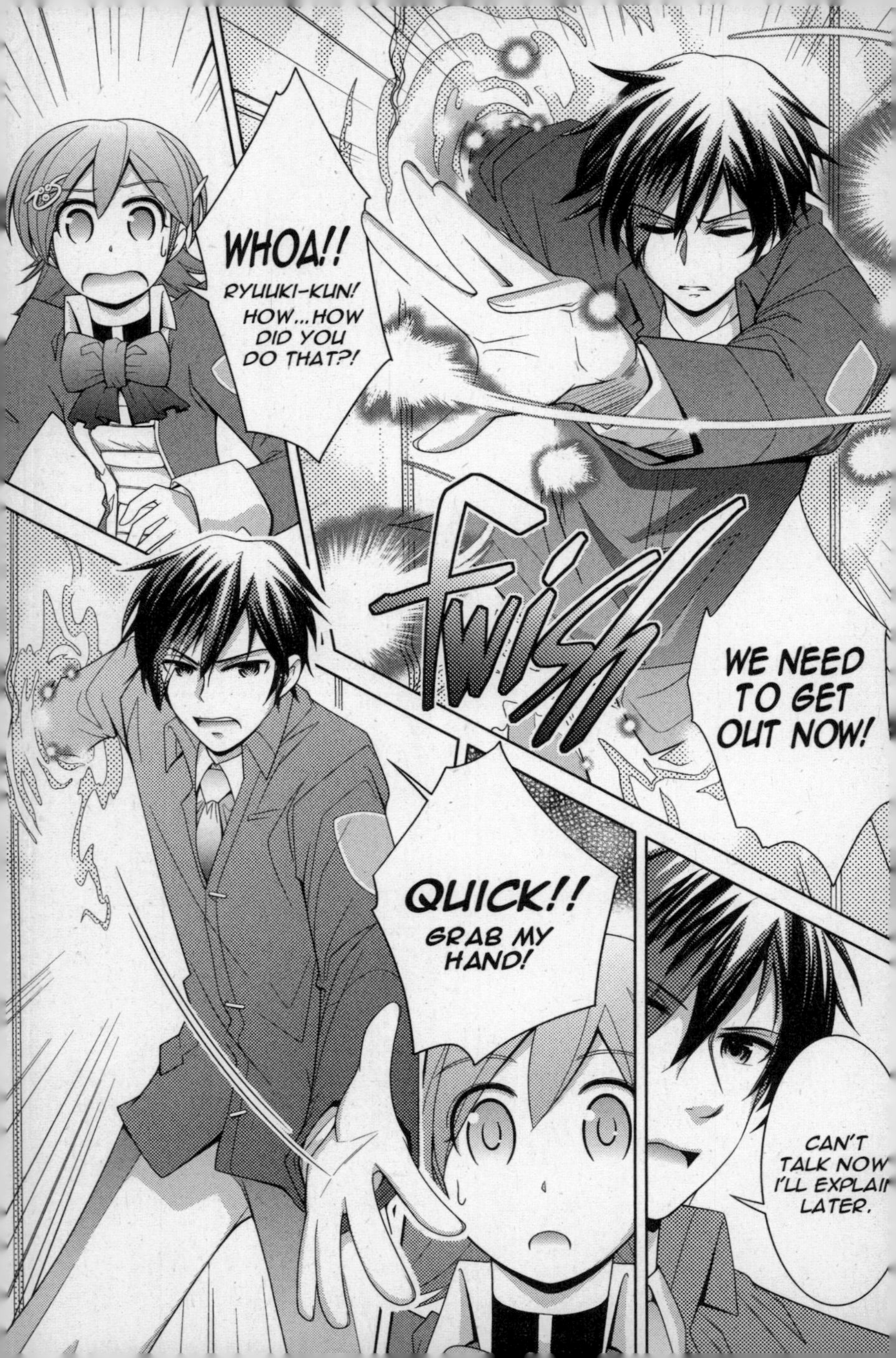
FWISH
WHOA!! RYUUKI-KUN! HOW...HOW DID YOU DO THAT?!
WE NEED TO GET OUT NOW!
CAN'T TALK NOW I'LL EXPLAIN LATER.
QUICK!! GRAB MY HAND!

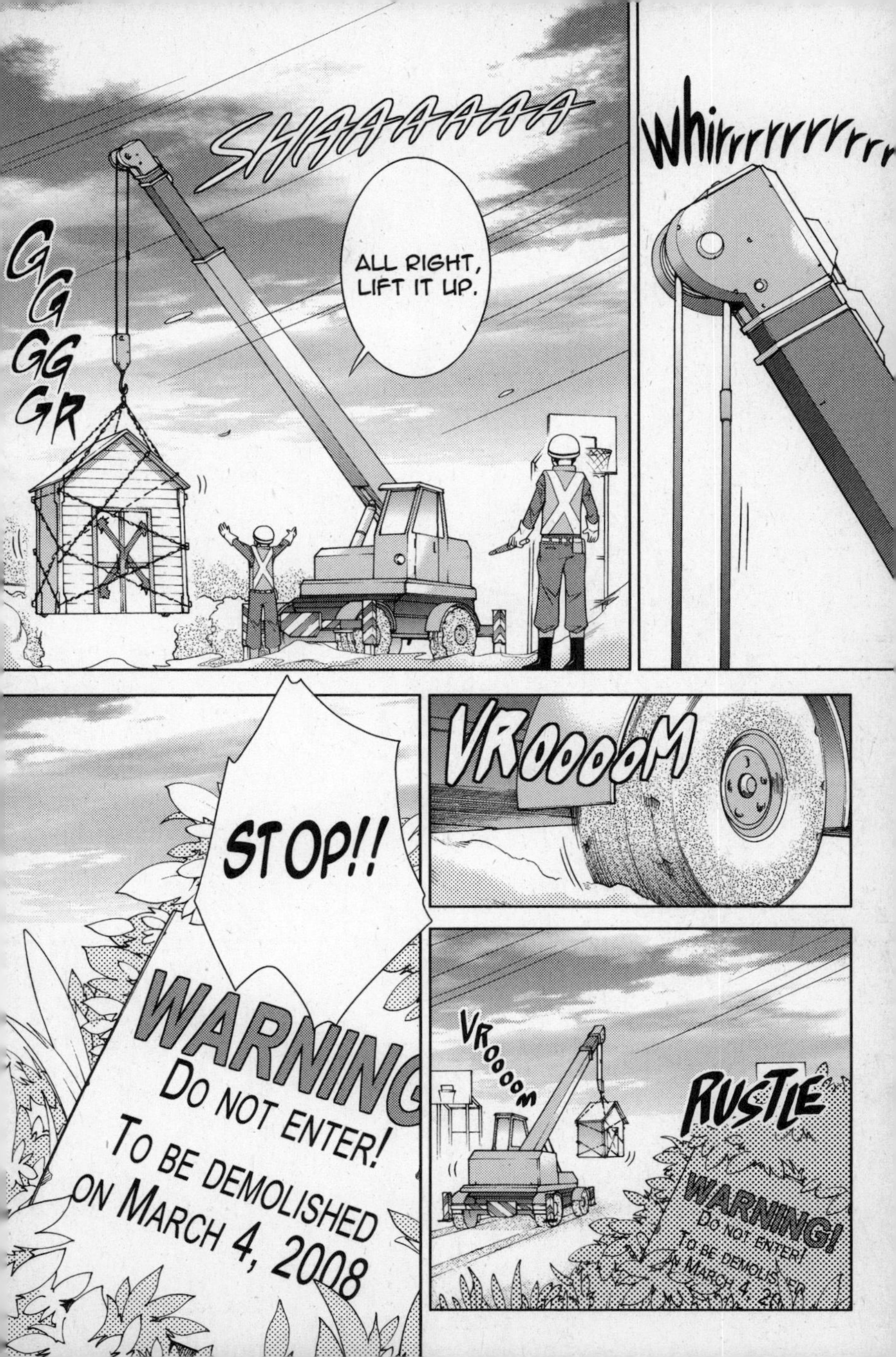

Whirrrrrrrrr
SHAAAAAAAA
ALL RIGHT, LIFT IT UP.
GGGGGR
VROOOOM
VROOOOM
RUSTLE
WARNING!
DO NOT ENTER!
STOP!!
WARNING
DO NOT ENTER!
TO BE DEMOLISHED ON MARCH 4, 2008

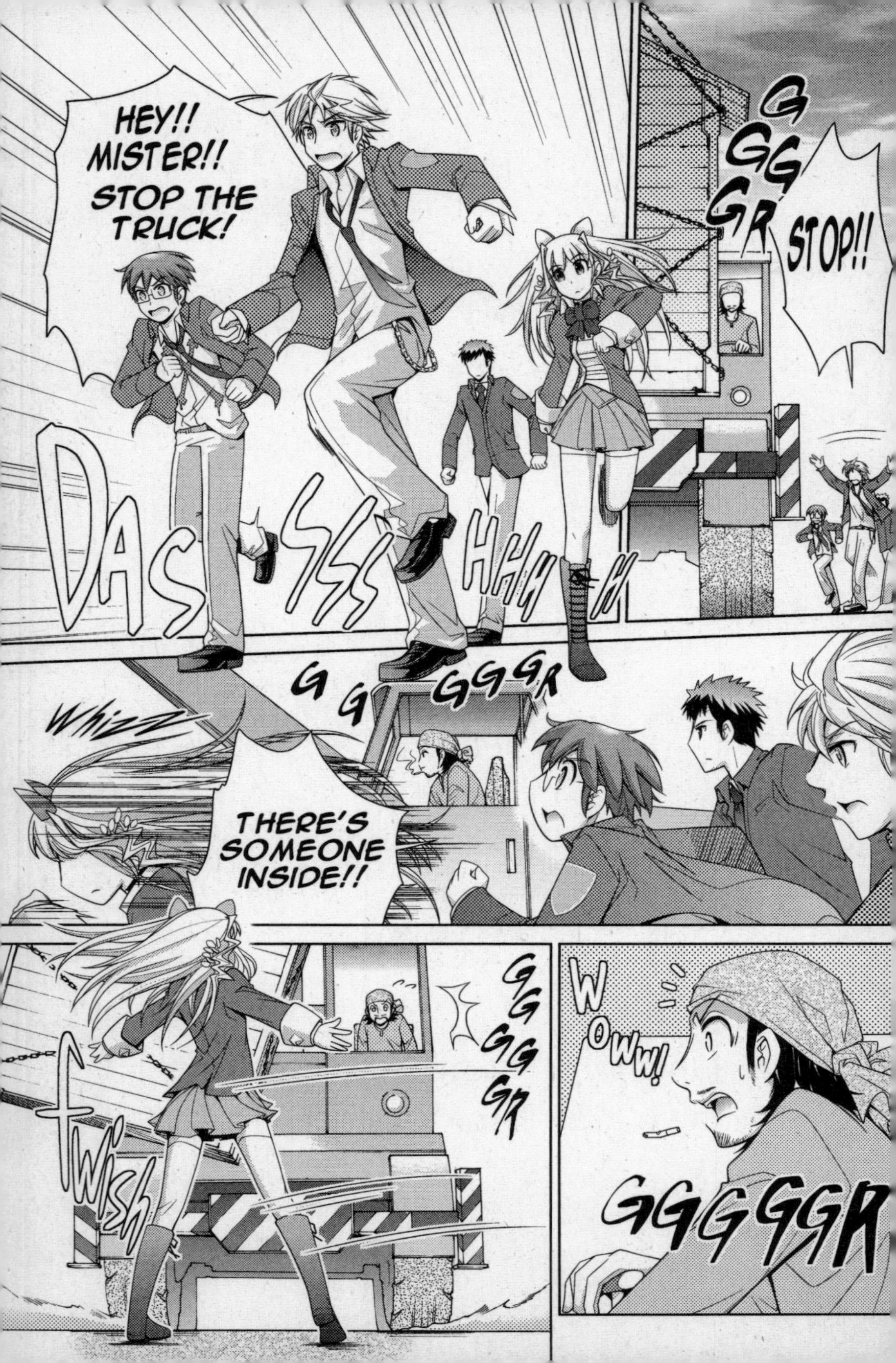
GGGGR
STOP!!
HEY!! MISTER!! STOP THE TRUCK!
DASSSSHHHHH
GGGGGR
WHIZZ
THERE'S SOMEONE INSIDE!!
WOWW!
GGGGGR
GGGGGR
TWISH

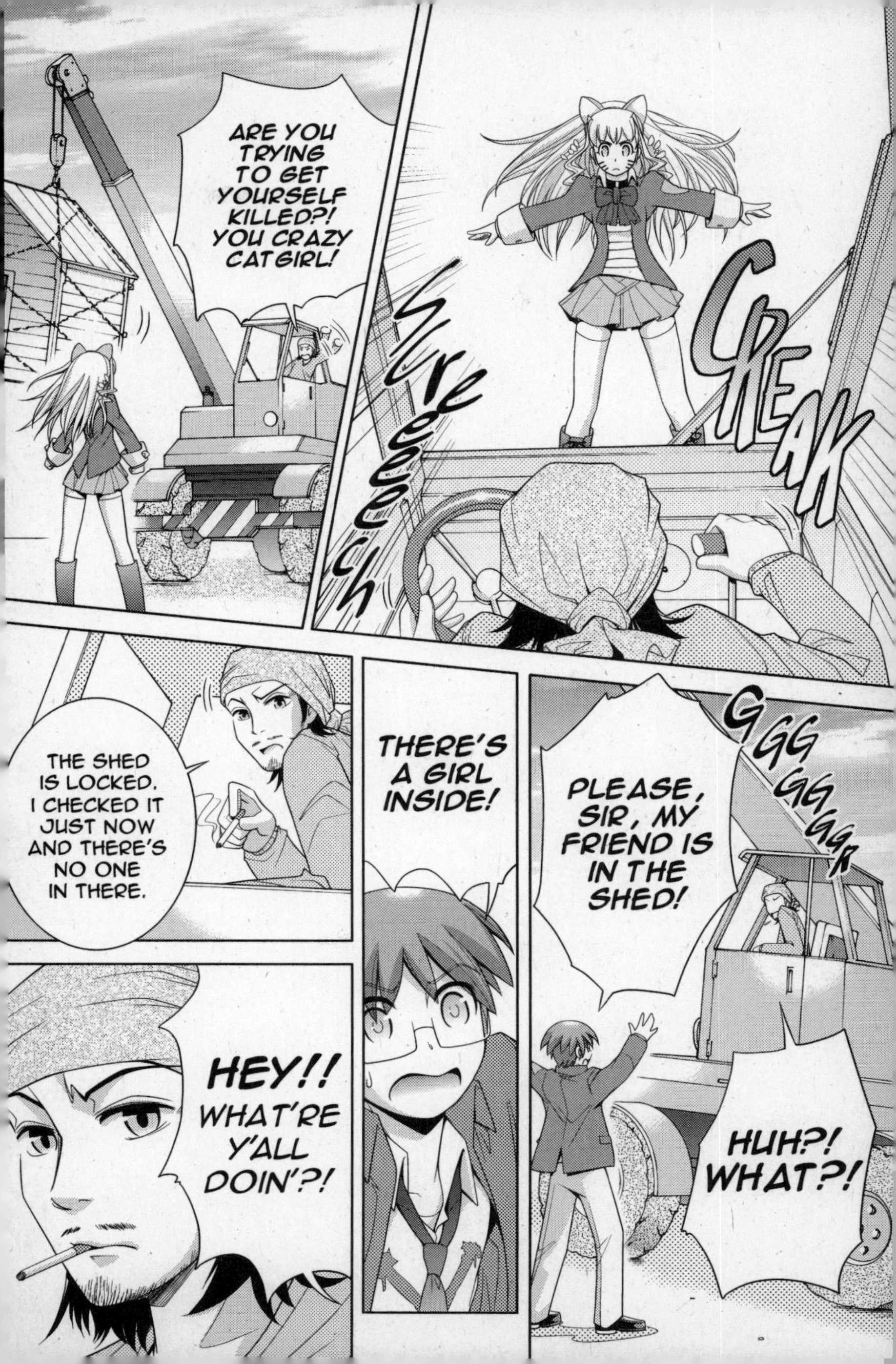
CREAK
Screeech
ARE YOU TRYING TO GET YOURSELF KILLED?! YOU CRAZY CATGIRL!
GGGGGGR
PLEASE, SIR, MY FRIEND IS IN THE SHED!
HUH?! WHAT?!
THERE'S A GIRL INSIDE!
THE SHED IS LOCKED. I CHECKED IT JUST NOW AND THERE'S NO ONE IN THERE.
HEY!! WHAT'RE Y'ALL DOIN'?!

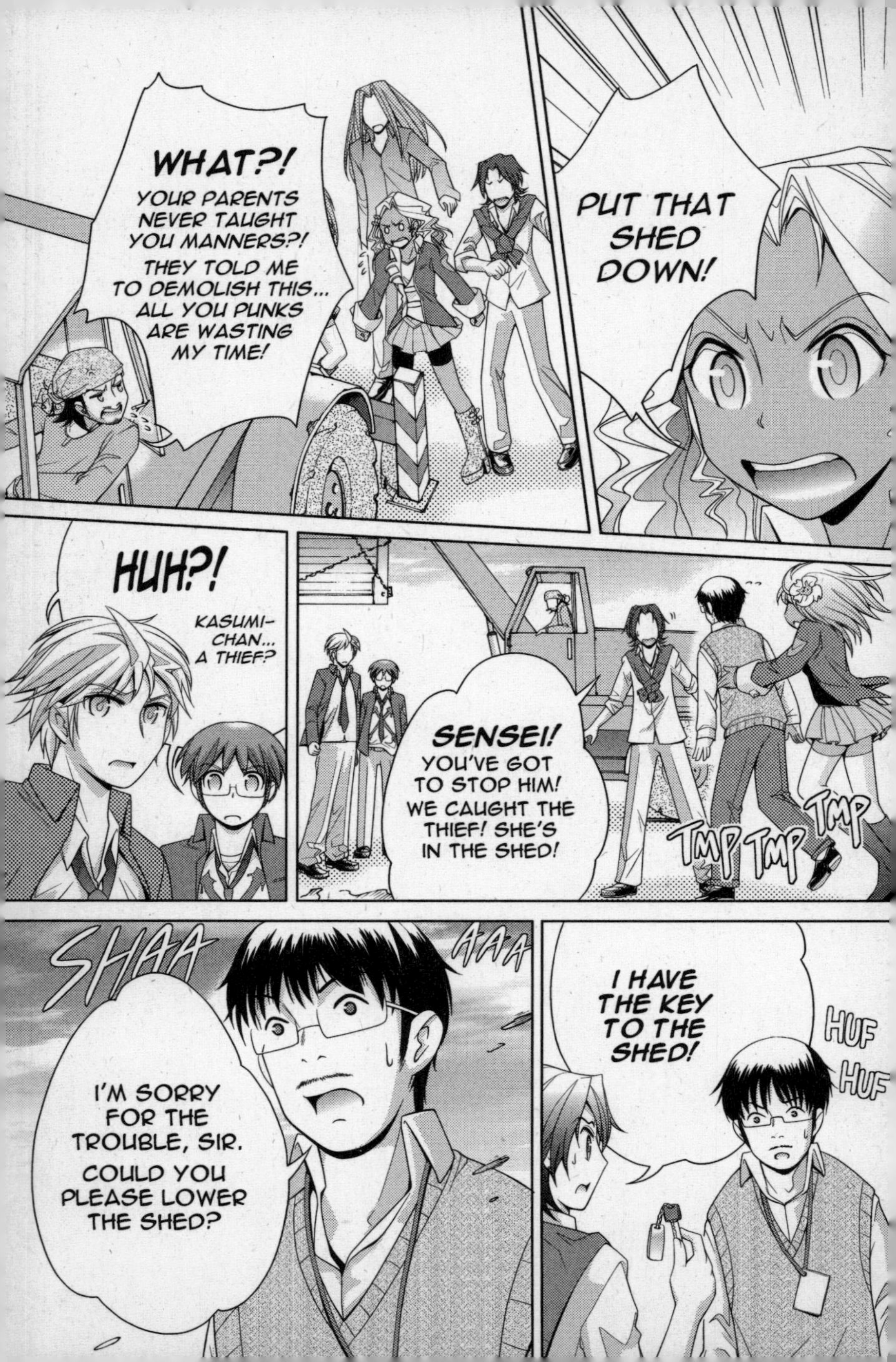

PUT THAT SHED DOWN!
WHAT?!
YOUR PARENTS NEVER TAUGHT YOU MANNERS?!
THEY TOLD ME TO DEMOLISH THIS... ALL YOU PUNKS ARE WASTING MY TIME!
TMP TMP TMP
SENSEI!
YOU'VE GOT TO STOP HIM! WE CAUGHT THE THIEF! SHE'S IN THE SHED!
HUH?!
KASUMI-CHAN... A THIEF?
I HAVE THE KEY TO THE SHED!
HUF HUF
SHAAAA
I'M SORRY FOR THE TROUBLE, SIR.
COULD YOU PLEASE LOWER THE SHED?

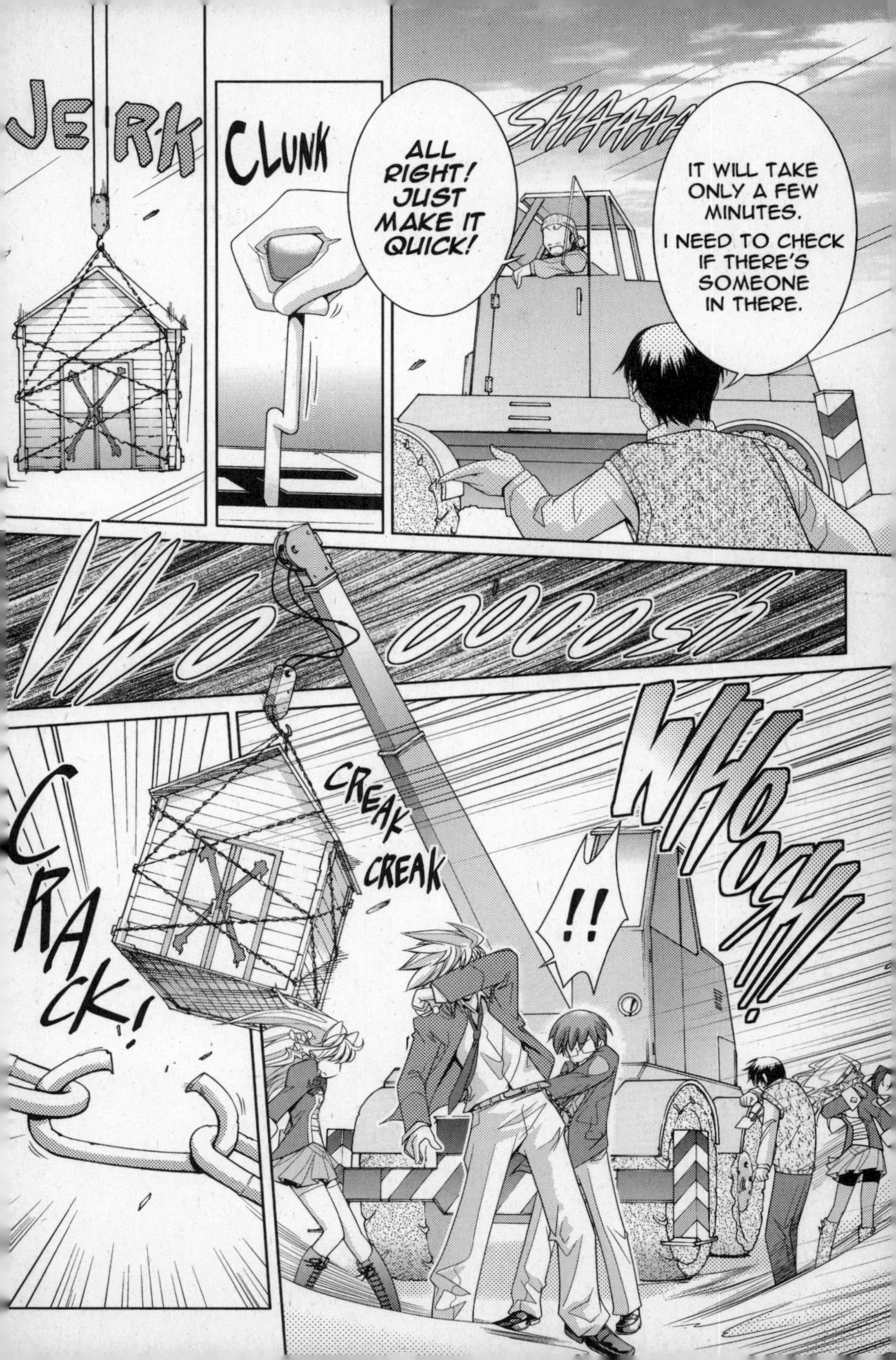
IT WILL TAKE ONLY A FEW MINUTES.
I NEED TO CHECK IF THERE'S SOMEONE IN THERE.
SHAAAAA
ALL RIGHT! JUST MAKE IT QUICK!
CLUNK
JERK
Whoooosh
WHOOM!!
!!
CREAK
CREAK
CRACK!

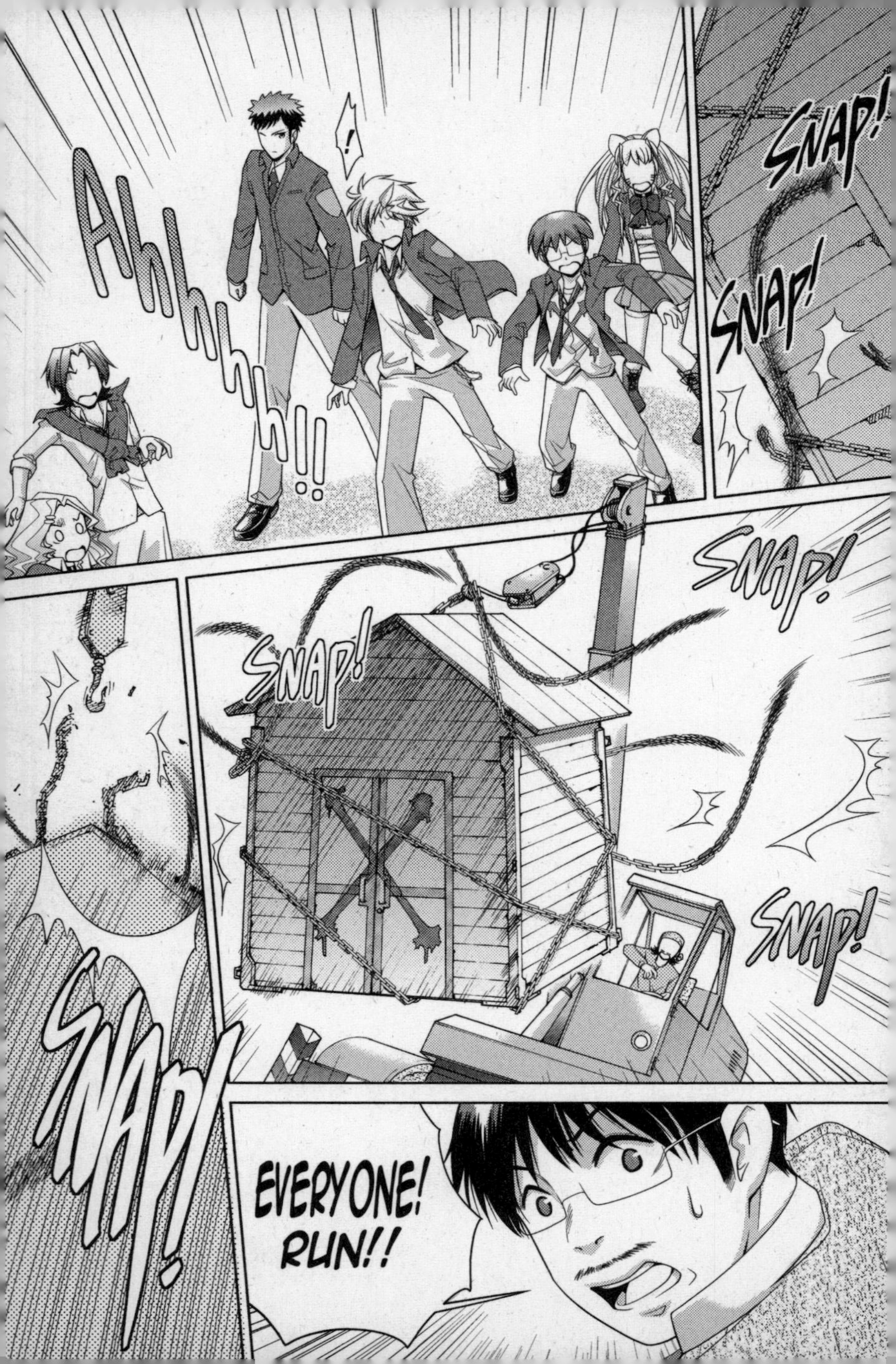
SNAP!
SNAP!
!
Ahhhhhh!!
SNAP!
SNAP!
SNAP!
SNAP!
EVERYONE! RUN!!
SNAP!

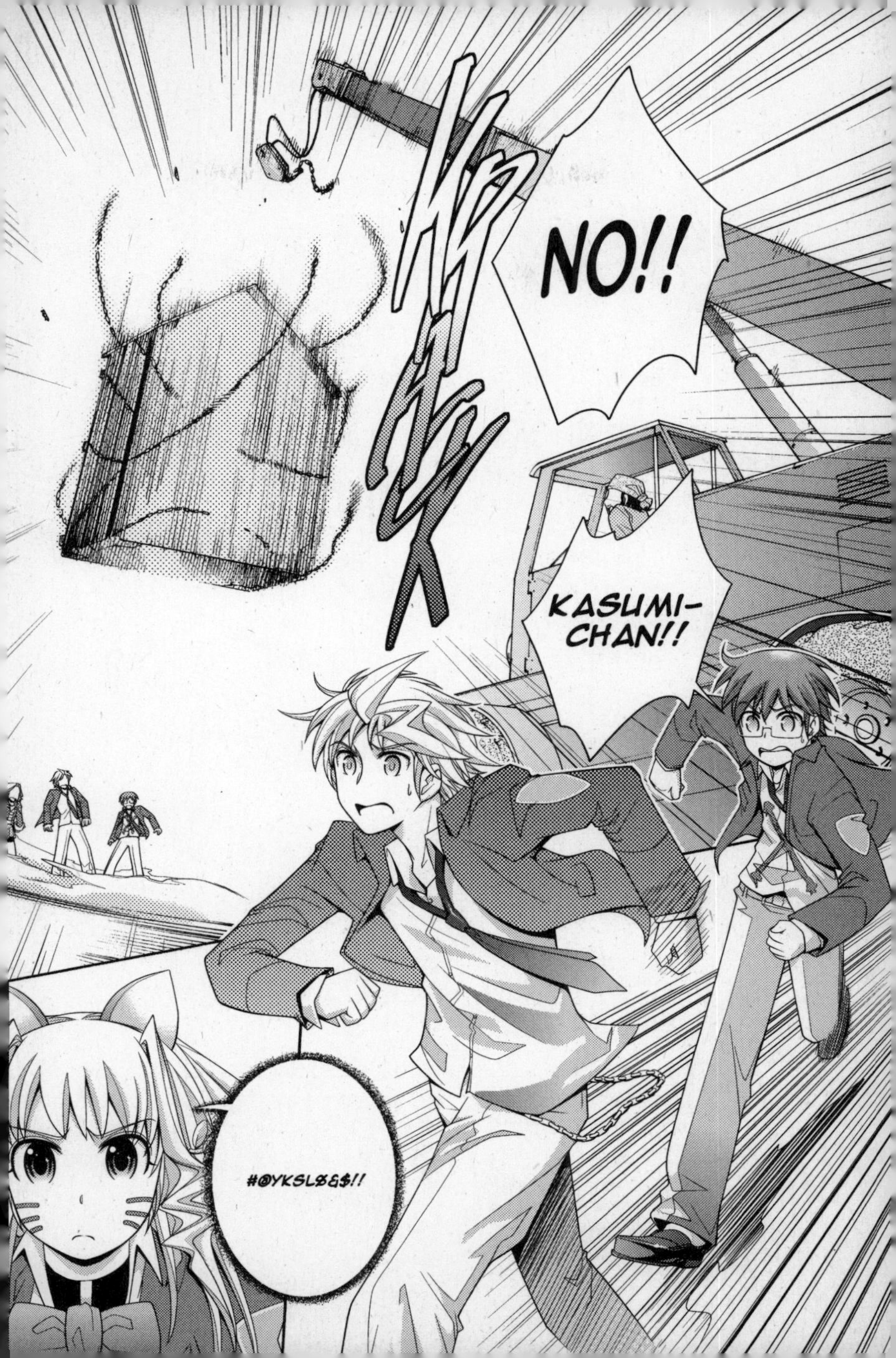
NO!!
KASUMI-CHAN!!
#@YKSLØ&$!!

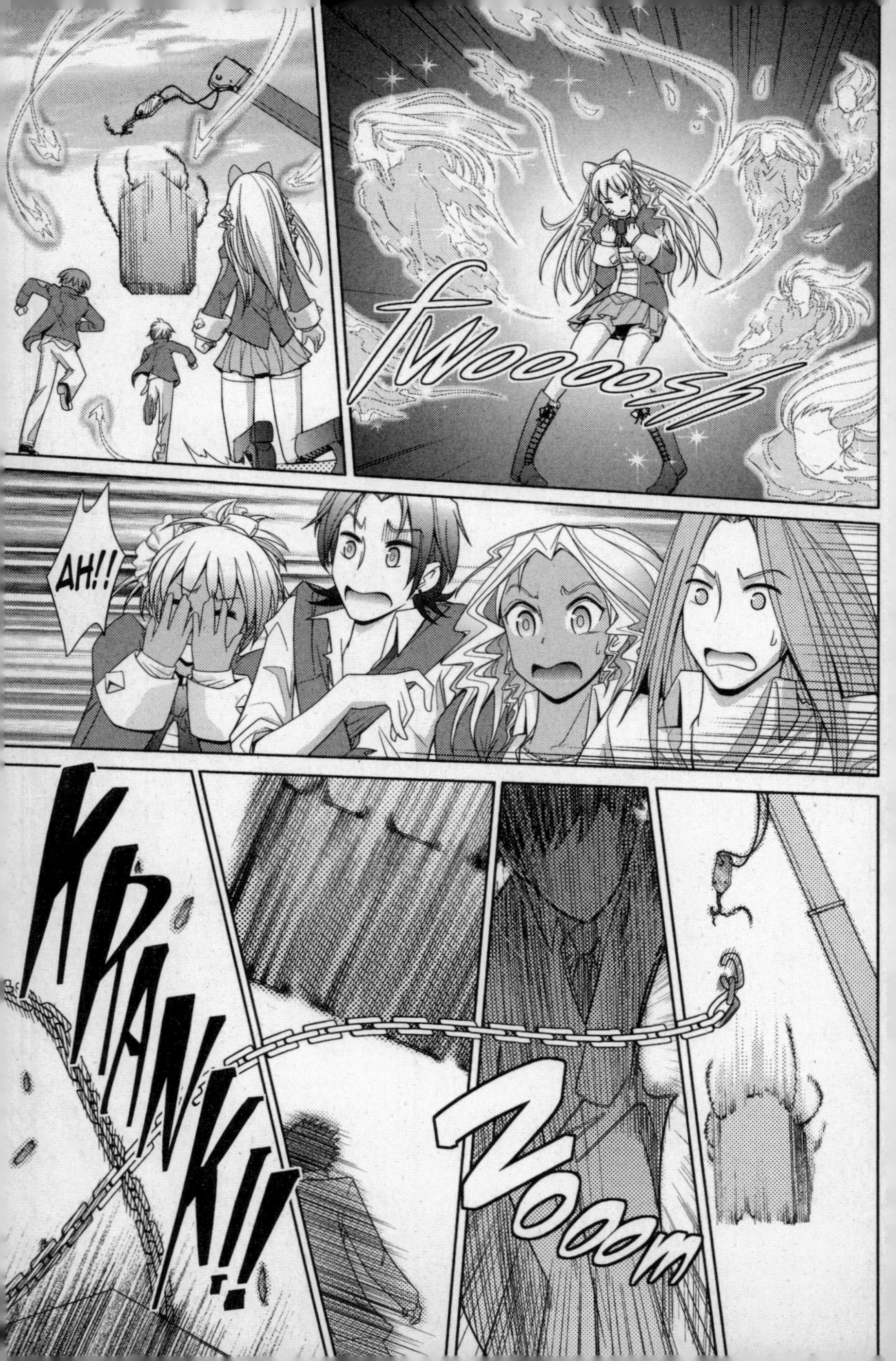
fwooosh
AH!!
Zooom
KRANK!!

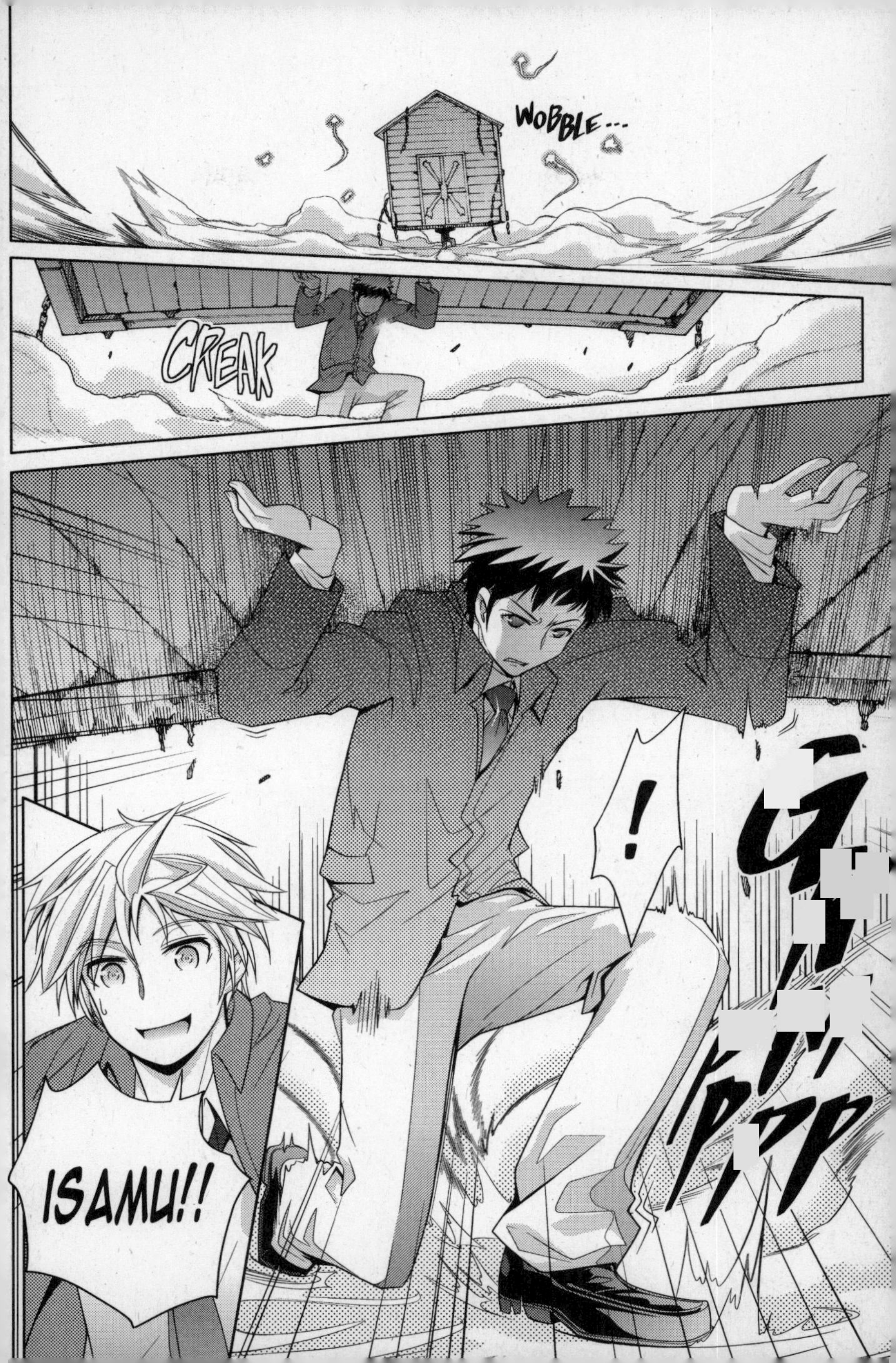
WOBBLE...
CREAK
!
ISAMU!!

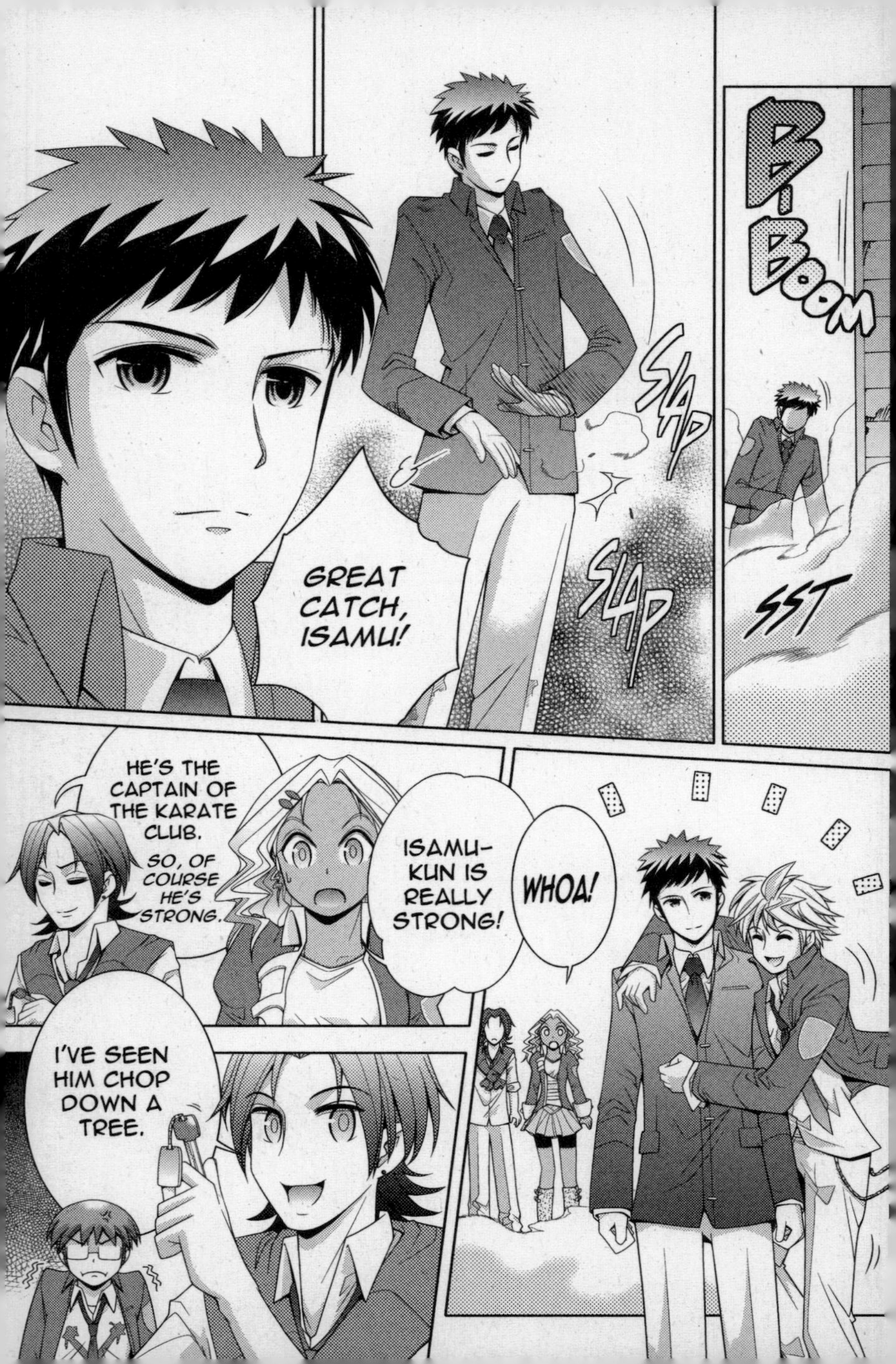
B-BOOM
SST
SLAP
SLAP
GREAT CATCH, ISAMU!
WHOA!
ISAMU-KUN IS REALLY STRONG!
HE'S THE CAPTAIN OF THE KARATE CLUB.
SO, OF COURSE HE'S STRONG.
I'VE SEEN HIM CHOP DOWN A TREE.

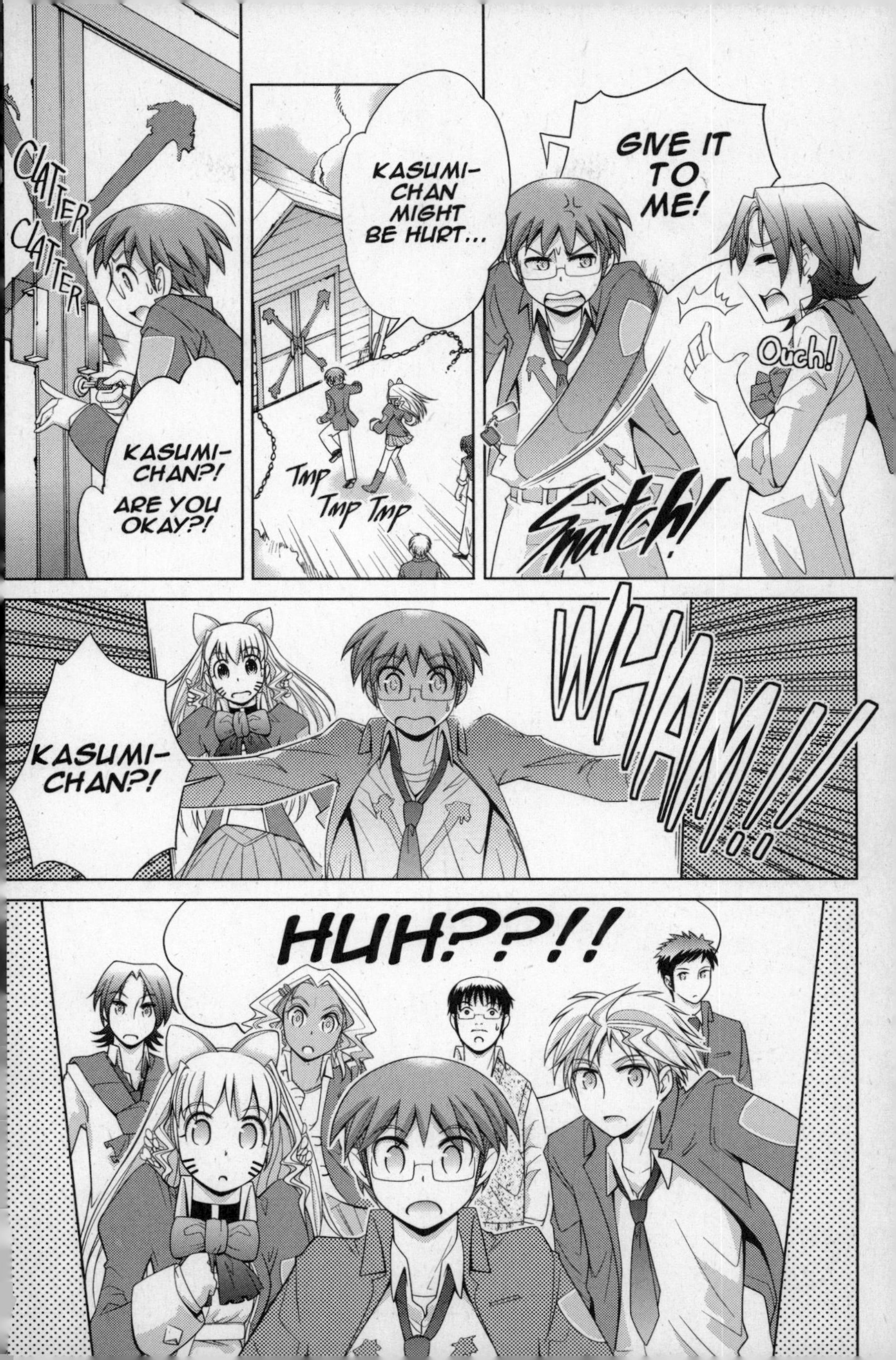
GIVE IT TO ME!
Ouch!
SNATCH!
KASUMI-CHAN MIGHT BE HURT...
Tmp Tmp Tmp
CLATTER CLATTER
KASUMI-CHAN?! ARE YOU OKAY?!
WHAM!!
KASUMI-CHAN?!
HUH??!!

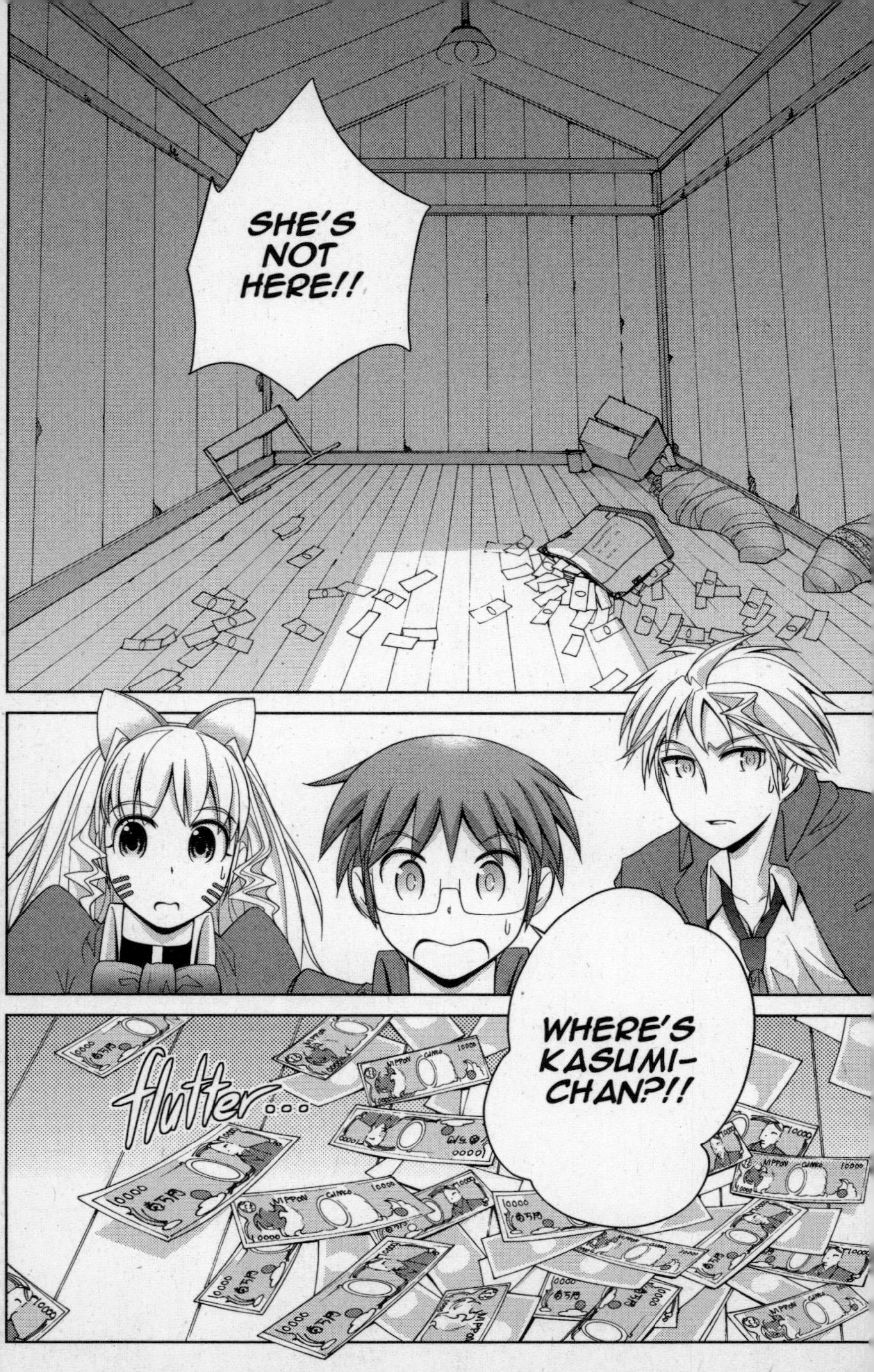
SHE'S NOT HERE!!
WHERE'S KASUMI-CHAN?!!
flutter...

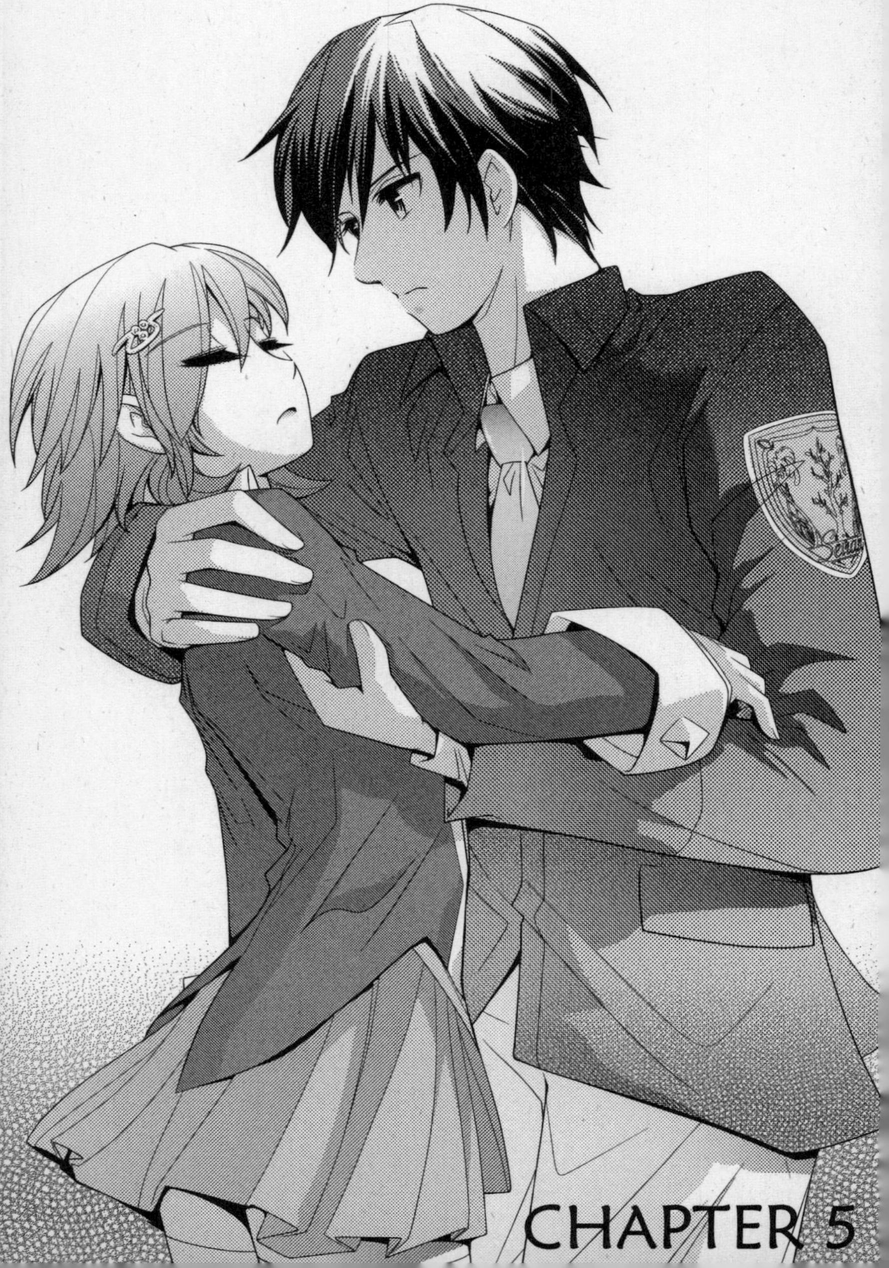

CHAPTER 5

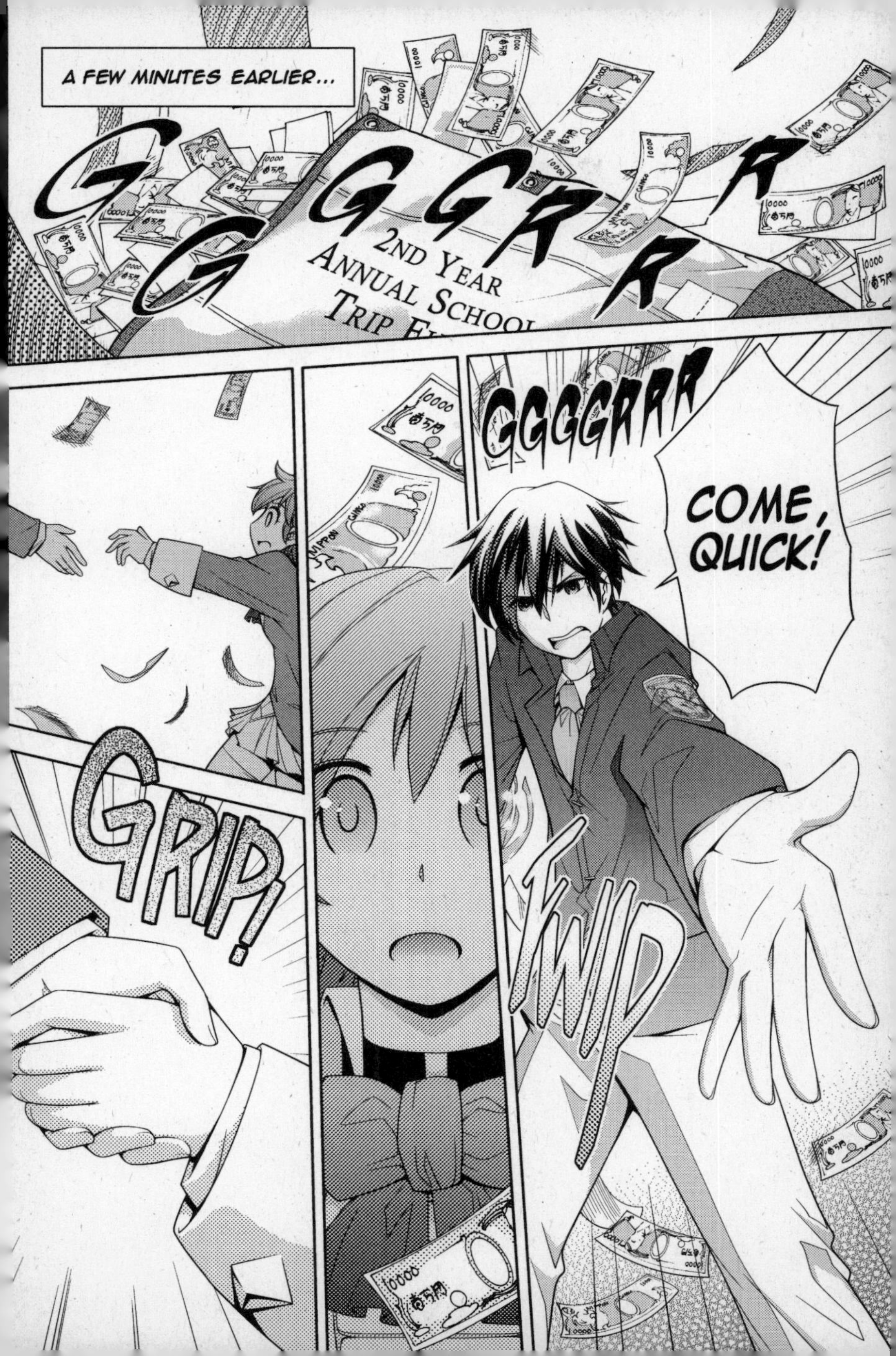
A FEW MINUTES EARLIER...
GGGGRRRR
2ND YEAR
ANNUAL SCHOOL
TRIP
GGGGRRR
COME, QUICK!
TWIP
GRIP!

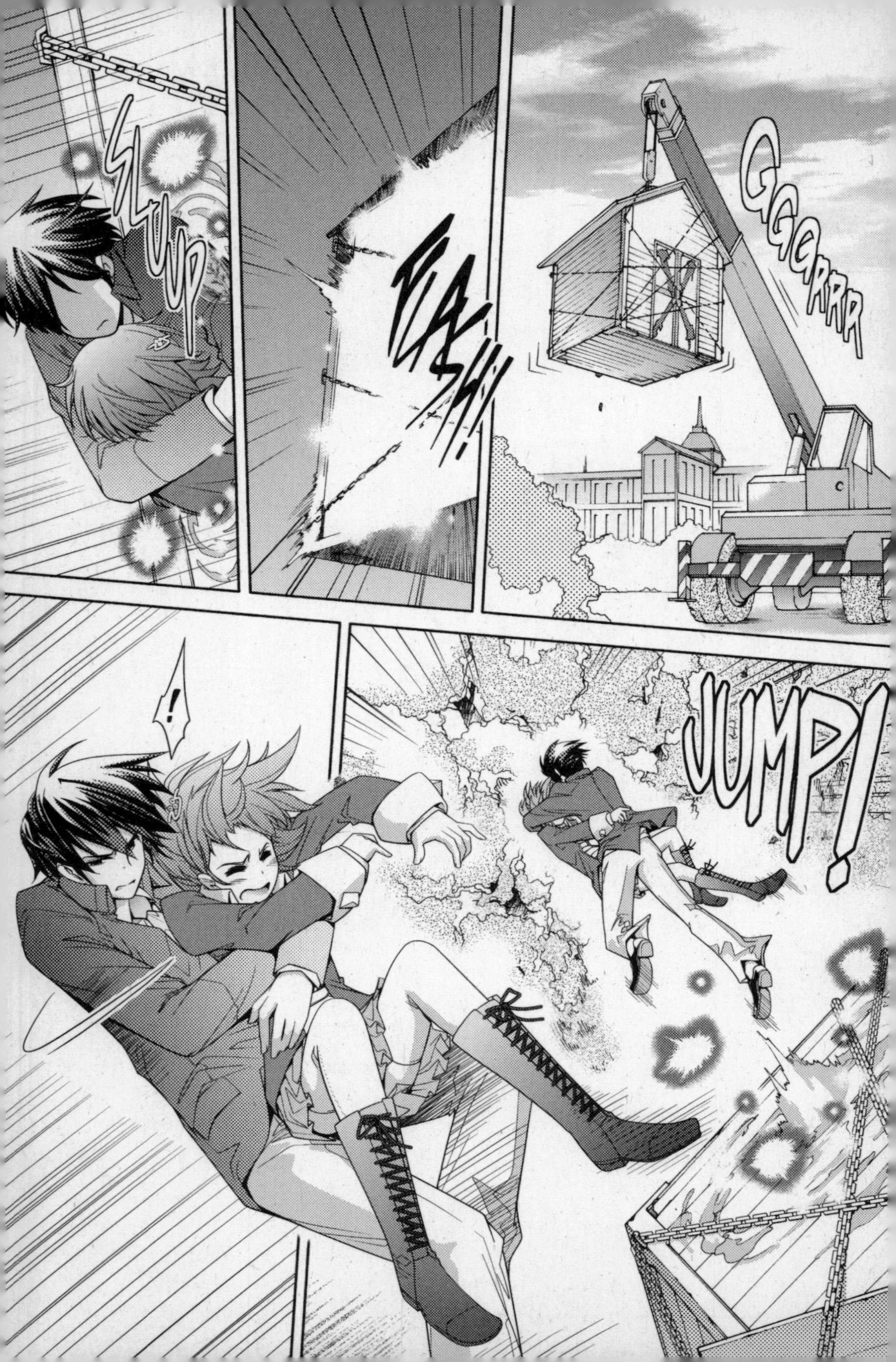
GGGRRRR
FLASH!
SLUUP
JUMP!
!

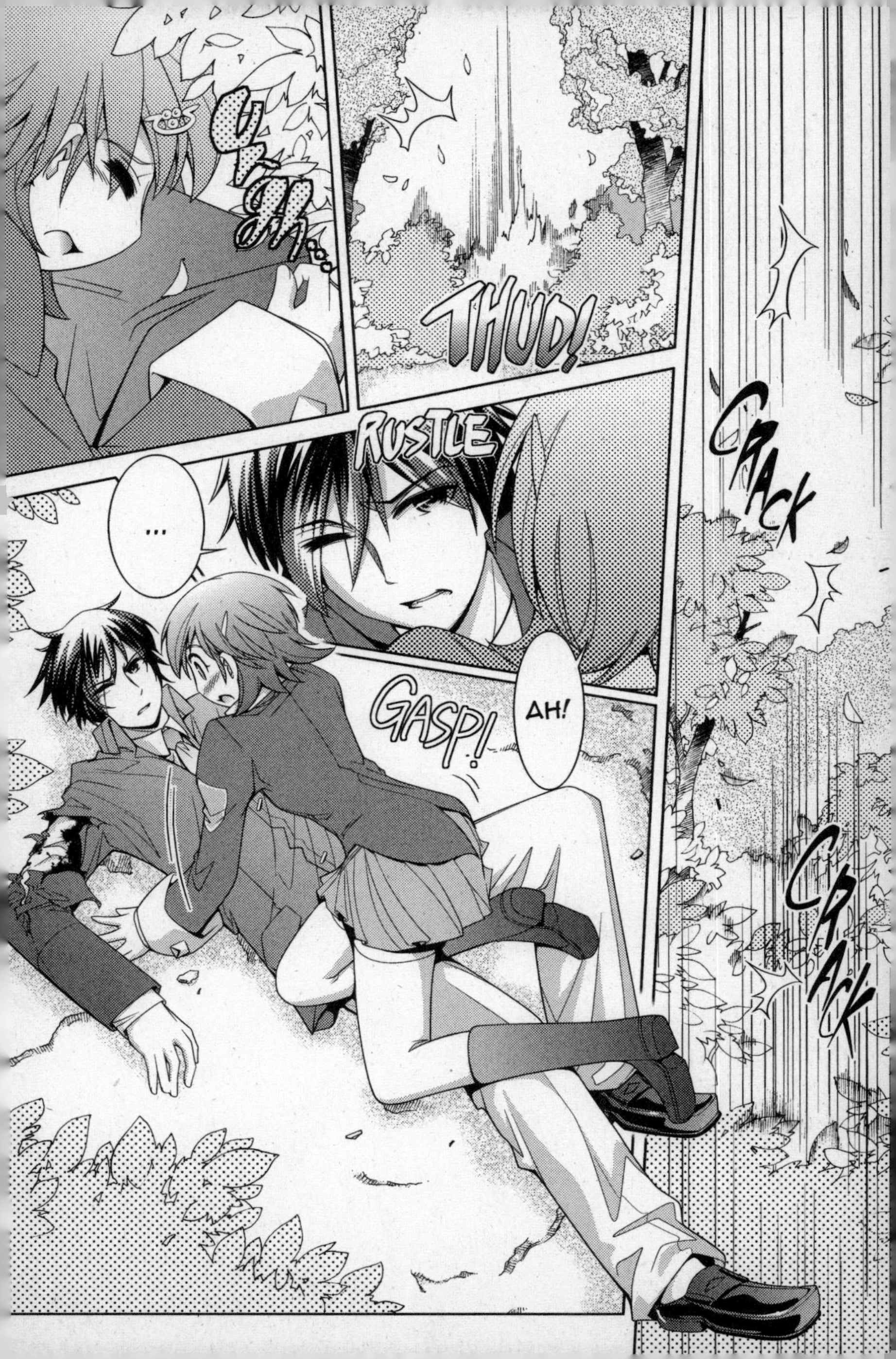
CRACK
CRACK
THUD!
UGH...
RUSTLE
...
GASP!
AH!

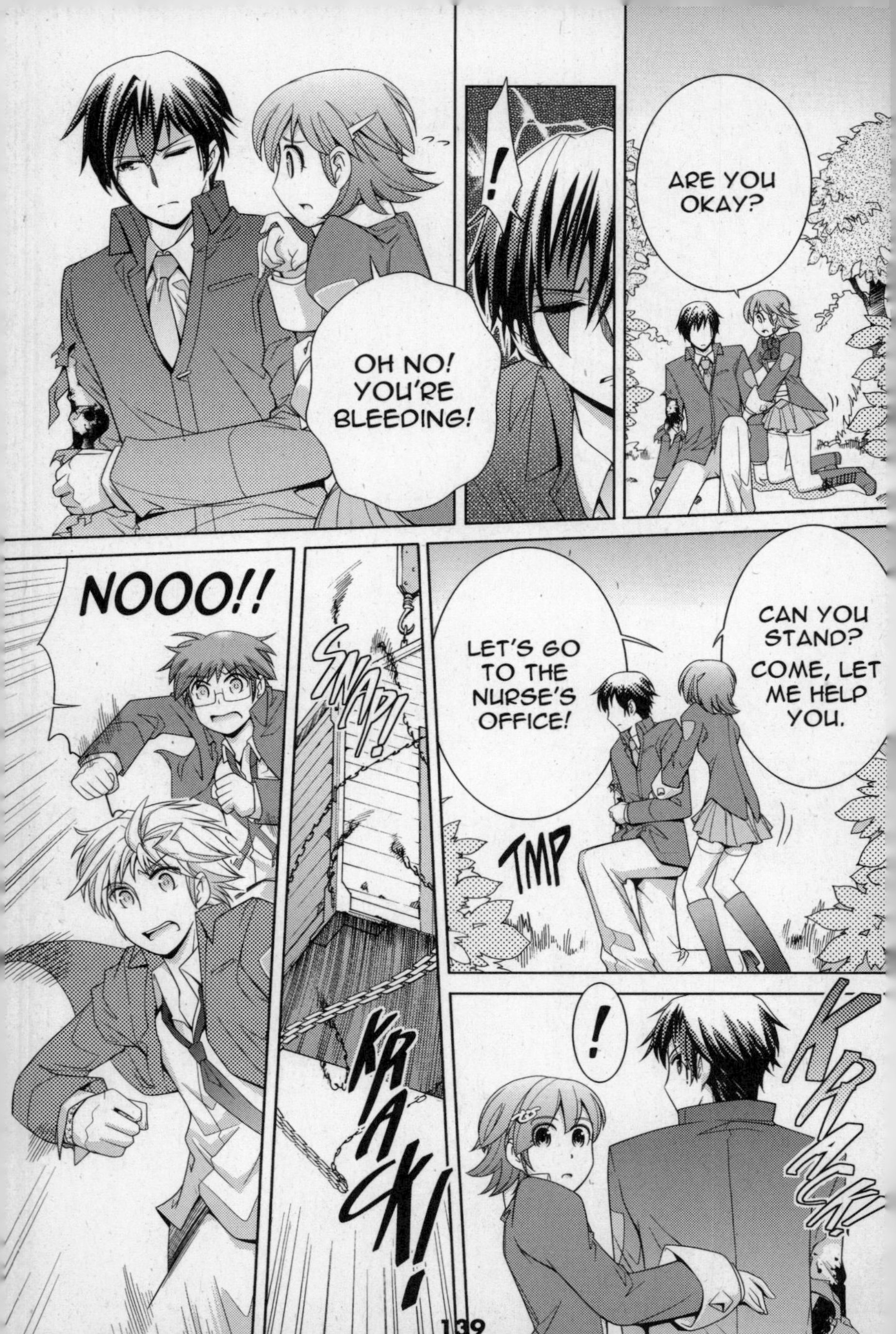
ARE YOU OKAY?
!
OH NO! YOU'RE BLEEDING!
CAN YOU STAND? COME, LET ME HELP YOU.
LET'S GO TO THE NURSE'S OFFICE!
TMP
!
KRAACK!
SNAP!
KRACK!
NOOO!!

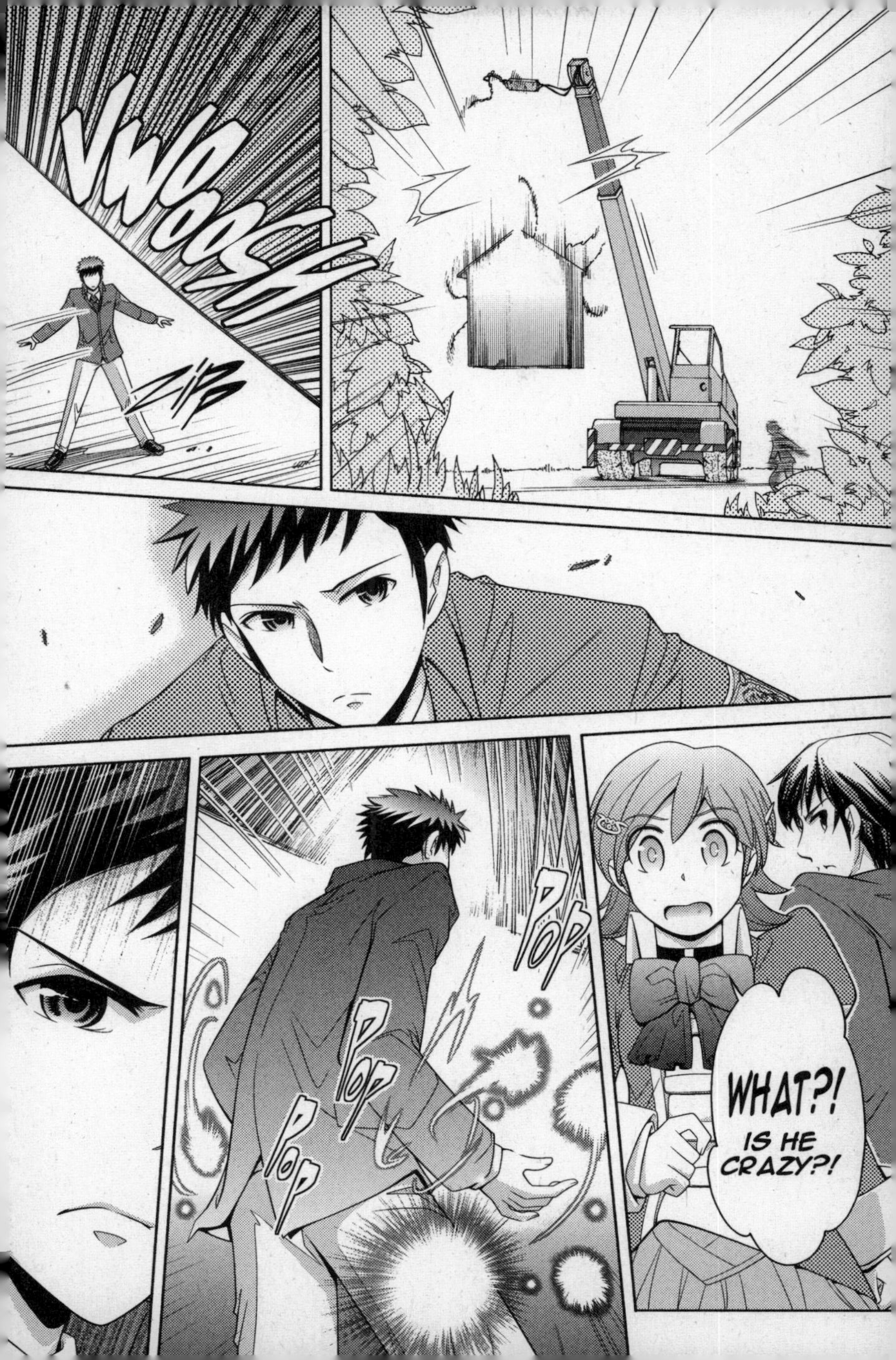
VWOOSH
ZIP
POP
WHAT?! IS HE CRAZY?!
POP
POP

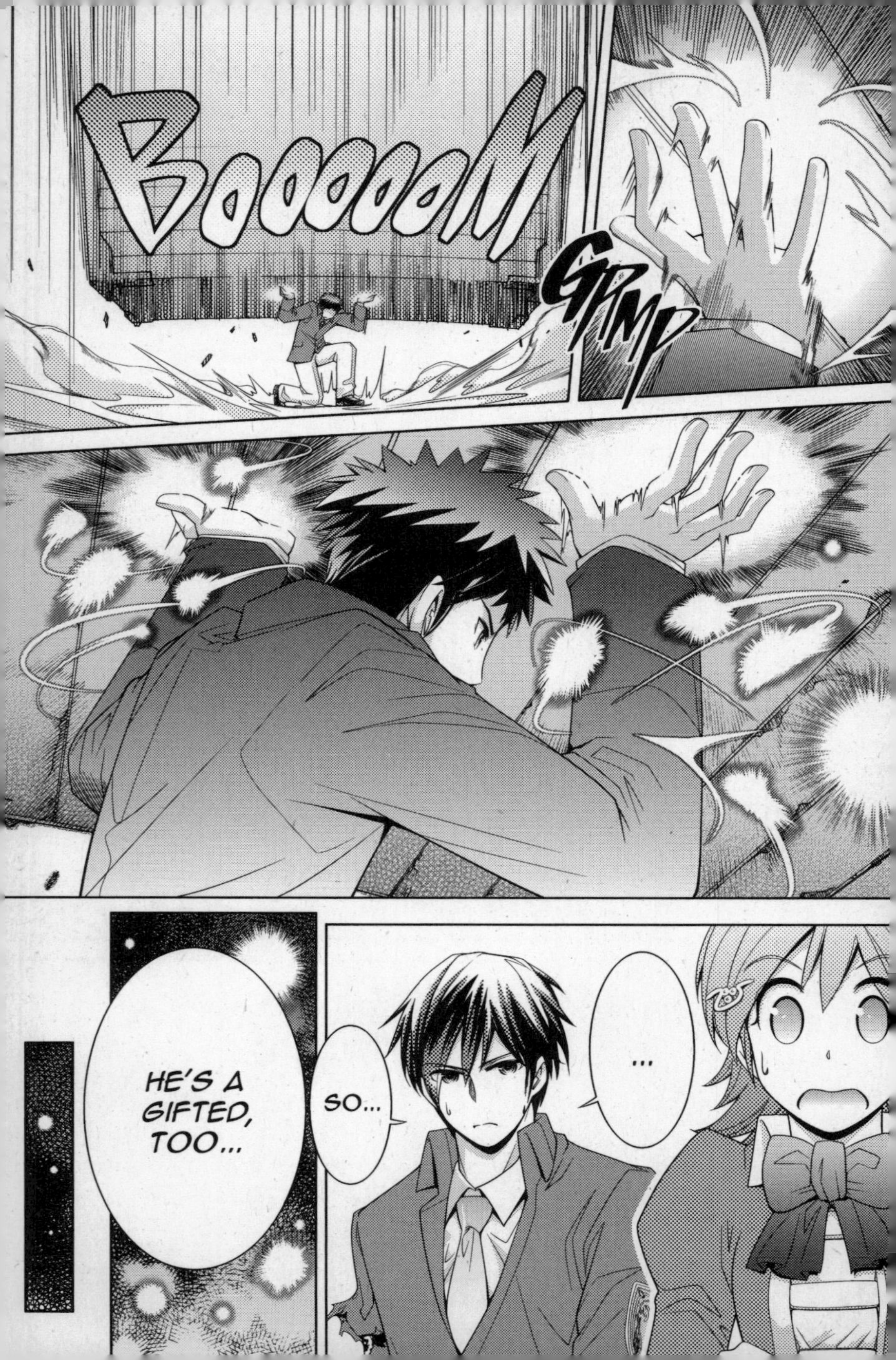
GRMP
BOOOOOM
...
SO...
HE'S A GIFTED, TOO...

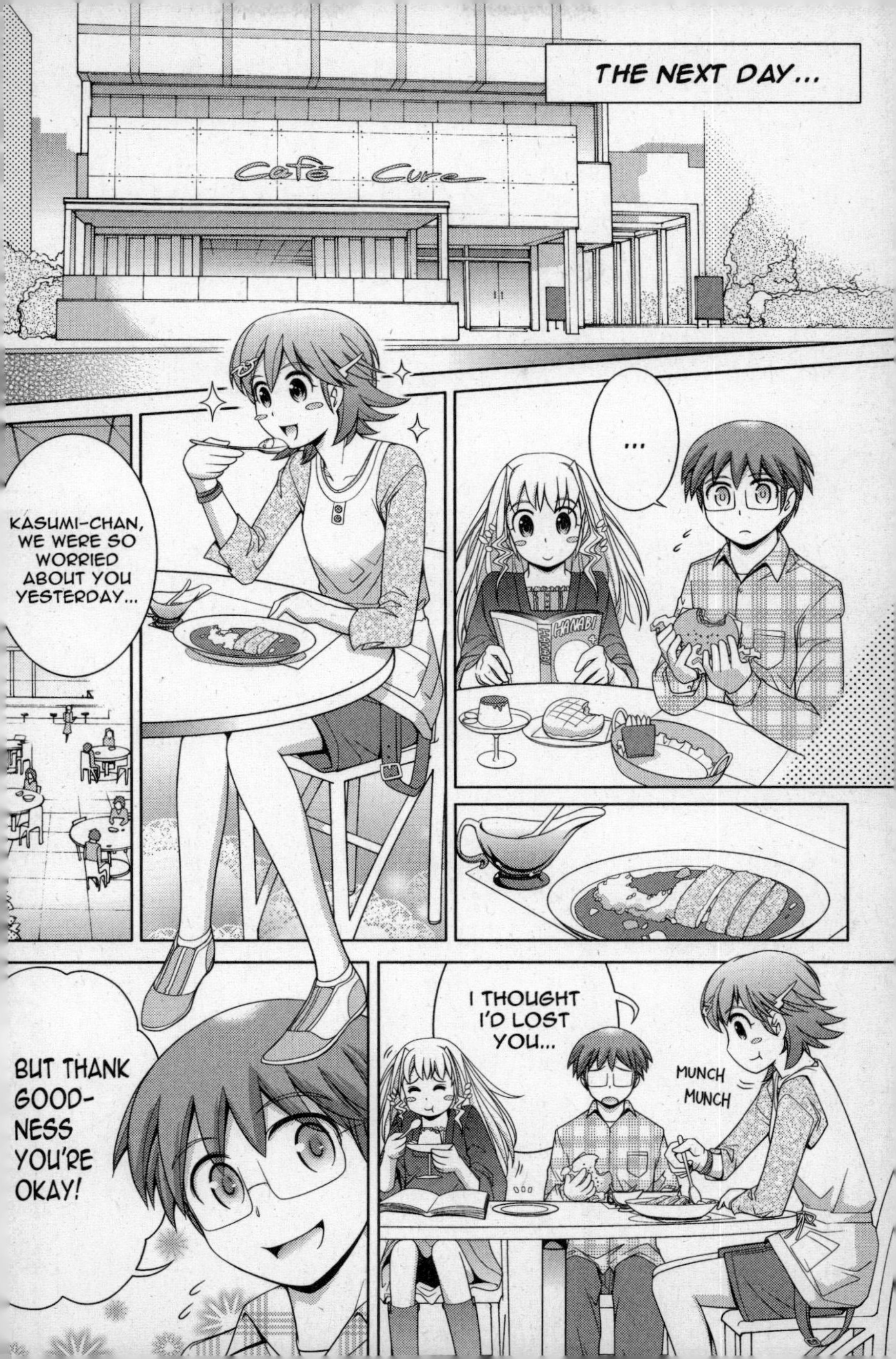
THE NEXT DAY...
Café Cure
...
KASUMI-CHAN, WE WERE SO WORRIED ABOUT YOU YESTERDAY...
I THOUGHT I'D LOST YOU...
MUNCH MUNCH
BUT THANK GOODNESS YOU'RE OKAY!

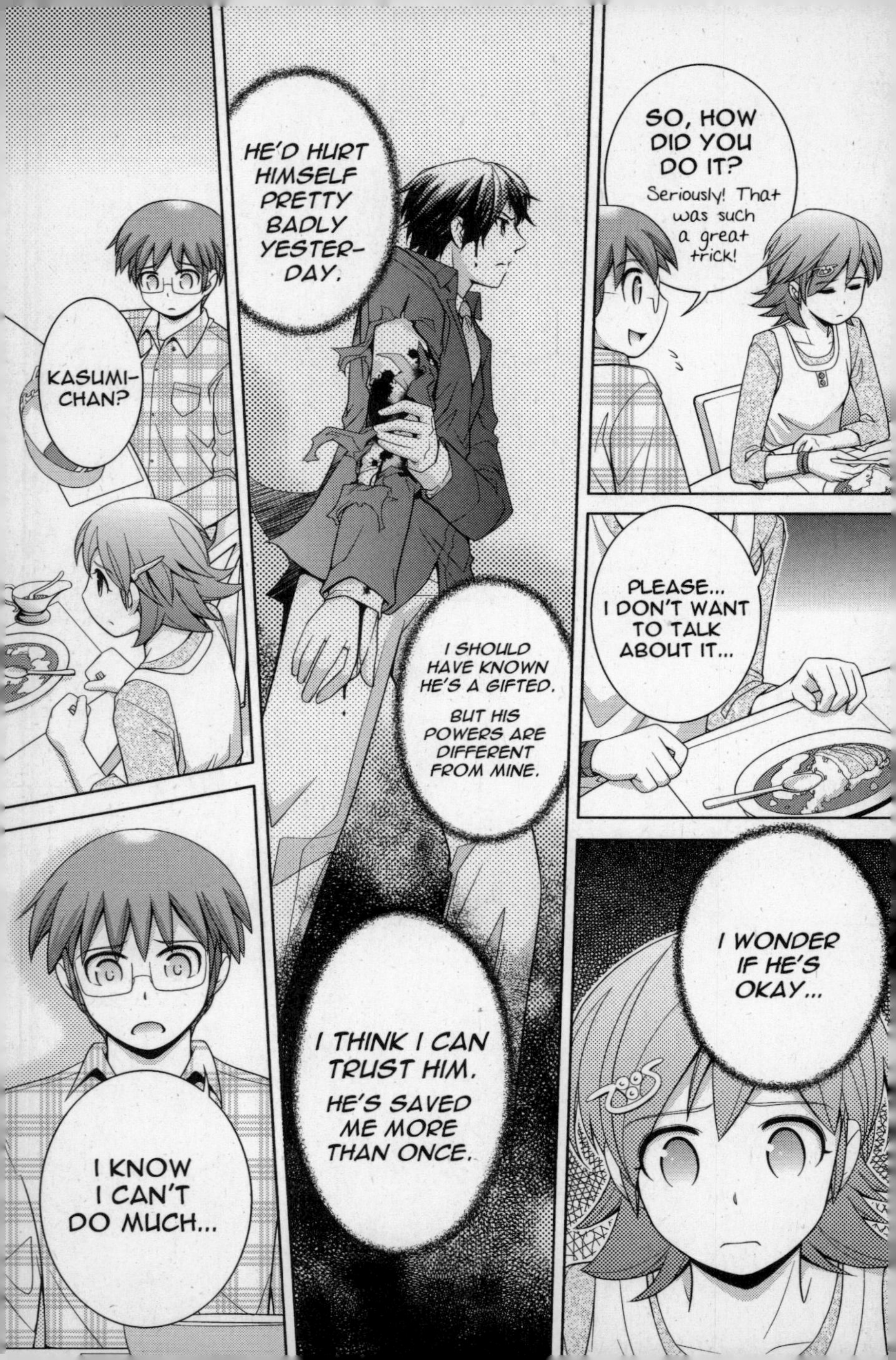
SO, HOW DID YOU DO IT?
Seriously! That was such a great trick!
PLEASE... I DON'T WANT TO TALK ABOUT IT...
I WONDER IF HE'S OKAY...
HE'D HURT HIMSELF PRETTY BADLY YESTER-DAY.
I SHOULD HAVE KNOWN HE'S A GIFTED.
BUT HIS POWERS ARE DIFFERENT FROM MINE.
I THINK I CAN TRUST HIM.
HE'S SAVED ME MORE THAN ONCE.
KASUMI-CHAN?
I KNOW I CAN'T DO MUCH...

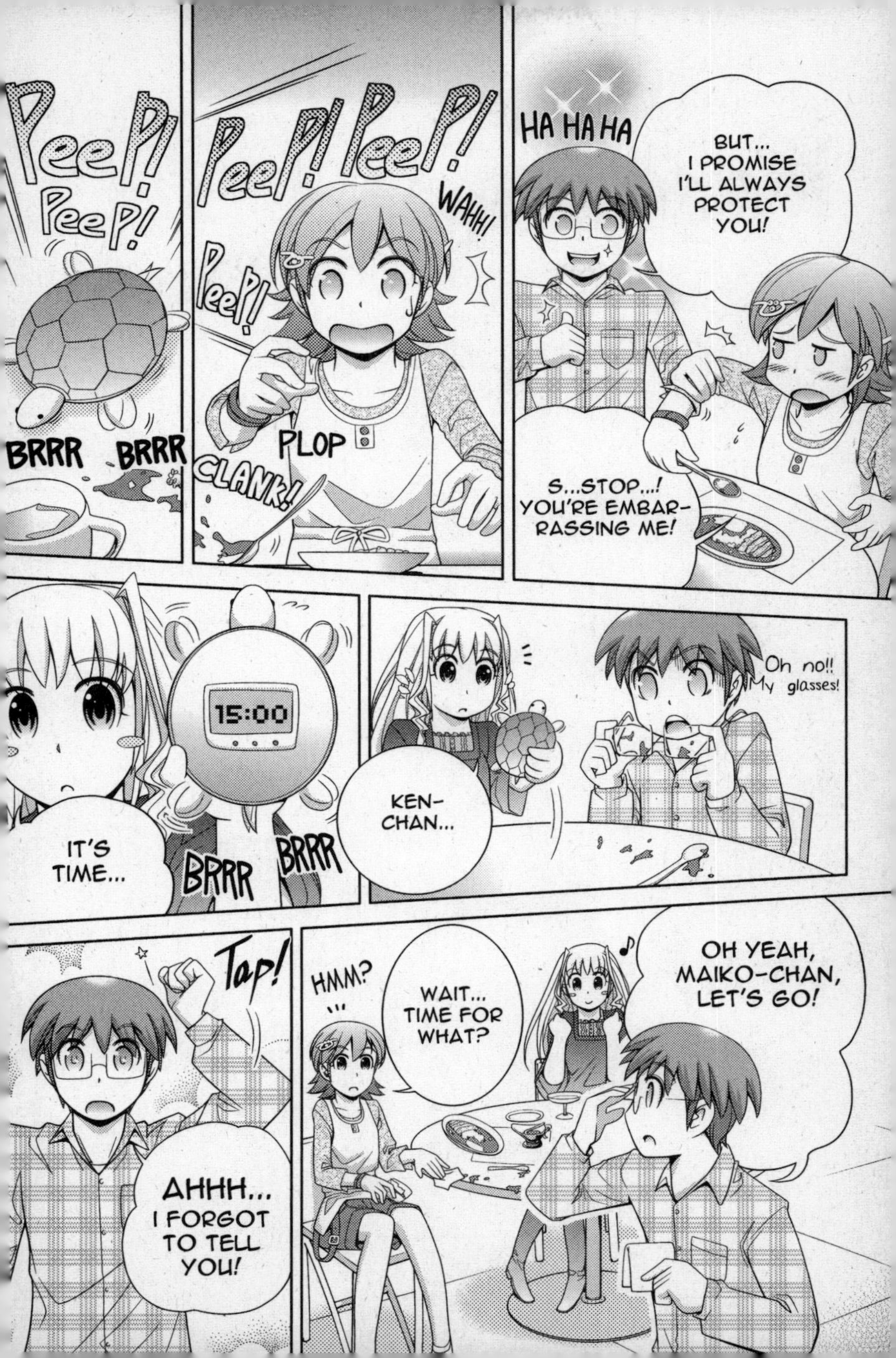
HA HA HA
BUT... I PROMISE I'LL ALWAYS PROTECT YOU!
S...STOP...! YOU'RE EMBARRASSING ME!
PEEP! PEEP!
WAHH!
PEEP!
PLOP
CLANK!
PEEP! PEEP!
BRRR
BRRR
Oh no!! My glasses!
KEN-CHAN...
15:00
IT'S TIME...
BRRR
BRRR
OH YEAH, MAIKO-CHAN, LET'S GO!
WAIT... TIME FOR WHAT?
HMM?
Tap!
AHHH... I FORGOT TO TELL YOU!

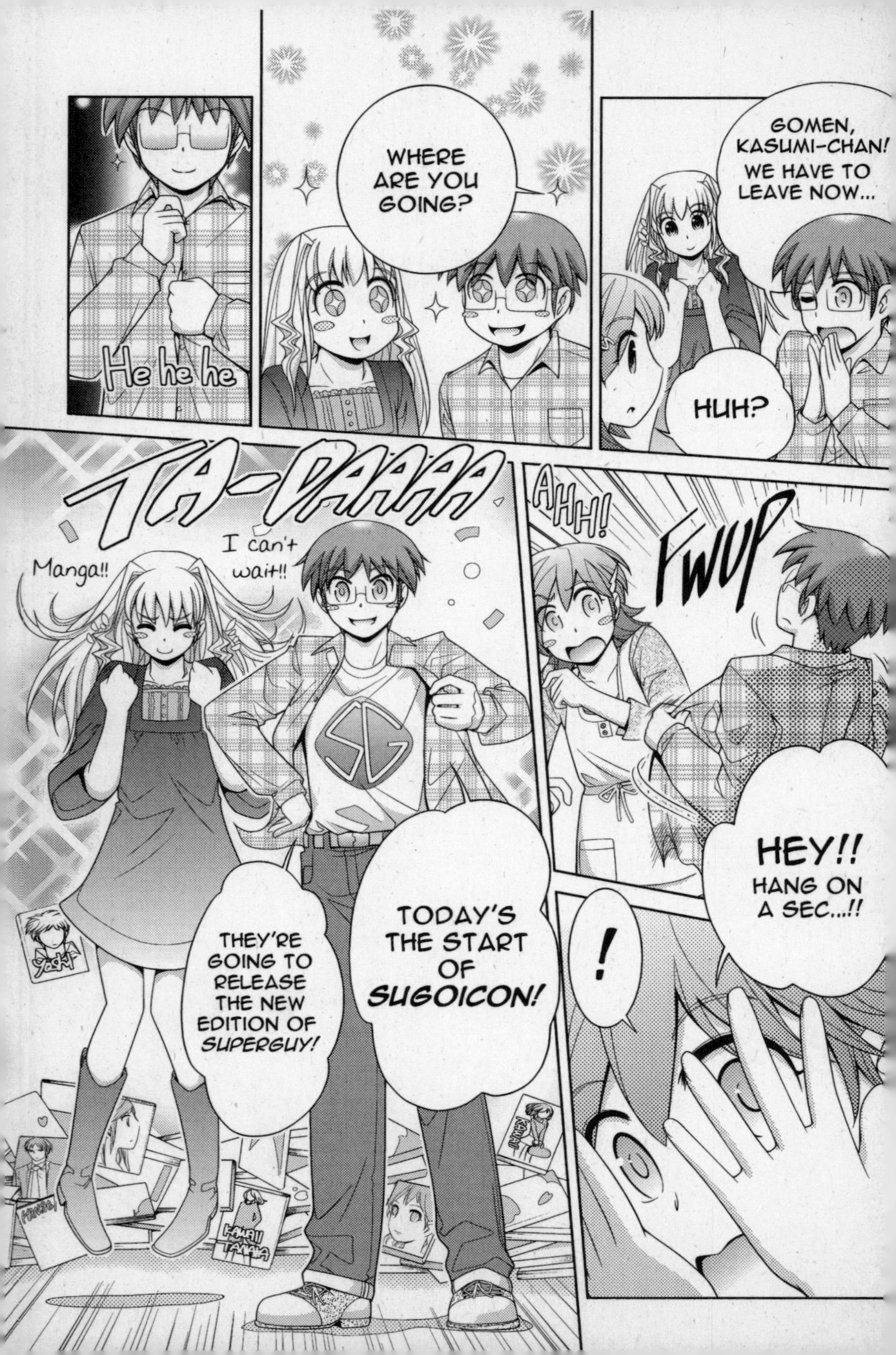
GOMEN, KASUMI-CHAN! WE HAVE TO LEAVE NOW...
HUH?
WHERE ARE YOU GOING?
He he he
AHHH!
FWUP
HEY!! HANG ON A SEC...!!
!
TA-DAAAA
I can't wait!!
Manga!!
TODAY'S THE START OF *SUGOICON*!
THEY'RE GOING TO RELEASE THE NEW EDITION OF *SUPERGUY*!
KAWAII TANAKA

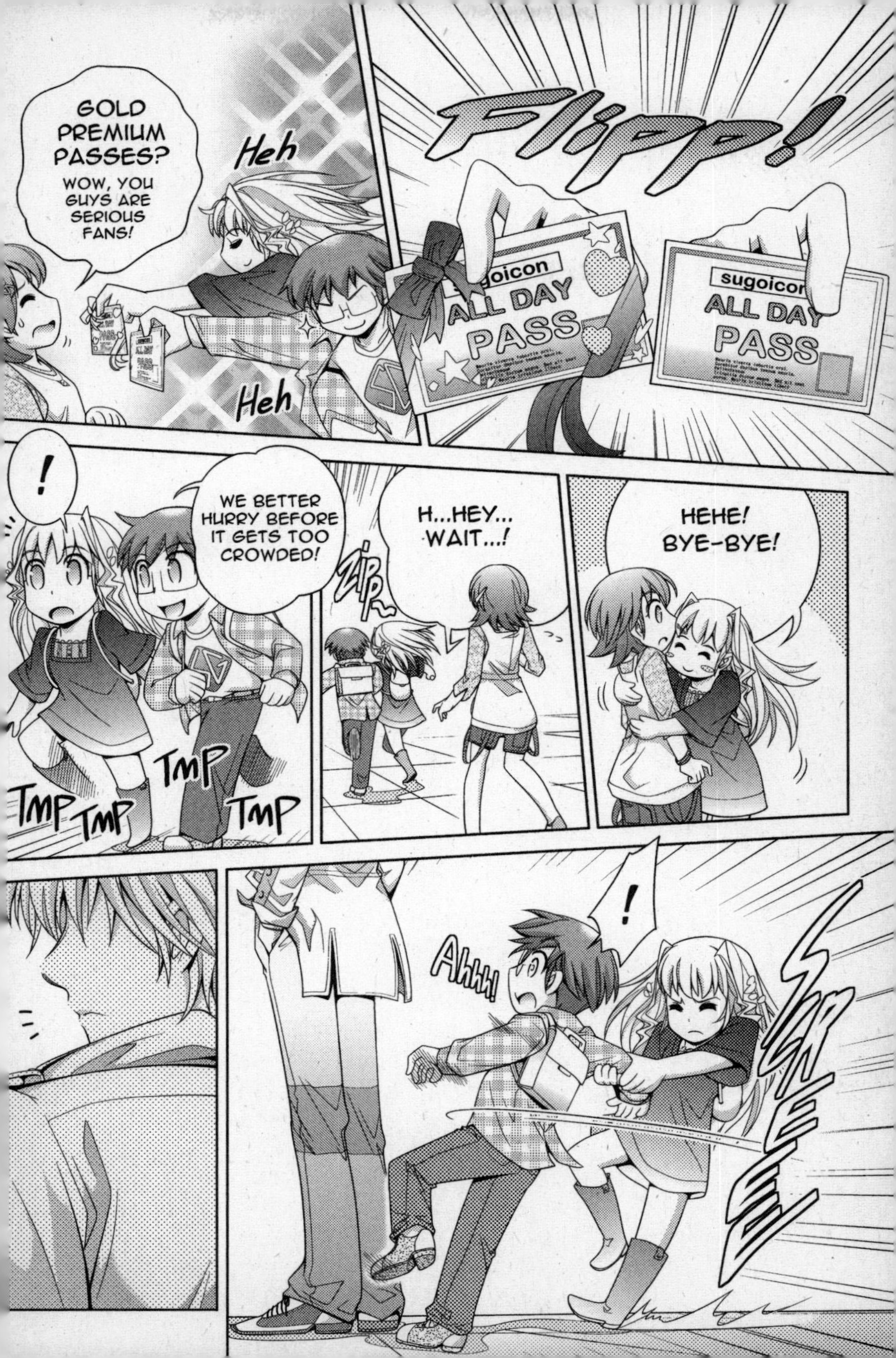
Flipp!
sugoicon
ALL DAY
PASS
sugoicon
ALL DAY
PASS
GOLD PREMIUM PASSES?
WOW, YOU GUYS ARE SERIOUS FANS!
Heh
Heh
HEHE! BYE-BYE!
H...HEY... WAIT...!
Zipp~
WE BETTER HURRY BEFORE IT GETS TOO CROWDED!
!
TMP
TMP
TMP
TMP
!
Ahhh!

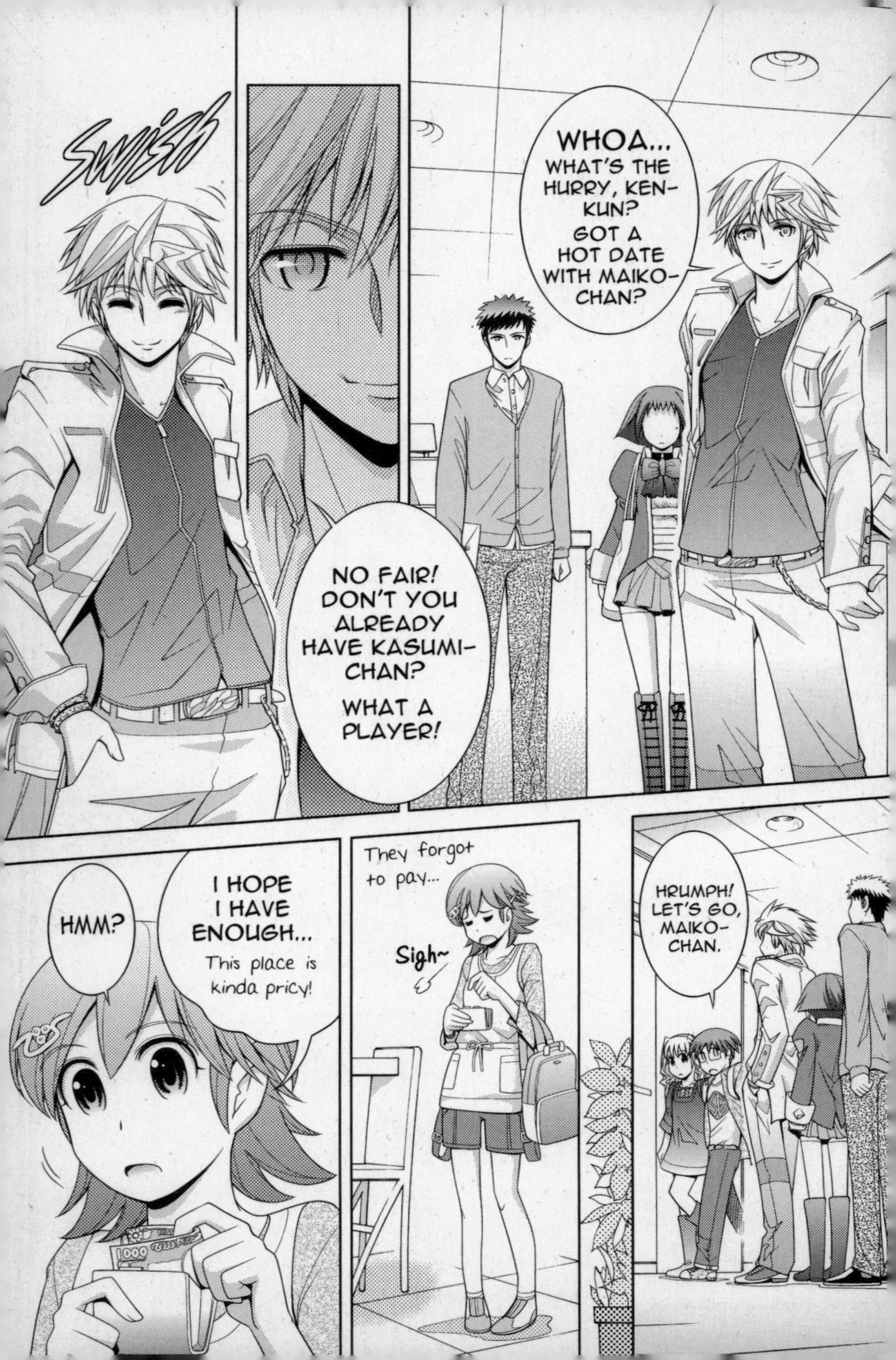
WHOA... WHAT'S THE HURRY, KEN-KUN? GOT A HOT DATE WITH MAIKO-CHAN?
NO FAIR! DON'T YOU ALREADY HAVE KASUMI-CHAN? WHAT A PLAYER!
Swish
HRUMPH! LET'S GO, MAIKO-CHAN.
They forgot to pay...
Sigh~
I HOPE I HAVE ENOUGH...
This place is kinda pricy!
HMM?

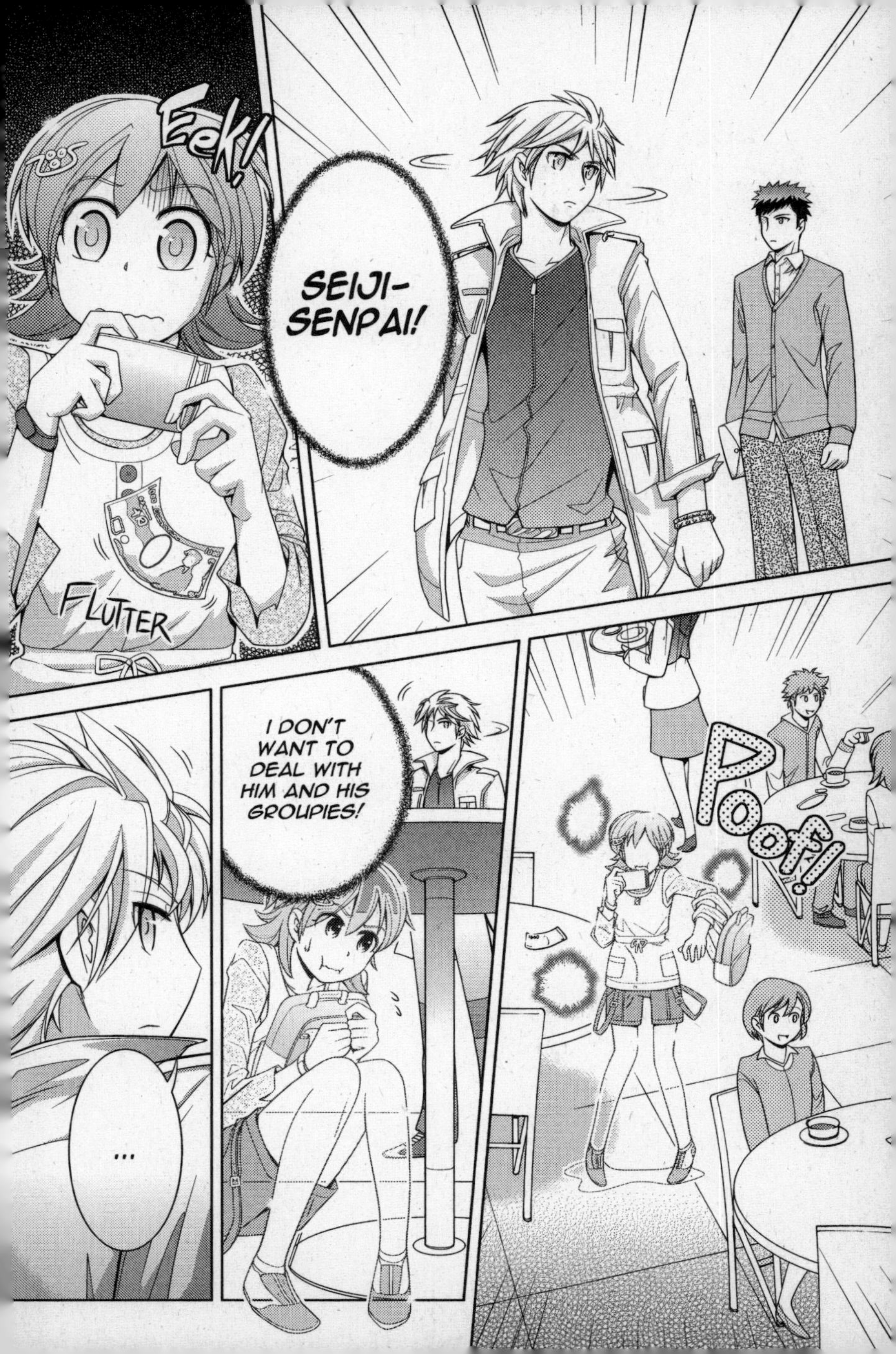
SEIJI-SENPAI!
Eek!
FLUTTER
Poof!
I DON'T WANT TO DEAL WITH HIM AND HIS GROUPIES!
...

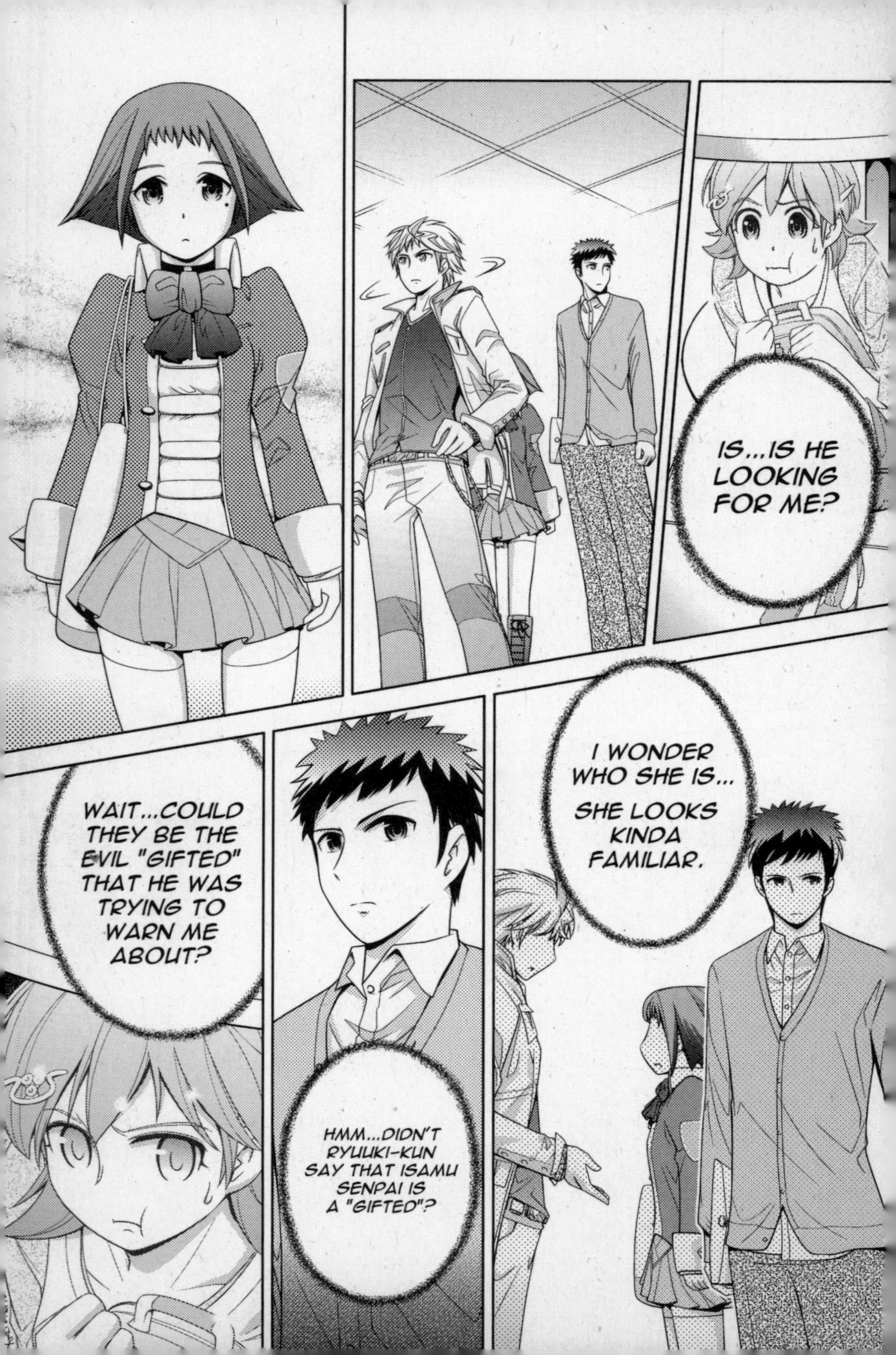
IS...IS HE LOOKING FOR ME?
I WONDER WHO SHE IS...
SHE LOOKS KINDA FAMILIAR.
HMM...DIDN'T RYUUKI-KUN SAY THAT ISAMU SENPAI IS A "GIFTED"?
WAIT...COULD THEY BE THE EVIL "GIFTED" THAT HE WAS TRYING TO WARN ME ABOUT?

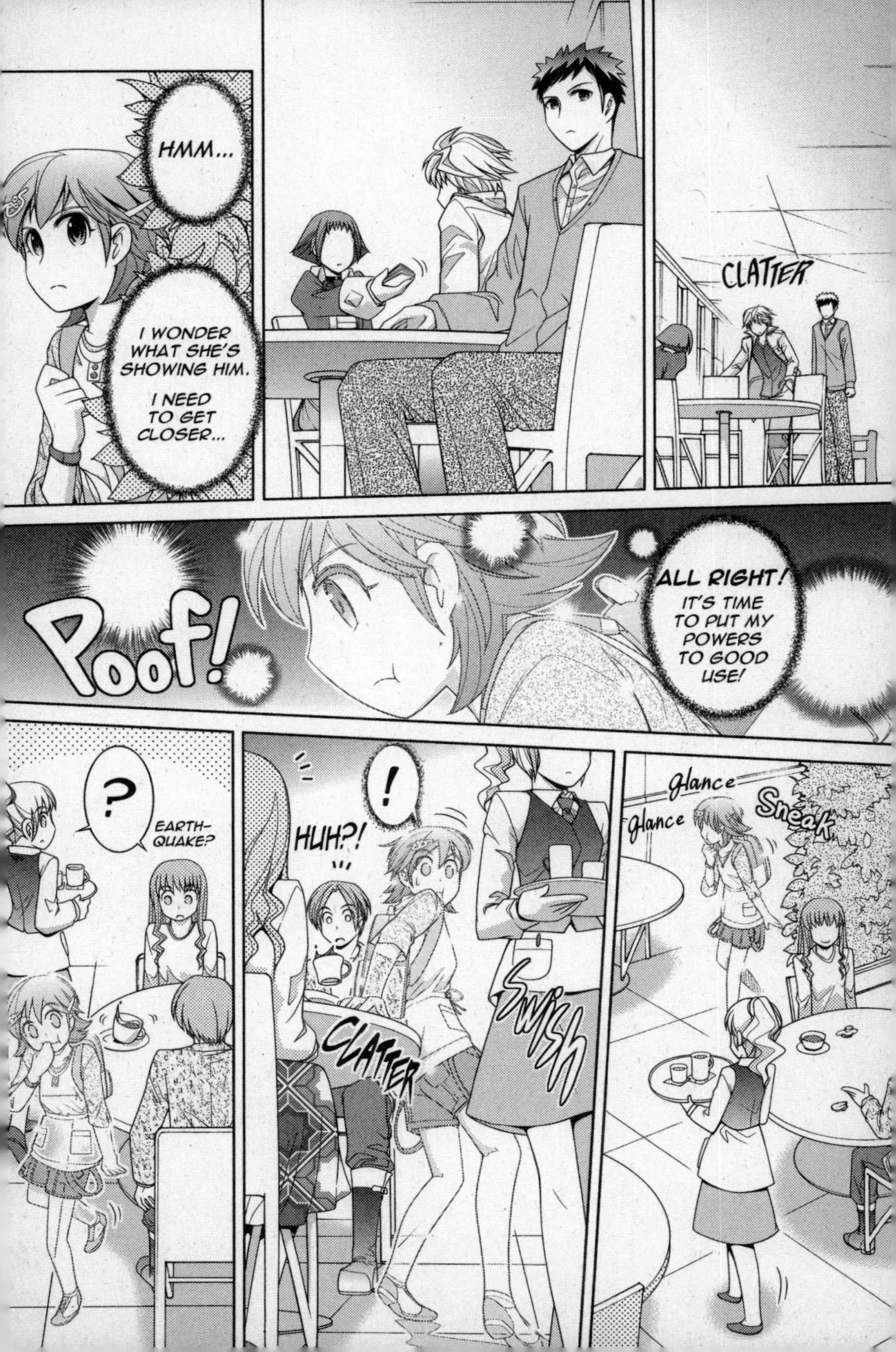
CLATTER
HMM...
I WONDER WHAT SHE'S SHOWING HIM.
I NEED TO GET CLOSER...
ALL RIGHT! IT'S TIME TO PUT MY POWERS TO GOOD USE!
Poof!
Glance
Sneak
Glance
!
HUH?!
Swish
CLATTER
?
EARTH-QUAKE?

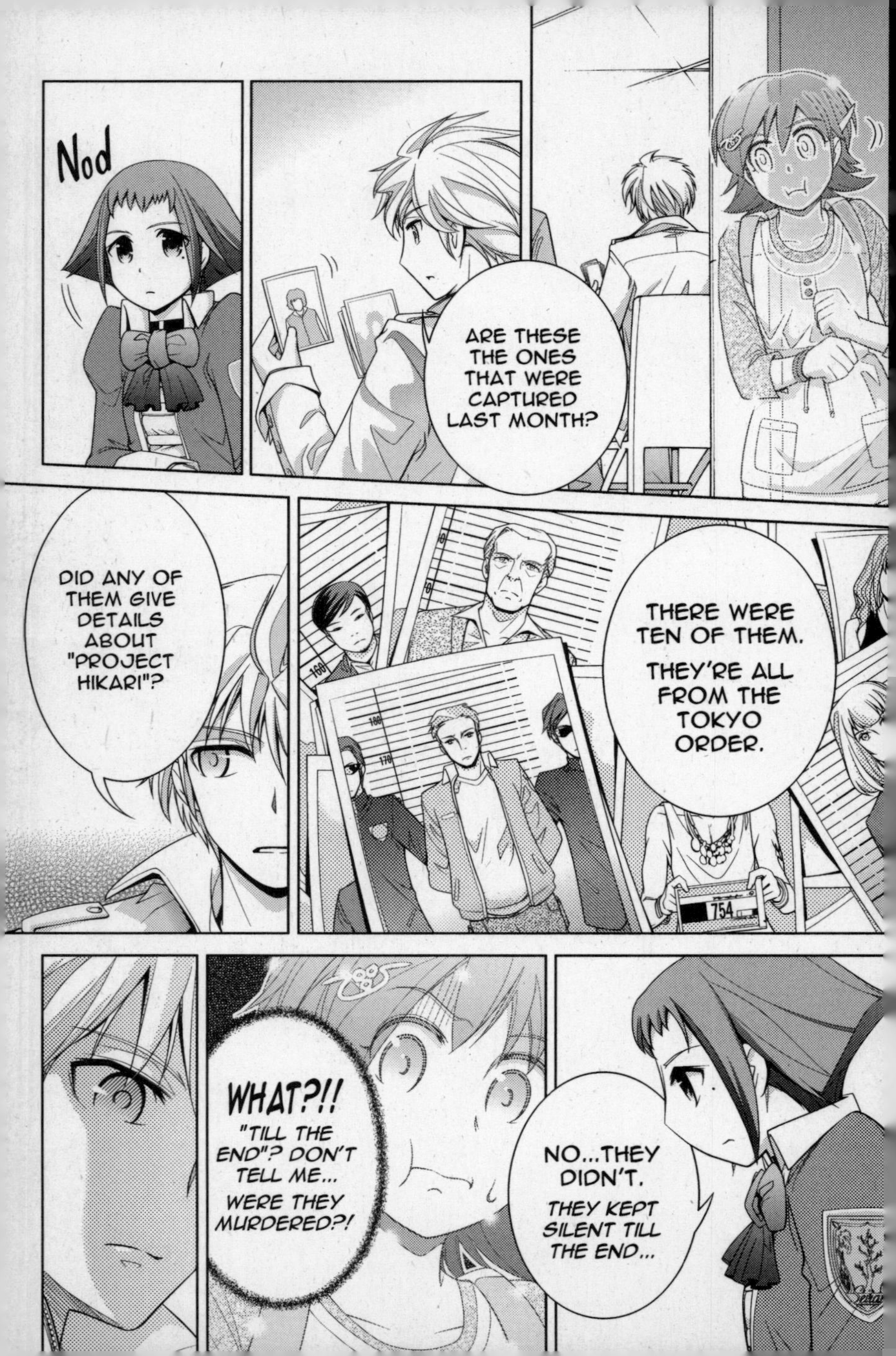
ARE THESE THE ONES THAT WERE CAPTURED LAST MONTH?
Nod
THERE WERE TEN OF THEM.
THEY'RE ALL FROM THE TOKYO ORDER.
754
DID ANY OF THEM GIVE DETAILS ABOUT "PROJECT HIKARI"?
NO...THEY DIDN'T.
THEY KEPT SILENT TILL THE END...
WHAT?!!
"TILL THE END"? DON'T TELL ME...
WERE THEY MURDERED?!

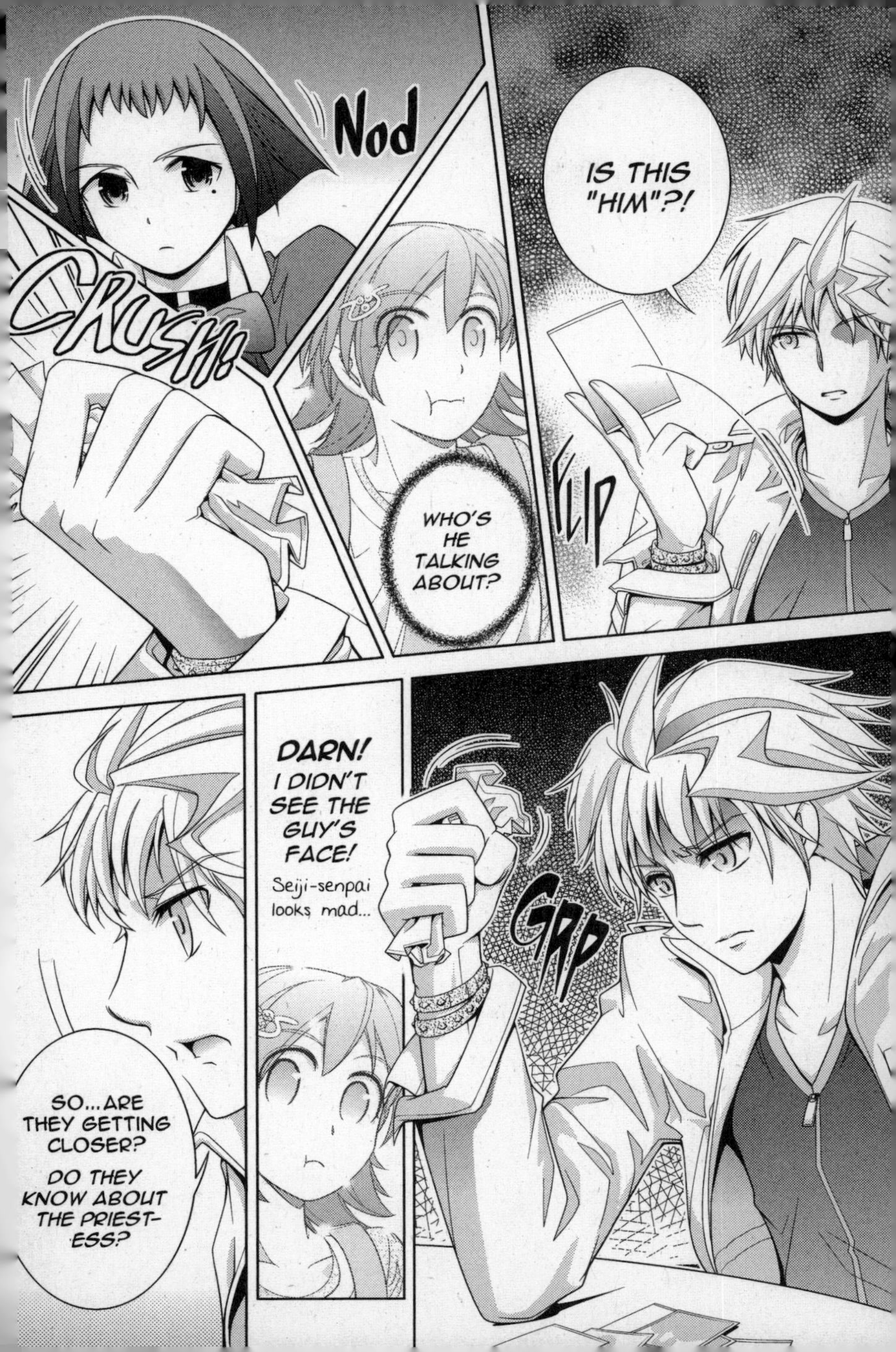
IS THIS "HIM"?!
FLIP
WHO'S HE TALKING ABOUT?
Nod
CRUSH!
GRIP
DARN! I DIDN'T SEE THE GUY'S FACE!
Seiji-senpai looks mad...
SO...ARE THEY GETTING CLOSER?
DO THEY KNOW ABOUT THE PRIEST-ESS?

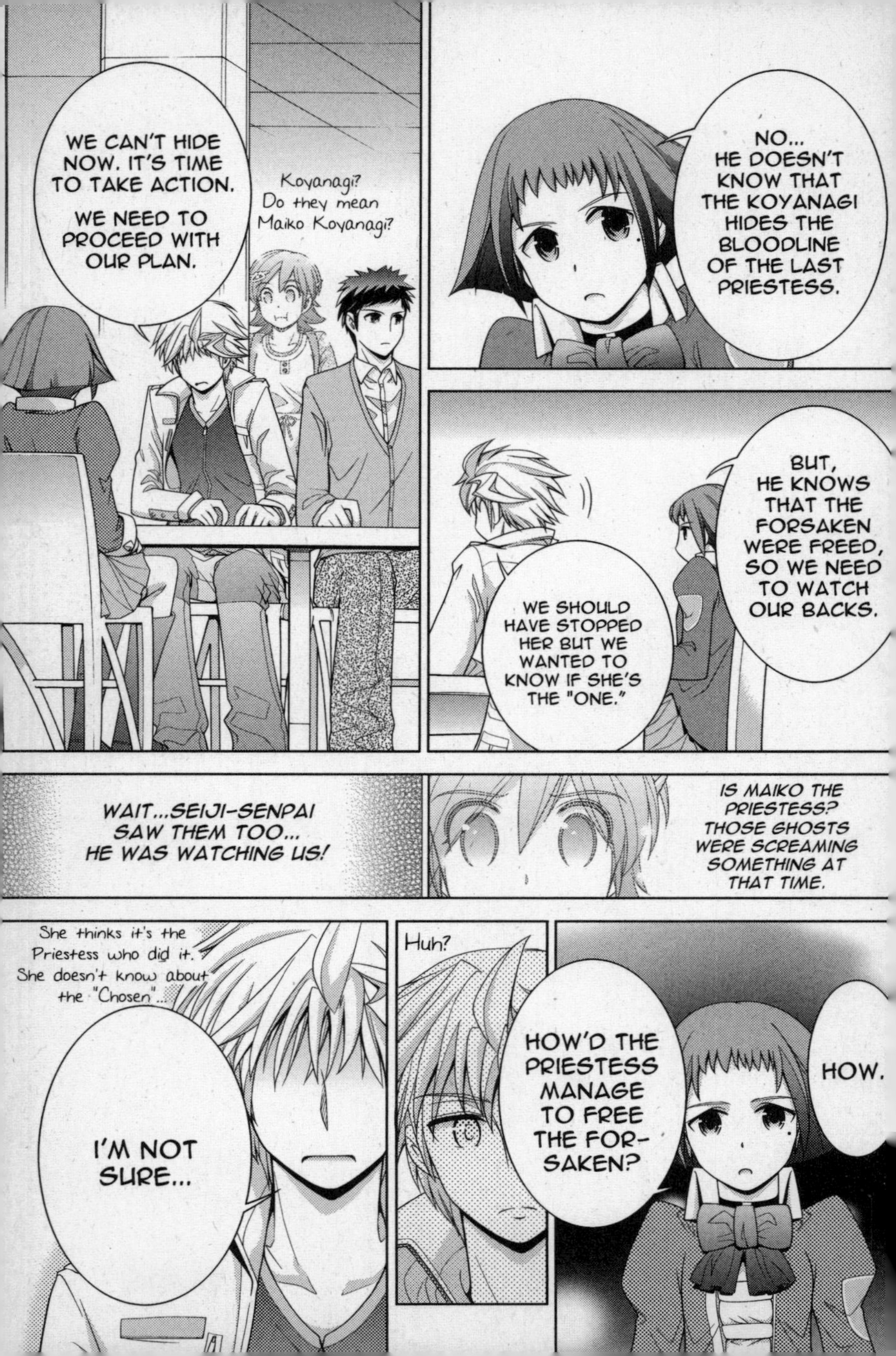
NO... HE DOESN'T KNOW THAT THE KOYANAGI HIDES THE BLOODLINE OF THE LAST PRIESTESS.
BUT, HE KNOWS THAT THE FORSAKEN WERE FREED, SO WE NEED TO WATCH OUR BACKS.
WE SHOULD HAVE STOPPED HER BUT WE WANTED TO KNOW IF SHE'S THE "ONE."
WE CAN'T HIDE NOW. IT'S TIME TO TAKE ACTION.
WE NEED TO PROCEED WITH OUR PLAN.
Koyanagi? Do they mean Maiko Koyanagi?
IS MAIKO THE PRIESTESS? THOSE GHOSTS WERE SCREAMING SOMETHING AT THAT TIME.
WAIT...SEIJI-SENPAI SAW THEM TOO... HE WAS WATCHING US!
HOW.
HOW'D THE PRIESTESS MANAGE TO FREE THE FOR-SAKEN?
Huh?
She thinks it's the Priestess who did it. She doesn't know about the "Chosen"...
I'M NOT SURE...

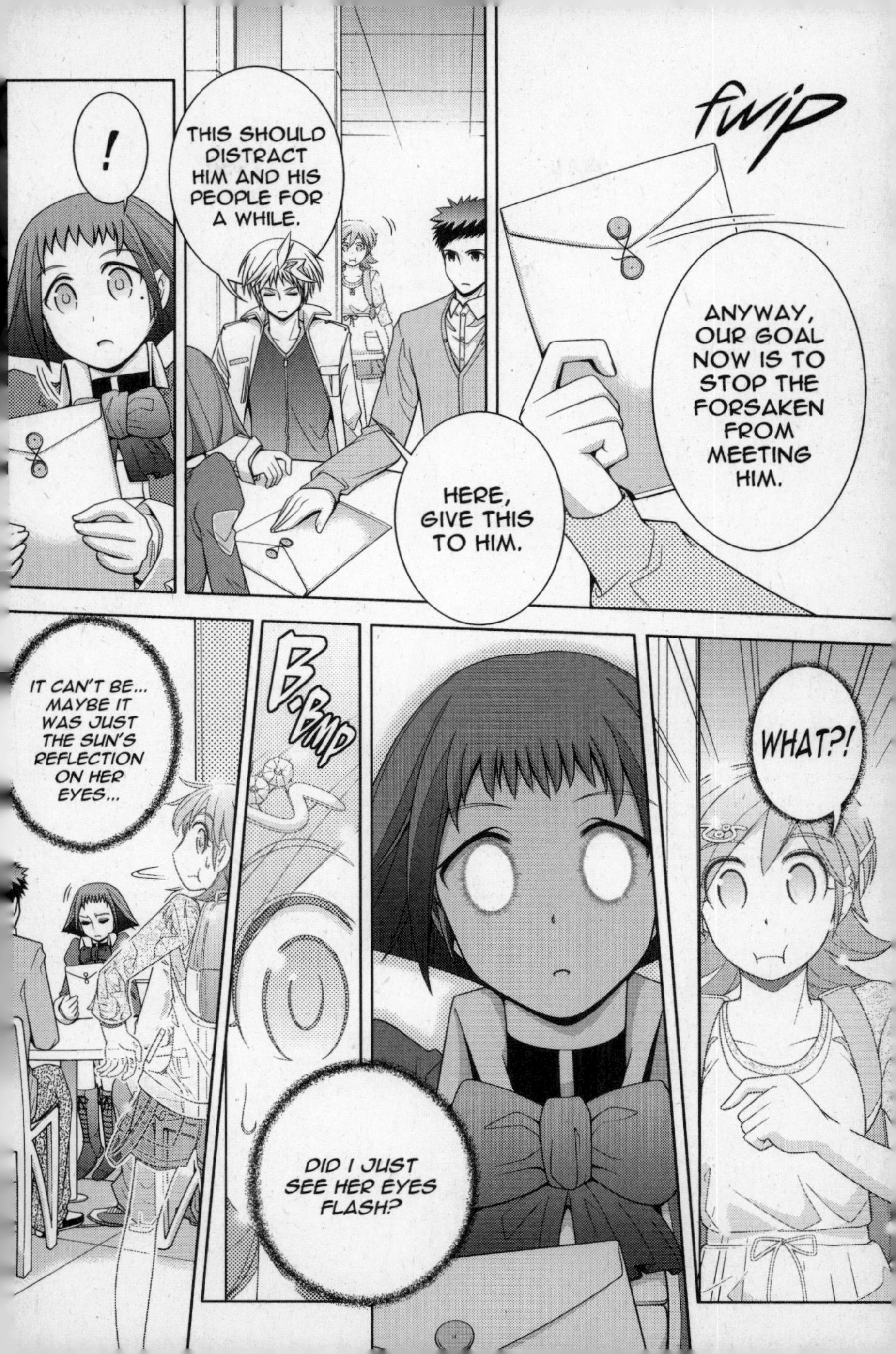
fwip
ANYWAY, OUR GOAL NOW IS TO STOP THE FORSAKEN FROM MEETING HIM.
HERE, GIVE THIS TO HIM.
THIS SHOULD DISTRACT HIM AND HIS PEOPLE FOR A WHILE.
!
WHAT?!
DID I JUST SEE HER EYES FLASH?
B-BMP
IT CAN'T BE... MAYBE IT WAS JUST THE SUN'S REFLECTION ON HER EYES...

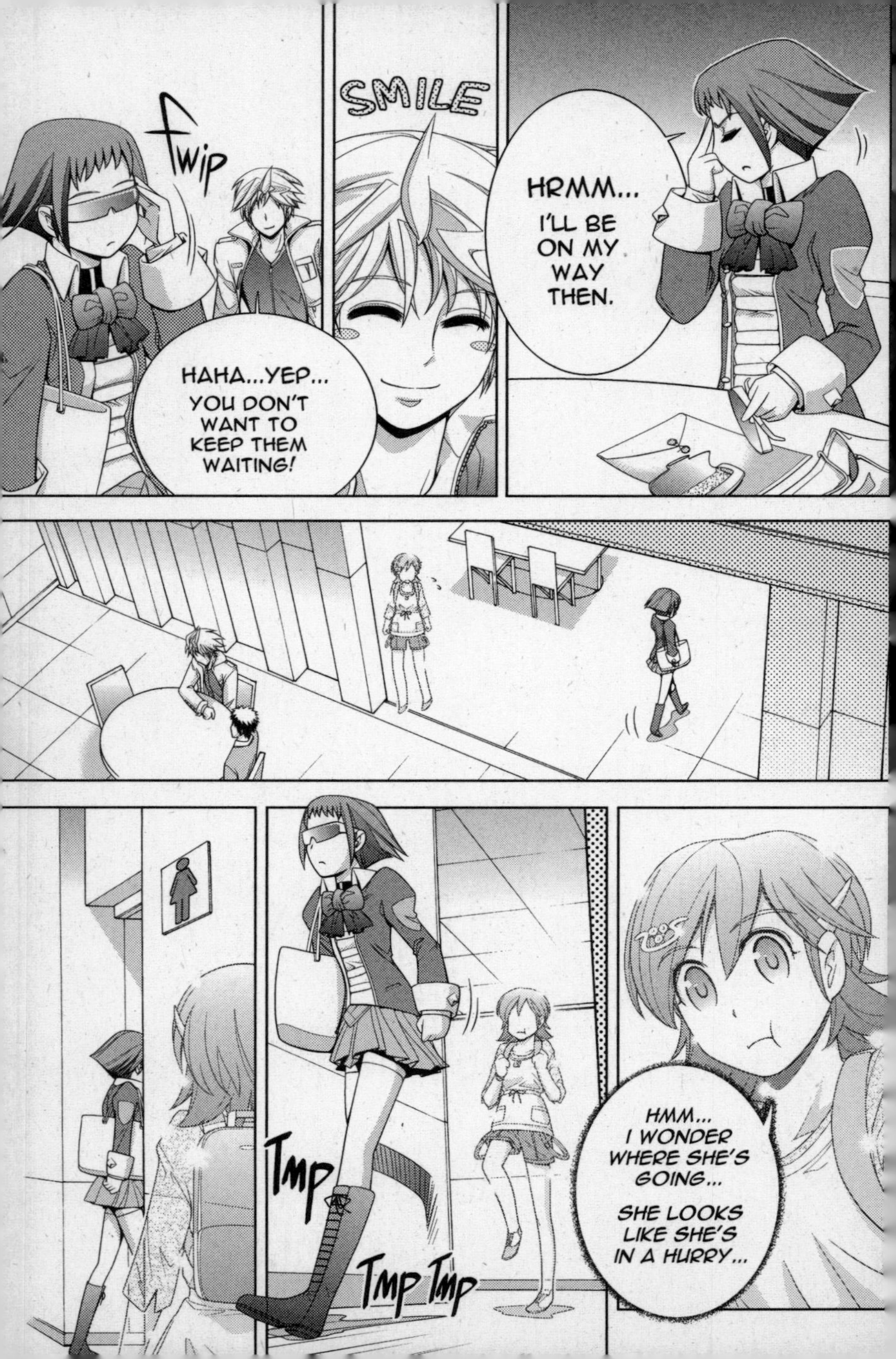
HRMM...
I'LL BE ON MY WAY THEN.
SMILE
HAHA...YEP... YOU DON'T WANT TO KEEP THEM WAITING!
Fwip
HMM... I WONDER WHERE SHE'S GOING...
SHE LOOKS LIKE SHE'S IN A HURRY...
Tmp
Tmp Tmp

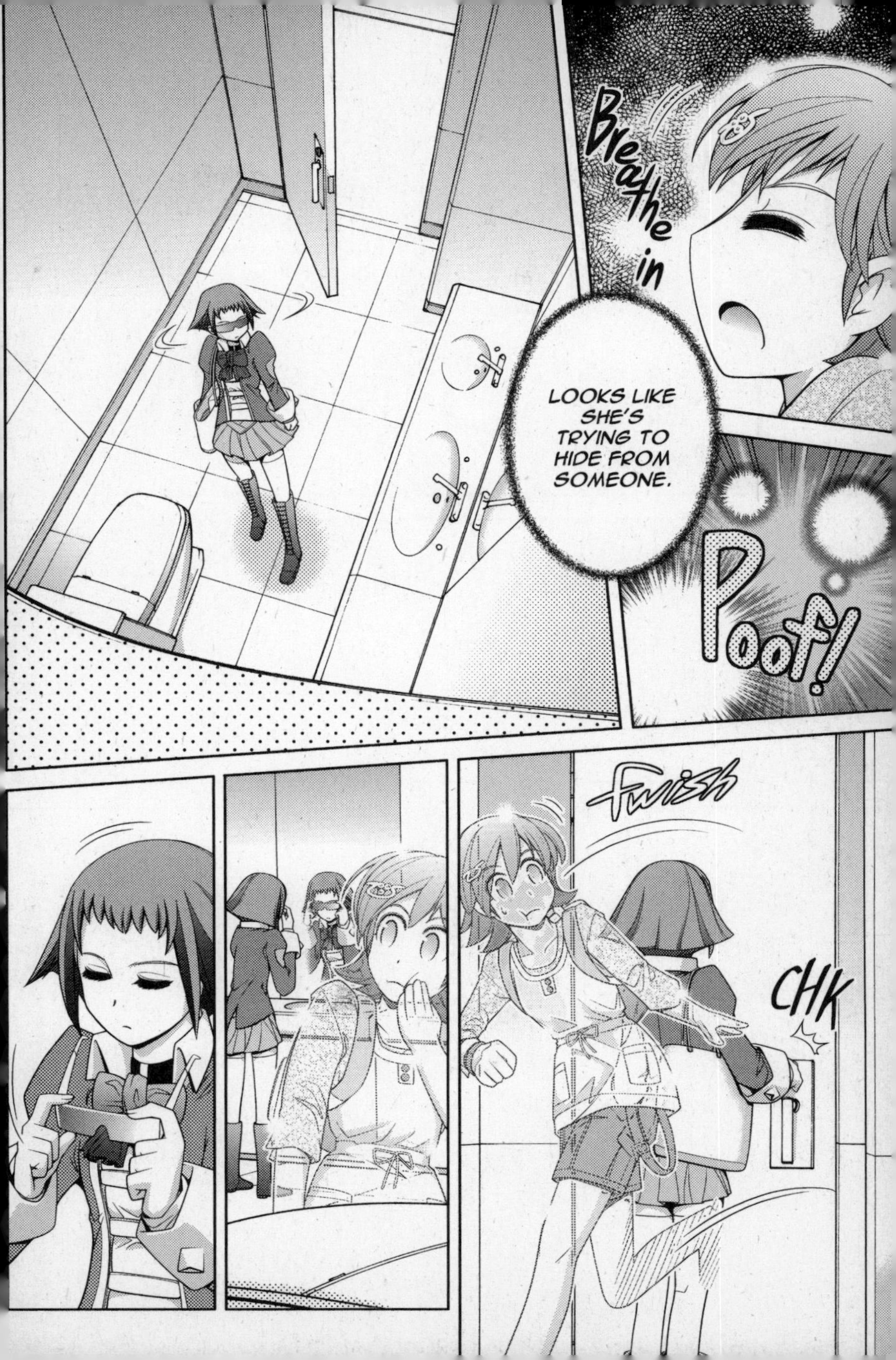
Breathe in
LOOKS LIKE SHE'S TRYING TO HIDE FROM SOMEONE.
Poof!
Fwish
CHK

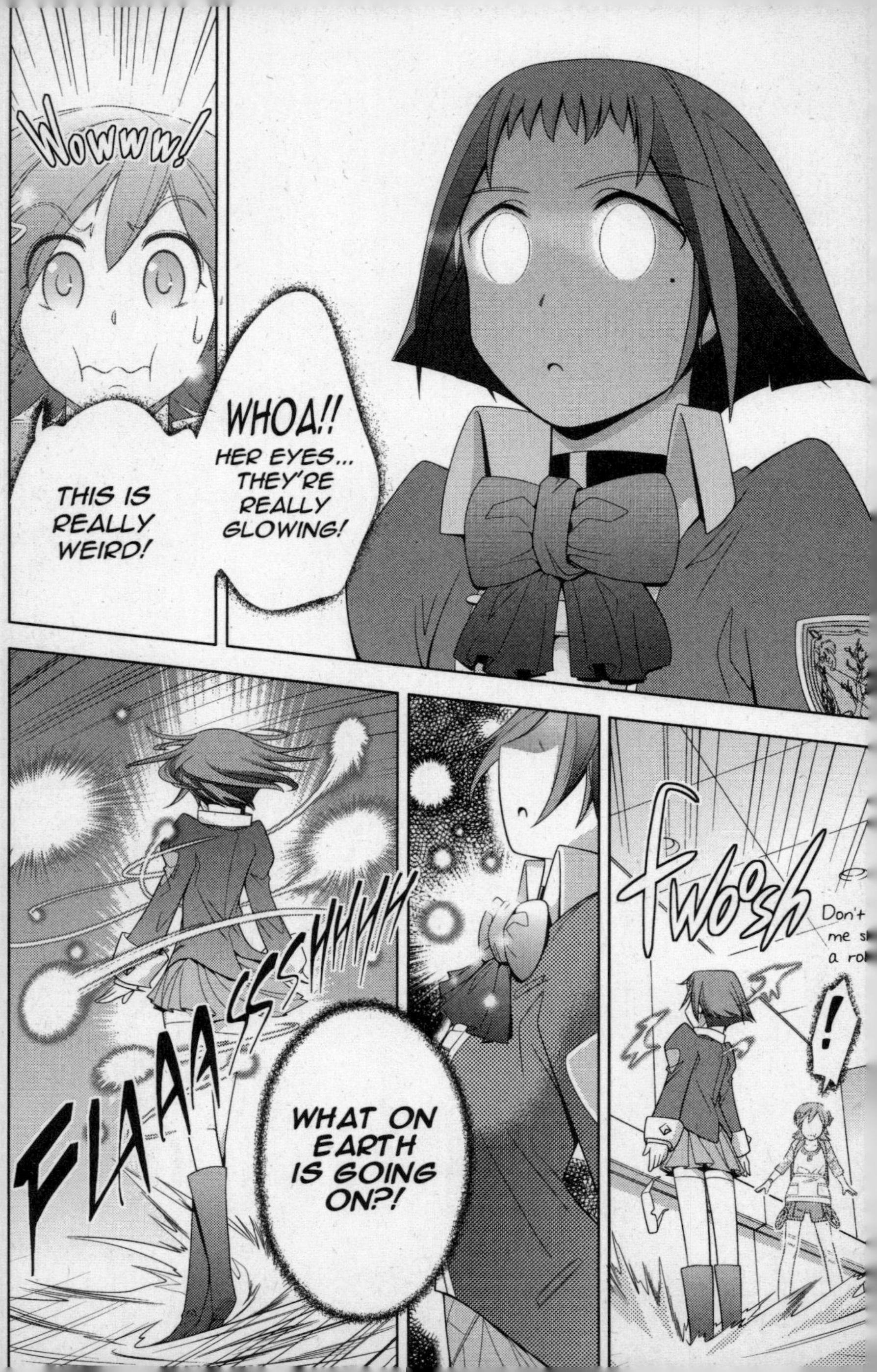
WHOA!! HER EYES... THEY'RE REALLY GLOWING!
THIS IS REALLY WEIRD!
Wowww!
fwoosh
Don't
!
WHAT ON EARTH IS GOING ON?!
FLAAASSSHHHH

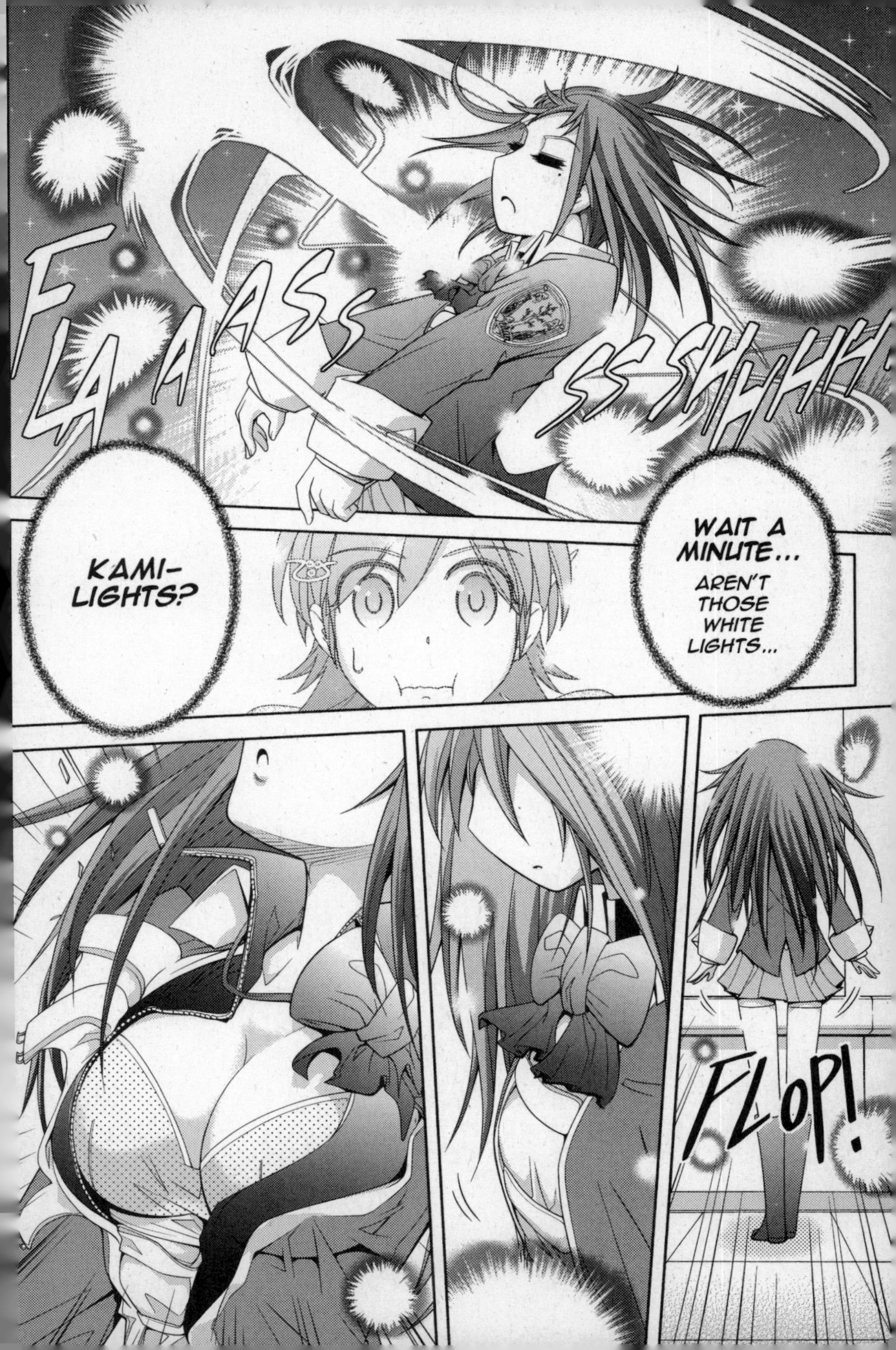
FLAAASS SSSHHHH
WAIT A MINUTE... AREN'T THOSE WHITE LIGHTS...
KAMI-LIGHTS?
FLOP!

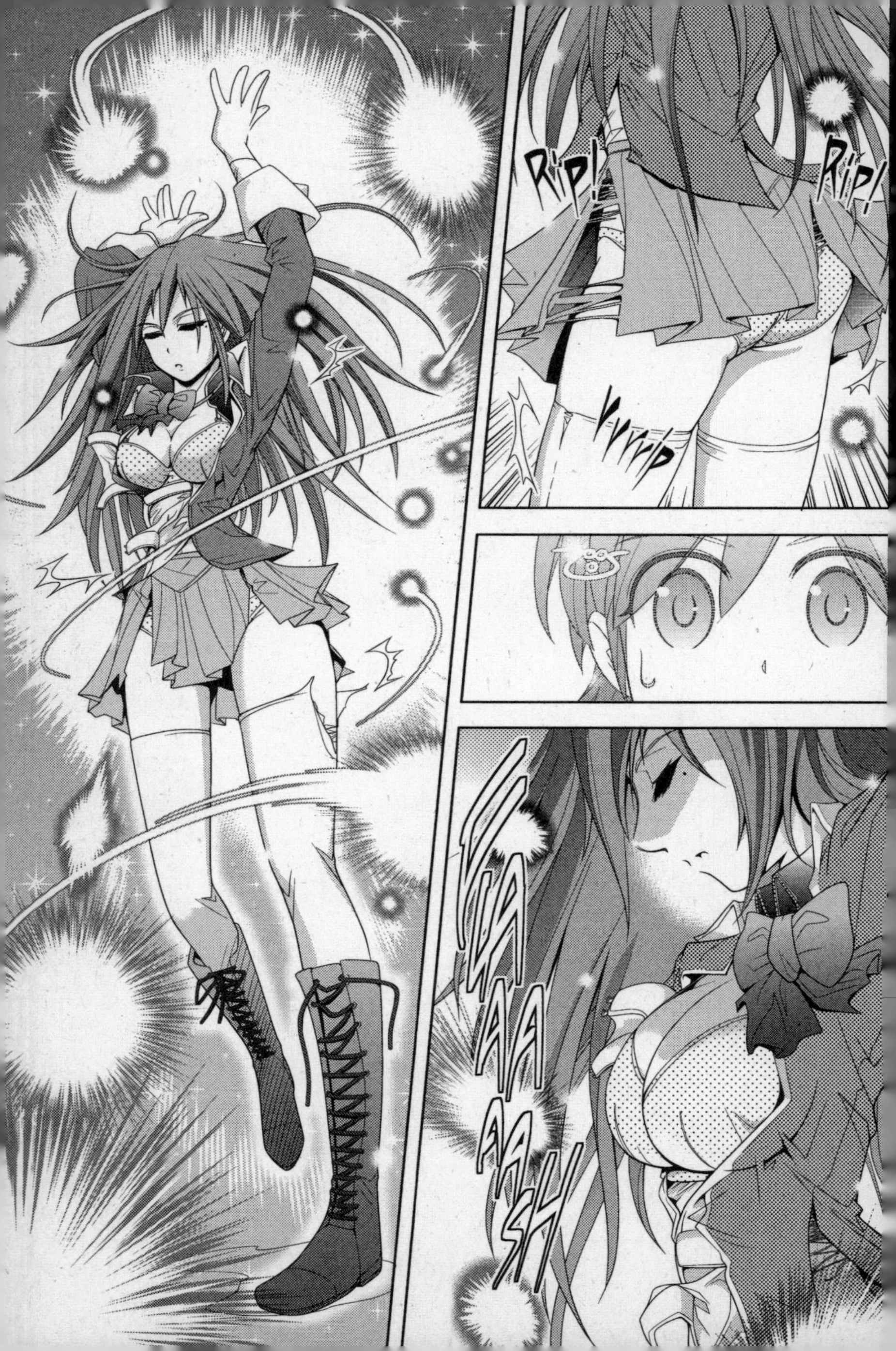
Rip!
Rip!
Vvvrip
FLAAAAASH

FWOP

FWOP

EEEK!

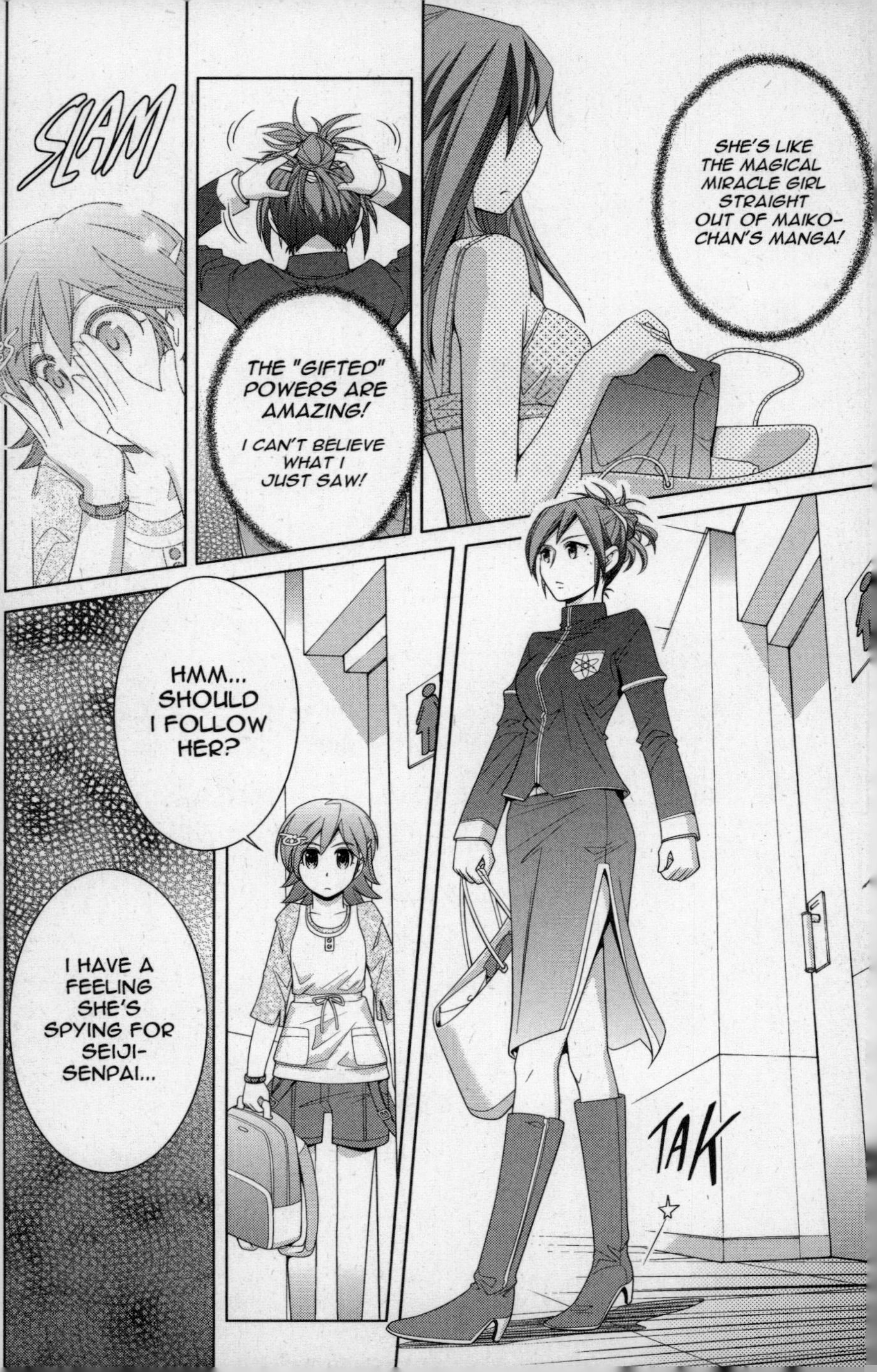
SHE'S LIKE THE MAGICAL MIRACLE GIRL STRAIGHT OUT OF MAIKO-CHAN'S MANGA!
THE "GIFTED" POWERS ARE AMAZING!
I CAN'T BELIEVE WHAT I JUST SAW!
SLAM
TAK
HMM... SHOULD I FOLLOW HER?
I HAVE A FEELING SHE'S SPYING FOR SEIJI-SENPAI...

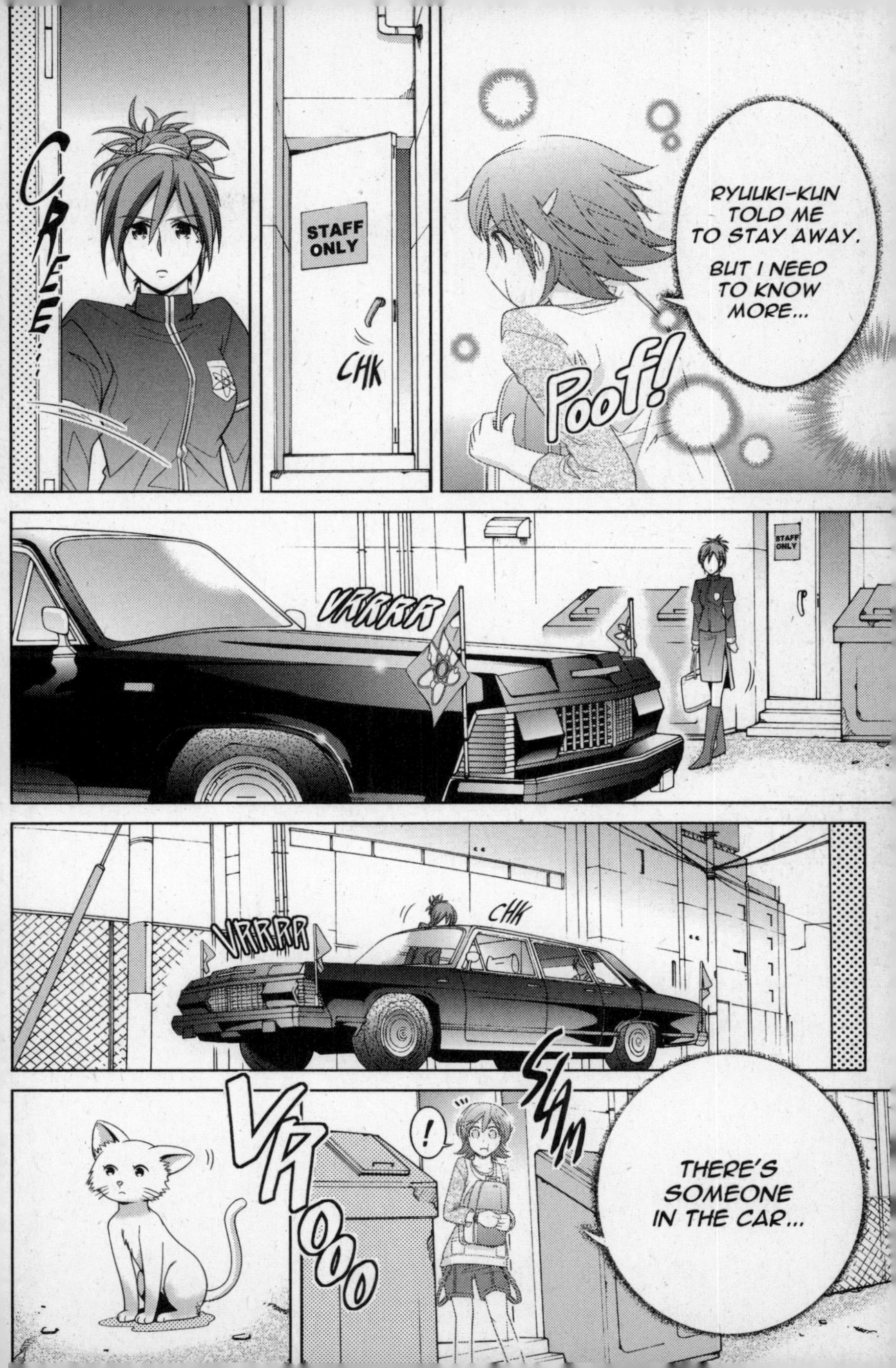
RYUUKI-KUN TOLD ME TO STAY AWAY.
BUT I NEED TO KNOW MORE...
Poof!
STAFF ONLY
CHK
CREE...
VRRRRR
STAFF ONLY
CHK
VRRRR
SLAM
THERE'S SOMEONE IN THE CAR...
!
VROOOO

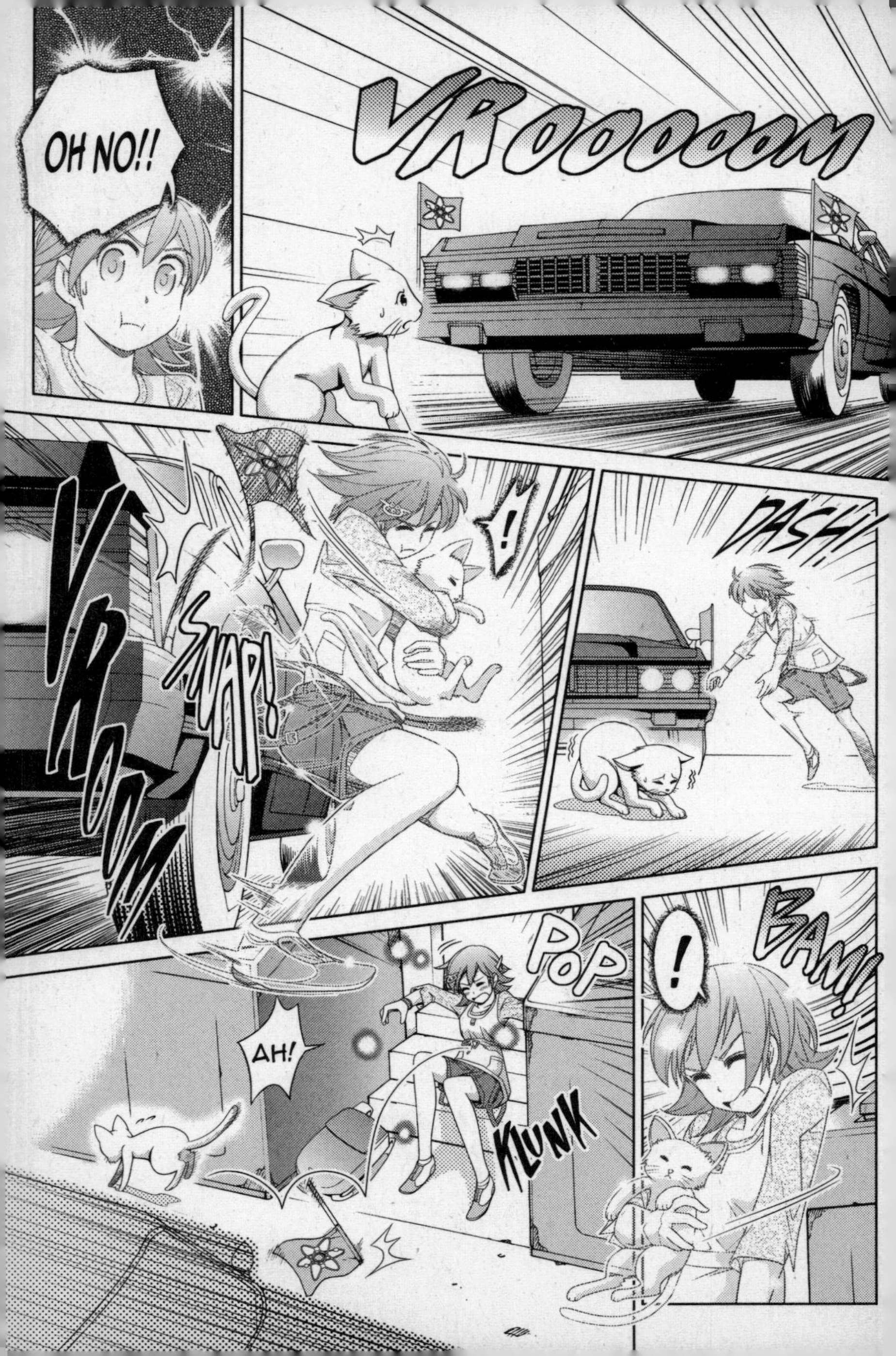
VROOOOOM
OH NO!!
DASH!
!
SNAP!
VROOOM!
BAM!
!
POP
AH!
KLUNK

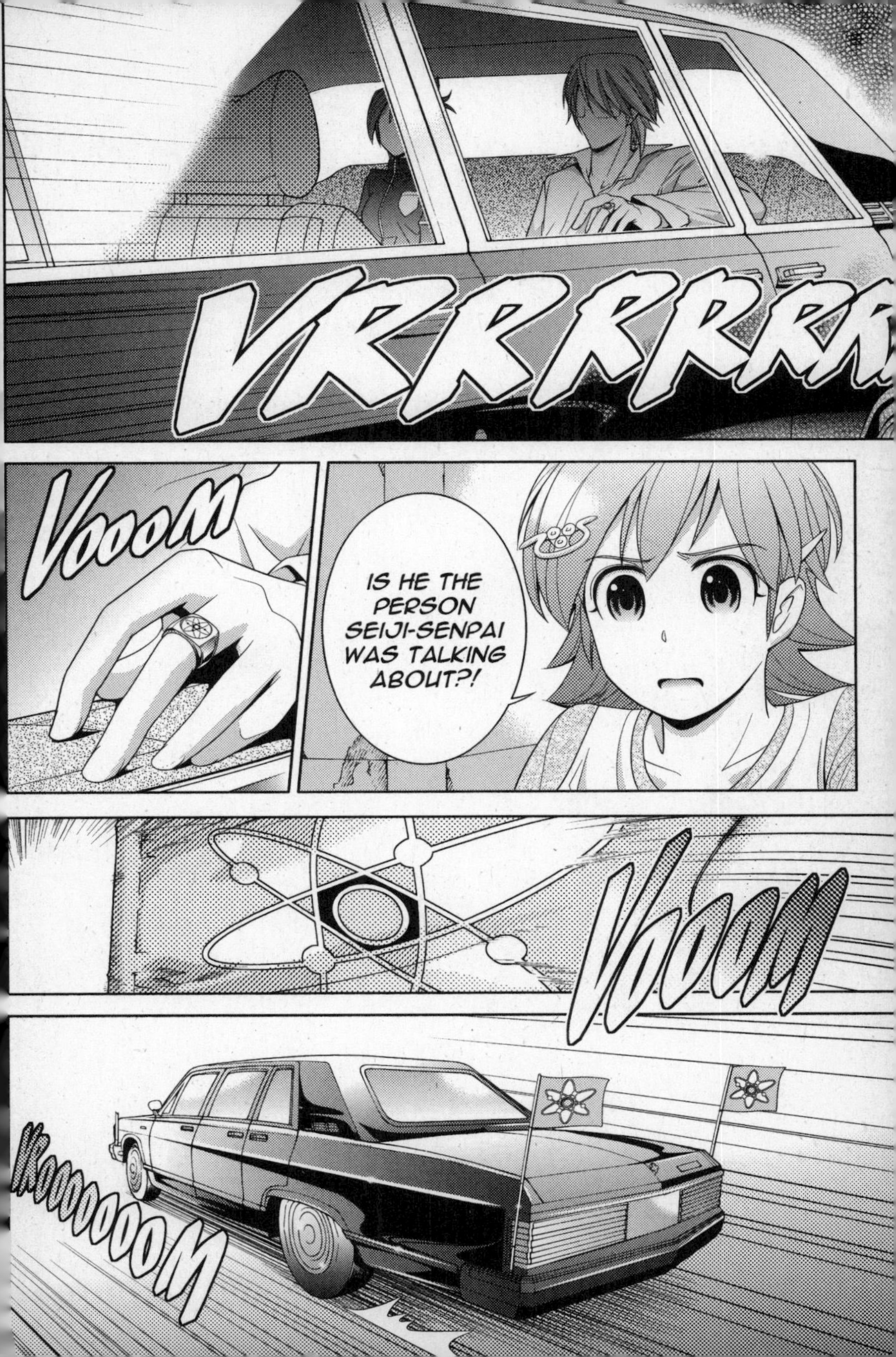
VRRRRRR
IS HE THE PERSON SEIJI-SENPAI WAS TALKING ABOUT?!
VOOOM
VOOOM
KROOOOOOM

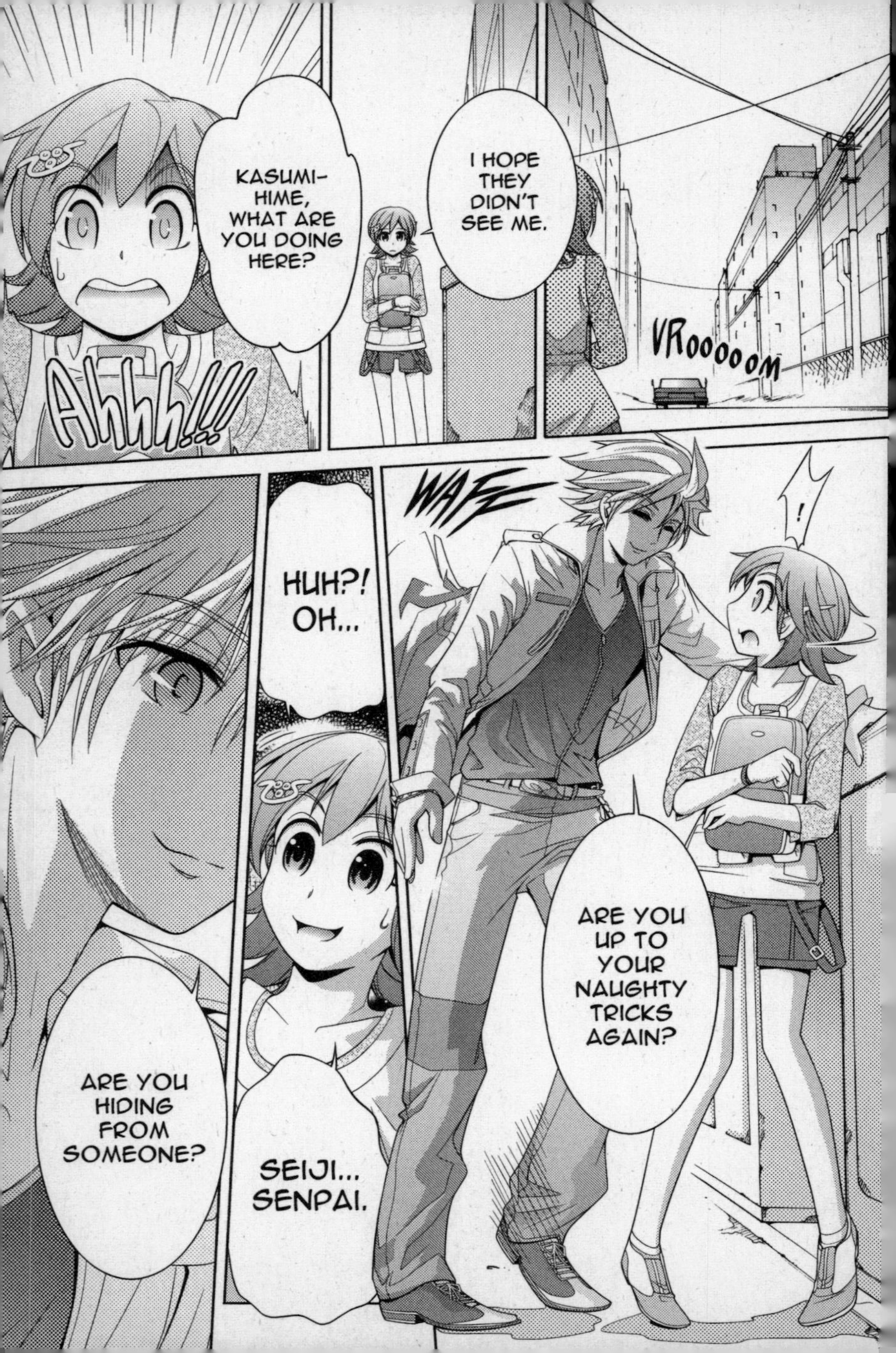
VROOOOOM
I HOPE THEY DIDN'T SEE ME.
KASUMI-HIME, WHAT ARE YOU DOING HERE?
Ahhh!!!
WAFF
!
ARE YOU UP TO YOUR NAUGHTY TRICKS AGAIN?
HUH?! OH...
SEIJI... SENPAI.
ARE YOU HIDING FROM SOMEONE?

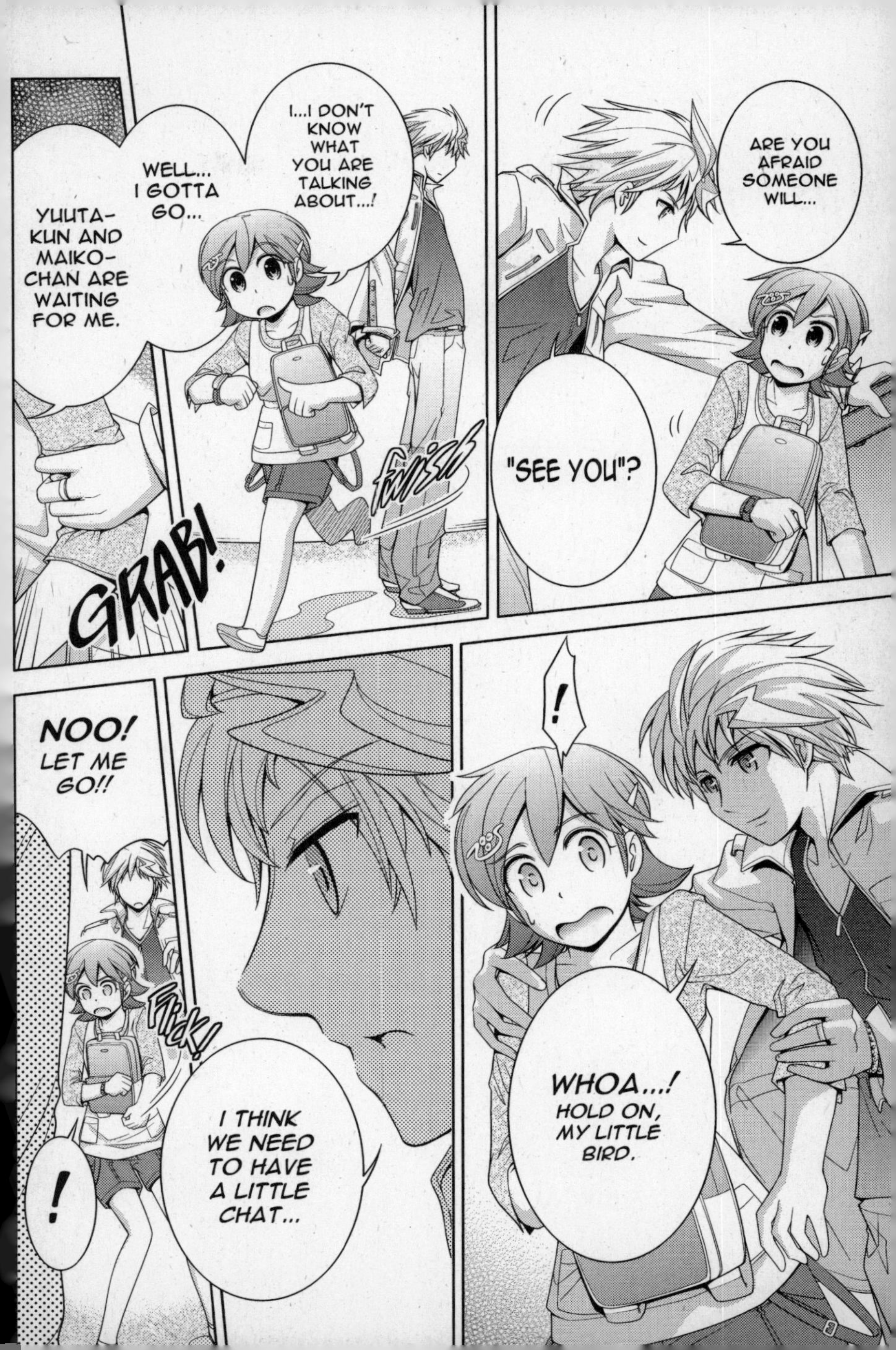
ARE YOU AFRAID SOMEONE WILL...
"SEE YOU"?
I...I DON'T KNOW WHAT YOU ARE TALKING ABOUT...!
WELL... I GOTTA GO...
YUUTA-KUN AND MAIKO-CHAN ARE WAITING FOR ME.
fwish
GRAB!
!
WHOA...! HOLD ON, MY LITTLE BIRD.
I THINK WE NEED TO HAVE A LITTLE CHAT...
NOO! LET ME GO!!
Flick!
!

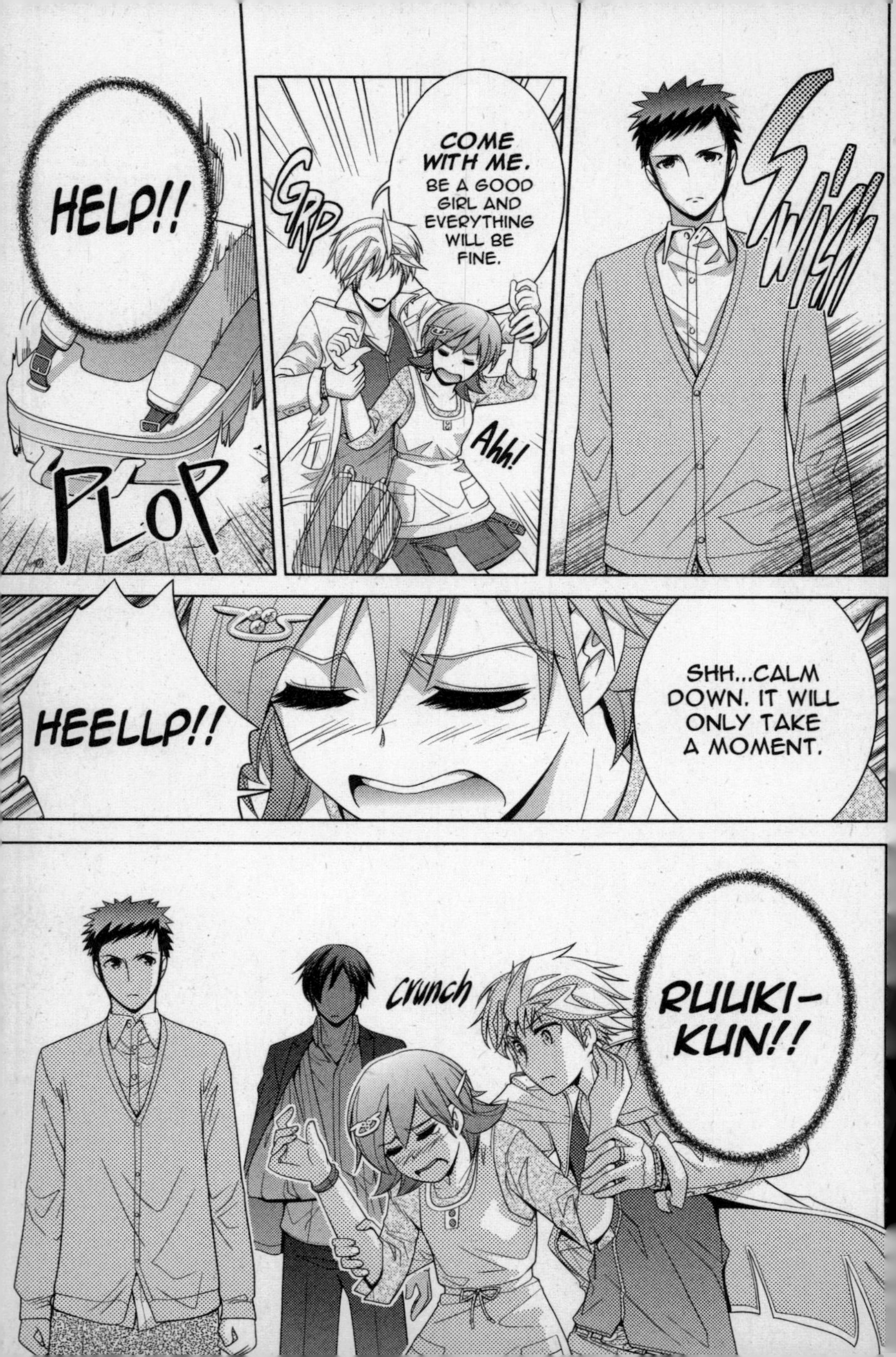
SWISH
GRP
COME WITH ME. BE A GOOD GIRL AND EVERYTHING WILL BE FINE.
Ahh!
HELP!!
PLOP
SHH...CALM DOWN. IT WILL ONLY TAKE A MOMENT.
HEELLP!!
RUUKI-KUN!!
Crunch

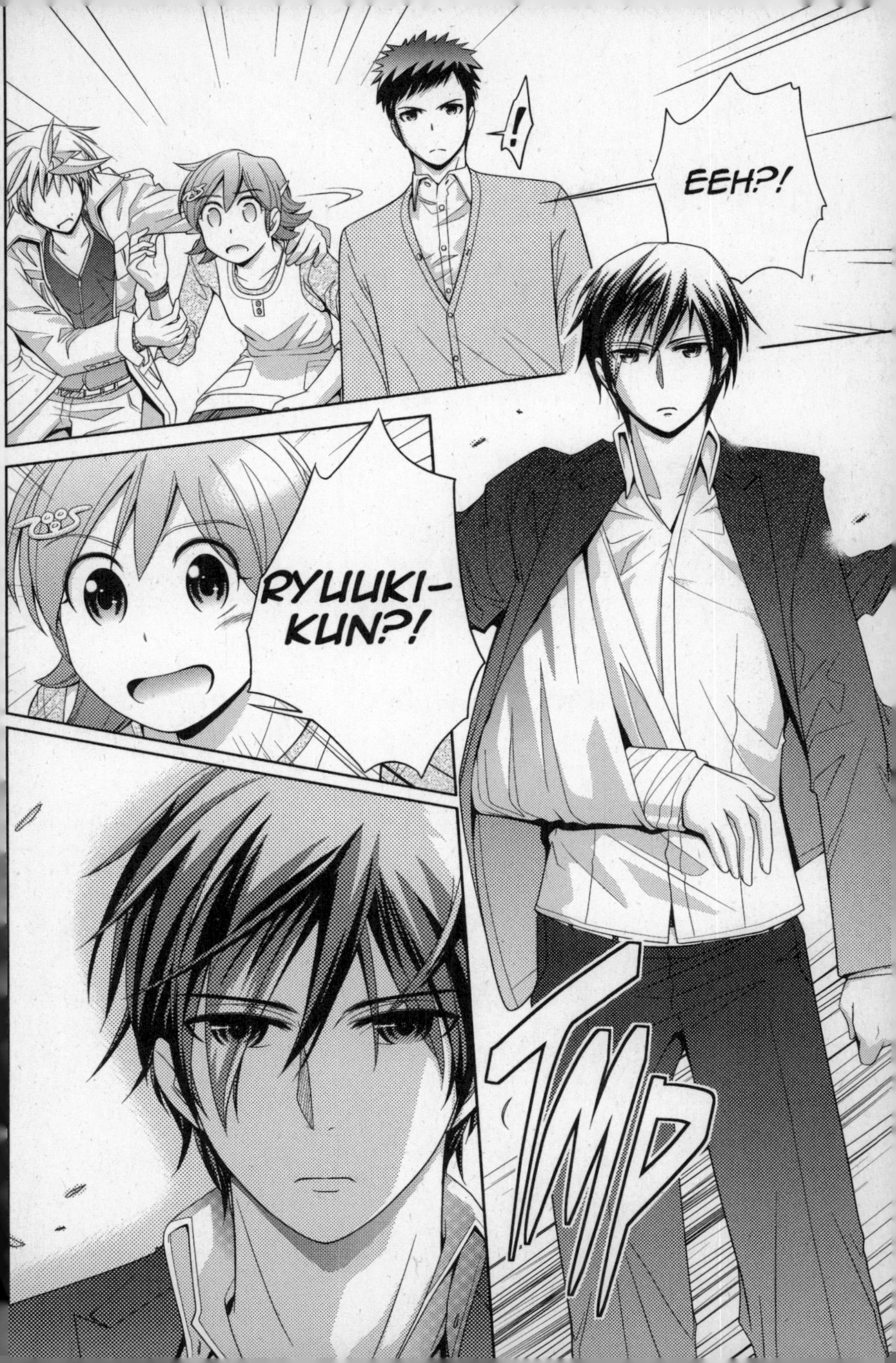
EEH?!
!
RYUUKI-KUN?!
TMP

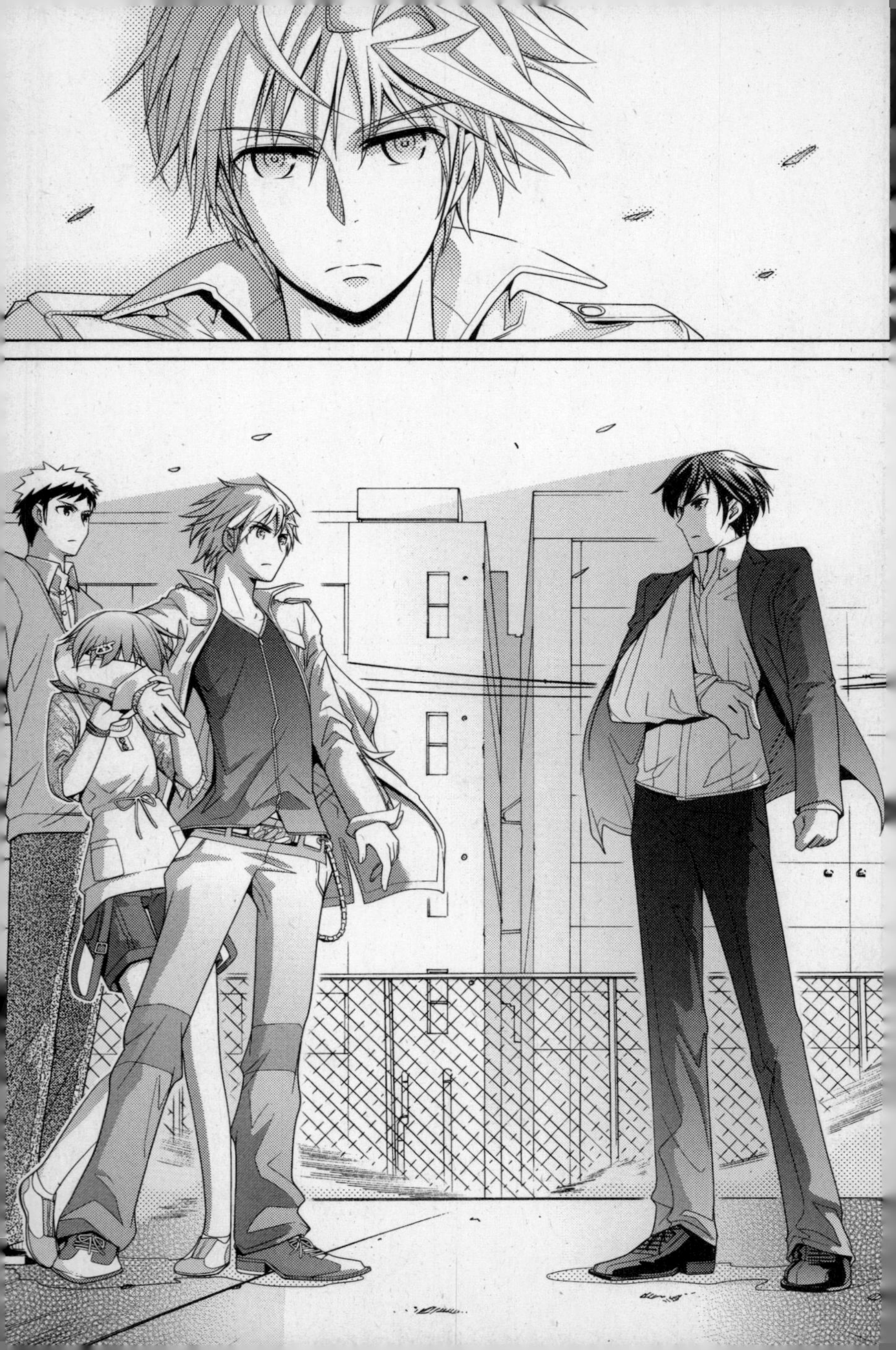

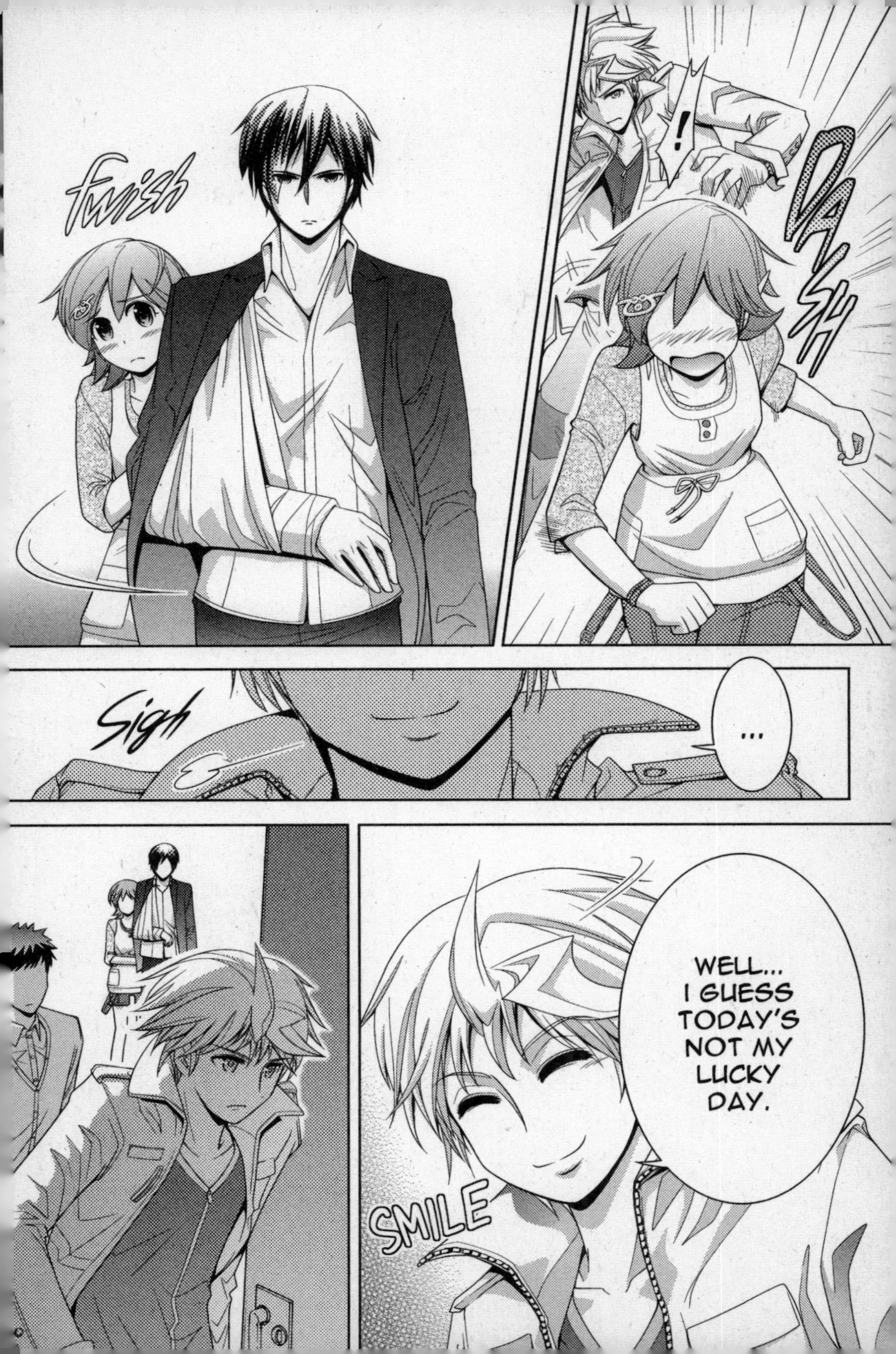
!
DASH
fwish
...
Sigh
WELL... I GUESS TODAY'S NOT MY LUCKY DAY.
SMILE

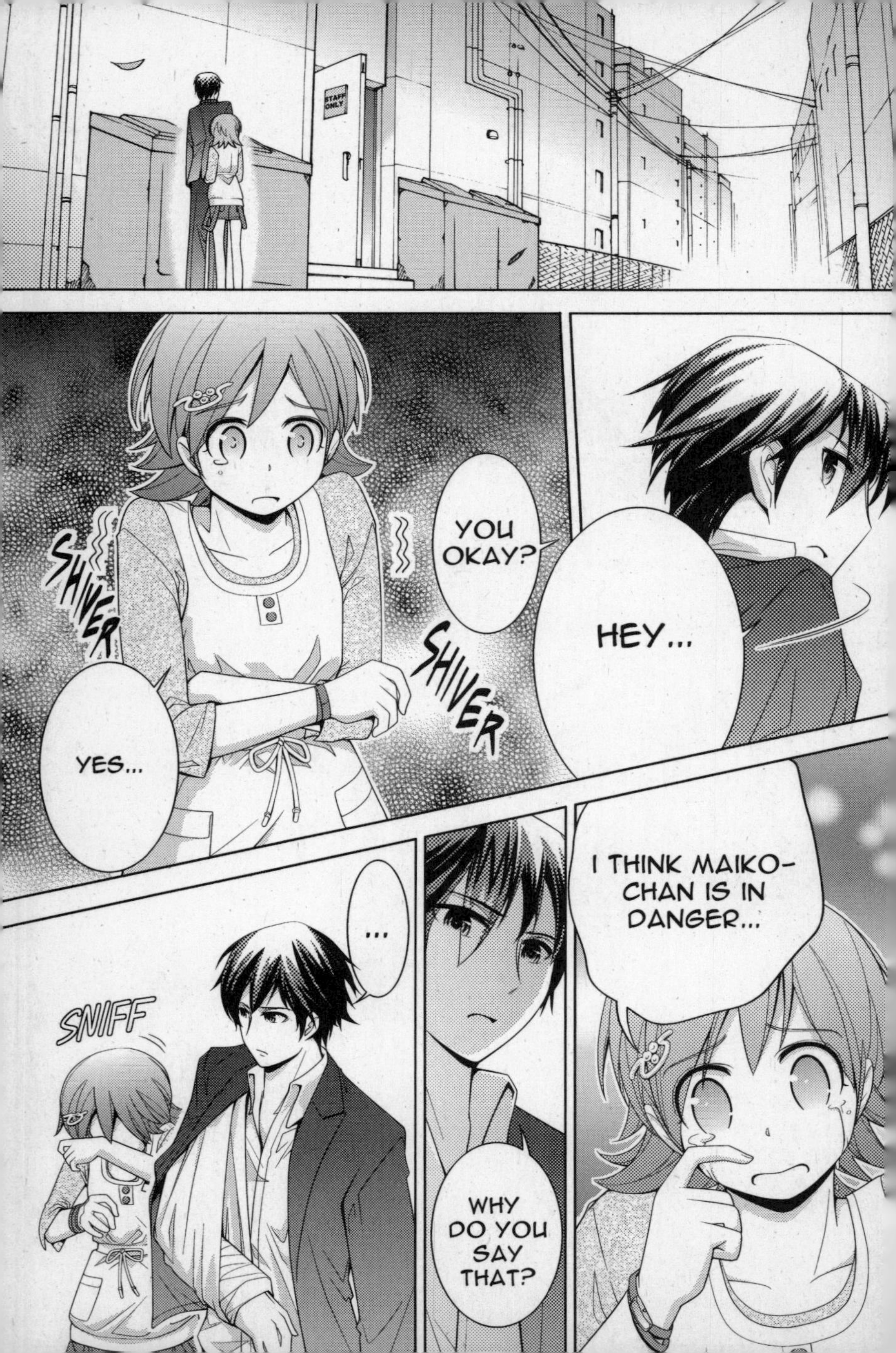
HEY...
YOU OKAY?
SHIVER
SHIVER
YES...
I THINK MAIKO-CHAN IS IN DANGER...
WHY DO YOU SAY THAT?
...
SNIFF

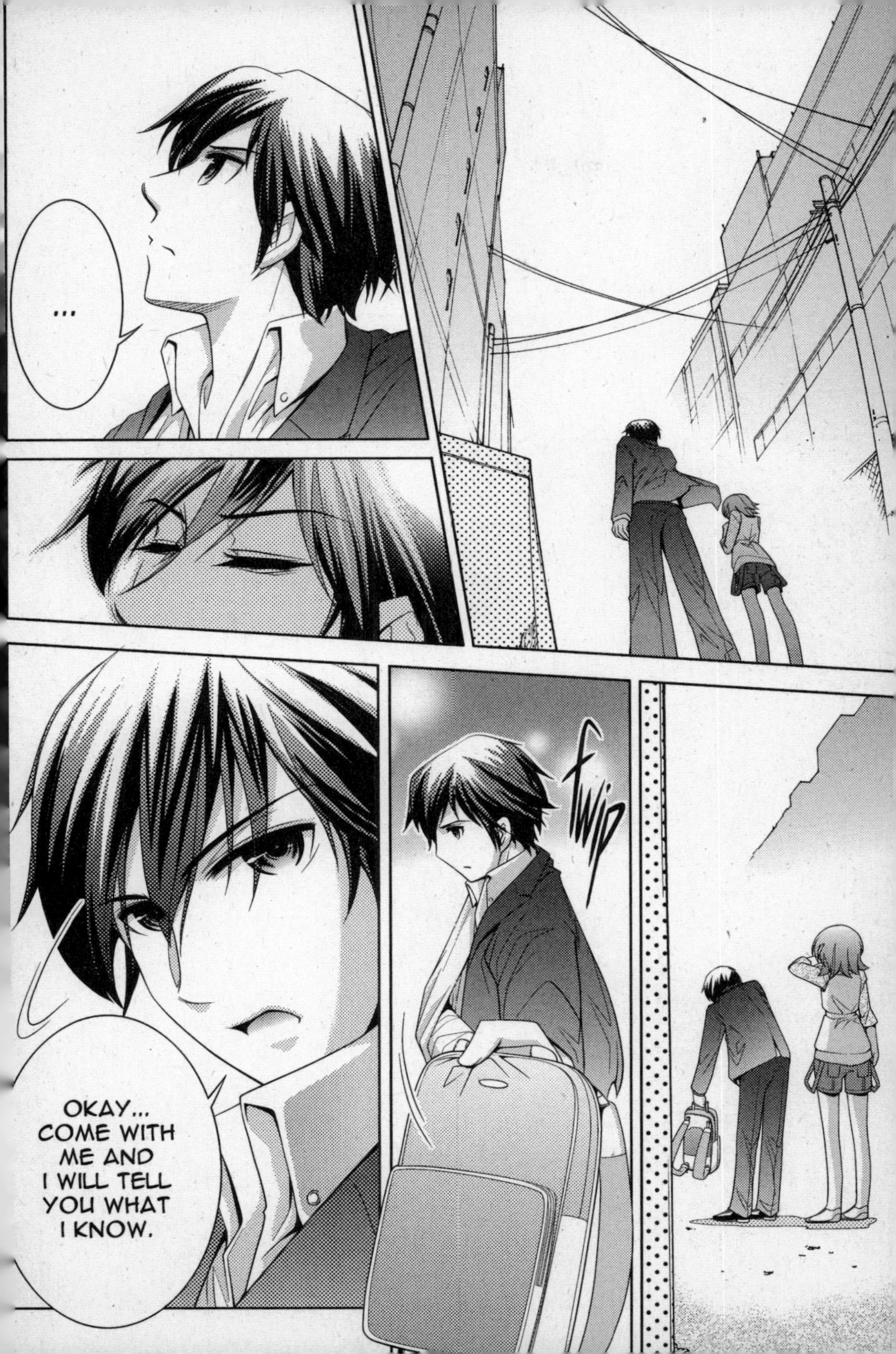
...
Fwip
OKAY... COME WITH ME AND I WILL TELL YOU WHAT I KNOW.

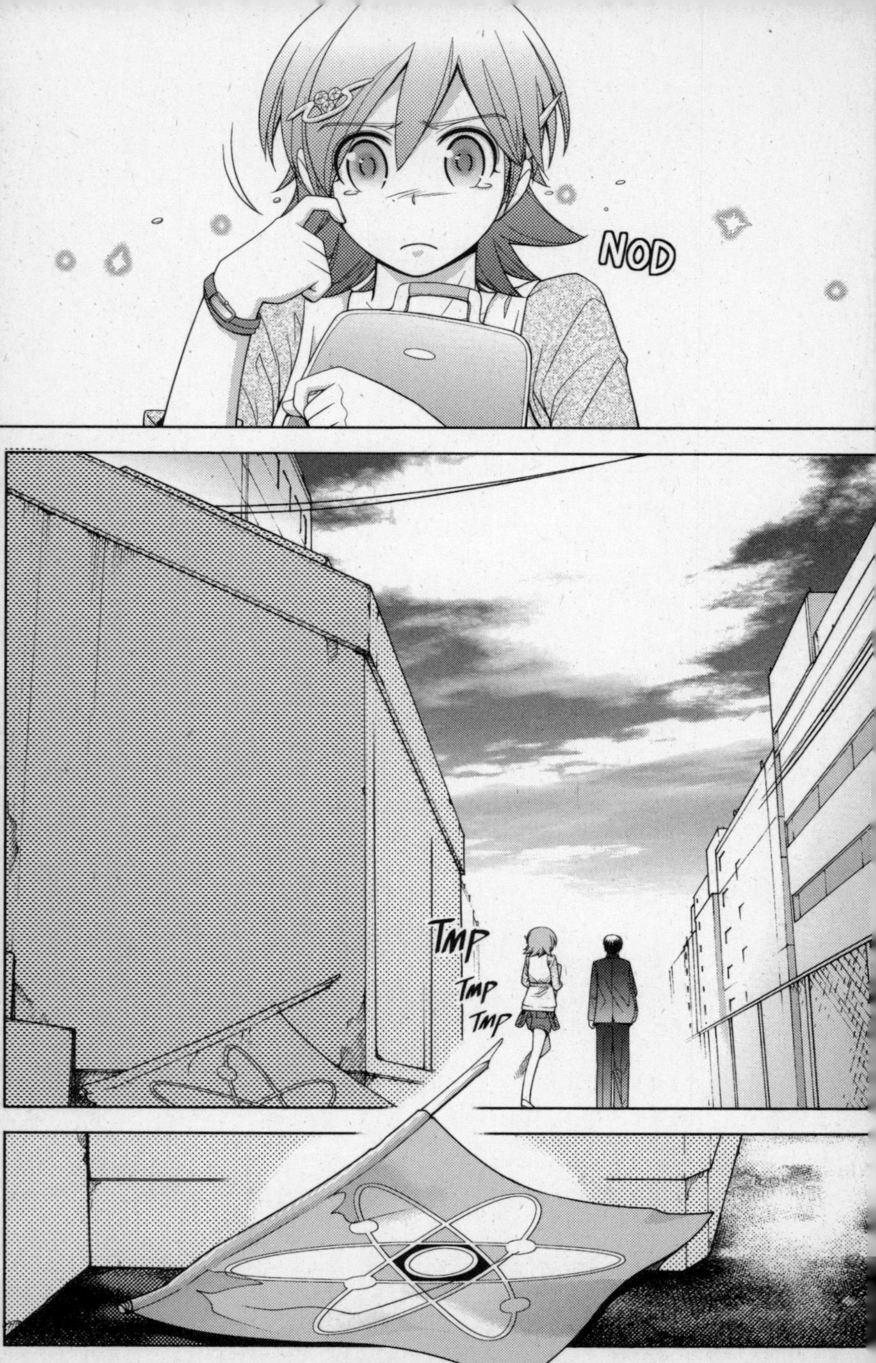
NOD
TMP
TMP
TMP

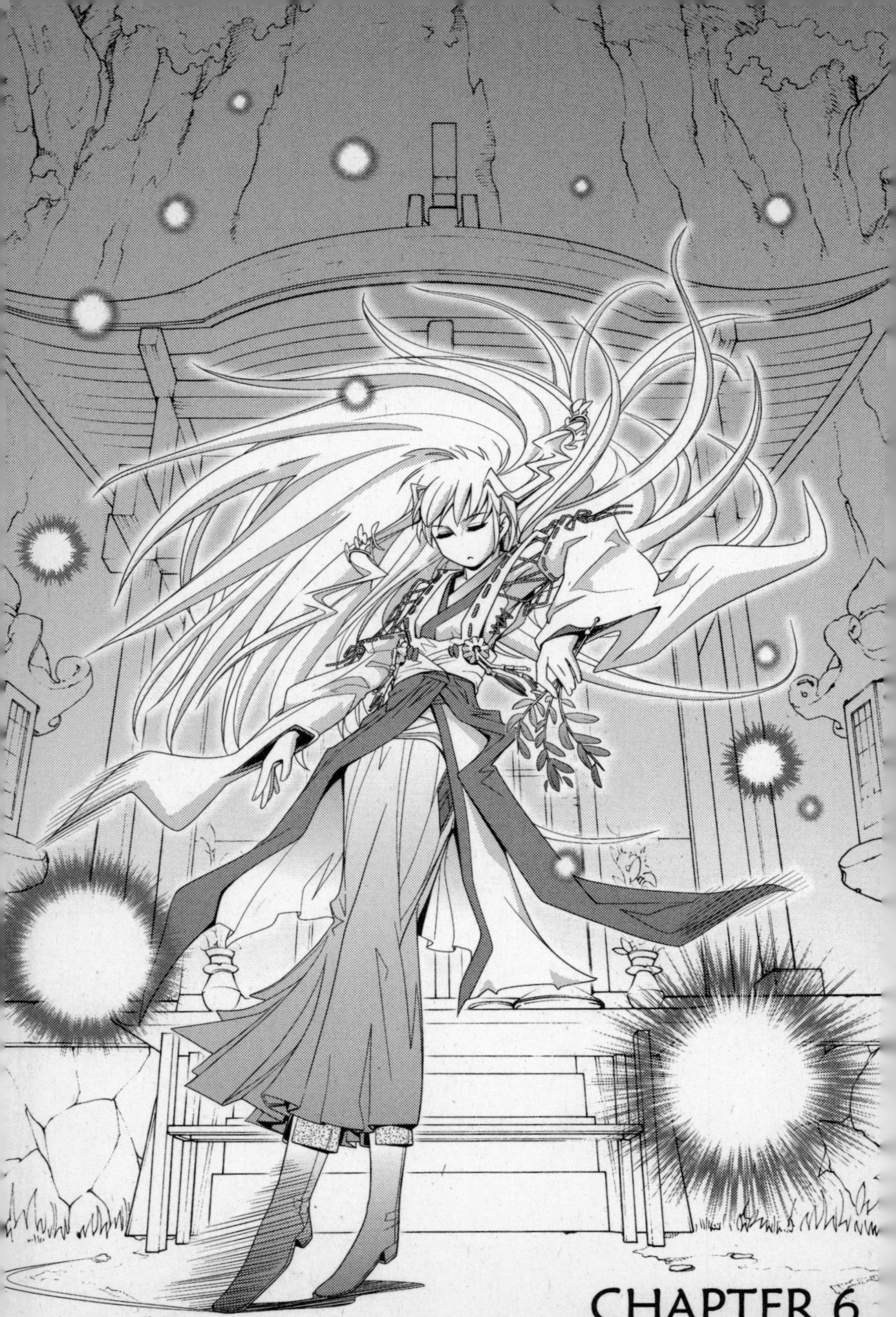

CHAPTER 6

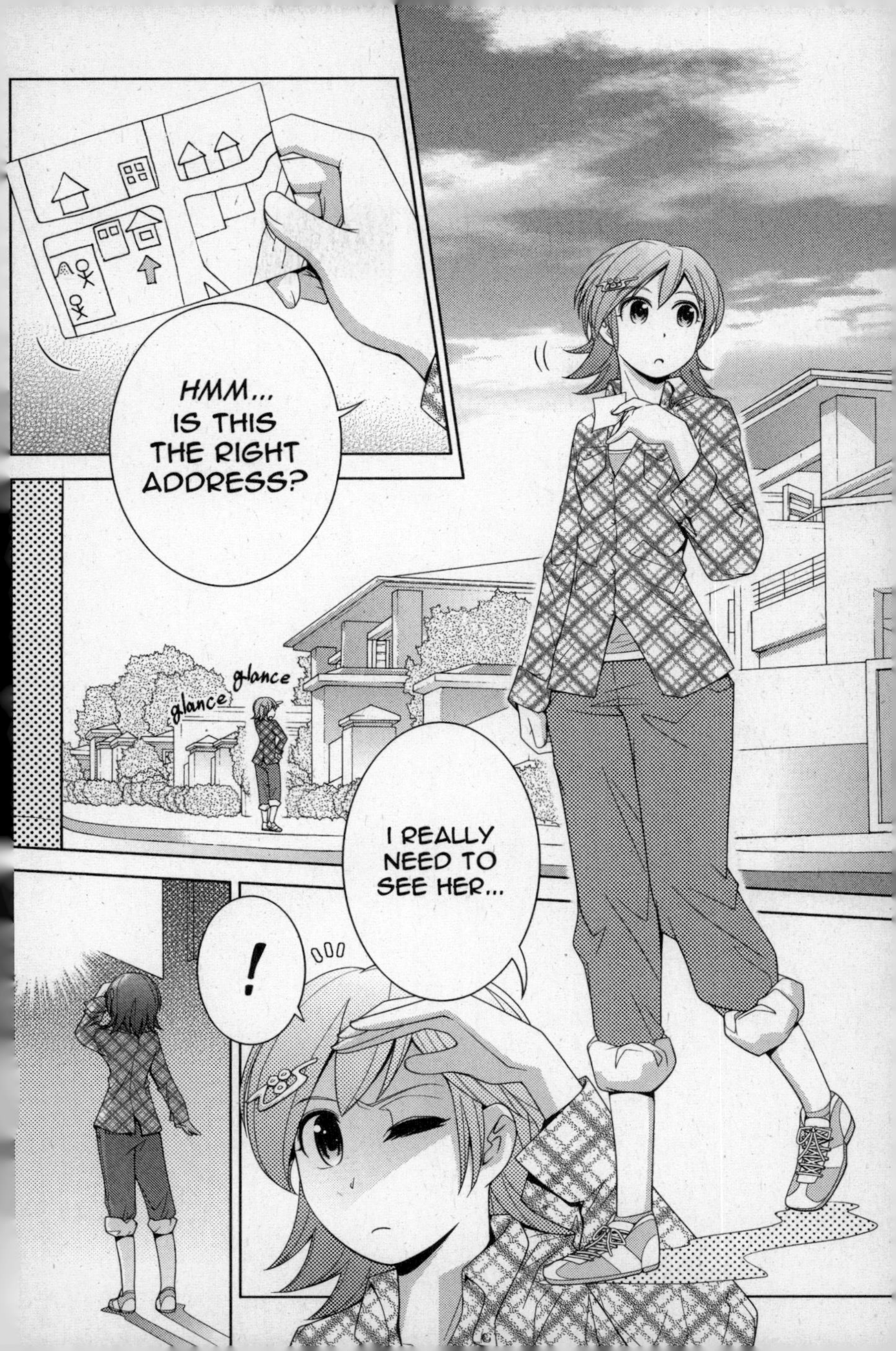
HMM...
IS THIS
THE RIGHT
ADDRESS?
glance
glance
I REALLY
NEED TO
SEE HER...
!

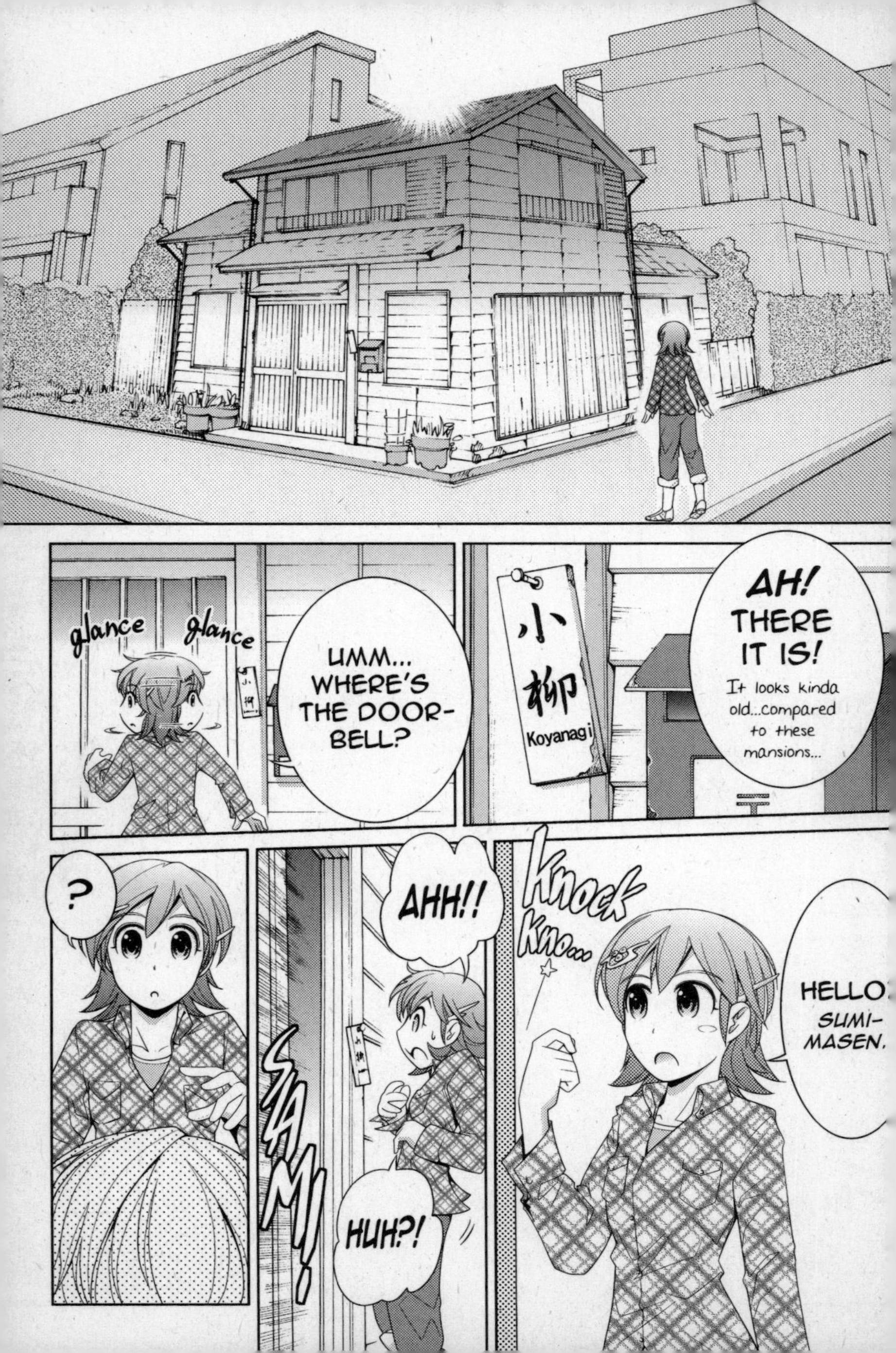
小柳
Koyanagi
AH! THERE IT IS!
It looks kinda old...compared to these mansions...
glance glance
UMM... WHERE'S THE DOOR-BELL?
Knock
Kno...
HELLO? SUMI-MASEN.
AHH!!
SLAM!
HUH?!
?

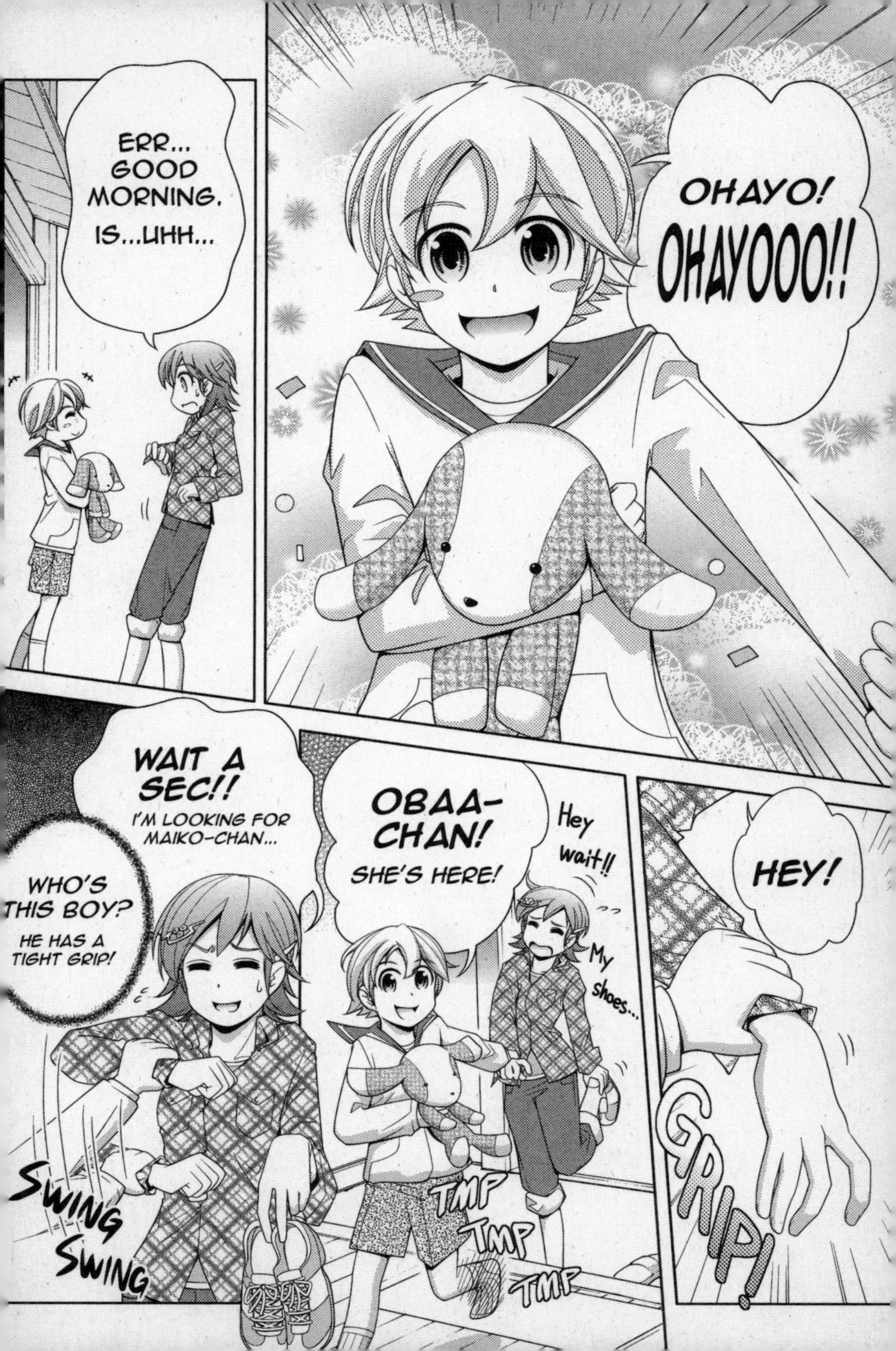
OHAYO! OHAYOOO!!
ERR... GOOD MORNING. IS...UHH...
HEY!
GRIP!
OBAA-CHAN! SHE'S HERE!
Hey wait!!
My shoes...
TMP TMP TMP
WAIT A SEC!! I'M LOOKING FOR MAIKO-CHAN...
WHO'S THIS BOY? HE HAS A TIGHT GRIP!
SWING SWING

Hi everyone!

I'm Surt, author of Kasumi. Thanks a bunch for buying and reading Kasumi, vol. 2! I assume that you've also read vol. 1 and I want to thank you all for your continuous support! Sugimoto-san and I are very grateful for your faith in us! *bow* *bow*

It's not easy to write under pressure...so to relax, I like to listen to jpop, read manga, and watch J-doramas. Sugimoto-san and I like to share music so we can inspire each other. Sometimes, I would tell him the song I was listening to when I wrote the chapter so that he can listen to it, too, and better understand my feelings and thoughts at that time. ^_^

There were times when I wondered what on earth I was thinking about when those weird ideas popped into my head...like the Jello prank that Kasumi would play on the RSF in the library. Imagine globs of slimy Jell-O... >_<

Apparently, I was the only one who thought it was funny! *Hazukashii!* I was the only one laughing when I described the plot. I'm so embarrassed... let's just say it didn't get the green light from the rest of the team... What was I thinking? @_@;

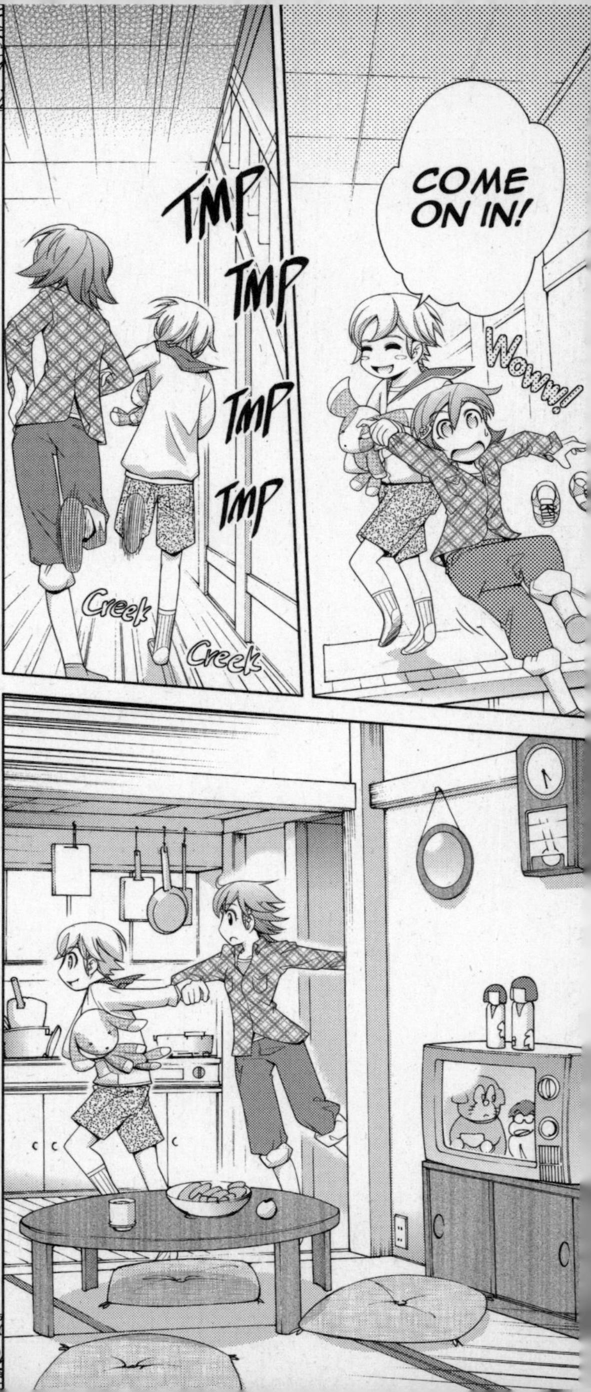
COME ON IN!
Wowww!
TMP
TMP
TMP
TMP
Creek
Creek

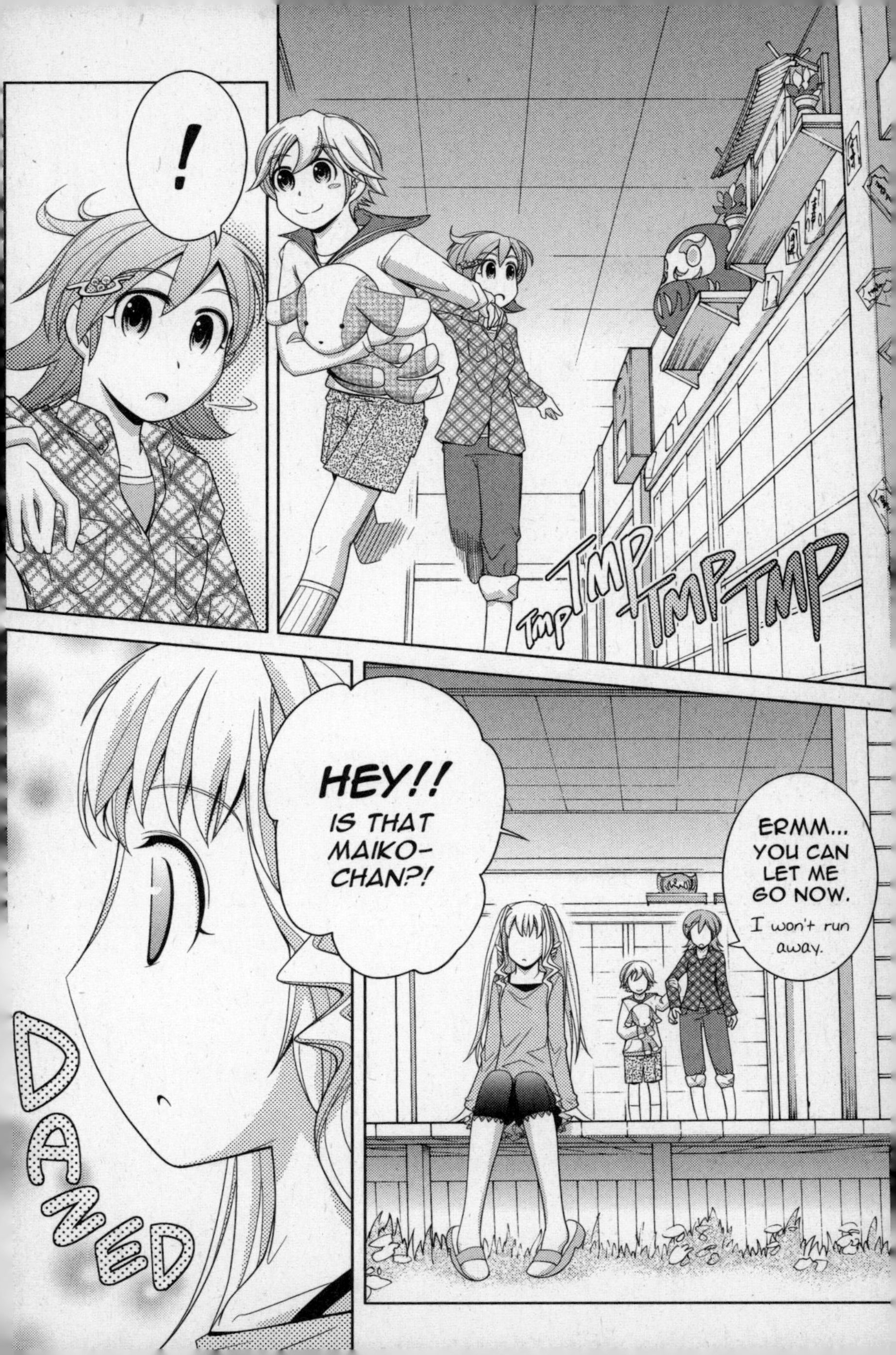
Tmp TMP TMP TMP
!
ERMM... YOU CAN LET ME GO NOW.
I won't run away.
HEY!! IS THAT MAIKO-CHAN?!
DAZED

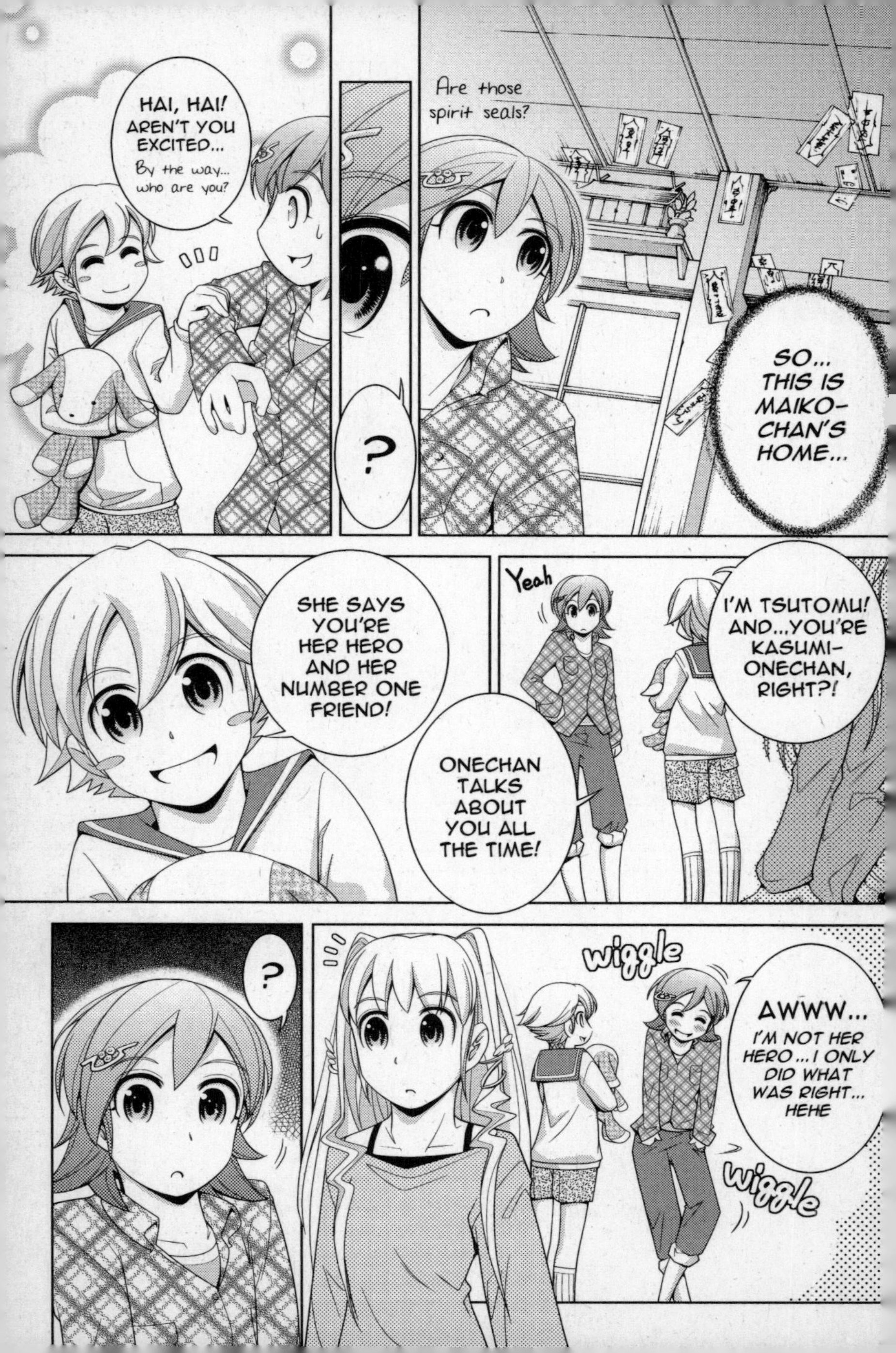
SO... THIS IS MAIKO-CHAN'S HOME...
Are those spirit seals?
?
HAI, HAI! AREN'T YOU EXCITED...
By the way... who are you?
I'M TSUTOMU! AND...YOU'RE KASUMI-ONECHAN, RIGHT?!
Yeah
ONECHAN TALKS ABOUT YOU ALL THE TIME!
SHE SAYS YOU'RE HER HERO AND HER NUMBER ONE FRIEND!
AWWW... I'M NOT HER HERO... I ONLY DID WHAT WAS RIGHT... HEHE
wiggle
wiggle
?

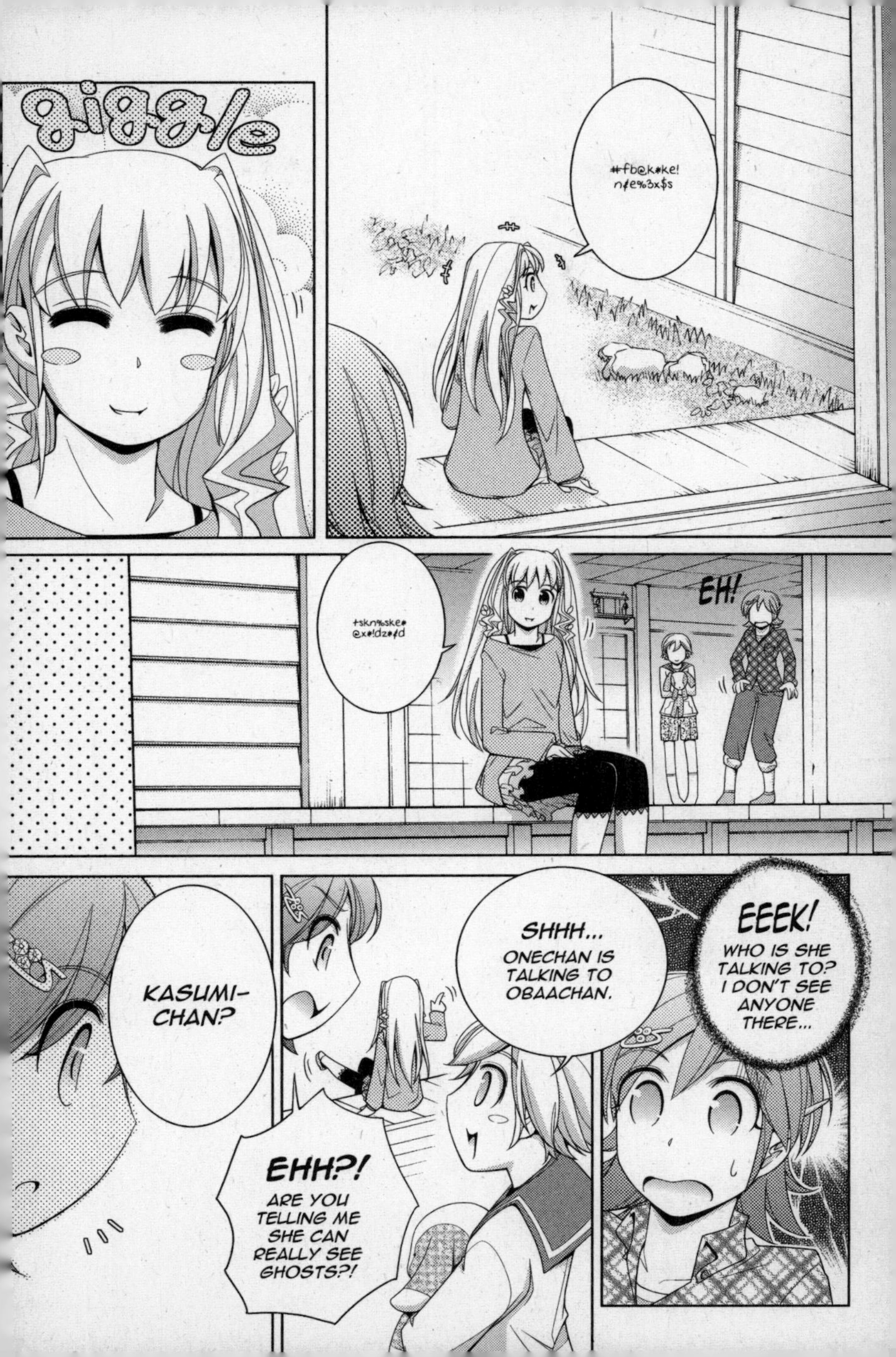
#fb@k*ke! n¢e%3x$s
giggle
EH!
tskn%ske* @x*!dz*¢d
EEEK! WHO IS SHE TALKING TO? I DON'T SEE ANYONE THERE...
SHHH... ONECHAN IS TALKING TO OBAACHAN.
EHH?! ARE YOU TELLING ME SHE CAN REALLY SEE GHOSTS?!
KASUMI-CHAN?

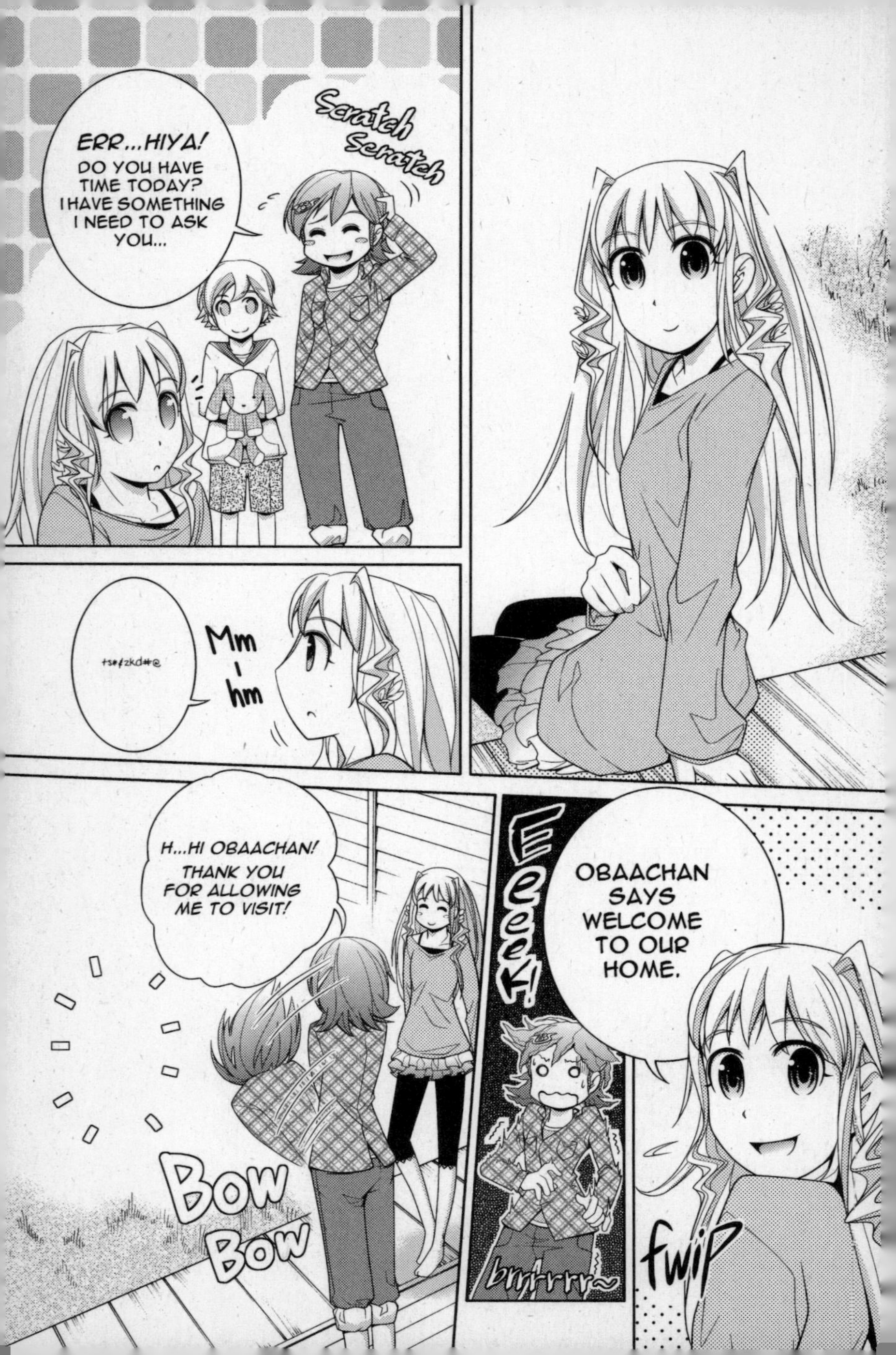
ERR...HIYA! DO YOU HAVE TIME TODAY? I HAVE SOMETHING I NEED TO ASK YOU...
Scratch Scratch
ts#≠zkd#@
Mm hm
OBAACHAN SAYS WELCOME TO OUR HOME.
fwip
Eeeek!
brrrrrr~
H...HI OBAACHAN! THANK YOU FOR ALLOWING ME TO VISIT!
Bow Bow

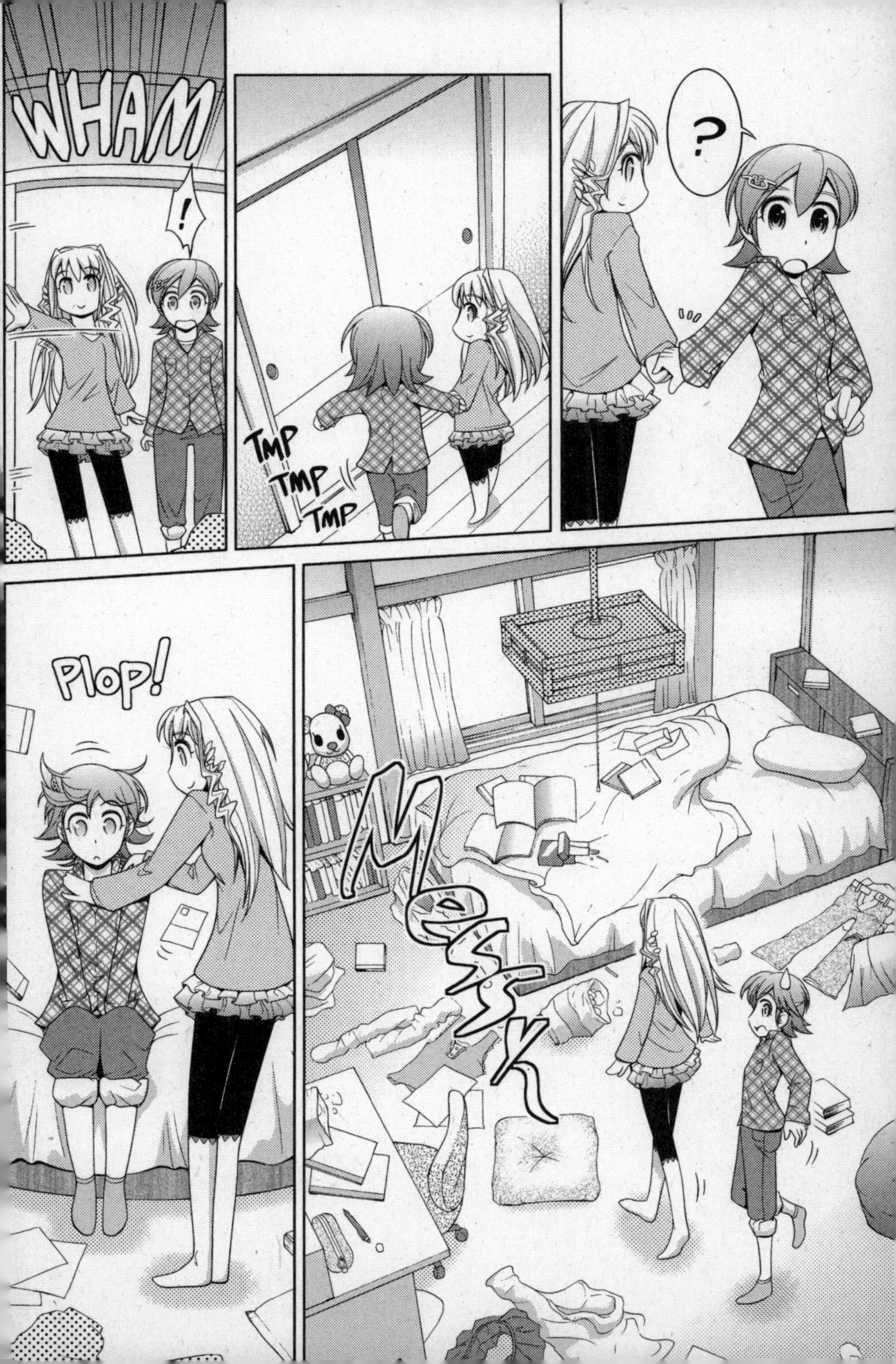
?
TMP
TMP
TMP
WHAM
!
Messy
Plop!

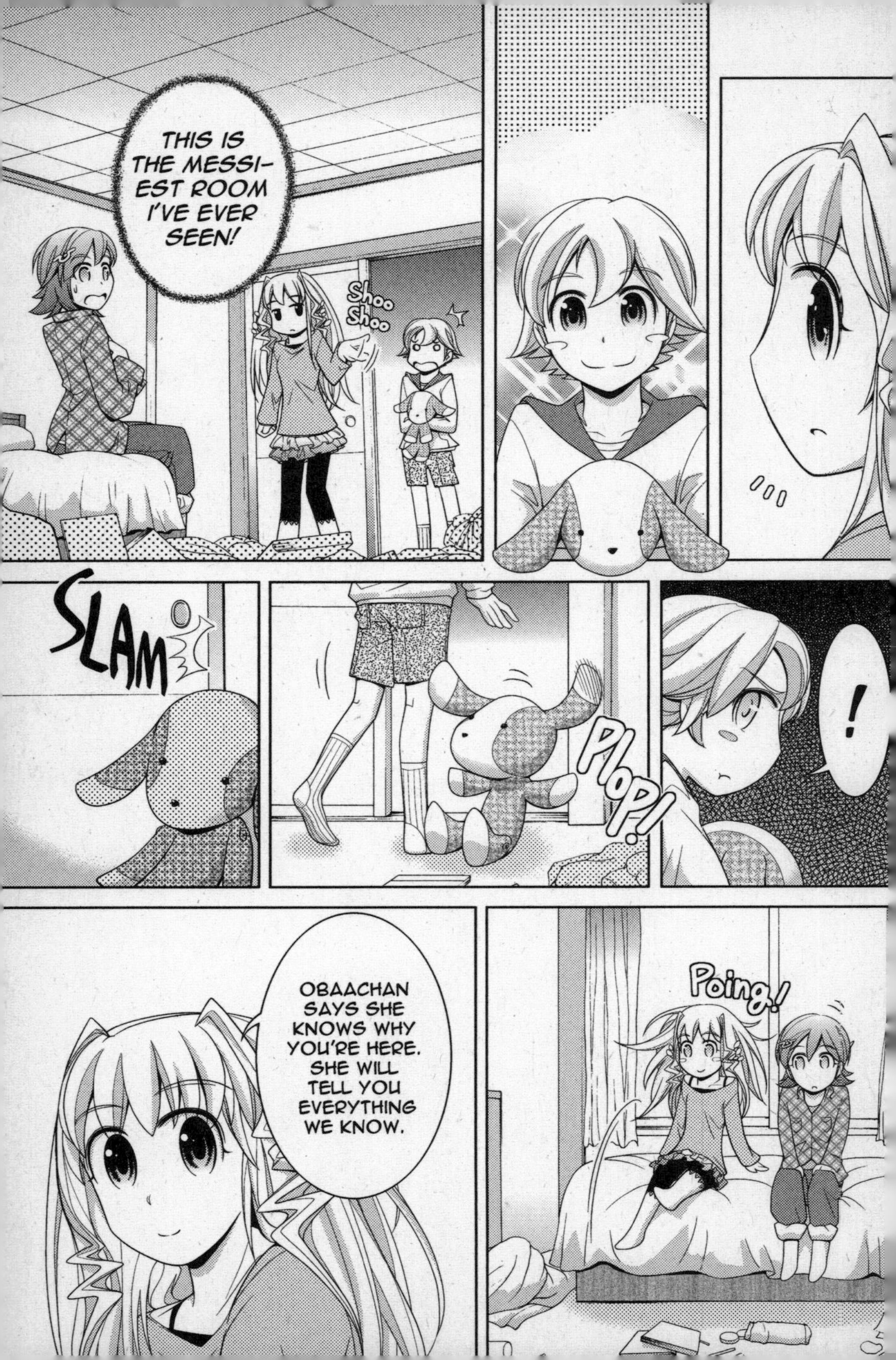
THIS IS THE MESSI-EST ROOM I'VE EVER SEEN!
Shoo Shoo
!
PLOP!
SLAM
Poing!
OBAACHAN SAYS SHE KNOWS WHY YOU'RE HERE. SHE WILL TELL YOU EVERYTHING WE KNOW.

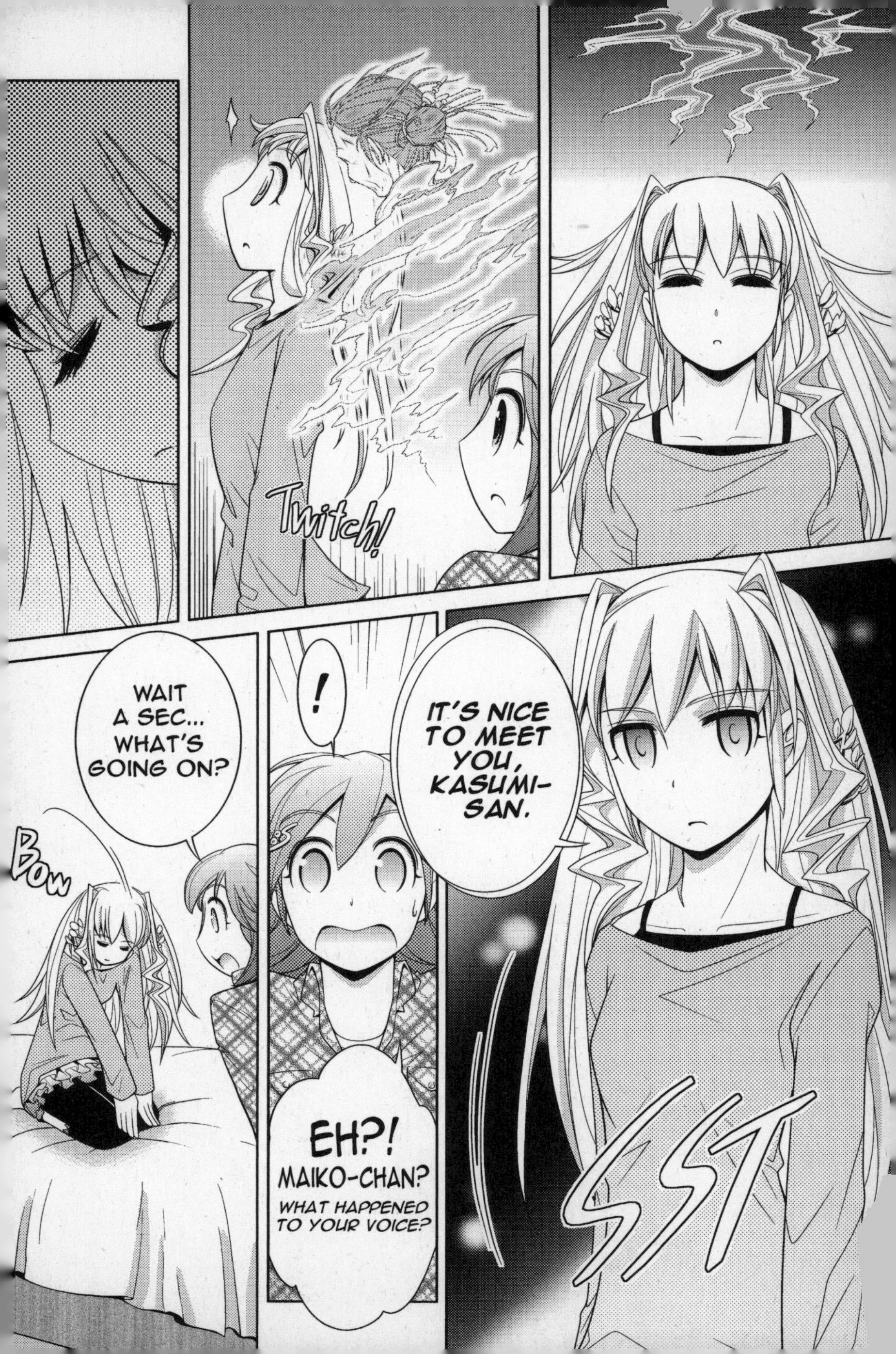
Twitch!
IT'S NICE TO MEET YOU, KASUMI-SAN.
SST
!
EH?! MAIKO-CHAN? WHAT HAPPENED TO YOUR VOICE?
WAIT A SEC... WHAT'S GOING ON?
Bow

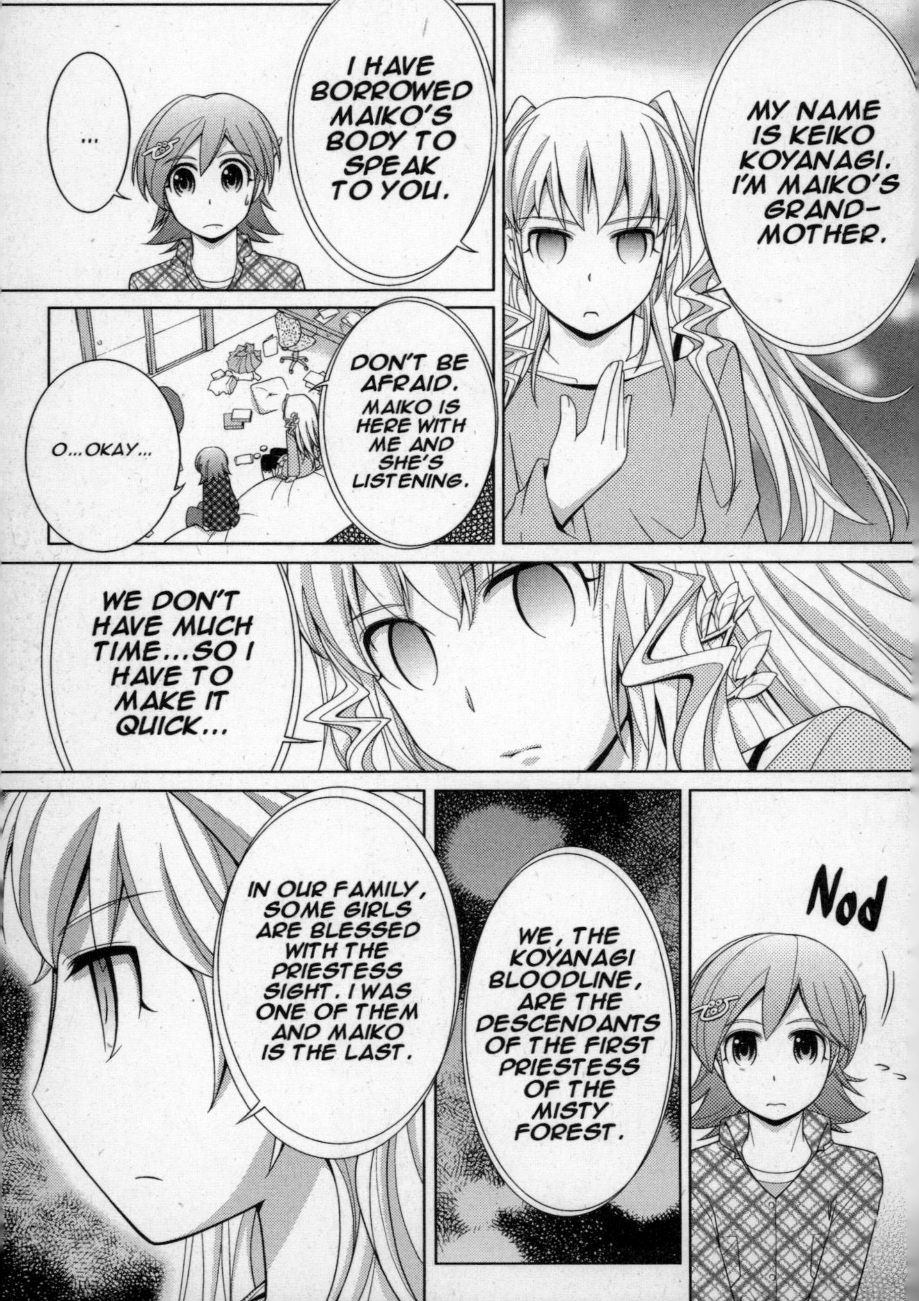
MY NAME IS KEIKO KOYANAGI. I'M MAIKO'S GRAND-MOTHER.
I HAVE BORROWED MAIKO'S BODY TO SPEAK TO YOU.
...
DON'T BE AFRAID. MAIKO IS HERE WITH ME AND SHE'S LISTENING.
O...OKAY...
WE DON'T HAVE MUCH TIME...SO I HAVE TO MAKE IT QUICK...
Nod
WE, THE KOYANAGI BLOODLINE, ARE THE DESCENDANTS OF THE FIRST PRIESTESS OF THE MISTY FOREST.
IN OUR FAMILY, SOME GIRLS ARE BLESSED WITH THE PRIESTESS SIGHT. I WAS ONE OF THEM AND MAIKO IS THE LAST.

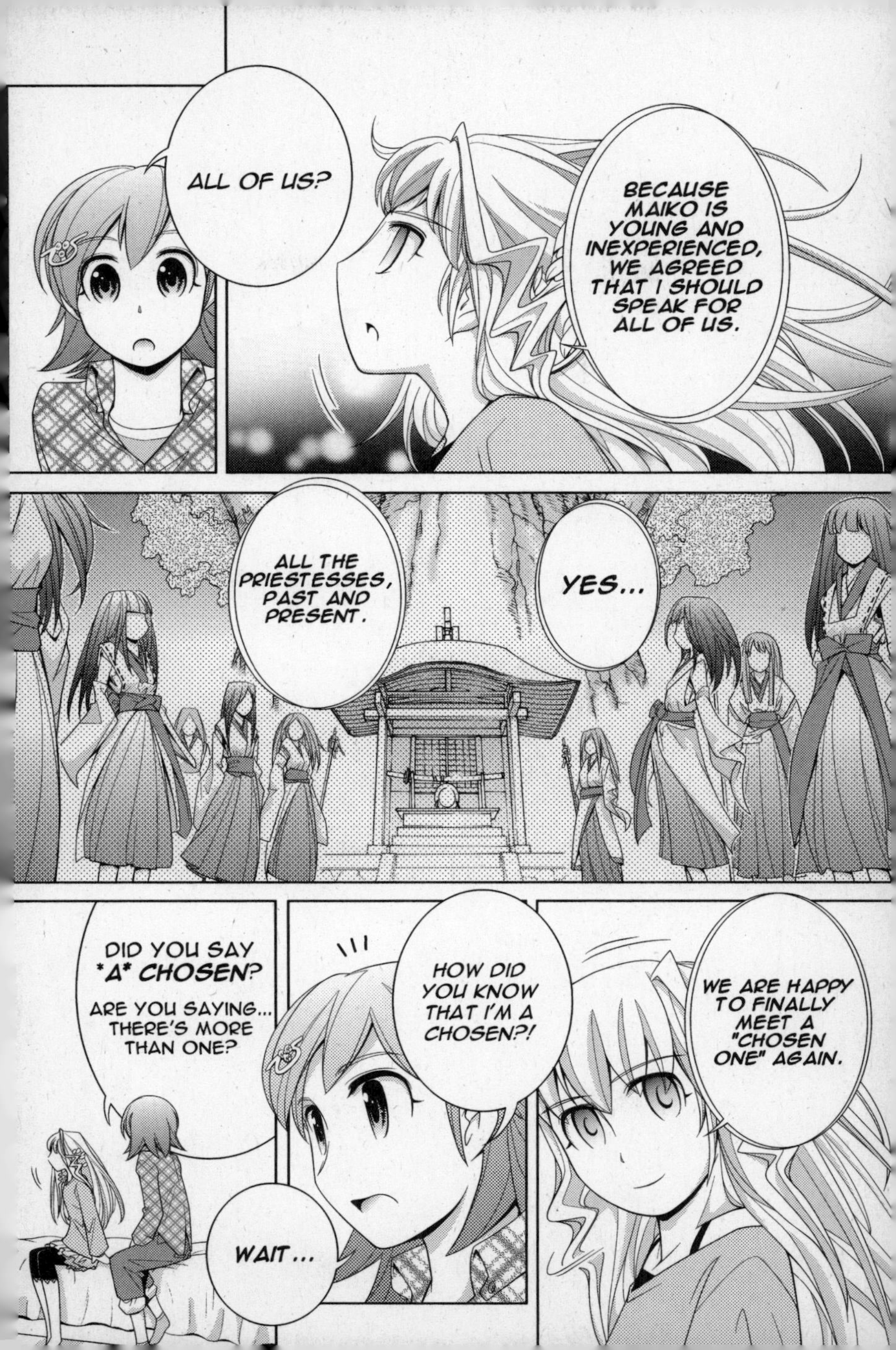
BECAUSE MAIKO IS YOUNG AND INEXPERIENCED, WE AGREED THAT I SHOULD SPEAK FOR ALL OF US.
ALL OF US?
YES...
ALL THE PRIESTESSES, PAST AND PRESENT.
WE ARE HAPPY TO FINALLY MEET A "CHOSEN ONE" AGAIN.
HOW DID YOU KNOW THAT I'M A CHOSEN?!
WAIT...
DID YOU SAY *A* CHOSEN?
ARE YOU SAYING... THERE'S MORE THAN ONE?

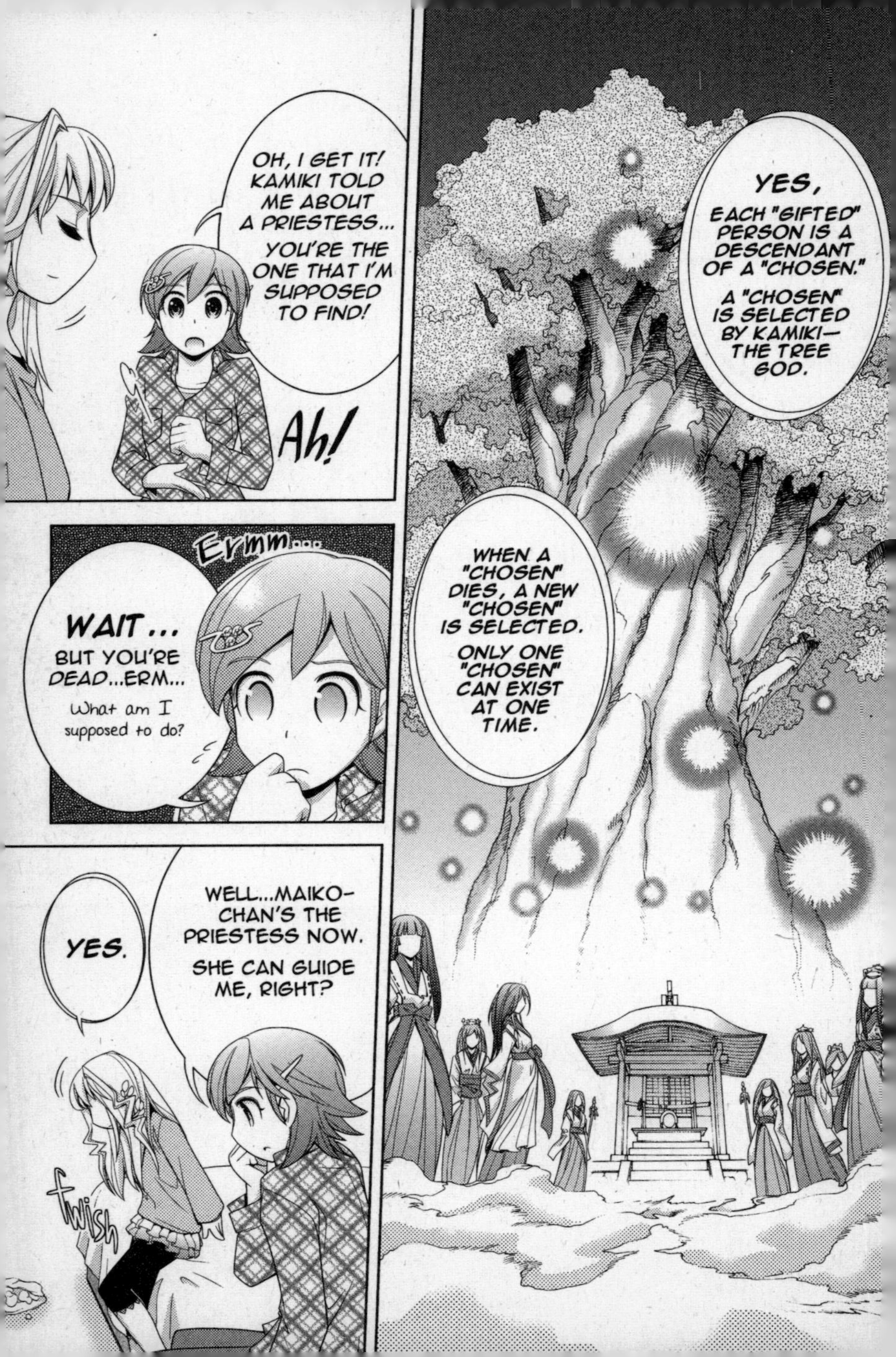
YES, EACH "GIFTED" PERSON IS A DESCENDANT OF A "CHOSEN." A "CHOSEN" IS SELECTED BY KAMIKI— THE TREE GOD.
WHEN A "CHOSEN" DIES, A NEW "CHOSEN" IS SELECTED. ONLY ONE "CHOSEN" CAN EXIST AT ONE TIME.
OH, I GET IT! KAMIKI TOLD ME ABOUT A PRIESTESS... YOU'RE THE ONE THAT I'M SUPPOSED TO FIND!
Ah!
Ermm...
WAIT... BUT YOU'RE DEAD...ERM... What am I supposed to do?
WELL...MAIKO-CHAN'S THE PRIESTESS NOW. SHE CAN GUIDE ME, RIGHT?
YES.
twish

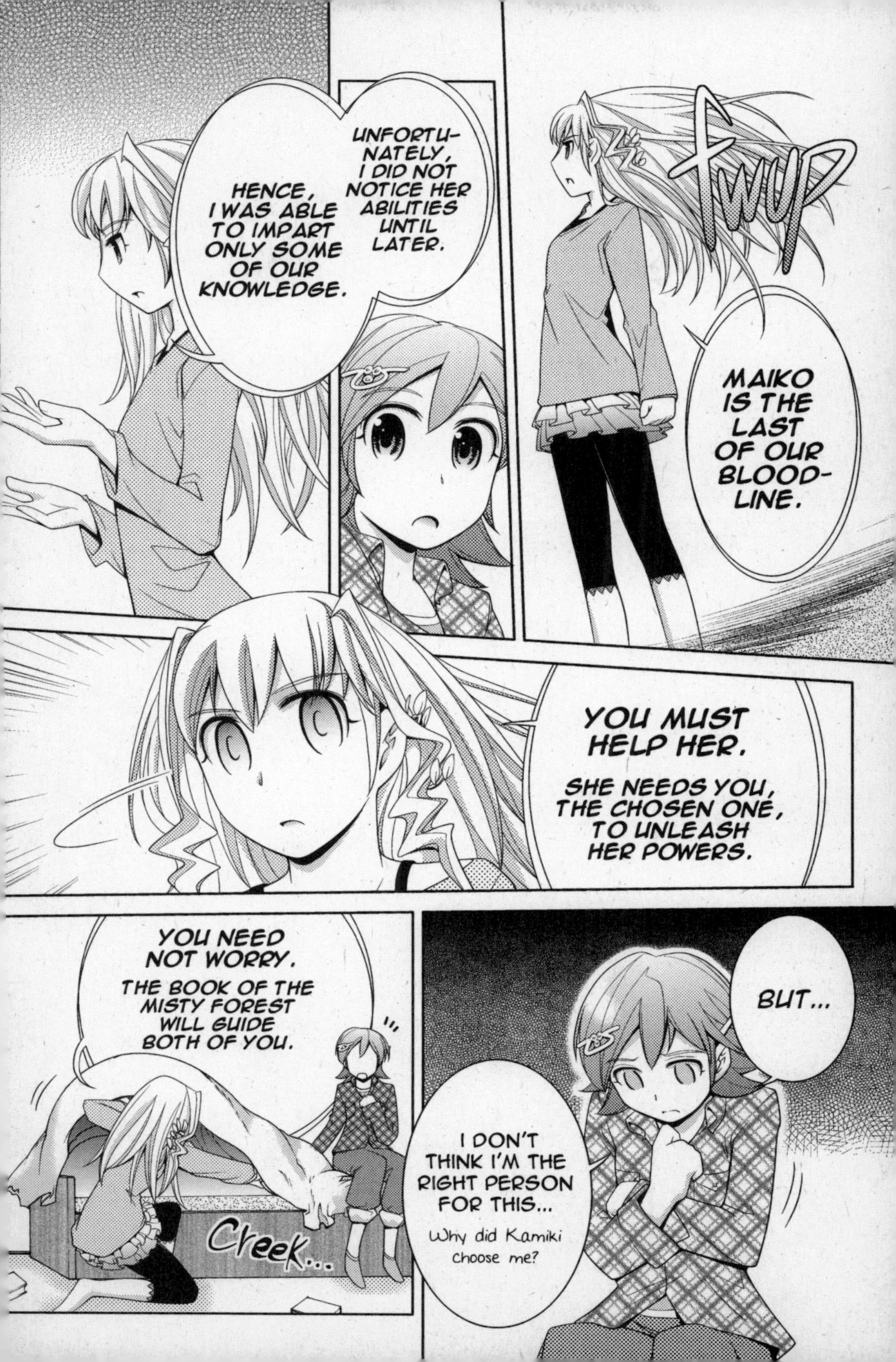
FWUP
MAIKO IS THE LAST OF OUR BLOOD-LINE.
UNFORTU-NATELY, I DID NOT NOTICE HER ABILITIES UNTIL LATER.
HENCE, I WAS ABLE TO IMPART ONLY SOME OF OUR KNOWLEDGE.
YOU MUST HELP HER.
SHE NEEDS YOU, THE CHOSEN ONE, TO UNLEASH HER POWERS.
BUT...
I DON'T THINK I'M THE RIGHT PERSON FOR THIS...
Why did Kamiki choose me?
YOU NEED NOT WORRY.
THE BOOK OF THE MISTY FOREST WILL GUIDE BOTH OF YOU.
Creek...

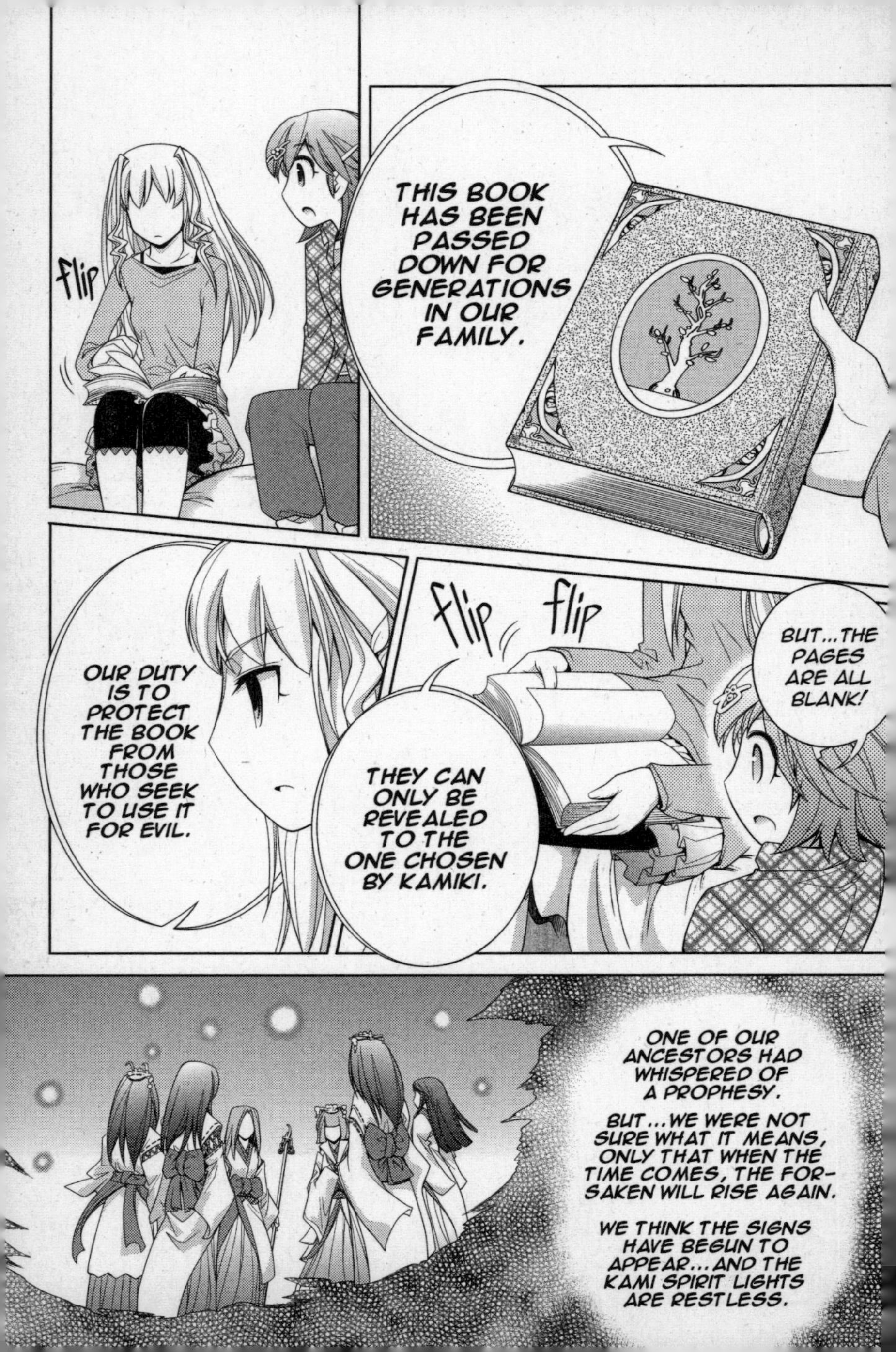
THIS BOOK HAS BEEN PASSED DOWN FOR GENERATIONS IN OUR FAMILY.
flip
BUT...THE PAGES ARE ALL BLANK!
flip flip
THEY CAN ONLY BE REVEALED TO THE ONE CHOSEN BY KAMIKI.
OUR DUTY IS TO PROTECT THE BOOK FROM THOSE WHO SEEK TO USE IT FOR EVIL.
ONE OF OUR ANCESTORS HAD WHISPERED OF A PROPHESY.
BUT...WE WERE NOT SURE WHAT IT MEANS, ONLY THAT WHEN THE TIME COMES, THE FOR-SAKEN WILL RISE AGAIN.
WE THINK THE SIGNS HAVE BEGUN TO APPEAR...AND THE KAMI SPIRIT LIGHTS ARE RESTLESS.

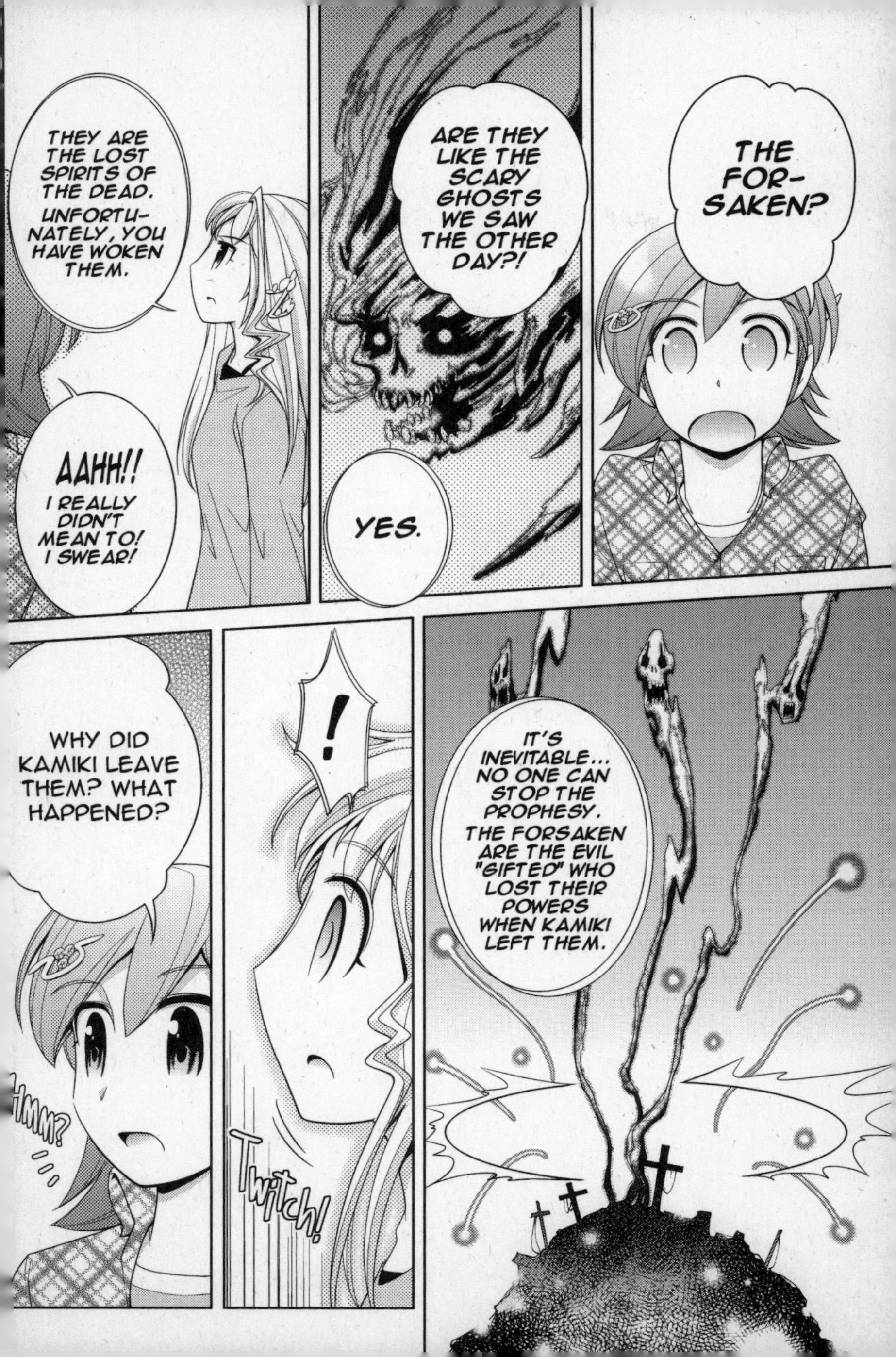
THE FOR-SAKEN?
ARE THEY LIKE THE SCARY GHOSTS WE SAW THE OTHER DAY?!
YES.
THEY ARE THE LOST SPIRITS OF THE DEAD. UNFORTU-NATELY, YOU HAVE WOKEN THEM.
AAHH!! I REALLY DIDN'T MEAN TO! I SWEAR!
IT'S INEVITABLE... NO ONE CAN STOP THE PROPHESY. THE FORSAKEN ARE THE EVIL "GIFTED" WHO LOST THEIR POWERS WHEN KAMIKI LEFT THEM.
!
TWITCH!
WHY DID KAMIKI LEAVE THEM? WHAT HAPPENED?
HMM?

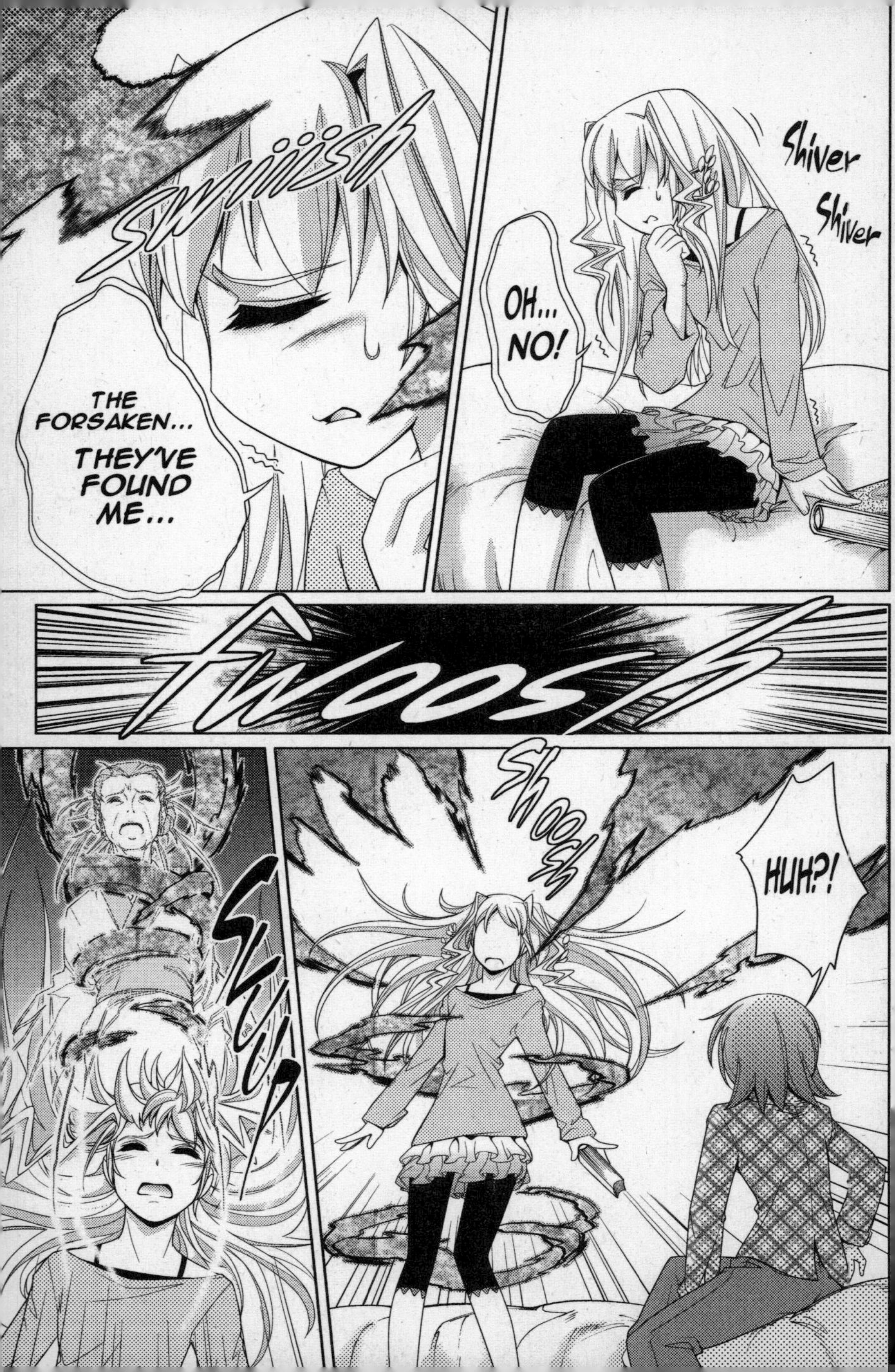
Shiver
Shiver
OH... NO!
Swiiiish
THE FORSAKEN...
THEY'VE FOUND ME...
fwoosh
Shoosh
HUH?!

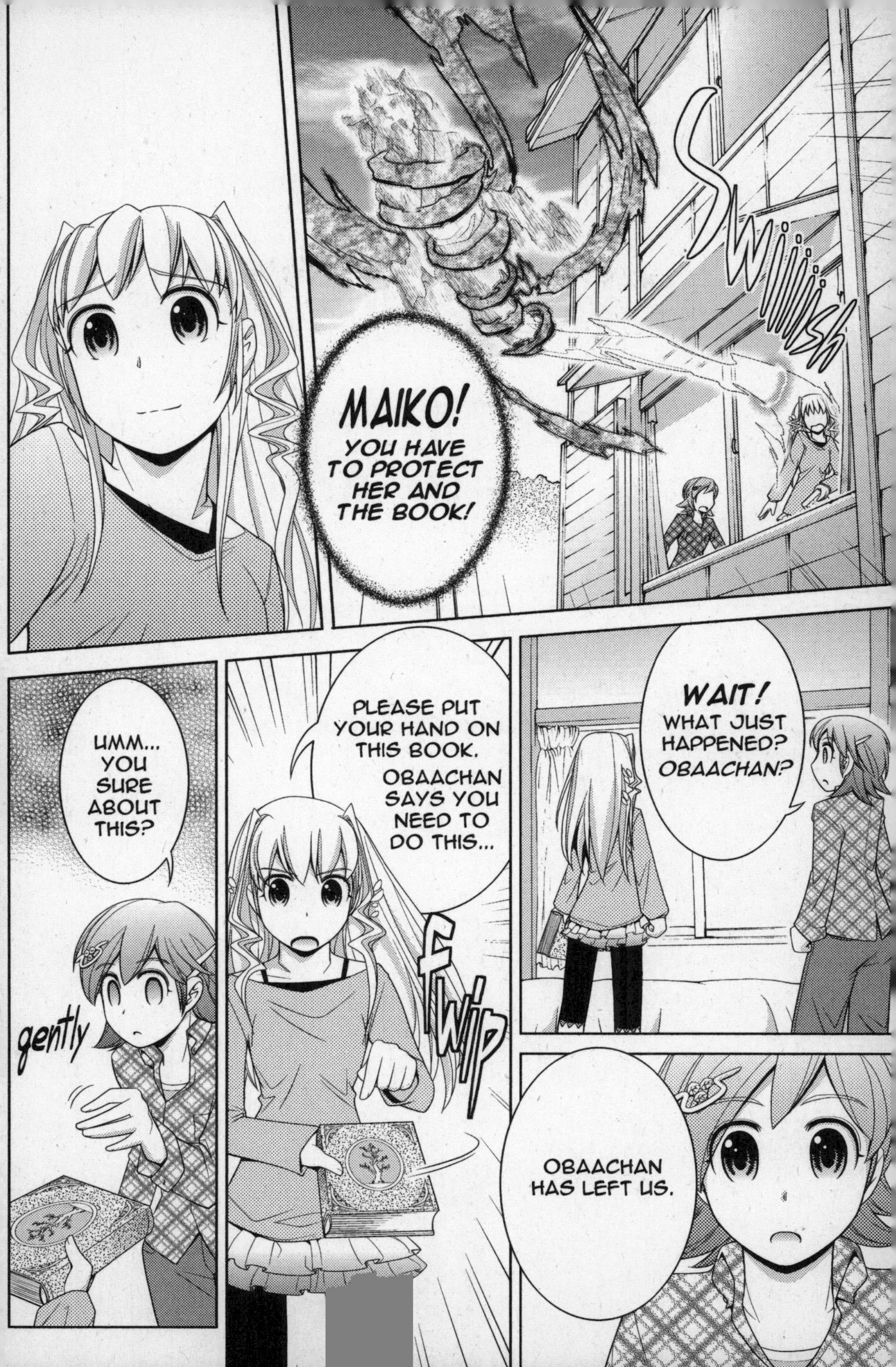
Swiiiish
MAIKO! YOU HAVE TO PROTECT HER AND THE BOOK!
WAIT! WHAT JUST HAPPENED? OBAACHAN?
OBAACHAN HAS LEFT US.
PLEASE PUT YOUR HAND ON THIS BOOK.
OBAACHAN SAYS YOU NEED TO DO THIS...
fwip
UMM... YOU SURE ABOUT THIS?
gently

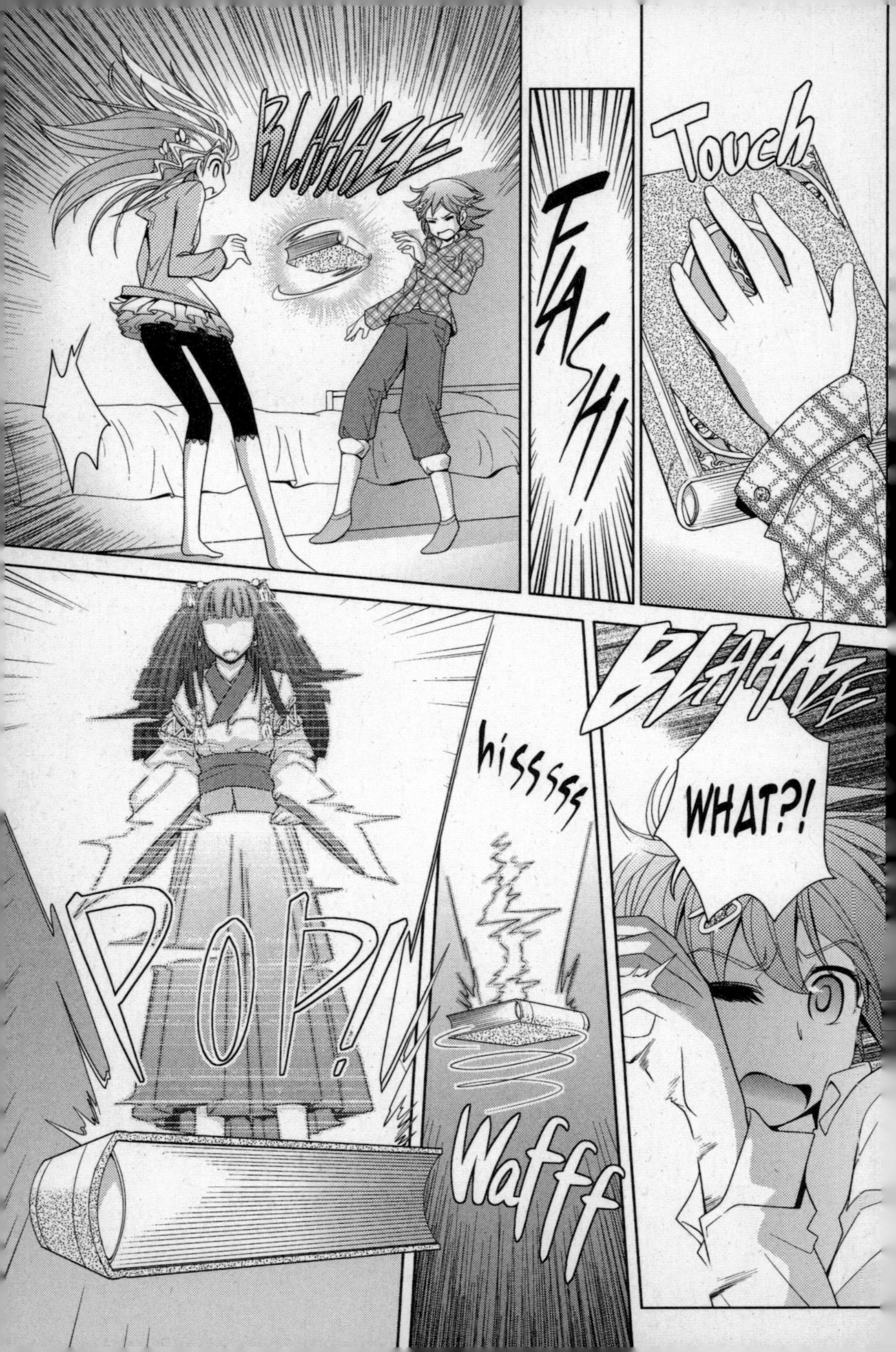
Touch
FLASH!
BLAAAZE
BLAAAZE
WHAT?!
hisssss
Waff
POP!

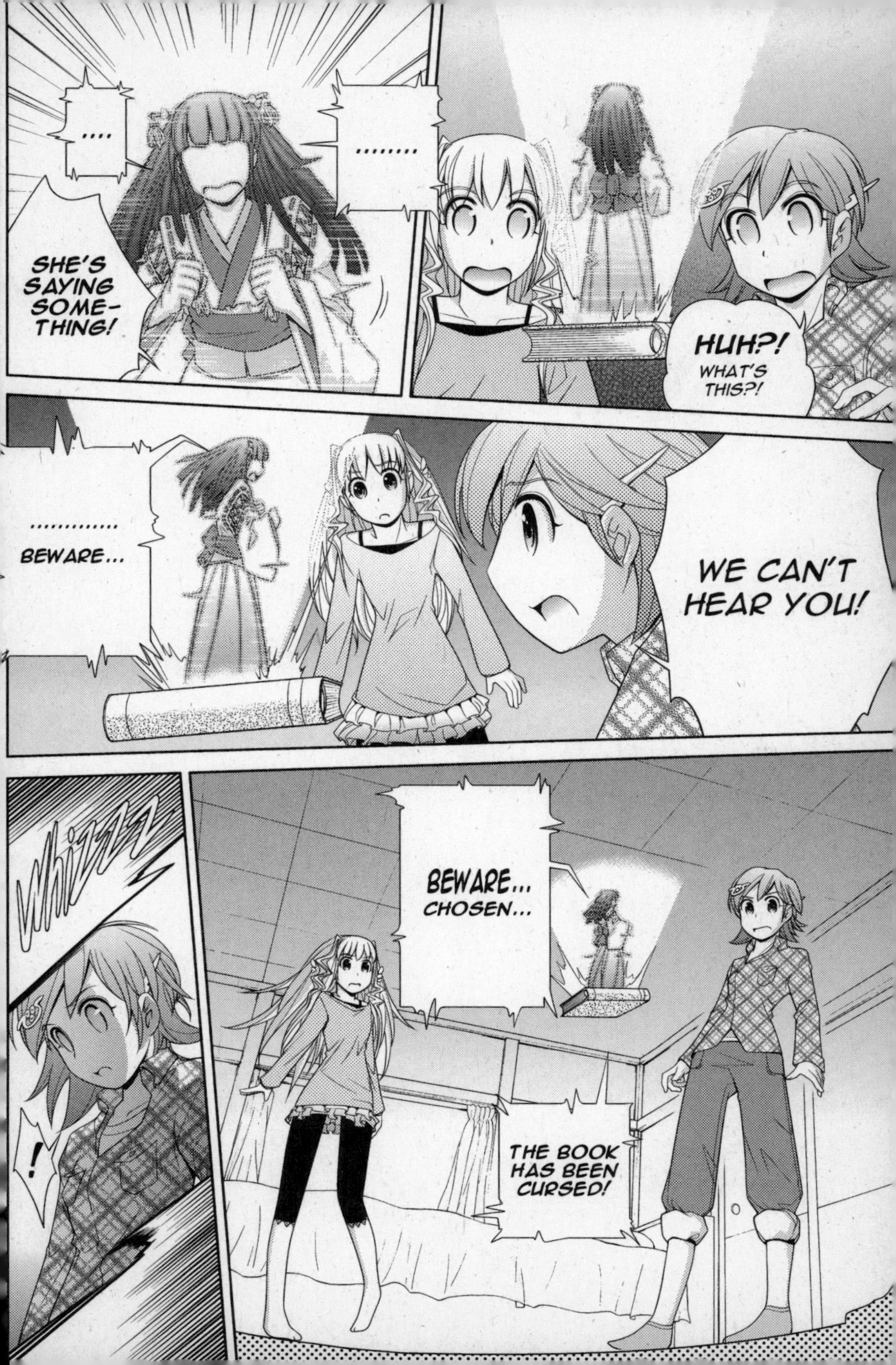

HUH?!
WHAT'S THIS?!
....
....
SHE'S SAYING SOME-THING!
WE CAN'T HEAR YOU!
....
BEWARE...
BEWARE... CHOSEN...
THE BOOK HAS BEEN CURSED!
whizzzz
!

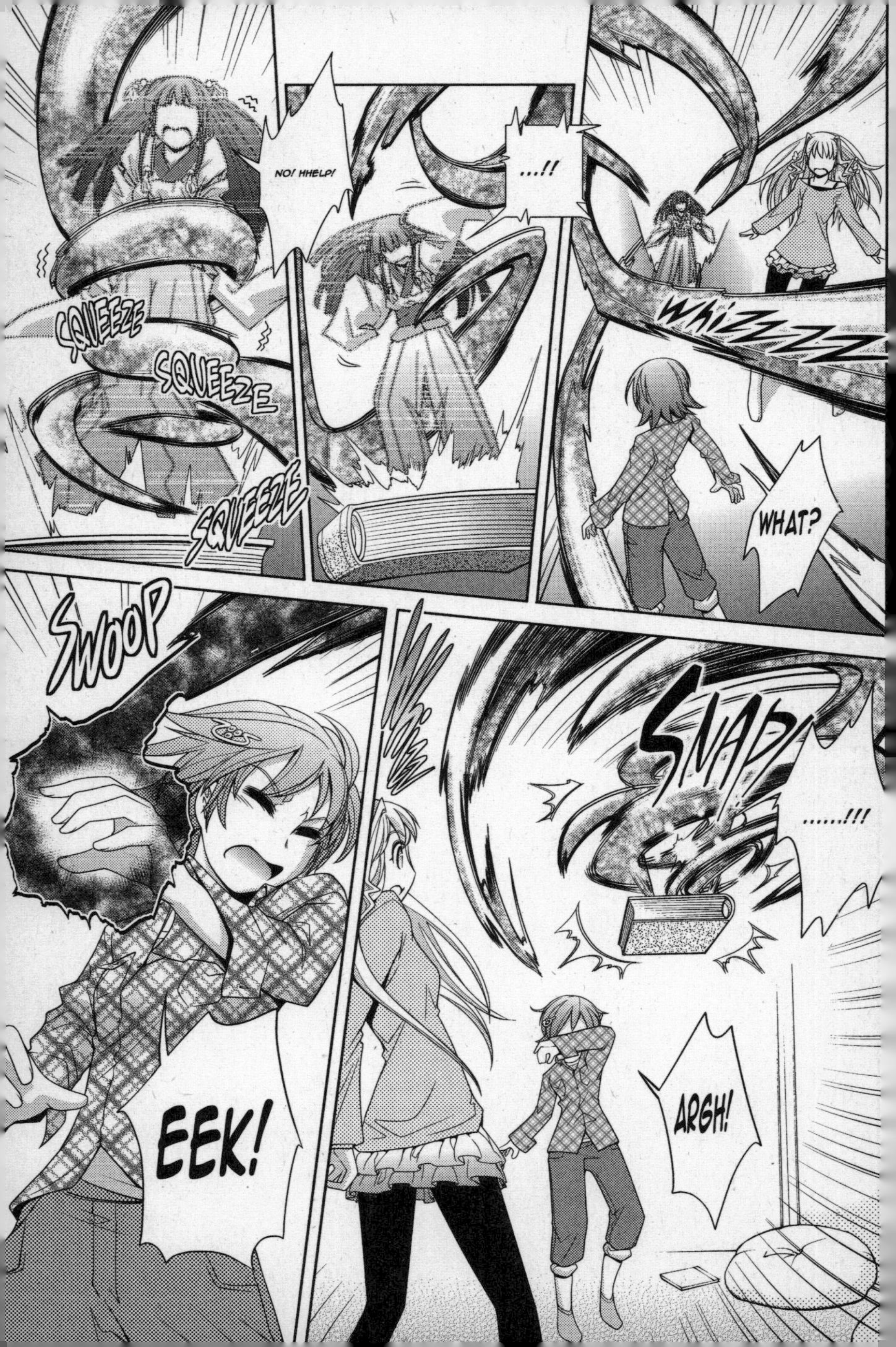
...!!
WHIZZZZ
WHAT?
NO! HHELP!
SQUEEZE
SQUEEZE
SQUEEZE
......!!!
SNAP!
ARGH!
SWOOP
EEK!

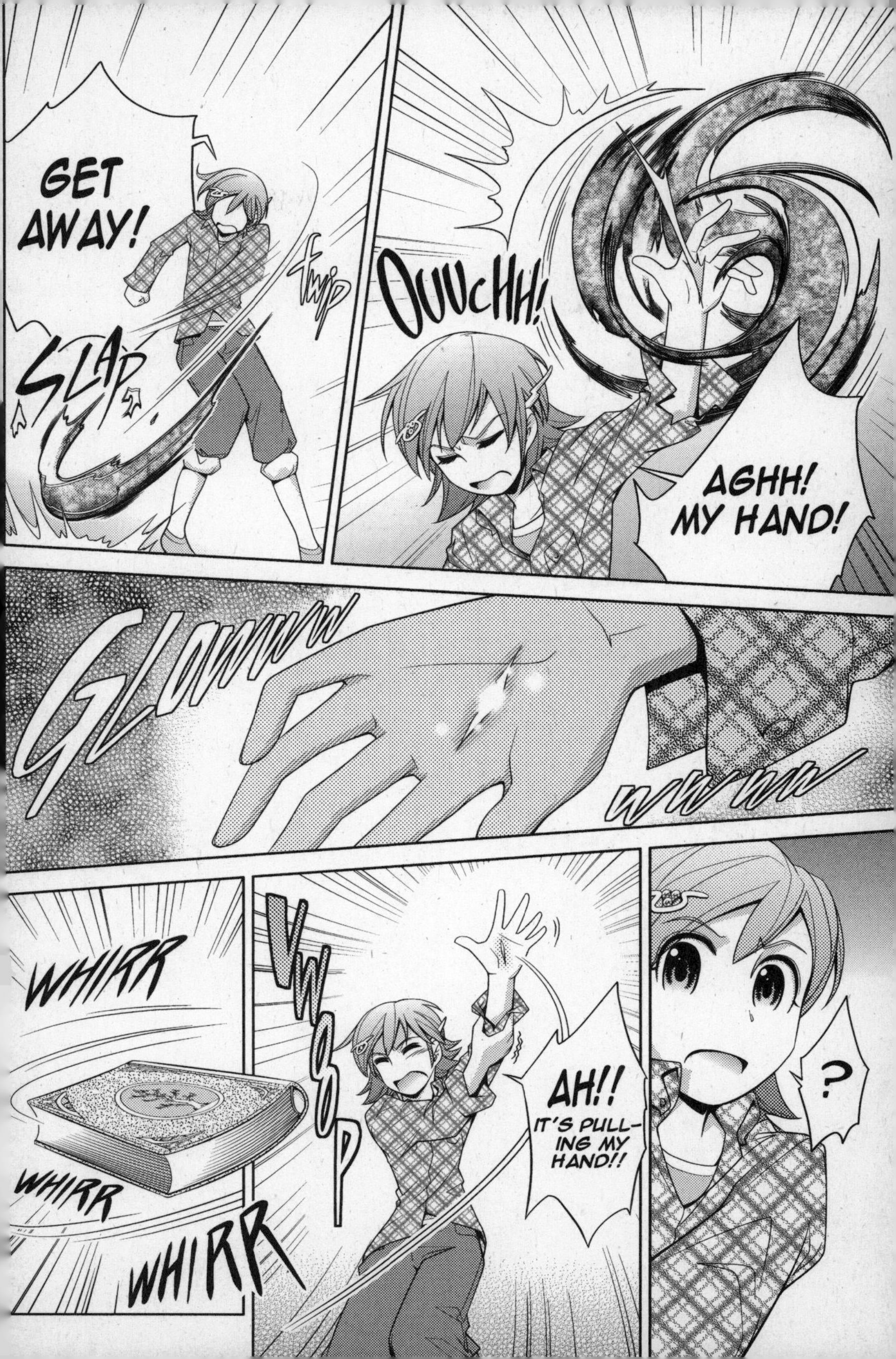
OUUCHH!
AGHH! MY HAND!
GET AWAY!
fwip
SLAP
?
VWOOOP
AH!! IT'S PULLING MY HAND!!
WHIRR
WHIRR
WHIRR

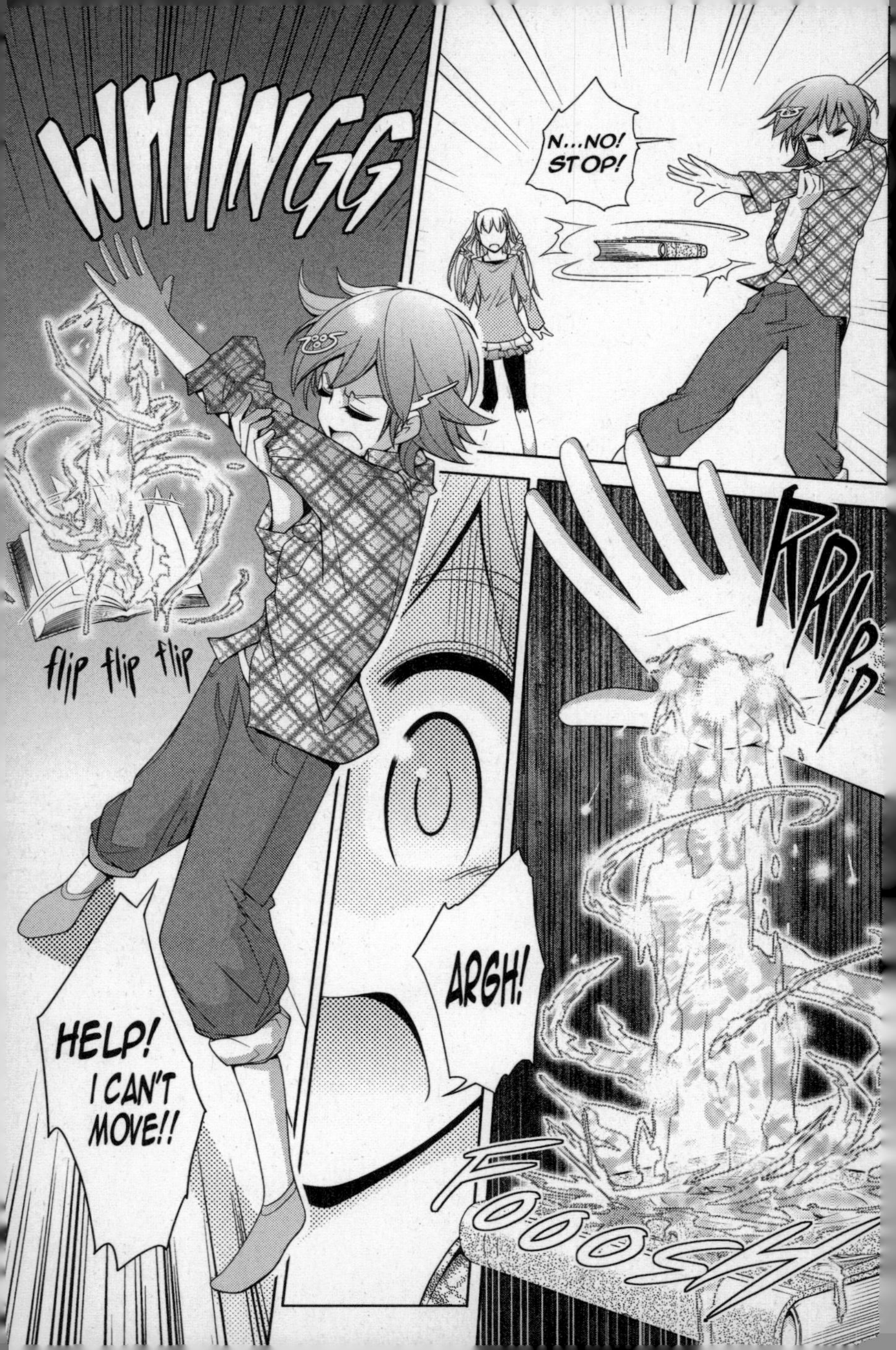
N...NO! STOP!
RRIPP
FOOOSH
ARGH!
WHINGG
flip flip flip
HELP! I CAN'T MOVE!!

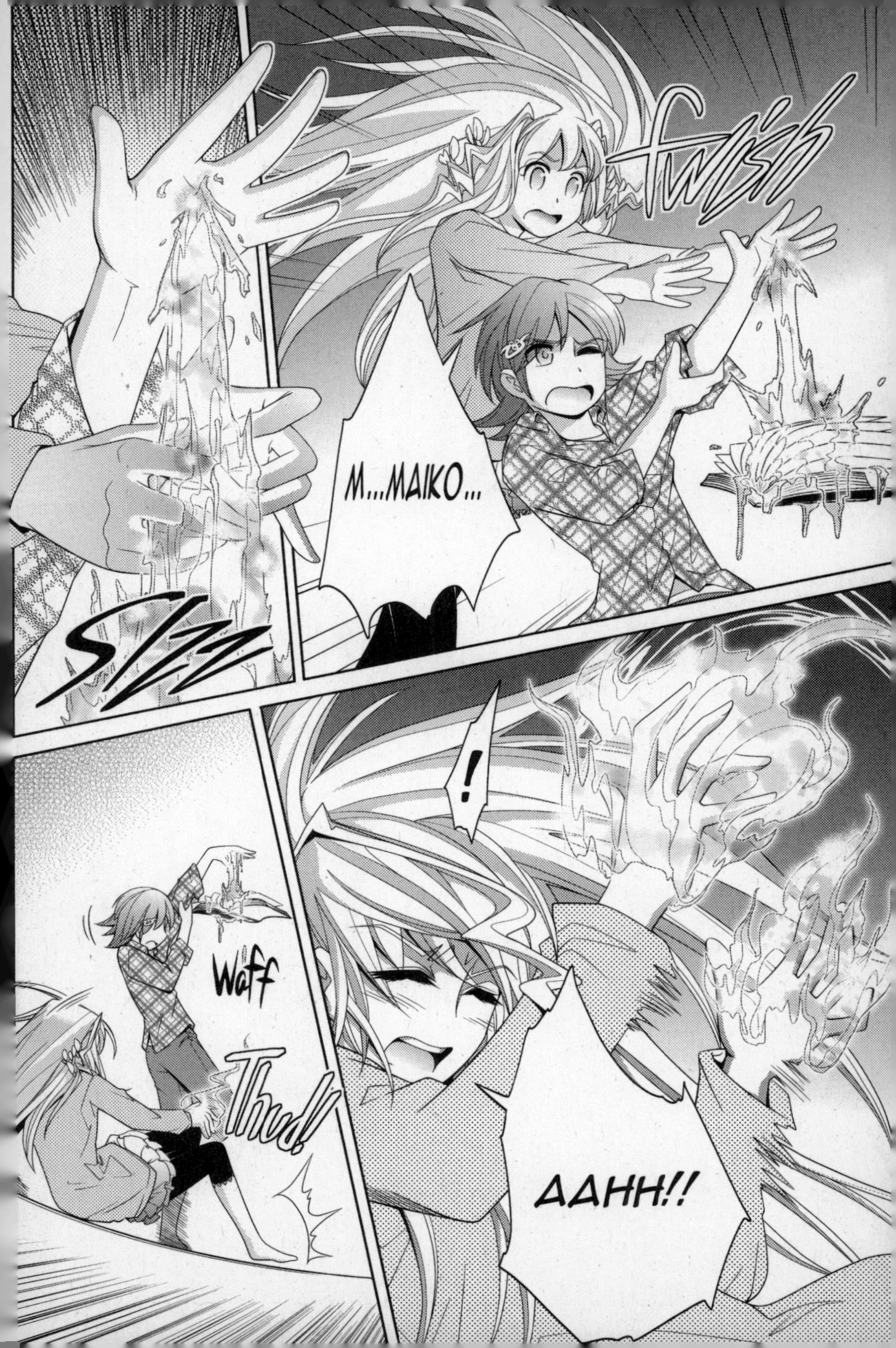
fwish
M...MAIKO...
SIZZ
!
AAHH!!
Waff
Thud!

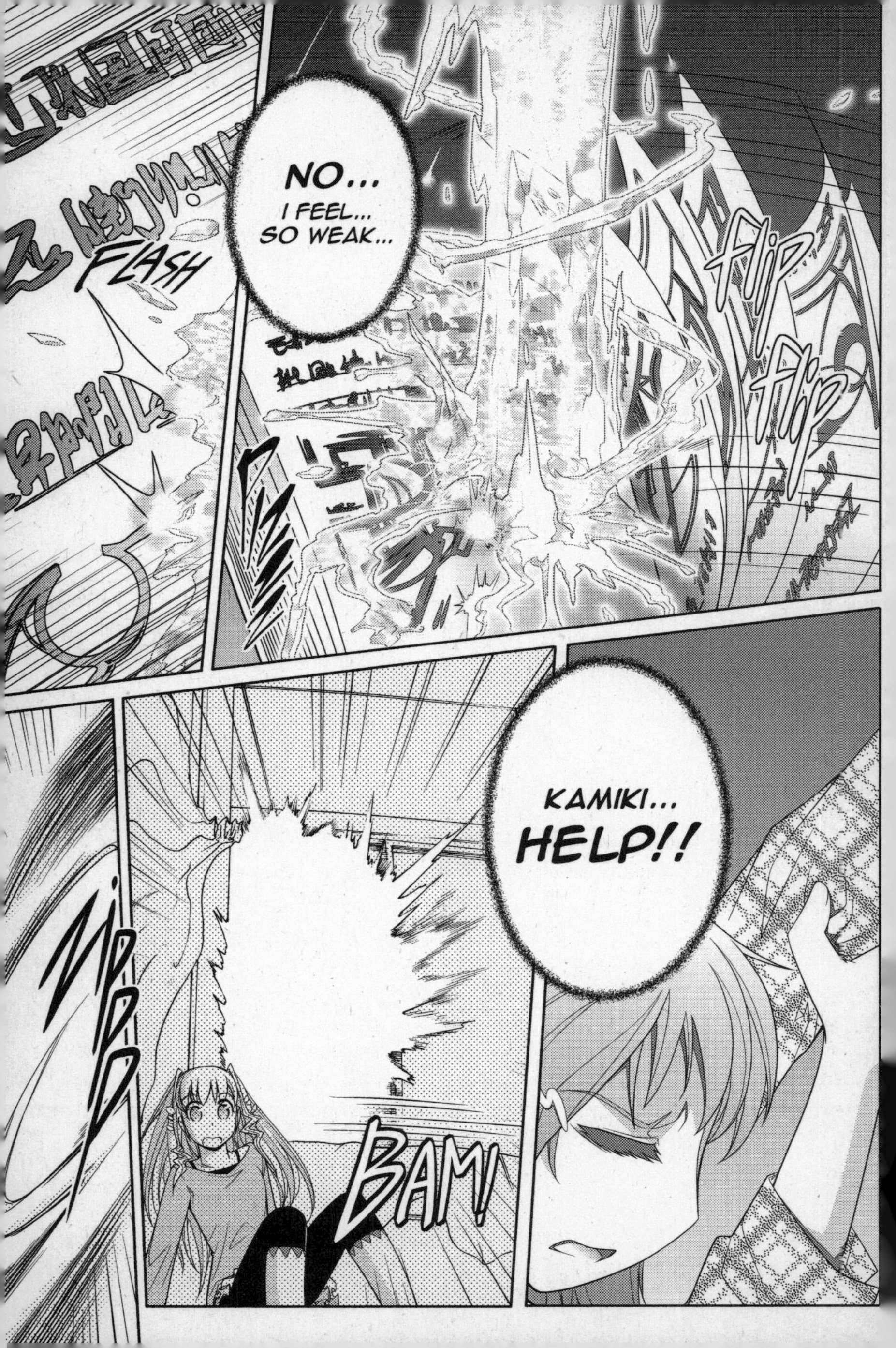
NO... I FEEL... SO WEAK...
flip
flip
FLASH
KAMIKI... HELP!!
BAM!

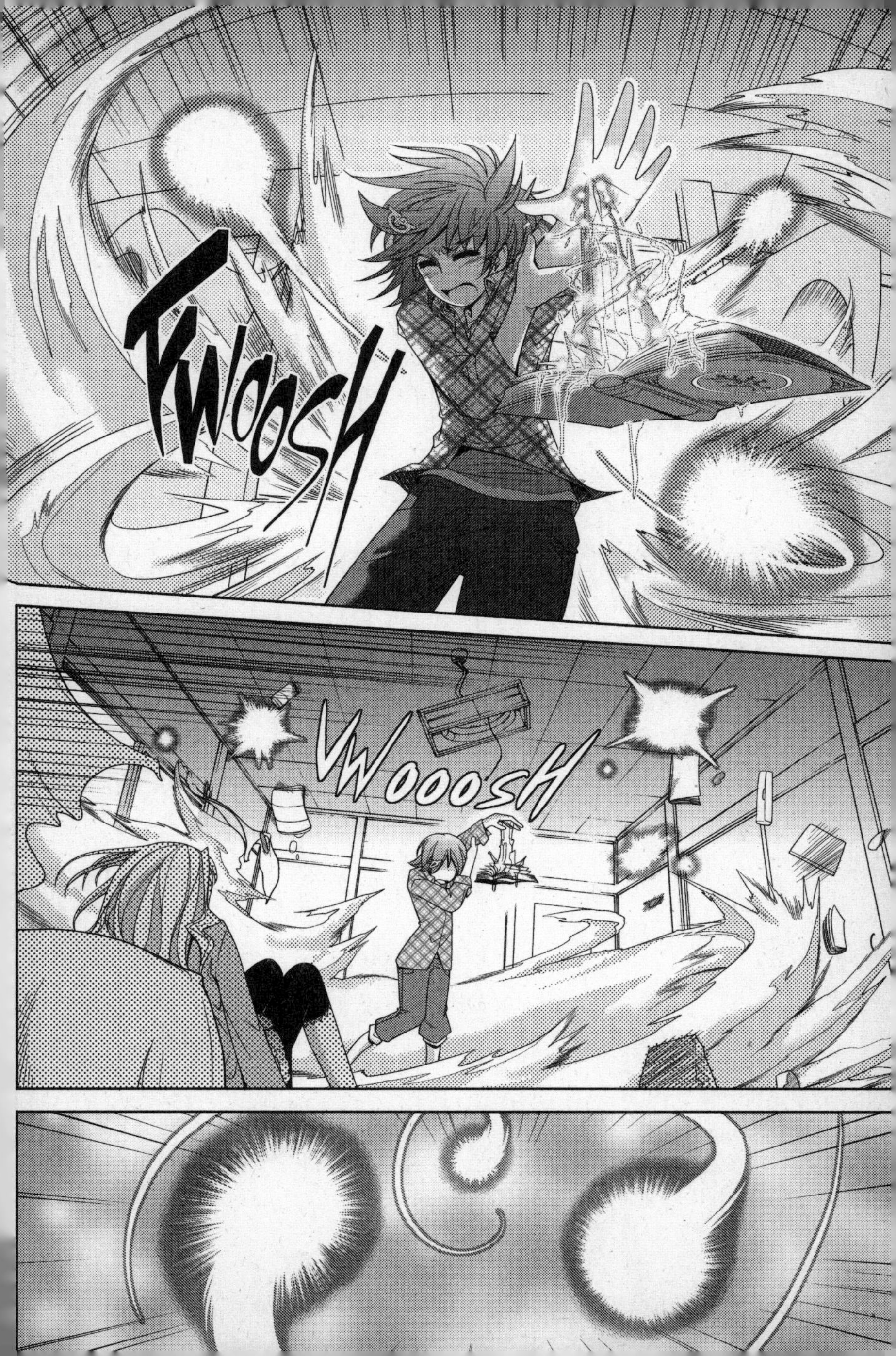
FWOOSH
VWOOOSH

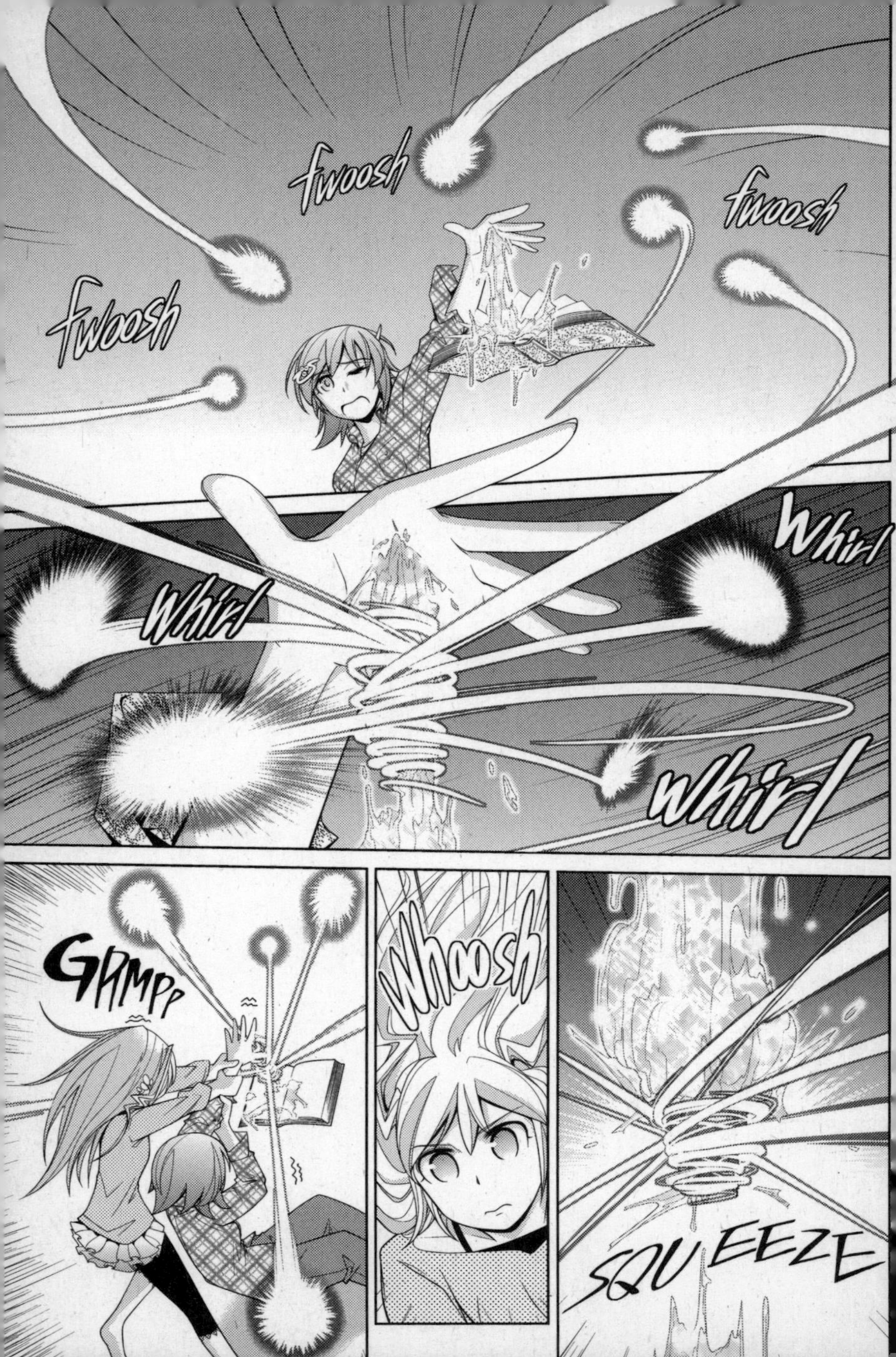
fwoosh
fwoosh
fwoosh
Whirl
whirl
whirl
SQUEEZE
Whoosh
GRMPP

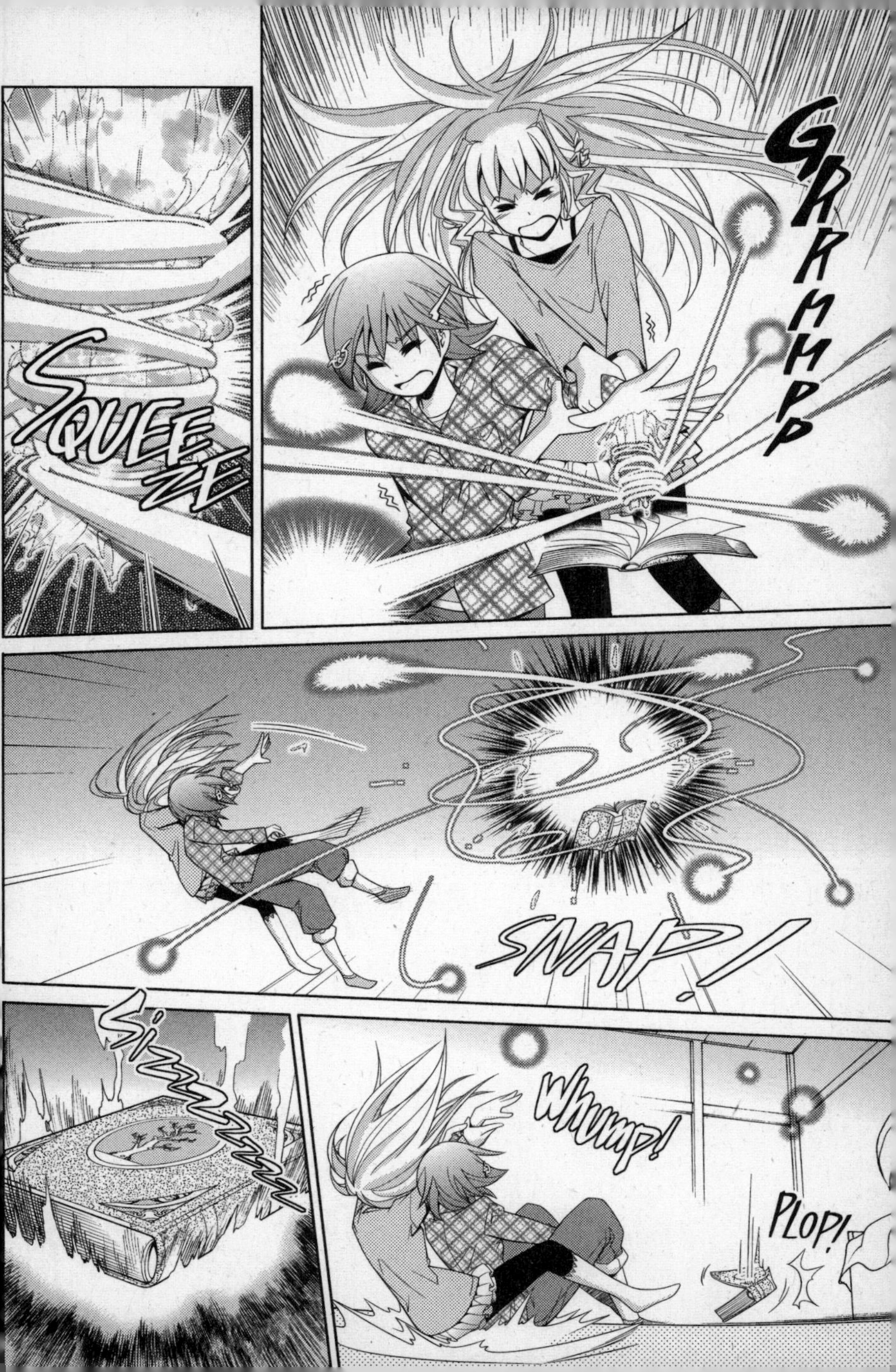
GRRMMPP
SQUEEZE
SNAP!
WHUMP!
PLOP!
SIZZZZZZZ

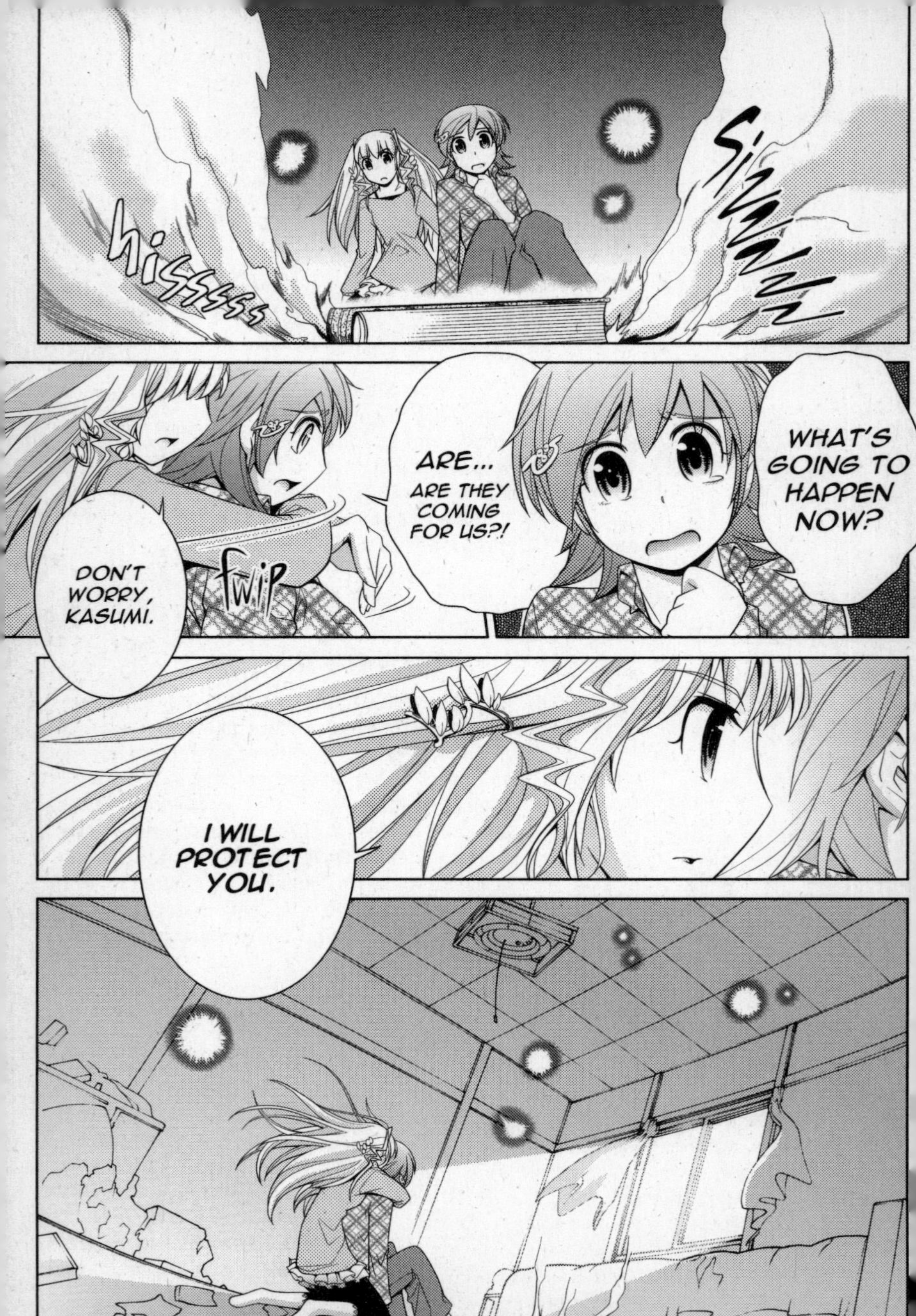
SIZZZZZZZ
hisssss
WHAT'S GOING TO HAPPEN NOW?
ARE... ARE THEY COMING FOR US?!
fwip
DON'T WORRY, KASUMI.
I WILL PROTECT YOU.

Yuuta's Guide to Japanese Words and Culture

Here, I, Yuuta Goodwin, the cultural expert, will explain the words and references to Japanese culture that come up in the story. Okay, here we go!

The Shrine

In Chapter 2, we found a shrine in the *Windy Garden*. It was built to appease the spirits. But Kasumi-chan somehow broke the spiritual barrier when she touched the spiritual rope and the evil spirits escaped! Oh my gosh, that was super scary!

Kogals vs. Ganguros

The girls that appear in Chapter 3 as Seiji-senpai's fans are "Kogals." Kogals are high school girls with dyed light brown hair or streaked hair, who wear lots of makeup, short skirts, loose socks, and leather loafers. They're always trying to be different and are known to have the latest gadgets and newest designer accessories. These rich girls sport an artificial Californian suntan and love to buy expensive brand-name items like Louis Vuitton and Burberry. By the way, those Kogals with dark faces who use dark foundation or undergo excessive tanning are called "Ganguros."

Bishonen

In Chapter 3, Seiji-senpai's male fans are called "Bishonens." It means "beautiful boys" and usually refers to somewhat fragile, not too muscular, trim looking, beautiful-faced boys. Does that mean I'm a bishonen, too? Hmm... Seiji-senpai's bishonen, are the famous boy band "STARZ." They like to hang out with Seiji-senpai, who's Seiran's principal's only son and the most popular and handsome guy in Seiran.

Seiza

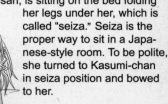

In the picture below, Maiko-chan, actually her obassan, is sitting on the bed folding her legs under her, which is called "seiza." Seiza is the proper way to sit in a Japanese-style room. To be polite, she turned to Kasumi-chan in seiza position and bowed to her.

Katsu curry and melon pan

In Chapter 5, Kasumi-chan is eating "katsu curry," which is a beef curry rice dish with deep-fried pork cutlet. And the round bread on the right is called "melong pan," which means "melon bread." I've heard that it's named after its look. It has a lattice-shaped pattern on the surface like netted melon. Melon pan is green and sweet and has a sweet biscuit cover over the bread. You can find it in almost every bakery in Japan and it's Maiko-chan's favorite pan.

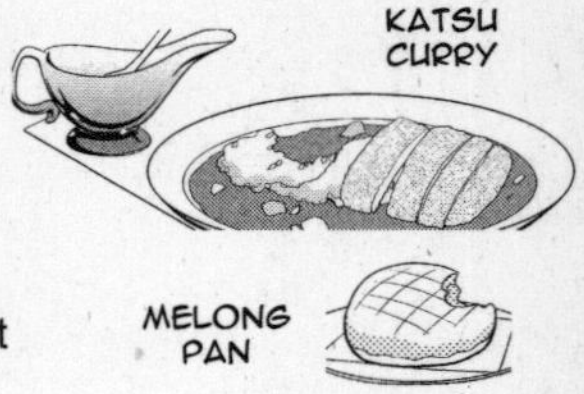
KATSU CURRY
MELONG PAN

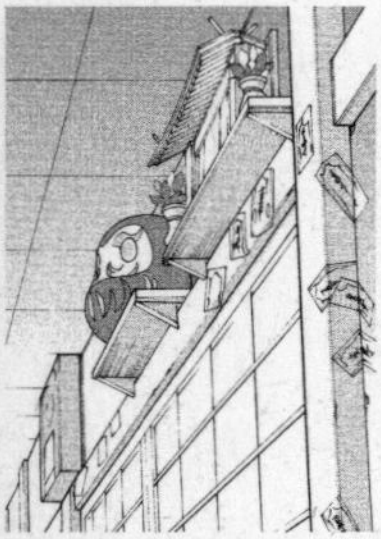

Household altar and talismans

This picture of Maiko-chan's house in Chapter 6 shows a small altar called "Kamidana." It is placed high on the wall to enshrine a kami god. The papers that are pasted on the pillars, which Kasumi-chan calls "spirit seals," are talismans to ward off evil spirits. They're called "ofuda" or "gofu." Since they're there, it must mean that Maiko-chan's place is haunted! It must be tough to be able to see ghosts all the time!

The following are some Japanese words that came up in this book. These words are used in everyday conversations.

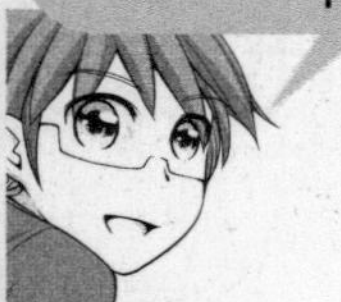

"Gomen"

The word "gomen" means "sorry." It's used when you apologize casually. I was so excited about the ComicCon that I forgot to tell Kasumi-chan that we can't go home with her. Oops!

"Onegai"

You may be able to guess from Kasumi-chan's expression on the right. "Onegai" means "please." It's used when you ask someone for a favor or for permission. How can I resist her plea for help, especially when she needs me so much?

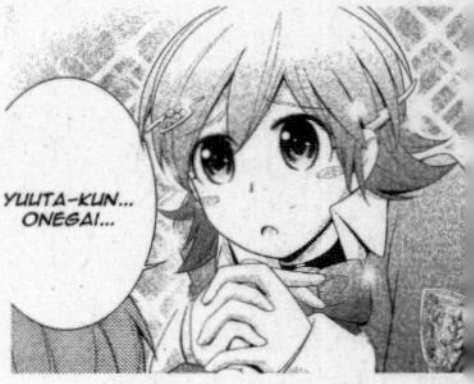
YUUTA-KUN... ONEGAI...

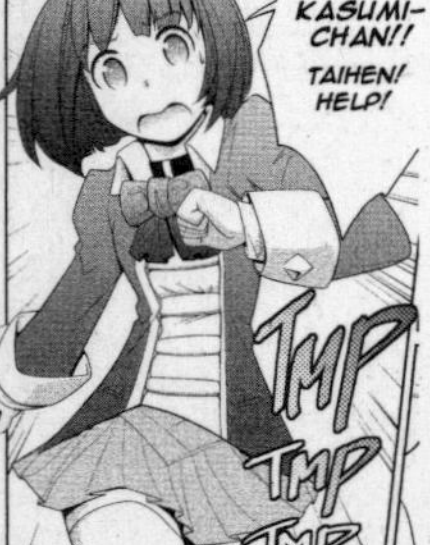
KASUMI-CHAN!! TAIHEN! HELP!
TMP
TMP
TMP

"Sumimasen"

"Sumimasen" means "excuse me" or "sorry." In Chapter 6, Kasumi-chan was standing at the front door of Maiko-chan's house, Kasumi-chan is checking if anybody's home. She is saying that she is sorry for disturbing.

"Taihen!"

When the word "taihen" is used in a sentence it means "very, much, great, serious, etc." But when used alone, it may mean "Oh no!" or "Terrible!" On the left, Noriko-chan is informing Kasumi-chan that there's big trouble.

Bonus Feature:
SugoiCon

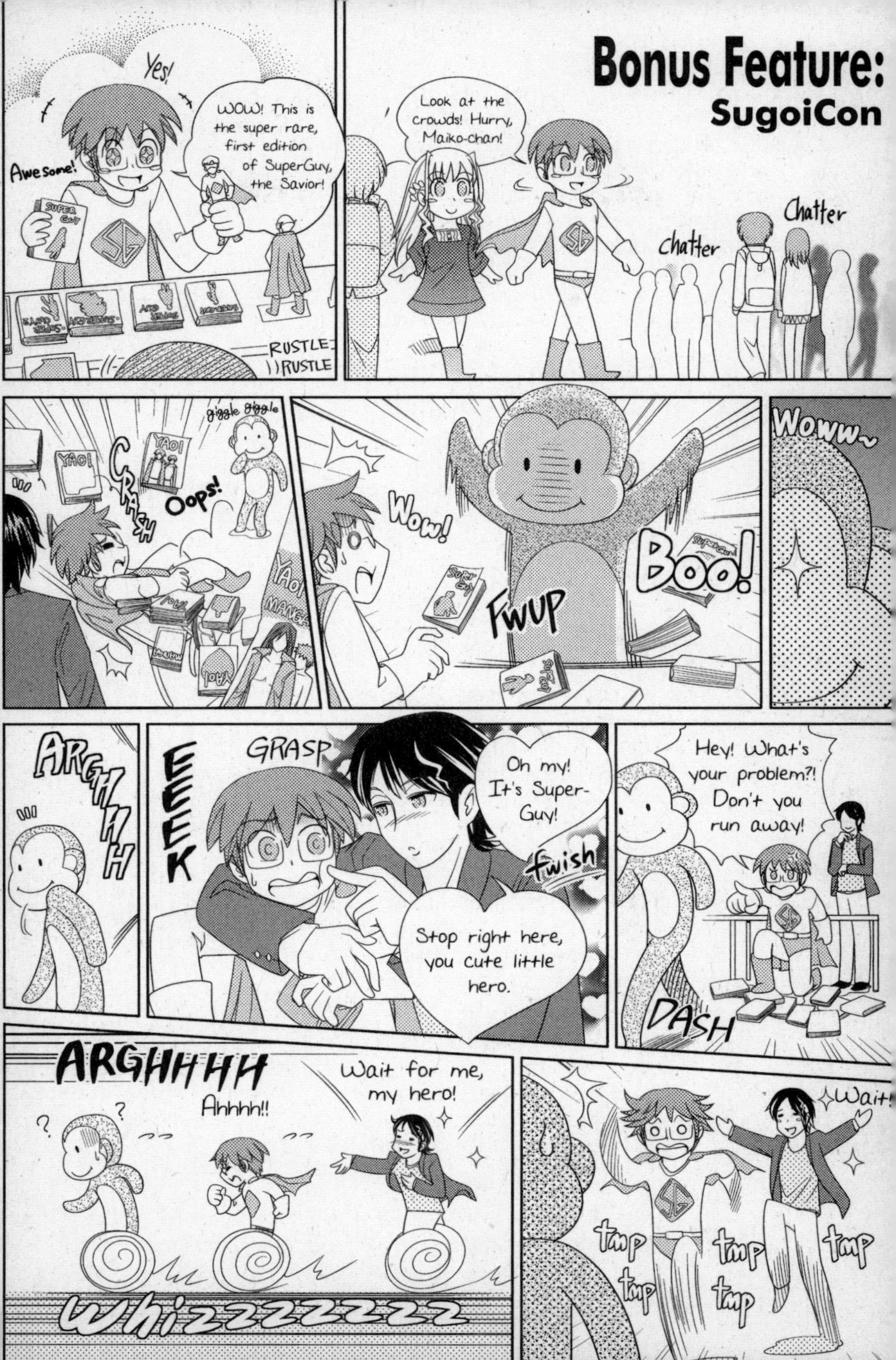

Look at the crowds! Hurry, Maiko-chan!
Chatter
Chatter
Yes!
WOW! This is the super rare, first edition of SuperGuy, the Savior!
Awesome!
SUPER GUY
RUSTLE
RUSTLE
Woww~
Wow!
Boo!
FWUP
giggle giggle
YAOI
YAOI
CRASH
Oops!
YAOI MANGA
Hey! What's your problem?! Don't you run away!
DASH
Oh my! It's Super-Guy!
GRASP
EEEEK
fwish
Stop right here, you cute little hero.
ARGHHHH
Wait!
tmp
tmp
tmp
tmp
tmp
tmp
ARGHHHH
Wait for me, my hero!
Ahhhh!!
Whizzzzzzzz

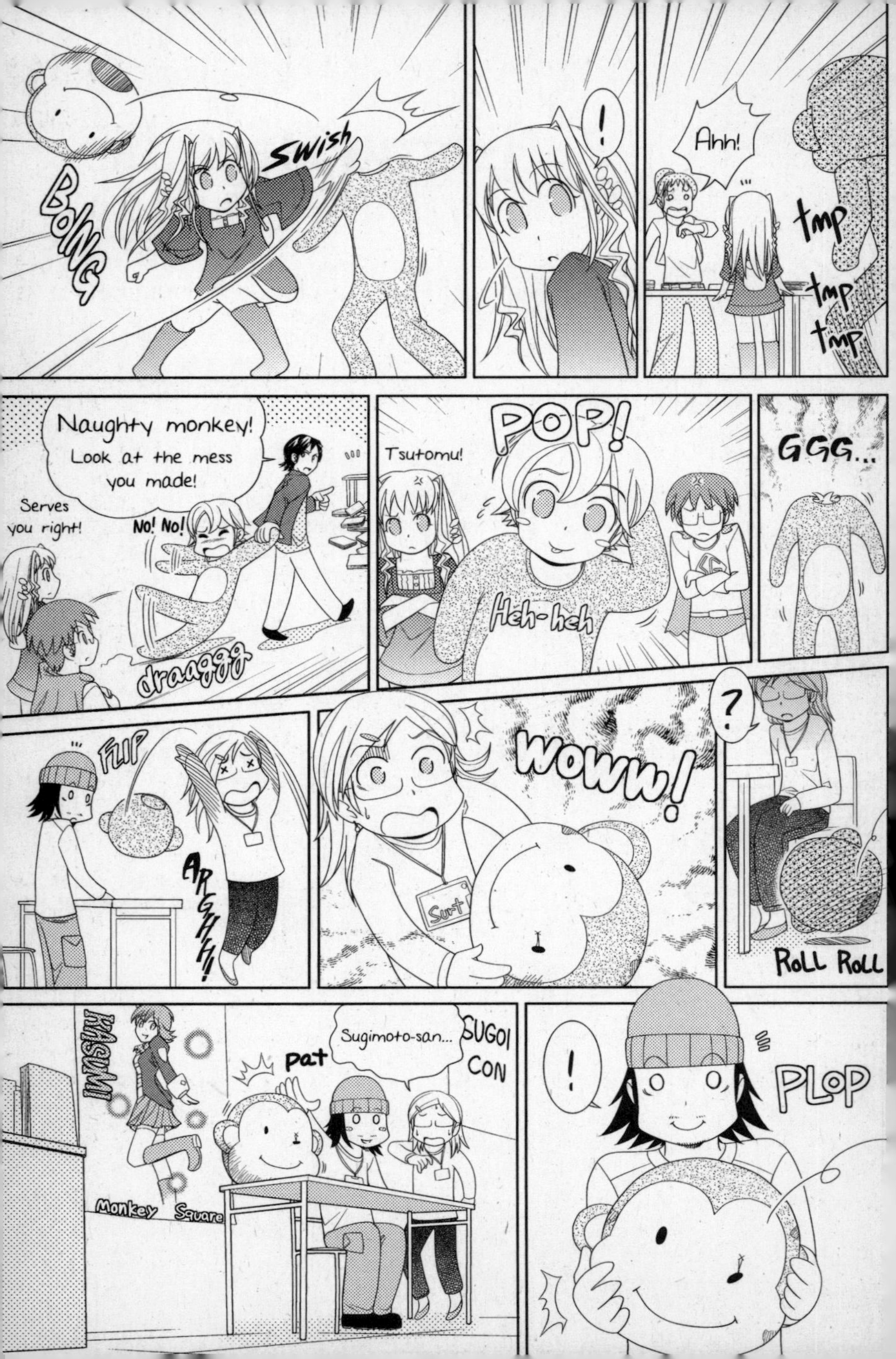
Ahh!
tmp
tmp
tmp
!
SWISH
BOING
GGG...
POP!
Tsutomu!
Heh-heh
Naughty monkey! Look at the mess you made!
Serves you right!
No! No!
draaggg
?
ROLL ROLL
WOWW!
FLIP
ARGHH!!
!
PLOP
SUGOI CON
Sugimoto-san...
pat
KASUMI
Monkey Square

Isamu Harada
勇　原田

5 FOOT 11 INCHES
BLOOD TYPE: A
17 YEARS OLD
TAURUS

SPECIAL POWERS:
HE HAS SUPERHUMAN STRENGTH WHEN HE BENDS HIS KNEE.

HOBBIES:
- KENDO
- VISITING ONSEN (HOT SPRINGS)
- WATCHING PERIOD DRAMAS

FAVORITE PHRASE:
NONE. HE DOESN'T SPEAK MUCH.

FAVORITE FOODS:
- NOT PICKY. HE EATS ANYTHING THAT SEIJI EATS.
- LIKES TO DRINK OCHA (GREEN TEA)

PERSONALITY:
HE'S A SILENT GUY WHO KEEPS TO HIMSELF AND BECAUSE OF THAT, HE DOESN'T HAVE MANY FRIENDS AND HIS ONLY CHILDHOOD COMPANION IS HIS COUSIN, SEIJI.

HE CARES FOR SEIJI DEEPLY AND WOULD DO ANYTHING FOR HIM. ISAMU IS AN EXCELLENT MARTIAL ARTIST AND ALWAYS WATCHES SEIJI AND PROTECTS HIM FROM HARM.

HE SHOWS HIS BRAVERY AND HIS BIG HEART WHEN HE RUSHES TO SAVE KASUMI, DESPITE THE DANGER OF HURTING HIMSELF.

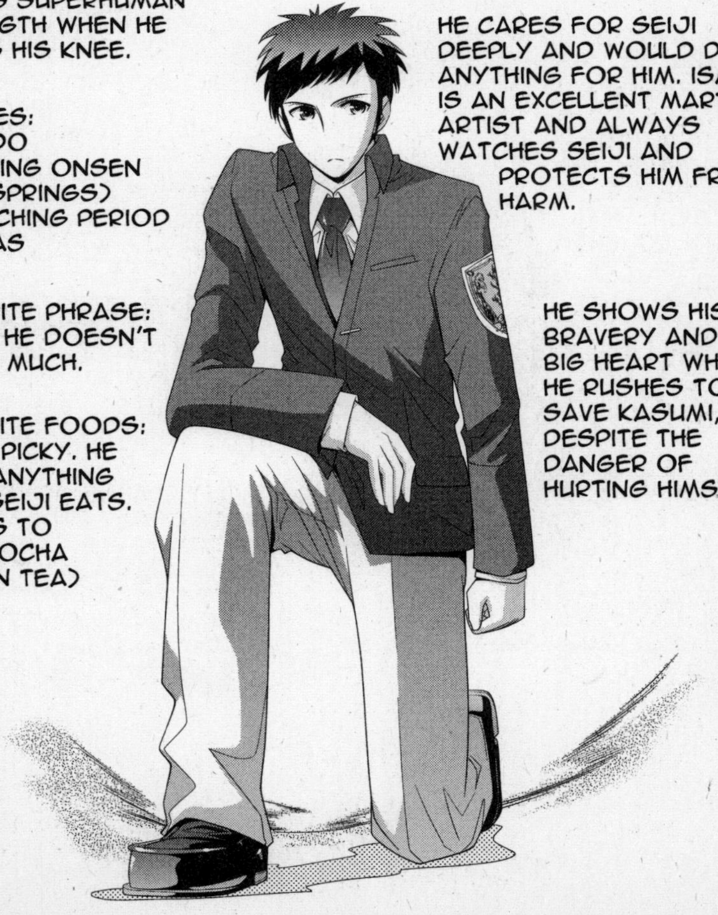

Seiji Nishimura
誠司　　西村

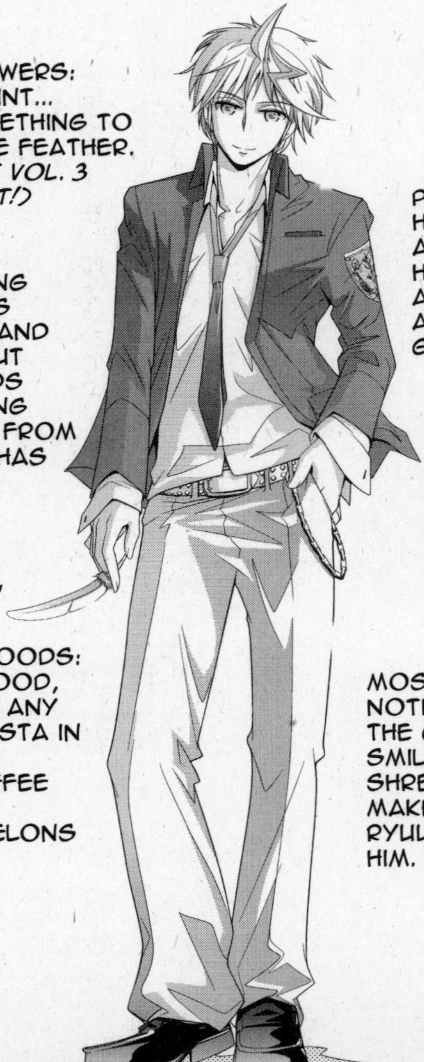

5 FEET 10 INCHES
BLOOD TYPE: B
17 YEARS OLD
LEO

SPECIAL POWERS:
A SECRET HINT...
IT HAS SOMETHING TO DO WITH THE FEATHER.
(CHECK OUT VOL. 3 TO FIND OUT!)

HOBBIES:
- COLLECTING GIRLFRIENDS
- CLUBBING AND HANGING OUT WITH FRIENDS
- COLLECTING SOUVENIRS FROM PLACES HE HAS BEEN TO

FAVORITE PHRASE:
"MY DEAR..."

FAVORITE FOODS:
- ITALIAN FOOD, ESPECIALLY ANY TYPE OF PASTA IN RED SAUCE
- DARK COFFEE
- GELATO
- SWEET MELONS

PERSONALITY:
HE'S FRIENDLY, FLIRTY, AND EASYGOING. HE LIKES TO HAVE FUN AND IS A CHARMING AND CHARISMATIC GUY.

HE HAS A VERY LOYAL GROUP OF FANS AND WOULD HAVE BEEN THE MOST POPULAR GUY IN SCHOOL, IF NOT FOR RYUUKI.

MOST PEOPLE DON'T NOTICE THAT BENEATH THE CAREFREE AND IDLE SMILE, LIES A GLINT OF SHREWDNESS, WHICH MAKES KASUMI AND RYUUKI SUSPICIOUS OF HIM.

Reina Takemoto
麗奈　竹本

SPECIAL POWERS:
SHE'S NOT A "GIFTED" BUT SOMETHING HAPPENS LATER IN THE STORY...

HOBBIES:
- SHOPPING, SHOPPING, AND MORE SHOPPING!
- READING GOSSIP MAGS
- GOING TO THE SPA

FAVORITE PHRASE:
"*HOW DARE YOU...*" AND ANYTHING ELSE SARCASTIC AND DEMEANING.

FAVORITE FOODS:
- ANYTHING HIGH-CLASS AND EXPENSIVE, AS LONG AS IT'S AT A POSH RESTAURANT.

- HER SECRET CRAVING (THAT SHE "*WOULD NOT BE CAUGHT DEAD EATING THIS*") IS ROASTED CHESTNUTS.

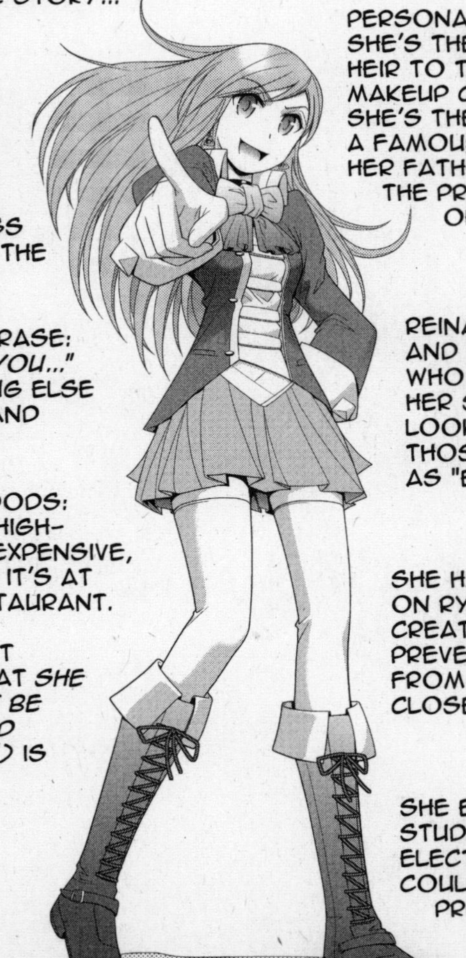

5 FOOT 4 INCHES
BLOOD TYPE: B
16 YEARS OLD
GEMINI

PERSONALITY:
SHE'S THE ONLY CHILD AND HEIR TO THE TAKEMOTO MAKEUP CONGLOMERATE. SHE'S THE DAUGHTER OF A FAMOUS ACTRESS AND HER FATHER IS RELATED TO THE PRIME MINISTER OF JAPAN.

REINA IS A SPOILED AND BEAUTIFUL GIRL WHO LIKES TO FLAUNT HER STATUS AND LOOKS DOWN ON THOSE WHO AREN'T AS "ELITE" AS HER.

SHE HAS A HUGE CRUSH ON RYUU-SAMA AND CREATED THE RSF TO PREVENT OTHER GIRLS FROM GETTING TOO CLOSE TO HIM.

SHE EVEN RIGGED THE STUDENT COUNCIL ELECTIONS SO SHE COULD BE HIS VICE PRESIDENT.

Maiko Koyanagi

舞子　小柳

SPECIAL POWERS:
SHE SEES AND TALKS TO SPIRITS. SHE CAN ALSO SUMMON THE KAMI-LIGHTS BY DANCING.

HOBBIES/OBSESSIONS:
- READING AND COLLECTING MANGA
- COLLECTING AMIGURUMI PLUSH TOYS
- DAYDREAMING
- DANCING

FAVORITE PHRASE:
NONE. SHE HARDLY SPEAKS.

5 FOOT 5 INCHES
BLOOD TYPE: O
16 YEARS OLD
PISCES

PERSONALITY:
SHE'S ECCENTRIC, QUIET, AND FORGETFUL. HOWEVER WHEN FACED WITH HER OBSESSIONS, SHE'LL STOP AT NOTHING TO GET WHAT SHE WANTS.

SHE'S ALSO PROTECTIVE OVER THE PEOPLE SHE CARES FOR AND IS TRAINED IN THE SECRET ART OF NAGINATAJUTSU.

SHE'S A LITTLE SOCIALLY INEPT AND IS CLUELESS TO THE FACT THAT SHE ACTUALLY HAS A SECRET FAN CLUB WHOSE MEMBERS WORSHIP HER ETHEREAL BEAUTY.

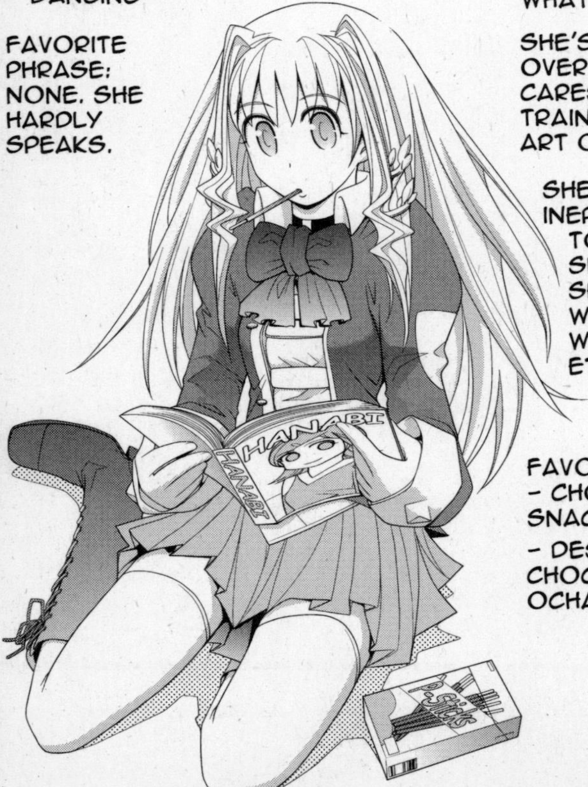
HANABI
HANABI
HANABI
P-Sticks

FAVORITE FOODS:
- CHOCOLATE-COVERED SNACKS
- DESSERTS, ICE CREAM, CHOCOLATES, CAKE, AND OCHA (GREEN TEA)

Get to know Kasumi's Team

(Guess what food we think is yucky!)

Koyadofu (freeze-dried tofu). It's the kind you boil in dashi soup. It's supposedly healthy but to me it tastes like a sponge!

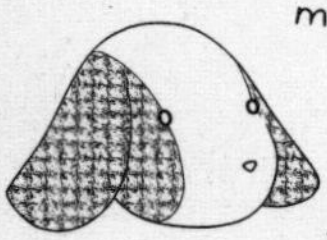

Boiled chicken skin! The white skin looks gross, tastes gross, and is gross.

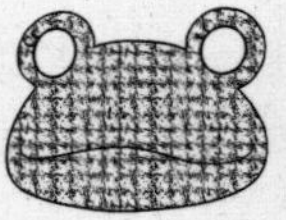

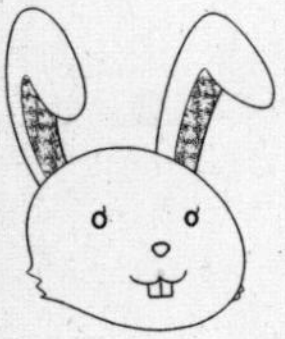

Green Peppers are too bitter!

I like everything...but if I were to pick, I would say Umeboshi (pickled plums), especially the ones with seeds.

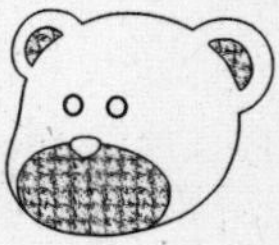

Raw Salmon eggs. I don't like how they taste like the beach and not in a good way...

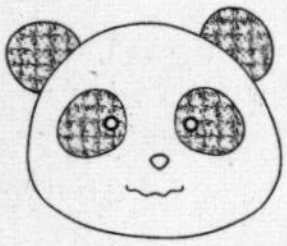

Nato with raw squid and raw egg. The sticky, gooey texture and the raw smell of the sea make me feel sick!

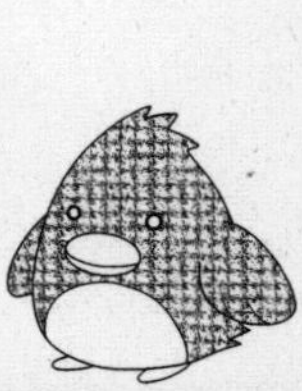

Are you a fan of Kasumi? Send us your fan art and we'll post it on our site and send you a special gift! ^_^

Answers: Dog (Harumi), Frog (Stanley), Rabbit (Natuki), Bear (Komamiya-san), Panda (Sugimoto-san), Chick (Surt)

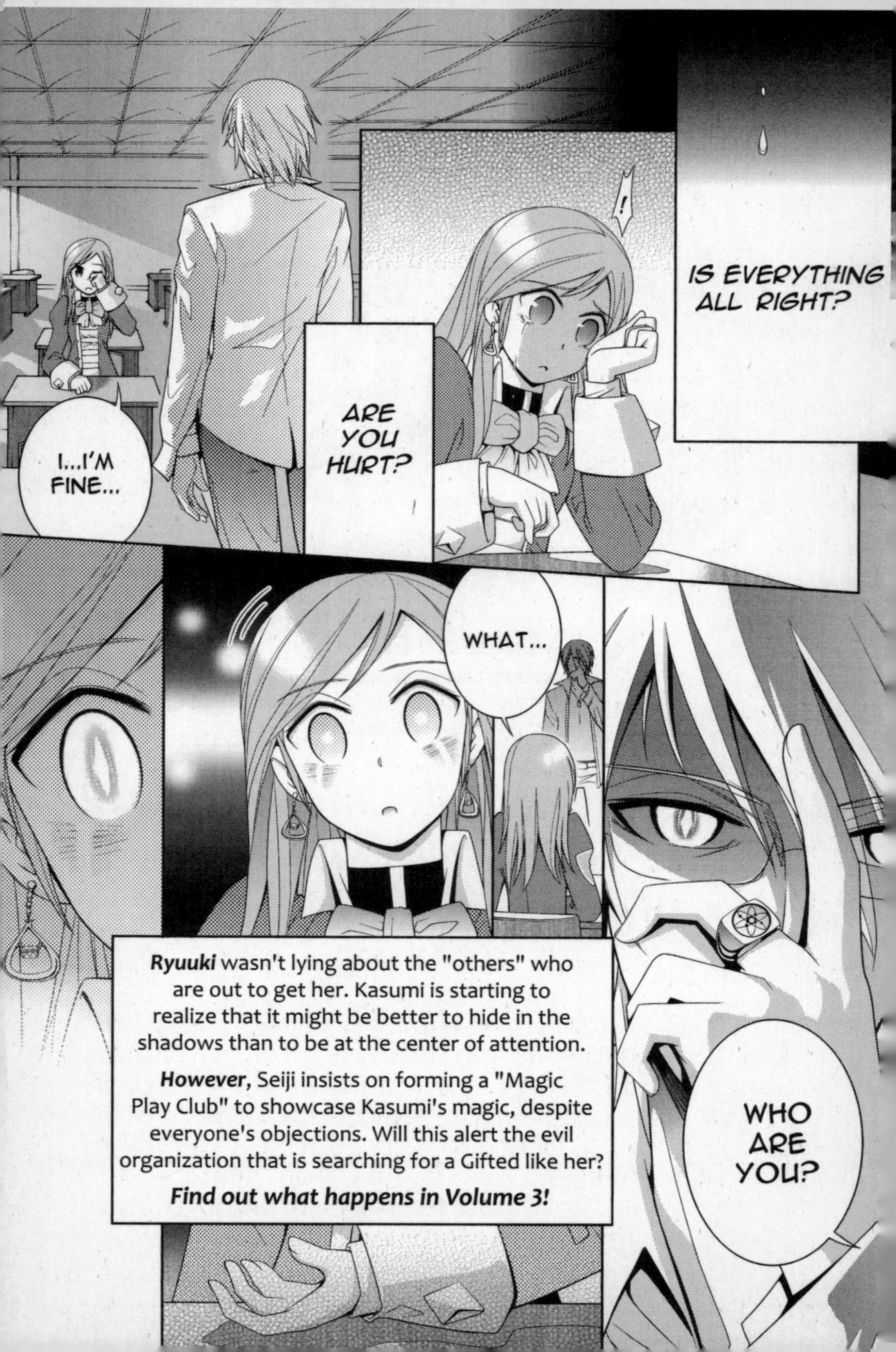
IS EVERYTHING ALL RIGHT?
!
ARE YOU HURT?
I...I'M FINE...
WHO ARE YOU?
WHAT...
Ryuuki wasn't lying about the "others" who are out to get her. Kasumi is starting to realize that it might be better to hide in the shadows than to be at the center of attention.
However, Seiji insists on forming a "Magic Play Club" to showcase Kasumi's magic, despite everyone's objections. Will this alert the evil organization that is searching for a Gifted like her?
Find out what happens in Volume 3!

You're going the wrong way!

Manga is a completely different type of reading experience.

To start at the *beginning*, go to the *end*!

That's right! Authentic manga is read the traditional Japanese way—from right to left. Exactly the opposite of how American books are read. It's easy to follow: Just go to the other end of the book, and read each page—and each panel—from right side to left side, starting at the top right. Now you're experiencing manga as it was meant to be!